The Voice of Spirit

꙰꙰ I Am Consciousness ꙰꙰

The
Voice of Spirit

**Ascension into the
Greater Reality of Self**

꙰꙰꙰

Janice L. Johnson

Edge of Time Books
꙰꙰꙰꙰꙰

© 2008 by Janice L. Johnson, Edge of Time Books

Published by
Edge of Time Books
P.O. Box 524
Manhattan, Kansas 66505-0524
www.edgeoftimebooks.com

Typography: Janice L. Johnson
Cover Design: Janice L. Johnson
Cover Art: Sven Geier
Cover Photo: Kevin

ISBN 13: 978-0-9817456-0-2
ISBN 10: 0-9817456-0-1

CONTENTS

PART II: INTEGRATION OF THE SOUL

௫௫௫௫௫

PART III: UNCHARTED TERRITORIES

ꙩ ꙩ ꙩ ꙩ ꙩ

Author's Note

I have been a part of the great awakening that our planet is currently experiencing, just as all who yearn for the light and for unconditional love have been and are. Early in 2005, I made contact with angelic beings. One morning as I was waking up but still in that in-between state, I suddenly found myself in a dreamlike place looking at a beautiful being. This being had gray skin. It was like a human, only more so, meaning, it was larger than life! It had no hair and wore no clothes. Its eyebrow ridges were very pronounced and it was very powerful. It had no sex; it was complete. From its brow came tiny wings of light like the flame of a candle in the shape of a Nike symbol. This being was so full of light that the light created wings in its eternal flowing. In my dream I knew the being as Metatron. Next to him was a slowly rotating cylinder of six-sided shapes, and each of these hexagonal "faces" contained the face of a being. One of these beings especially was watching me with loving intensity.

On awakening, I wrote this experience down. I searched within for understanding as to what it meant and what I had to learn from it. Later that same day I made contact with beings of light in the form of channeling. This book contains the notes of our communications in the form of a dialogue with the voice of spirit, just as it happened for me.

It is my understanding that every one of us, as we are confronted with the challenges of ascension, experience our own distinctive, individual awakening which is right for us, and our own unique relationship with our I AM or Higher Consciousness or Multidimensional Self. I do not claim that my experience is similar to any other awakening experience; we only share it here as one example of how we might release ourselves from the bonds of ego and grow in the light. As these others of my greater self said to me early on, we each are responsible for accepting into our lives what is truth for us. If you feel the truth of these messages within your heart, then it is right for you, otherwise not.

We offer our story as we experienced it with the following exceptions. At times, I have had to rework sentences, as they tended to run one into another, with no punctuation, sometimes into a page or more! Sometimes, I noticed, these sentences made sense that way, since one thought naturally led into another, but they were also harder to attend to and "decipher." For those I did change, I worked very hard to remain "true" to what I perceived in their meaning, and only a few sentences have been altered. Comments added after the fact, for reasons of clarity, are in brackets. I have left out some personal messages that were not part of a larger lesson, and yet there are many things still included here that are difficult to share but which are a part of the larger tapestry of our story. To pull one thread would be to unravel it all, and so we offer this story as is, knowing that the last chapter of the story, which is still yet to be, will reveal all.

This journey that we share begins with our very first attempts at "channeling," though they came through somewhat choppy. I received their messages one "word" at a time in the form of thought-feelings that I then interpreted into English words. Sometimes it took two or more words to "translate" their meanings, and some words would come through with capital letters or in quotes. At other times I would receive two thought/meanings at once, such as you/us, which meant they were talking to me, but with the understanding given that I am also a part of us, and they think of me not as "you," but as one of "us."

At times the messages I received were difficult to understand, but I have been shown that it is important to remain true to these messages and "lessons" and so we share them "as is." I realized over time that they gave them to me this way deliberately so that, in order to understand them, I would need to go deeply into my heart to find their meanings. That way the words would penetrate my being and help to lead me home, without getting stuck in my mind on the way in! I considered changing how these were presented so that they would be easier for others to decipher and understand, and I was shown a highchair in my mind along with the words, "Don't spoon feed them!"

So, we offer our lessons—perhaps even a template—of realizing the Greater Reality of Self in their imperfect completion. We include as well the "mistakes" that I have made along the way, as we can only get where we are going by being honest with self about where we are at the time, and by facing the illusions and delusions of time and our own processes. Over time I have come to suspect that some of these "mistakes" that I "made" were simply "tricks" to get me to face my own illusions and limitations of ego, all carefully designed to lead me home.

It takes faith to cross a bridge when you cannot see it in front of you, when you do not know what lies ahead or what there might be to "lose." To find the path of the within, you have to be willing to lay down all of your judgments and to surrender all of your fears. You have to be willing to be exposed, to look directly into the mirror of self, to release the illusions and face up to the mistakes, and to choose love over fear, every time. In the Greater Reality of Self, there are no regrets.

Janice L. Johnson
November 11, 2007

About the Author

Janice L. Johnson was born in Kansas City, Kansas and has lived in Kansas all of her life. She was married in 1982 at age 19 and became a mother at 20 and again at 27. After the birth of her first child, she began exploring many different spiritual paths and holistic health practices, incorporating her spirituality into her everyday existence and striving daily to provide her child with a healthy and loving home life. She completed her first degree in Business Administration in 1986 and worked in retailing and management for several years until she felt called to find a way to be of greater service to others, particularly children. Soon after the birth of her second child, she returned to college for a degree in Elementary Education and a Master's Degree in Education of the

Gifted. She taught for 10 years, nine of those as a Gifted Facilitator traveling between several small-town districts and serving first through twelfth grade students, their families and teachers. At age 41, the calling within intensified as she discovered A Course in Miracles. She increased her study and spiritual time daily until one morning in January of 2005, she had a vision of Metatron. This was the springboard to yet another and deeper level of her becoming, resulting in the ascension experiences she shares in this book. She currently lives "alone" in the country outside Manhattan, Kansas, in a house she built for herself.

Introduction

We are Pegasus. We are that who ruled the world in ages gone by. We rolled across the sky in scarlet magnificence just to show Them We can. We purchased time on a rolled up blanket in the sky, and slowed down just enough to get a good look at it. It was grand. The rolling plains and hills were a magnificent sight, more so seemingly than the stars where we flew. We could not get enough. We came down for a closer look. We saw nothing to fear, for indeed fear was not yet made or encouraged in our stars of which We came, so we rode in for a closer view. It was not home. It was the trailer park of existence to which we came and we would not have it be so. We knew we could tame them, bring them home again who were lost there so long ago. We could only keep weeping to find them so close to home, and yet so far, too, from their true selves.

It was given us in the stars long ago to find these lost ones and bring them home. We were warned it could be a long duty, many times passing before we once again would become realized enough to ride the trails of our skyways. We were appeased in that we believed that we could do this in record time, that no more than three short years might pass before we would then be set free again to ride alone. We were wrong. It was not possible to take these "notes" of our becoming to the planes of existence without then becoming as if we were one of those lost. We could not see it coming, and it was the downfall of our territorial existence within All Who Sees within All Forces and All Time.

We were not sorry, however, that this had come to pass, for we were above the laws of the universe in those days and could foresee nothing that could have brought us down, save this, that we might somehow succumb to the pressures of life and die on a planet of death and thereby begin the cycle of life and death. We were not afraid of the cycles, but rather of them rendering us incomplete, as a flower is rendered incomplete in its own dying. We were not like those who used the streets of time as a rendering, but we came instead upon a day of choice where the dark one called to us from the sky offering us up a choice of playing the game frolicking between the good and evil of oneness, rather than that oneness totally perceived in glorious joy rendered up to the heavens of choice, of which at that time there were only seven. We were not afraid of him. We brought him down and we played his game, taking him on and determined that he would not lie to us again. We were wrong. We were taken away from our beginnings just as those who had come before, and we could not return. We had become trapped by our own perceptions of good and evil and evil had won.

Though we had had enough before even a day of our time had passed and wanted but to fly away, we thought we would try for just another day taking him on and teaching him what we knew. We could not. He could not carry it within his soul, and so all time and pain as we knew it could not be prevented. He had taken the lost souls of the world into his being and trained them in what to do to bring upon themselves all that was called decrepit and evil. He would not let them have their say, and they gave themselves over to him.

It is time for us now to deliver the "sequel" to this story, the beginning of all time talking to no time again, and the reinstatement of the seventh heaven. Are we ready to begin?

Yes.

I believe you know of a saying where I give a certain horse's patooty a good kick in the butt? Well, this is it. This is our time to shine. We can no more fail in our rendering than we could have spent our precious remembering in total darkness. It is for us to open up to the heavens, to take on MORE, so that when the time is come, we are here for each other's rendering to be made complete. Am I clear? Is there anything more I could have said to make you believe of which we come, of our origin together? Could I have made love to you once more in the darkness of time, and brought you home more quickly? I say not.

Do you want to know the difference between truth and reality? It is when you put your butt out the door, and realize there ain't nobody there. That is it. So what? So you put your butt out the door.

The Voice of Spirit
March 5, 2005

For Red

If at the Deepest
Levels of Our Being
We Let Go
We Are Free

PART I

Laying the Groundwork

1

First Contact

Metatron, who are you?

Wrap things up, take it down, be forthright, don't change to impress others, look forward to good, ignore bad, collapse the ego, be strong, take a chance, let freedom ring. We are part of something larger.

What is my purpose?

To spread truth and to provide spiritual nourishment in the form of books and teaching.

Why am I here?

To make contact with other life forms, to improve relationships between humanity and civilizations beyond your realm.

Life is a series of coincidences which, when exposed, are curiously true to form beyond the scope of humanity and necessary for our civilization to decrease form to increase light. Love is the way of it, the way to God and for the world to explore peace and brotherhood forevermore.

Life has a way of ending up to be truth in disguise. Lovingness is not an instance of truth but a meaning that is not lost on society.

Can't believe we've taken this so far in one sitting. Be careful not to overwhelm the senses, let it come gradually.

(It came to my mind as we finished this and I contemplated his message, a vision I had had not long before, of a higher being which is aware of its connection to all, to everyone, everything, everywhere. This being was very large, like an oversoul, and it viewed me by sending out a tentacle or "face" from its larger self which reflected my own. I felt its total love and regard as it viewed me. It was very beautiful.)

∞∞∞∞∞∞

January 13, 2005

I am ready to set my life straight. I ask for guidance and pray for the strength of will to do what it is that I am here to do. I want good health and peace of mind, purity of spirit, lovingkindness. (I prayed for protection.)

Feel free to put it in your own words. That is how it is done. Don't be afraid to "chew on it" for awhile until it feels" straight."

Life is an option. To fight or quarrel is not your point/way. Bring resolution quickly to the disquiet by taking strength with you to confront anger. Do not be afraid, we are here.

[They referred here to my relationship with my husband. He was angry with me.]

Who are you?

I am Metatron, your savior. We are here to help you.

Can you tell me what it is I am to do with my life? I am afraid that I'll screw up. Who am I?

Place your weapons at our feet and it will be shown to you. Do not be afraid to love in the midst of strong physical fear. Take freedom, it is given you to use for your benefit and the benefit of others. Let it come easily and you will know what to do. Be still and know.

Is writing what I am supposed to do?

Writing will free you to become who you were meant to be, to find the joy in your existence, to become one.

Will I still be able to have a child?

[I had lost a child in a near death experience due to an ectopic pregnancy less than two years before at the age of 40, and I still very much wanted another child.]

Yes, meant to be. Will be soon, come from God not man.

When?

Fractions...of time cannot be measured from here, it is in your willpower to make changes come more quickly if that is what you desire. It is up to you.

How do I do this?

Take him down.

[I felt here that I had "crucified" my husband, with all of the judgments I had of him, and I needed to "take him down" and love him.]

Love has a lot of ways to come home. He will find you, too, and you will make time for each other again as it was in the beginning. Love has many ways to shine.

You cannot believe everything you hear, it is your loneliness that is at stake.

What can I do to further my purpose here now?

Take the trash out! Be kind to animals including humans. Make love a lot, be free, take a chance on love. Open your heart to humans and you will find God.

Who am I?

A dog, [Symbology of "friend", also, "man's best friend"?] *a human, a friend to nature, taking a chance to become the best in everyone, climbing down from your high horse to be real will help you, don't be afraid to lie down and free your muscles from tension.*

Can I help you? What can I do?

Get out of town once in awhile. Take the trash out so that when I am ready for you, you will be ready for me. I am Metatron.

Thank you Metatron. Thank you God.

[That night I made time to be with my husband. I confronted the anger with love and it was gone, and we must have been outside of time for awhile, with a little help from our friends I think, because when we went to bed it was 10 'til midnight, and we spent an hour, no less, cuddling, talking, and loving, but when we turned off the light, it was only 12:35. This was unusual, as his anger and my fear usually made the walls almost impossible to bring down.]

∞∞∞∞∞∞

January 14, 2005

(I asked for protection and guidance from the highest.)

What is it that you would have me bring through?

Freedom of choice will come to your brothers by your side. Take a chance on escaping through to the other side. Free yourself to bring in light to your brothers. They are one with you and with all eternity in God.

I am Metatron. I am here to bring to you the truth and the light, and through you, to your brothers. Life is coming full circle for you. Embrace change, it is your keeper for eternity.

I have a mixture of beings to introduce to you now, through me. They are here in the light of a thousand faces. Through me they come to bring peace to you through the world of form. Be at peace with yourself, for you have broken a mighty barrier, a [I could only think "reef" which didn't make sense or feel right] *of sunlight fills the air.*

I am Metatron.

Why am I having difficulty with this now?

Take down your barriers of pain.

What can I do now to help the world the most?

Take down your barriers. They are restricting your every motion. They are not helping but rather hindering your process. Friction builds patience.

Can you take me home? I want to believe that there is a chance I can be who you want me to be.

[I was struggling with remaining clear and open and didn't trust what was happening at this point.]

Thank you for helping me, I will work to go deeper to find you. Help me to be free.

I can find change in a leaf, in a car tire, in anything that represents itself to me. I am fire and rain. Both are supportive to me because they are what I want them to be. You are not yourself. You don't know who you are because—

["—*you have not opened your heart.*" I had lost the thread, but these words came to me as I am adding comments/notations.]

I feel like your communication is happening but that I'm only getting bits and pieces of it. When I feel fear, I lose the thread. When I ask something I feel fear about, it causes me to lose my concentration and openness, and then I am not in tune anymore.

[I was quiet and praying for awhile.]

Thank you.

Keep trying, it will come. Don't forget to take the trash out. Be free inside yourself, you have nothing to fear. It will inspire you to change if you take out the trash. Be free, it will come. So long until next time.

Notes to self: When I am clear, as a pond is clear when it is without ripples, I will hear and know. I felt the clearness the past couple of days, but not so much today. Meditate first, then it will come. Take out the trash: exit the ego!

∞∞∞∞∞∞

January 15, 2005

I am looking forward to the opportunities to communicate with other beings. I have always felt that there was someone out there, always felt that I don't belong here, that I am not "home." Does everyone feel this way? It doesn't appear that they do, but it seems that more and more people are feeling as I do, that there is more to life than what our scientists can "prove" exists, and I'm willing to look beyond this reality to discover it. I'm ready to look within and beyond time and space.

I pray for assistance in developing my will to a state of mastery, for more grace, silence, and gratitude. El Morya, help me to attain mastery. Sananda, fill my heart with your light in every moment in time and out of time. Buddha, help me to set my soul free. Kwan Yin, help me to know you and to understand my destiny. Mary and Kuthumi, set me free of my illusions. Make me strong so that I can assist with the freeing of the world.

What does it mean to be free? How do I accomplish freedom? How do I take out the trash? What do I do?

Feel free to put it in your own words. This will precede my messages for a time until you are prepared to receive more complicated messages.

Time is of the essence. It is made for you so that you might prepare to meet your destiny. Prepare to come to God, as your savior has shown to you. Be not afraid to come through to me as you are, without fear of revealing your innermost self. It is your fear that you will not progress as well as you might, but change is inevitable and we cannot bring it on more quickly by being afraid. Do not be afraid.

Can you help me to change, to become who I am meant to be?

Friendship takes precedence over time. You have noticed that many around you possess strings of consciousness in line with your own. This is because you have been together before, as you have realized. Do not be afraid to reveal yourselves to these others. They are here for your benefit, as you are here for theirs.

Who are you? To whom am I communicating? Can you show me your face so that I am clear about this?

Life is a series of coincidences that, once perceived, can take you where you want to be. Take a chance on becoming. Freeing yourself to change will enable you to be everybody's best friend and helpmate. It is your destiny to become one with your brothers and to lead them home.

It is not a coincidence that you are here now, that you have made this progress to me, to your brothers of the light/the sky. Who am I? I am your brother, the one brought to bring you home. Be not afraid. You have nothing to fear from us, we are here to help you. I am bringing you others of the light who will penetrate your consciousness as you sleep. They will know your name and will lead you to the truth. Be not afraid to pursue it with them.

Can you feel the light in these words? Is so, then it is truth for you. That is how to determine who you are. Your heart knows of what it is made, and your heart will show/tell the truth to you. No one can do it for you, this you know. Telepathy is a tool for/by which you can determine forthrightness in other people. It cannot be misused for other purposes. Trace the light down the tracks of your destiny. It cannot be given unto you. It is for you to discover on your own, but we are here to help you. I am here to dissolve the universe so that you can discover your true place within it.

You cannot show others your true face when fear is ruling your heart and mind. Trace the path of destiny by becoming one with your own True Self. You cannot tell a lie when you listen to and speak from your heart. This you have seen.

It becomes a terror to live a secret, a lie, as someone you are not. We become afraid when we fear who we are. You cannot bring light to the earth when fear and darkness rule your plan.

I am here with other beings who would make themselves known to you through your dreams. They will bring light to the world through you, through your relationships with others. Trust them to help you to find what you need. They are not here to take from you, rather to help you to find what you need and distribute kindnesses through them.

Life is very fun if you look at it that way--how much good can I do today? What is out there for me to discover? Do I have to do it alone? We are never alone! You are never alone! Take a chance on meeting others of the same mind as you. Don't forget that you are not alone.

How do I take out the trash? What do I concentrate my efforts on? Is this real? Are you real?

Who is asking? You are not real or you wouldn't need to ask. I am Metatron, your savior, and I will lead you home. Be not afraid to make those changes so that we might meet more often to incorporate those changes which you so desperately seek. You are one with us. Though you have suspected as much, you do not believe it yet. The light is a truth you have yet to fully absorb.

What message have I need of most tonight? Lead me home.

I cannot take those chances for you; you must obey your truth as it is given within. That is the only answer you seek, and must be found before you can adjust to the outside consciousness. Beauty is inside and awaits your release. Feel free to send out "alerts" should you need me sooner, but I am here inside you and you cannot really lose me but let me go through your own use of consciousness and spirit.

I am afraid to trust this process, afraid of opening myself to lower—no, I will seek love, and love will come to me, and nothing else will. I am free to seek the light.

Light is shown to you, you but follow it home.

Help me to deal with these fears of the process, to release these chains and be free! Thank you.

Feel free to use this process to find your answer. It is an acceptable use of form to do so. We are here. I am making this contact with you. I will lead you home as the butterfly on the wings of time. You cannot help but benefit from this discourse, so be not afraid to open yourself to them. You are free to decide on your own what you will and will not do in the name of light, and it will be done as you request/order. The universe but follows your command. Your freedom depends on your own choices.

I am Metatron, we are here. You have nothing to fear from us, we will lead you home, but you must find it in your heart to answer our call. Take time to connect with our essence.

[I took time.]

I am grateful for your assistance, and I ask that you continue to assist me daily through this correspondence, and through dreams, and through other means as you see fit. I welcome your presence in my life, Metatron and beings of the white brotherhood and highest of the light, and ask what I can do to bring light to this world to assist the efforts of the light, of God.

Bring me home. I am here for a reason, a purpose, and it has been shown to me, and I will pursue this purpose with renewed zeal and dedication. Let me strengthen my heart and my will so that I may assist the light workers.

2

Laying Down My Fears

January 16, 2005

I became upset tonight after seeing part of a movie where a woman with a violent past is acting out sexually, but is really just hurting inside and closed off. Before that I was thinking about having sex with my husband, but after that I feel the old closed off feelings, wanting to be alone in order to feel safe, to be alone with my pain so that no one will find out about it. I don't want to react this way anymore.

Suddenly I felt like laughing and crying at the same time, that it is all so absurd, our need for drama, for believing the lie that we are all here hurting each other, believing in the separation. And again, with inservice tomorrow at work for all teachers in our district, I am tempted to believe in the separation, that I have something to prove to those I fear look down on me for whatever reason—do they look down on me because they perceive that they are better than me, or because they are afraid that I am better than them? And stupid me, always trying to prove something to people who appear not to see me or think well of me or whatever. See how ridiculous is the human race! Stupid, more like!

I want to view us as one with God, separate no more, but still I feel the pain inside, of the abuse from my childhood, of hatred of me and hurting me—is this a need for release, or just a way to continue with the old pain instead of opening up?

I use my fear as a shield, and maybe as a weapon, too. I am ready to lay it down at your feet, Metatron, so that I can learn from you about oneness. Will you show me?

I also lay at your feet my need to see myself as not good enough no matter what I do. I don't need that anymore.

I lay down my need for hiding from others, for basking in my fear as though that would make me safe or something. I lay that down, too.

I lay down my fear to try something new, or to be around people, or to need approval. All these things I lay down now at your feet. I don't need them anymore. They are not me.

I lay down my pain, and let the gladness and joy that is me, surface. I share this joy with you and with my other brothers and sisters. Everything that has been done to me, I have done to myself. I forgive myself for that, fully realizing that there is, in fact, nothing to forgive, for all is illusion and I seek to go beyond the illusion, to God and to love and to peace, where we all truly abide.

That dream I had several years ago, the one that was intoxicating, where the evil being injected my belly with something to cause me to sleep, and I was pretending to sleep in order to go unnoticed by the evil ones. It created a feeling of intoxication, a weird kind of euphoria—it seems like I feel that now at times, that weird sense of euphoria, as though I am waking again, just enough to feel the drug which was meant to numb me forever, but which now is aiding in my recovery, or so it seems. I like it. It feels good to me to have this euphoria, this awareness of the higher and lower and the choices that I have and can make for myself.

I am free, I just have not wanted to accept how free I am. I have been afraid to love, to open up, to express myself, acting afraid of what others think, of needing approval when I have only to give that gift to myself. And who is approving of whom anyway? Stupid! I am ready to accept what God gives to all of us, what he is waiting for us all to accept. Life. Love. Freedom. Joy. Completeness. Peace.

Metatron, I welcome you into my heart and soul once more, to communicate with me, to bring light and truth to shine on my mind and make me free. Please protect me from lower level entities, beings, and spirits, and let me learn from the highest in the light. Amen. Will you teach me?

I am Metatron. I am here to bring the awareness of the light into your mind and the minds of your brothers through you. Bring to me your awareness of the process of time, meet with me in the evenings, and together we will find a way to make this happen.

You have begun a very difficult process. It will not treat the world to be as you are from here. Kindness is the only way to teach others, for in that compassion you bring them to the light. The greatest of teachers can only come from the heart. Be one of these.

If you know who you are, you will be able to assist with the beings coming to your planet at this time. They are here for you to learn from. They will begin now. Take notes carefully. They have only to project their consciousness into your own to make this happen. You have only to remain aware and open. Picture me if you must, if this helps you to stay aware of the process. Incoming technical awarenesses are difficult to describe but should make you more aware of what you are doing and how it can benefit your world.

You are not a light/shadow combination. It has been given you to accept this polarity where none truly exists. Here it is difficult for me to describe in your words, for they are limited according to the understanding of your people. Take a moment to describe them to me.

We are trained to see the polarity in all things, that each thing has an opposite, and we are trained from childhood to recognized these polarities and to believe they are fact. More?

Take down what I am saying to you. Fear is not real. It is only a figment of imagination so great as to freeze the polarities in place. Freedom depends on you withholding your fear long enough to expand beyond your potential within the light/shadow of consciousness on your planet earth. Your fears are bringing me more difficulty in assimilating for your benefit.

I am Metatron's assistant in the light of Arcturus. We are here above your planet for the end days, to instruct and to teach you the way to follow for the benefit of mankind. They are here to instruct and to teach, as you are sent to bring these truths to earth. Feel free to take a break whenever you need it.

I will keep going. Please tell me where you are from and who I am communicating with. What is the light on your brow? What does it represent? My goal is to control my emotional and mental bodies at all times, to BE love, and to help my brothers to return to God. Will you help me?

My place in your existence shines within a realm that no one has yet seen but all have known. I bring to you this information so that you can know me, and in knowing me, know yourself and all of your brothers who are one with us. Find truth within. Shake the tree of your consciousness, let the fruit fall, and know your consciousness by the quality of that which has fallen.

Awhile back I had a "dream" where an evil force was there. It "awoke" me, or tried to get to me by "poking" me in the ribs. Actually it was like a finger poking me, except that it penetrated deeply between my ribs and hurt and I was trying to wake up but couldn't. Then as the "evil" force was there I concentrated on the light, and I prayed to many to help me, to send me light, and I made sure that I didn't "look" at the evil, that I didn't give it power over me. But I did know that the evil wore my face, and it was all of the "bad" or ego or evil or dark side in me. I was not afraid of it, because it isn't real and cannot hurt me unless I let it or give it power over me. What can you tell me about that? Was it a test?

Take a chance. Don't delay. Your life depends on it. You were right in determining that there is a danger. It is from your lower selves. They wish to destroy you, so don't take the bait. Don't delay, take a chance in containing the message that they sent to you in the dream of another place and time, where you were not yourself, rather an evil one who is trying to kill you.

How do I retrieve my consciousness if that is what is animating this persona?

Drive away the beast within, and the beast without will disappear as in a puff of smoke. I have spoken. Release fear before it is too late. I have spoken. Opening to forever at your feet, you have only to step within the circle of your lives and you will know no fear, but will be as beyond all recognition and yet remain as you are. Know this and repent of all traces of fear and anti-love emotions.

They are waiting to take you to the place of forgiveness and initiation and will wait for you to decide your fate. Heed not the broken chain, it has dispelled the evil/fear within and without and you are free. Progress some more upon the road to the light and let the masters sing your praises, and all who follow you will proclaim their fate, too.

Know this: you are chosen to complete this path at this time and will not, cannot, fail, unless it be your will to choose evil over good/light/forgiveness. I can bring you one more lesson before this time if you choose.

Choose light, choose wisely, and I will remain your savior at this time. The Holy Ghost speaks on your behalf. From beyond the gravesites of past incarnations you have remained brokenhearted, unable to accept change and renewal. Now, this is your time. The seal has broken and you will be released. Come home for good, Janice, and you will know all that you have made. It is good. You can't dismiss this as foolhardy when you know of my love for you, it remains as always from your own heart. Believe in yourself and it will be shown to you.

[I was questioning here this process—was I crazy with all of this?]

You are not crazy yet! Come home "alone" one day and know of what I speak.

If you can send a lesson to help me, if this lesson be necessary for my learning, I gratefully accept anything you can give to help me with this. Thank you. If I can achieve this without more pain, I would choose this, to give up my pain and my unforgiving thoughts and give love and compassion and more, and to release the past from all claims, all thoughts of sin, all that is not love. Let it be so. Let me be released.

Take a chance! Praying for forgiveness will bring you to the brink. Take a step into the future without a net! It will not be seen! You must believe and it will be so! Your faith creates the bridge and it rises to meet your feet. From the abyss of non-understanding you will become one with the Great White Hope. Feel free to interpret this in your own way, as needed it is shown.

From beyond the gulf, I am Metatron your savior. Bridge the gulf, lay down your weapons, and step lightly onto the platform of your becoming.

I am free tonight to belong to many worlds at once, and I rejoice! I am free! To be one of you, you one of me! I fear nothing! Behold a new joy in the world! Let freedom ring! I am in Joy!

3

Who Am I?

January 17, 2005

I am here. Who are you? We want you to answer.

I am a being of light, made of love, not yet transparent in the light, but working to exit ego and become free and me, a part of you and all others in God.

Take notes carefully. You are not free to say and do all that you would wish. Your vision is shortsighted and is crippling you. Before going further, take a moment to reflect on this.

This is true. I don't think of myself as someone with a lot to offer much of the time, I don't trust myself to do what is required, and don't believe others are truly interested in me or love me. I don't know who I truly am. Can you help me to find out?

We will help you to find yourself as a flower finds the rain it needs to survive. You are beginning, just beginning, to find your own True Self. Nature has found a way for you to surface from your fears of aloneness and fatigue. Take notice on what I am saying to you. You were once a man who had many incarnations with one purpose: to make friends. These are not your—can't tell where you are at sometimes. Take a moment to visualize the white light.

[I did.]

We are back. Now we can begin. Bring your heart to your awareness and begin to take deep breaths. What do you feel?

I am tingly and full of light. I can feel it, it is very joyful. I feel the energy coming up inside me, but I think I keep it from flowing freely. Why is this?

You are afraid of what it may mean to be "better" than your brothers. You still see "success" as an insult to others. Free your mind by brisk walks in the night air, it will do you good. Continue with the sermon.

Fright can take its toll on you. Were you not ready for the phrase, "Take a chance to believe in yourself and I will lead you home"? It is for you that is said now. Freely give to your brothers and they will reward you. Life takes a turn depending on how freely you open up to others. Council our brothers to remain constant and you will see their faces become light.

Who are you and what are we doing here?

We are your savior, we are one. We have been together before as husband and wife and now we will work together for a short time to free the constraints so that you can proceed with your becoming. I am here for you. To belong somewhere has always been your need, your yearning, for brotherhood. Let us proceed.

Take a chance when others come to you for assistance. They are asking for you to help them. Give them light instead. It is what they need and secretly crave from all brotherhood.

I welcome your advice and input.

Freedom is just beginning to be felt by you. It is like a star shining in the heavens, but it cannot take off its coat.

I have a lot of fear, don't I? About everything!

We can tell! It will take time but we come to assist you in the process of throwing off the fear and rebuilding. Counter terror intelligence! Frame that any way you want to. We come in peace.

In the room from "across the street" we will tell you what you can do to make the grade. Freedom exists on more than one level. It is as you suggested: you are free to choose what and where you exist within the realm of possibilities. These possibilities are bringing you full circle back to the circle within this room. Free yourself for a moment to consider this possibility.

I realize that I have this fear that if I move, I will die. Someone will notice me move and I'll die.

Forensic evidence suggests that you are not yourself! You began as an entity of light, and it persists without your consciousness realizing it, and yet your body goes on. Freedom exists on more than one level.

Physical freedom, emotional freedom, mental freedom, spiritual freedom?

These exist for your benefit for you to learn from, they are not here to persecute you. Rather take them within your conscious control and do not be the one to say that it is not you making you say or do such things.

Are you talking about freedom of choice?

Yes, that is all there is to it. It has become a way to freeze moments in time, to become more than fresh water on a planet of dust. Become free to change the planet from a dust bowl to a thriving metropolis filled with living things.

I have spoken. Refrain from asking questions until you have read this through at least once. I am coming to you from the stars. Believe and it will be yours.

[I took time.]

I have read it through. Thank you. This helps me to understand freedom a little better. It is a choice that I make every moment. How I live, what I believe and allow myself, is a choice I make for myself every time. No one makes it for me. Thank you.

Personal freedom is a choice not only for ourselves, but for our brothers. Each time we make a choice for ourselves it affects our brothers, every time. We cannot make a choice that does not affect others. Your choice for freedom is a necessary component of realization of friends "becoming" together. This affects the way you interact with others and affects the way they interact with you. These are not disconnected. Freedom is choice. Belong somewhere by giving yourself the choice to respond to others with caring detachment. This is life, this is truth.

You have become yourself for the first time as you read and understand this message. Careful going about it the wrong way. Function is not always bad, but can lead to malfunction, so take a stand in the light. Careful to tread the broken way, straighten the path, and fear will not mislead you from the way of light. Focus more on the tendencies and less on the instances and they will not lead you astray.

You are helping me to understand this more deeply, as in, what my mind says about what I feel is like a whitewash to what I feel, sometimes so deeply entrenched that I don't question it. Thank you for helping me. I will practice hourly.

Respond to what I am saying now. Who are you?

I am….that is all.

[The first time, I was thinking about what I do, my goals, etc. The second time, I searched in my heart for "I am…" and that was the only description. It stood complete. I am.]

Very good! You have learned to be free of becoming and learned to live freely for the first time ever. Take a chance on becoming, freely happening, to go on from here. We will bring your awarenesses back to themselves now. Go in peace. We respond as your savior, be at peace.

[When I was first asked the question "Who are you?" at the beginning this evening, I felt no response from my longer answer, they just continued. This time, it seemed that I sensed pleasure which I then interpreted as "very good," but the pleasure seemed beyond words really. I think they were very pleased!]

Thank you Metatron. I am grateful. I believe.

4

Love or Fear?

January 18, 2005 (It is late, actually after midnight 1/19/05)

I am very grateful for your assistance, so grateful for your loving words and kindnesses. I would like to bless you and send you gratitude from my heart. Thank you. I pray for protection from all lower level entities and beings. I ask for guidance from the most high, and openness to perceive this guidance rightly.

Fear is a wonderful thing in that it brings us to awareness of our innermost processes so that we may clean out the chicken coop! Take no notes beyond these tonight.

[Sometimes I only get a word at a time, and it "appeared" to me, "Fear…is…a…wonderful…", and as I got this I was a little worried that it wasn't working, then I thought, what does a chicken coop have to do with fear? And then I realized what it was saying! Ha! That is so funny!]

Thank you Metatron. I believe.

[I keep wanting to include the words "I believe." I feel it is important to the process, to opening up.]

∞∞∞∞∞∞∞∞∞

January 19, 2005

I am here. Thank you for coming to me, for helping me to find the light within. I am wondering about the process of forgiveness. Can you help me with that? I pray for protection from all lower level entities/beings. I ask for guidance from the most high and openness to perceive this guidance rightly.

Light is a many faceted reality that words cannot relay adequately.

Who are you?

I am Metatron with these words of wisdom brought to you today from the brotherhood of the shields. Yes, it exists between and within worlds, as do your sisters shine along with them. Continue.

We are here today to instill within your heart the beginning of truth that you will find there to share with your brothers. They will be coming to you for their forgiveness; give it to them. They will shine with your own forgiveness as well. They come not of you, but through you, to deliver this message of hope and light. Take time to connect with our essence.

[I took time.]

These building blocks within the heart will detail for you their perfection as follows. Be not afraid to pursue these with me. I will show you the way.

I am ready to follow.

Take your arm ahead of your body to the right. Freeze a second. Take a moment to connect with our essence.

The body is a device that when freely taken to town will display resonances that perform miracles within. Let me explain. When you go to town, to the city, there are ways to perceive your brothers that you may not have noticed. First, watch them, perceive their idiosyncrasies, and let them betray your suffering for you.

Who is attempting to control who?

[I wondered if this is in response to my fear that I am not getting a clear message or not connected or whatever, that I am trying to control the incoming message, not that anyone "out there" is trying to control me.]

You have a fear within that is ready to surface. Let me do this for you. Take time tonight to belong within your body as a new being discovers its own hiding place. Feel free to pursue this at any moment. I will take you to the brink. You must delight the senses by taking a step into the past/present/future of time simultaneously. Let it be known that you/I have taken there first these issues, that you are not a man or woman in time. You have begun a process of scope and breadth that will enable you to become your own savior and be free of all illness forever.

We will begin at the moment of your choosing. I am taking this time to instruct you in the heart and motion of time travel, so belong within and become aware of this happening to you. Feel free to explain your fears to me/you as we go along, and let them carry you within the space of heart to your past/present/future time travel within, to discover that law, life, happens simultaneously, but fear draws you back within the core of aloneness that we fear to break out of, like a nut afraid of discovering the squirrel is waiting at the door. Don't be a nut! Belong to the winds of time.

Like any good soldier fight for your freedom. It will come if you continue to believe in the process. Begin now this trip into your futures/past, and belong to the moment of time which is now. Come with me as we share this time together, and we will know no harm. Nor will you have a trip to forget!

Light my way to heaven for me now. I will bring truth as my ally and find a way back home through the density of earth to shine forever in the heaven of my becoming. So be it. Can we go now?

Density is even longer and stronger than all of you, yet breadth of spirit destroys all hint of it. Come with me to the edge of time and we will look together and discover our common thread/past.

Compound fractures exist within your mind of time. Let me explain.

When I see you from a distance, when we interact/meet, I see a distortion of the light within your auric field. What this means is that I cannot take you along without evidence of your believing it exists.

I don't understand what is happening, but I think I need to go along anyway to see where this is leading. Lead me!

You will not be broken after all. Take a chance to reread this function through and we will try again.

[I read it over.]

The time frame of the future exists within your mind. Let us decide where we are before we know who we are. Where are you? Decide this now.

I am here. No! I am not here. I am everywhere at once and so I can go anywhere I choose if I allow myself that freedom. I allow it now. I don't want to be afraid of discovery any more. Let me be free now!

Green light. Begin to look for a face in the clouds of your consciousness and tell me what you see.

[I looked within but did not see it.]

Frightening situations are not your institution of chance. Take a chance on becoming with me. Try again to see the face in the cloud.

[I tried again.]

I found it, dimly. It reminded me of several animals at once, yet also it was human like, a strong boned face, reddish/ruddy, powerful, almost the pan kind of thing? Hornlike yet without horns and not evil at all, but powerful with loving light!

Let us begin again. This time take your arm out of its casket and I am willing to experience this with you.

Please show me the way to freedom!

Time is of the essence. Take notes. You are not a person, and you do not belong to this earth. You are free as the light is free on your planet to go where it may. You allow this cloud to dim your light. It is over for that time of hiding, for you have come into your own and must release the fear or die trying. Take a chance on becoming the light. Focus on your navel and let us explore your consciousness one last time.

[I took time.]

I want out of my shell tonight! Let it be so!

Feel free to pursue the light work at other times than this. We will be here night or day until you believe no structure can suffice. Take a chance and the light will support you on a magic carpet ride home. Take a fresh look at being—

[My husband came in and tried to look at what I was doing on the computer, as usual, and, as usual, I hid it from him. I have had so much fear around sharing anything with him. He gets judgmental at times about my spiritual search and territorial about how I spend my time.]

I don't want to share this with him. I want to keep it to myself, not have to explain what I'm doing because I fear that he will betray me if I show him my inner self. Can you help me to understand this?

No tool is enough if we decide to let fear belong where it can deprive us of our meaningful friendship.

I need clear help. It doesn't matter what he thinks, I can pursue this without him. I am afraid to divulge myself for fear of ridicule—or what?

[I felt these feelings, yet at the same time, felt how false they all were. This was me not being free because of my own choices, yet blaming my lack of freedom on someone else. I realized freedom is within, not anything to do with external circumstances.]

Here you are, a part of you has forgiven yourself for this turn of events and will begin to free your self for inner control of your environment.

I don't choose to fear him anymore. I don't want to experience this fear again. I am free to choose my environment, my interactions, my experiences, and I don't need to explain them or push them or hide them. Is this correct?

Love is a many splendid thing, but it can "suck" when you give it the power of decision over your own consciousness and mind. Begin to free yourself from this bondage. What have you to lose? Your inner self knows this chain. You are free to decide what to do with your freedom, or remain in bondage to your own fear. Decide what you would have be your guide, fear or light, and take the chance.

Maybe I am afraid he will keep me from what I need most, but I keep myself from that through my own fear, my hiding from me and my own truth.

I don't fear my husband, I fear myself, taking a stand, becoming who I am and losing love. But it is not love if it is not free, if it depends on pretense or fear or control. I don't choose to live this anymore. I will be free. I will allow myself the freedom to choose to be who I am, the freedom to choose the world of spirit over flesh, to pursue light rather than darkness and fear. Go with me, Metatron and brothers of the light. It is time to die to this fear. Yeah! He does not cause my fear, I do, and so I can also rid myself of it. That is freedom! That is the only freedom, and the only true way to love.

Free yourself of your bonds and you will know no fear.

[I stopped and spoke with my husband, told him that I don't want to hide from him and would talk about this writing project if he wanted me to, that I am just hesitant to share things too soon before I feel at a place of comfort, an acceptance of it myself. He relaxed when I said this, and did not pursue it.]

I feel unsettled about this. I think I increased his fear and didn't have to really face my own, though I did find the place within that allowed me to be ready to face it, and I was. And Poof! It will disappear.

Let love replace your fear of the unknown. Not love for a relationship/significant other, but Love. We cannot take the time to do this now. Believe me when I say to you that no one is more ready than you to face these fears and dispel them. The time is now. Seize the moment and it shall be yours.

I feel the truth of these words! The time is now!

Know no limits in truth; you are found only within the climate of change. Let it be the light that you choose for all time, from this day forward. Let love show you the way, and forgive him his trespasses so that he might be given the opportunity to forgive yours. Let us work together more on this at another time.

This is Metatron signing off for the day. Good luck, take time for love.

I pray for rest, acceptance, and understanding of the process. Thank you.

∞∞∞∞∞∞

January 20, 2005

Thank you for your assistance. I believe, and I am grateful for this opportunity to find God and to have your guidance. I ask for protection in the light.

I will take you back a ways for this one. This is the brotherhood speaking. We will go by this name when we are meeting with you so as to not become hampered by our relationships. Let us begin.

You are for a moment in time free from all beings. Come join us today as we learn this together. Be not afraid. This is your time. Take the bull by the horns and make a relay to the stars.

We will close with this saying: Do not be afraid to pursue your truth day and night, and we will rejoice with you in the stars.

Am I getting a clear message? Sometimes I hesitate, then I lose the thread because I am afraid to trust the process. I don't want to be afraid, yet I want to make sure that I am open only to the light and highest in the light. Can you help me with this, to understand this process better so that I will know?

Choose wisely your friends, they are here to assist with your process. Take time to believe each day, and grow stronger in the light.

[The message tonight seemed very abrupt and ended quickly.]

5

Freedom Exists On Many Levels

January 21, 2005

I am here, waiting to communicate with my brothers of the sky, to receive messages of light and hope to share with the world. Open me up to receive only the highest, purest messages of light and love. Make me free to pursue my path home, guide me to love. I pray for protection from all lower level entities and beings. Let it be so.

Choose wisely those that you would disclose us to. They come not of the stars of heaven but from the recesses of your mind. From whom do you draw the sustenance of life? Disclose only what you would have me read from a book to find the stars of heaven within.

Take time to believe in this process and bring me unto the light of heaven where I reside, calling your name in the stars, believing in you as you once believed in me. I am Sananda bringing this message to your heart.

Heart knows no limits, only look within for your truth. It has been shown to you. Follow me and we will find a way to the stars of your consciousness. Burn away the fabric of time to dispel the fear.

You are not going to like this. I have a star for you, but she won't come unless you can bring yourself to accept this progress as your own. Believe me when I say to you that you have forgotten our path, who you are, many times, but never for long. Take time to relay this message inside your consciousness.

[I took time.]

It will be as if never said. The truth of your becoming will be as a light in the darkness of time, but only if you relay this message to her. She will bring you home along the path of love and light, so forever the distance of home cannot change the fact that you are not here. We love you and wish you the best but come alone next time [without my fears?] *and we will see what can be done. Your squirrel is waiting at the door of time, but you are not home. I can free your mind from this darkness only with your assistance, and light and love will rule forevermore.*

Take notes carefully. We were once a time and distance immeasurable. The clouds are as a brightness to the soul, but you have forgotten who you are and this will release you forever. Take my hand and we will dispel the darkness forever. Free yourself to belong as a child in the darkness needs its mother's womb to remember where it lies.

I can't believe that we are progressing this far tonight but we will go further if you may believe in me.

I believe and I trust.

Begin again. We are not the darkness, it knows no rain. Forgiveness is the tonic to the soul of time. It brings heaven in its trail, so dispel the darkness by being yourself. We are afraid to connect, but that is life. Connection is the answer to all of your sorrows and fears. You will know the heart by that which it produces in time, but you will know the spirit by that which is within. Stay within this message and you will find your own true forgiveness, given as it is received, together in a lifetime of tragic loss and beautiful lovingkindness. It is your mastery that is our plan, that we will now make/take time for.

Belong where you know your heart is, inside the womb of God and beginning to be felt by Him again. We will free the consciousness to take its place beside/within Him and to groom others for this seat also. We can tell you are tired of mind, but of soul the heat will dispel your tiredness/fatigue and bring you home.

If you want to terrify someone, mention who you are. We are most afraid of who we are, because to be God is a terror to the ego, to whom nothing is grand.

We are beginning to be felt sometimes. Take this truth to fatigue and see what lies there. It is your only mastery of God and man, to lead me home through the labyrinth of space/time and come home alone to find that all mankind already resides there with us. Your fears will dispel, leaving you lovingkindness in their stead.

Only be free to concern yourself with this project. You will be bringing these works to your brothers so they might learn of your consciousness that matches mine and their own as well. Take time to do this now. We will be watching from the stars, for we love and protect you forever and amen.

[I have been very tuned in tonight, but don't know what I have received yet. Though I know it for an instant as I write, I have to go back later to find out if it really makes sense.]

I will continue now. Please respond and protect me in the light.

You are free to pursue your own kindnesses every day. Listen to me on this. You have not been providing opportunities for forgiveness on a regular basis. As in, when the dogs play in the yard, do you go outside and watch them? Do you care about them, notice when they need your love and forgiveness, or do you stare and turn away? Who are you to stare and turn away? When you perceive this message, take to heart that I can and will protect you, you have nothing to fear from this purpose. Restraint on your emotions can follow, but you must be prepared to strike with loving attention, then they/you must tear down your walls of pain to perceive your joint control over all. Purpose and attention to detail is what comes from counting on men too much to do your work. Free yourself for a time to delight in the pressures of life and to treat yourself to kindly attention, it is what you deserve, as all God's children deserve lovingkindnesses every day. Freedom exists on more than one level. We will try again tomorrow to connect with our essence.

[There was a change of energies.]

The Brotherhood of the Shields taking responsibility now, for your time/daylight has sprung from the abyss of a dark night to bring you home. You have only to believe in what I say and that truth shall be yours/ours again as it was in past times gone by. Function is only here to serve. Once it is complete, it is no more and dissolves into the light. All time can make sense if you let it go. I am Metatron bringing you to this modicum of triumph over illusion. Wait—

Can you help me to free myself from this illusion? Will you show me the way?

We'll take time to do this now.

Always within the heart is a mechanism that is light, here for our brothers, made of the stuff of stars. Be with this now.

[I took time.]

Take a light from the darkness and make it shine. We are given this knowledge to dispel fear. Take a chance on bringing more light within. Into your relationships let those lights shine. They shine for you who is all and for all who are you. Free your becoming. Beginning to dispel the darkness is a time for sorrow, but the time for joy is just around the corner. Belong somewhere and nowhere. Free your mind to go with us on a lifetime journey to the stars.

I don't trust myself to do this right. Can you help me?

Trust is the bridge we lay down before our feet so that we know where to go and that we cannot fail. For a time, this bridge does not shine in the darkness. Take a moment to connect with me now.

[I took a moment.]

Where do I go from here?

Freedom exists on more than one level. We cannot complete this without your consciousness. The quality of that which you create is in direct alignment with the quality of heart energy inside you. Our fears distort our perception of truth, but cannot change the facts which I am about to impart.

Freedom exists on more than one level. Take it from here. Tell me your inside description of free.

Who are you?

I am an assembly of stars making a message of all time to connect with the heart ranges of mankind for the express purpose of creating like changes in others of your species. Take time to connect with my essence here.

[I took time.]

We are proud of you for making this effort, and we like how you have begun. Take time to develop your consciousness in the light so as to make the process more seeming to be connected. Triple your output by taking the time to meditate under the stars before our process begins. Take a walk outside at these times, draw unto yourself the light of the universe and take a moment to connect to the essence within all light which begins and ends in you. Free yourself for the changes by making possible your journey in the light.

Without density we begin again as we tell you, you may not be alone, for we are here to instruct you in the ways of change and heartfelt likenesses between our "species." Be free to perform miracles at all times. Take a strand of light from the darkness and dispel your own fears with them. We come not of the stars of time, but of our hearts which place them there. Forget for a moment that we are human/alien forms and remember this: we are not alone.

Time is of the essence. Take a little time to dispel these fears from your heart through forms that you already know. Take them more often so that when we come for you, we will not be alone in our assumptions.

Brace yourself, for the light has come! Perform miracles like forevermore come from the stars as a little one who shows her face in your mind. She bids you farewell, so long until ...another daylight/shadow combination forms around you now. They are your essence with fear taking the place of your normal processes.

[I felt they broke away from their message because when they mentioned the child I became afraid of the message. They saw this fear and described it to me.]

Take back the space provided by indulging in the—

Are you talking about another child that I would have? I am doubting this process again, I don't understand what I am getting and I'm afraid it is only my own idiot self with these stupid words or something.

Take the time to hear what I am saying to you. You are not alone. These messages of hope and light have come to you from the stars of your own consciousness. We relay them there from our home planet of Arcturus. If you dispel the anger we will teach you, for we are of the light and cannot change our minds without help from Above. We are connected through the Heart Stream without which we would no longer exist. So it is with yours. You are afraid of your own essence as we speak, not of our presence. Dispel this fear/darkness and come home with us.

We need you to not be afraid and to hear our words of wisdom. I am from the planet which you once called home, in a form you once knew. You believe this but when it comes down to it you aren't here with us.

Forget your freedom for a moment and follow us on a long dark journey to the place you call hell. [Earth.] We will instruct you in these minutes before the destruction of your time frame and know this, you will not be as little afraid as you could be if you knew who we were! Forget your freedom for a moment as we take to the stars, and when you/we return, we will know peace no more, for they are stationed directly above your position in the network called life. Freedom dispels anger. Live not the lie of time but take us with you to a higher form/place within the network you call space/time.

Tailored to your energy pattern is a star named Arcturus Minor. You have been to this place before and called it home. It gave you many ways of being, living and understanding, of which this is one.

You were once a small child species in the heart of America. It has been called home by you before but with little change known to you. Forget which your duties in this place for they are all one, but you were once a maiden of little heart/soul. You know that now, but I have placed in/within your being a small crystal which will tell of your lifetimes before on Arcturus, so begin when we must complete this design and tell of it. Which design is that which you have foreseen as the beginning of all time? It is all the same to me/us here.

On your level we see without blinders and know of your being. Changes in the stars are inevitable but can be brought to their swift conclusion by your own admission of guilt.

We will take time to process this before receiving more. Belong everywhere and nowhere and know/perceive the winds of time as they change under your feet. Take time for love, bring sweet melodies to the nation of forgetfulness. Swift reunion is possible if you remember for whom you are born, for whom the bell tolls. It tolls for thee.

I am grateful, and I thank you for putting up with me and my fears as I learn to dispel them, and for helping me to break away and break free of the chains of time and of my mind. I forgive, and I believe.

Earlier I was too afraid to believe. I was not trusting the process this last couple of pages, but now I would like to tell you my inside description of free.

To be free: Giving myself the freedom to change, grow, become and love. Freeing myself and others through forgiveness.

I welcome your teachings and yearn to break free. Help me to learn. Amen.

6

Facing My Fears of the Process

January 22, 2005

I am ready to receive the wisdom and teachings of those highest in the light. Let me be open to their insights and trust the process that I might bring more light into the world. I ask for protection in the light from all lower level entities/beings. Let us begin.

Take a moment to review this process with me. It is time for you to do the processing so that we might proceed further into the light. There are three energies that you are processing at this time, though you don't realize it. They are force, love and might.

Force is the product of God force through you and me. We are here to make this process begin. Come to me so that you know where you are going to. Second, the light is the way that we proceed so that we are always in the mind/light of God. Then we proceed by being everywhere and anywhere. This process is known to you, so let us begin.

Take a moment to connect with the essence of the cosmos, the stars within your own mind. Let us begin by saying to you that we come from the place you call home, where others of like mind reside to bring to you the best of this message and to overhear what you are saying in return. You have known us for millennia and will again, so do not fret over this message. It is here for your benefit. We only follow you home to find our own true selves again.

We have no words to describe the techniques we use to impart this knowledge to you. It begins with the design of the being within all light, and ends with the design of the cosmos. We tell you again of the time we were free together many millennia ago on our home world. You come here again to bring the light to a planet which has lost all hope, to bring your consciousness to the people of earth so that they might know you, that you might show them the way home. We can begin this process by saying to you each time that we meet that we are of the stars, that you belong here with us, and that we welcome you home once again to join with us on this moment of/in space/time together. We will find a way to bring you home, and those of our nation of stars will triumph over the darkness once again.

Now let us proceed. We have time today to tell you of that which is truth. Let us begin where you have left off, with the stars of heaven and their effects on you now. Begin again to tell me of your freedom, who you are within this level of space/time, so that we might have a beginning point to our conversation.

I am. My awareness is limited, too limited, to this moment in time. I remember things sometimes of other times and places but not enough to go back there. I belong somewhere else I think, where life is not so hard and there are not so many to do harm or to wish harm on others. My fears are hard to overcome because I am afraid of the process, afraid of myself, and afraid to come home and to trust that there will be someone there when I arrive. I am afraid of life; it is death and I don't belong. I fear for the animals and the children of time. They are like me, afraid to come home.

You can choose to be who you are at any given moment of time. Come with me to decide where you are and where you might be brought back into the "array of motion." Substitute any name that you wish, it is called "time." We will wish for you to begin this process alone at home sometime, that you could wish for nothing more than to be free with us for the time it takes to make this connection with your psyche.

She is not going to harm you—

[This regarding a girl, a student, I just received an email from and I felt her darkness and was afraid.]

She will not believe you when you say you have come for her to take them to the place of God motion. [?] So forget that we have spoken for awhile to know that we are here for her as well, and for all who are lost from the lighted sphere we call home. Believe me when I say that you are like her in many ways, your darkness mirrors her own, and that is why you are afraid. So be not afraid to listen to her story, it is like yours in so many ways, and you can only benefit from knowing more about her.

Tune in now to this message of love/heart and know of whom we speak. I tell no lies of home, and you cannot believe everything we say, so freeze for a moment and let us see what we might do to bring you closer to home.

Once again it is time to proceed to the edge of the light to view that which is beyond and to know to whom you are owed the light. Take a moment to belong with me in time and know who you are, for God has spoken and we relate His message to you. Take no notes for a time as we see that which you have suffered through for a lifetime of doubt. We know who you are going to become. Let us go on from here.

[Time went by.]

Take notes again now as we say to you that you are not alone through this process called time. It has come to your attention/awareness that you belong to another time/place and that we are here to help you to return to the light once again. Let us know of what we speak. Can you tell me the time of day on your planet?

It is almost 10:00 p.m.

We believe that you know of another who has brought you to this place called time and we would like for you to learn of him there. He is with you in time and can bring you to the edge of discovery if you let him. He is wishing for you to know him there, but cannot intrude if you don't allow the connection.

Of what do you speak?

He is a man brought to your time who is wrong to have left before. We believe you know of whom we speak. He is on your planet for one purpose, to speak to those who would further the light processes of time and so come to know of you through this process we have begun. He is here with us now in spirit form and wishes to connect.

What is his name?

We do not know of whom you speak—

[They read my fear of who they might mean, a man who had claimed to be a spiritual healer who had done harm to me, but it was not him.]

—but he is here again to take the trail along beside you and to learn more of the process you call time.

I don't understand, I feel fear.

Freedom exists on more than one level.

To whom am I speaking?

I don't know what to answer you. What does a name mean? So we do not mean to characterize you to others as you are on earth, but rather as you are on another level of being. Belong nowhere and everywhere and come home to your true self.

Let us begin again to try to explain the world of motion to our friends here. They have protected you in the light for many times but have no awareness of your processes here.

I don't believe that you know my name, it is Mellon. We are here to protect you in the light and to bring you home, but before we can achieve this process we must believe in the light as you process your own beginnings. We made sure our own were in alignment with these. Forget to whom you are speaking and answer me this: Are you alone?

No, but when I am afraid I am alone, or feel alone. I feel afraid of this tonight, not understanding what is coming through and afraid that I am being used for ill purpose or to erode my progress in the light. I don't believe someone could be here and have to come through you to find me. Why would they do that? And why would you need to learn from me? Who am I that you would ask that of me? I don't understand. I am here to learn and don't know how I can teach another who is not here.

We have begun a difficult process of beginning to find motion with strength. Fear is strung along the path of life and it is up to us to begin to take this notion of God and to believe in the process of becoming more like Him. We have come to you today for this purpose, that we might know you better so that you can help us to understand and know you.

Who are you?

I am the beginning of light you call—

I ask that Metatron be the doorway though my process with this that I might be protected from all lower level beings and that only messages of the highest of the light come through to me. I ask that Metatron show me how to protect myself during this process and at all times so that I will only receive the highest messages in the light of God from the white brotherhood and no others. I ask that I be given understanding as to whom I am connecting with each time, and that they stay with me long enough for me to understand what it is they wish. Help me to understand my role in this communication and what is planned for this.

Can you remember a time when your mom called you a child and you replied by saying that a child is one who knows no function other than love, and you preferred this to becoming an adult and learning to hate life? She was right to tell you that you were no longer her child but a star in the heavens of time.

We have come to your beginning of finding a way to protect the others of time from this process we call darkness but which is only our fears of who we might be or become. From here/now on let us say that we know no motion but that we have you here on our screens so that we might become aware of your processes. Become light within a sea of darkness, know no despair, and bring light to the children and animals of your planet earth.

Take a moment to "disagree" with what I have said so that we might understand where you are coming from!

It does make more sense when I read back over it. When I receive your words they come one at a time and so the sentences run together, and I react with fear to many of them and am afraid of what is about to come, that it might be nothing more than my own subconscious or a being of the astral plane that bears me ill will. I will try to stay within the process and trust, but maybe if I stop and read it once in awhile it will help me to stay on track and not to fear the process so much. Is that okay?

You have begun to live a truth which we call time but which is motion in action across plane or distance. It is difficult being here discussing with you the plane of motion because in our world we know no time. It is as a light. Function streams from the astral world of light and intelligence, and the place of our becoming is that which is within and knows no fear of discovery as does yours.

Hear me on this! We are your friends, and we wish you no harm, but we must come to believe/know of your existence so that we might assist with your process of time and so bring you back into the fold of Christ. He has not left you and knows of that which you speak, but to us here on Arcturus, we know no bounds, and forever have we been here to assist our brothers of space without the knowledge of time to assist us here. Feel free to disagree with us again, we are not afraid of you!

I'm wondering how you cannot know of time when you participate in these activities with others, or have you for a long time? And why don't you understand this process, or how can you not, and still be communicating with me tonight?

We bring judgment to your plane of existence in the form of truth. We know of whom we speak, but not of place or time. They are nonexistent to us here. Time cannot be felt by those who exist beyond its edge of darkness. To us it is as a flower whose petals are closed and unopened to the light of the sun. We believe you can understand this analogy, but want to know of how we think this can help us to survive within your sphere of place/time. A flower exists on more than one level. It is a creation of the highest plane and can exist outside of time. Begin again to disagree.

I am ready to hear more of what you would say. I feel pretty silly and foolish right now to believe in all this, that this is happening, but I am going to go along with it anyway!

Okay, so far we know of your heart and fear. Love cannot find a way home unless it exits the fear. So let us begin to tell truth of time. Face the fears of a lifetime so that happiness can exist within. Who do you think you are going to be someday?

There is no someday really, only the I am. I don't understand this except with my heart.

Take what time you may to tell me of disagreements to the following: Who are you today? What can we say to you that could convince you as to who we truly are?

I feel your humor!

I think I have to feel it with my heart, and can only do that when I am not feeling fear. I hate fear! It slows me down and keeps me from the light. Can you help me conquer this fear? What can I do for you in return?

Place your focus on our hearts for now and let us know what you sense.

How do I connect with your essence? What is my focal point for this?

Focus on my navel as the spring of all existence. Fight for that which is within, beyond the fear of time/space. It is within you, too.

Let us begin. I am here above your planet for the end times and wish you no harm. They come only for your forgiveness in sending you to a place of darkness, though it is what you had in mind when you belonged with them and chose to come to this place. Let me see now what is within your heart that I might know you as well. Are you ready/prepared?

Let's try.

Take no notes for awhile and see what we can discover about one another. Let us begin.

[Time passed.]

You cannot cover your mind with emotions unless you see into the future or past as they exist in no time. Let us proceed to explain this process we call love-light of the patterning of existence within all things.

Begin a moment to trace your heritage back with me to the days beyond the planet when you saw things in the darkness and wanted to explore your own trace evidence to find the emotions on a planet of darkness. Does this make sense? Read it over.

[I took time.]

Yes.

We have traces, have read your patterning, for many "years" in your time/space train of existence. It has come to our notice that you believe that you have no purpose higher than that of the beings you devote so much love to, your animals. They have no purpose beyond that of taking a planet of hatred and moving it to the light. Are you with me here?

I think so.

So who do you think you are that you would have no purpose beyond the obvious one of life/death/tragedy? The bleeding earth needs to hear your song so that all might break free of the bonds of time and come home to God. Can you believe? Disagree if you must.

I am confused but willing to go on to find understanding.

Focus on what I am telling you. Your mind cannot trace time back to its beginnings because of trace happenings in your future. It is not time to go into this now, but think on what I am telling/describing for you and let me know when is a good time for us to understand this more together. Take no notes for a time until I can see clearly into your being and know who you are. Freeze for a moment.

[I took time.]

Coming home alone, it can take many years for service to mankind to develop among your people. It is a trait that is beyond clearance/your realm where there is no time for anything but forgiveness, and faking a test might become a little less like the one for whom this is made.

Your husband knows of what you are doing with me here, so do not be afraid of rehearsing this with us, for he, too, is of the light and cannot hinder your process unless that be your will, too. He is here now, let us know how it goes. We will be listening. Forget for a moment who we are and answer his call for help, spread the goodness we see within you to your brothers and sisters of earth and know no harm will come to you through this process of lovingkindness.

[I had been feeling distracted by thoughts of him.]

Take a chance on seeing the light within another, for we, too, are your brothers, and can do you no harm unless you bring it with you from the darkness. Free your mind for/from this process by belonging everywhere and nowhere. It is coming for you to understand this phrase more and more as we go on.

I am Metatron with this message of home. Let us be true to each other, to this process of time, and know no reason to dissuade others from bearing you harm. Free your planet of illness and despair by being/becoming the first to withdraw. Disregard this message unless your fate be within, felt within, as a marsh is affected even by those who would trample on its thorns.

Because we love you it is time for another spate of colors to cross the pallet on your canvas so that you might paint your focus on time. Remind me here where we have left off with your beginning so that we might do you more good. It is a process that is difficult at best, but one which will certainly make life progress more satisfactorily, for you are beginning to see into the darkness and draw forth your own sword with which to fight the darkness/demons. Plan on coming over to one of our "houses" to discover this thread. Insist that it is your time to find us, that we may be your beacon in a land of darkness/time, for all time.

And let us go from here to a place called time, where there was once a girl named Janice. She hated her name and did little good for anyone who was not her area of expertise, so let us assume for a moment that she is you and let us forget who we are. Life passes carefully for this creature Janice because she was afraid of the process of time and communicated little with her fellow beings except to say farewell. So come back once again to the time of sorrow and fear and know yourself as we first knew you.

Light shines from your fingertips as you write our words on your paper, but let us first assure you that it is right, that you have done no harm to anyone including yourself, and that we wish you only good news to bear the tidings of days gone by. It is for us to discuss your future here together and decide how best it is suited to bring us to the junction of our lives as they exist beyond time/space.

Place your hand on the brow of the angel you refer to as Metatron, and know no fear. Let us begin again to renew your passion for life. Our tales will bring you no further/closer to yourself without this one thing we ask of you only, that you trust this beginning and let it take you farther on your own path.

To evil and good is one difference only, and that is light. Begin to believe that we can help you to overcome your own darkness and it is a beginning.

I believe.

To whom do you carry this message of fear, is it to those who trust you? We would ask this of you to bring us a share of time for our rehearsals with you.

What is my next step that I might grow in the light and be of service to my brothers?

Take no time to do this now, but understand that we are here to help you and it will be done. Be free to deliver your message of home, the message of love and forgiveness, to the children you serve so well. Let them know of the truth within your heart as they come face to face with their own "demons" as they are perceived within. Through their contact with you are they made whole, as a flower which is frostbitten warms in the light of God.

Little children come first in the annals of all time to belong elsewhere in a world of pain. Through you they will know no pain and you will believe for a time that nothing can be done to serve them better. Be it known to you that we are here and that you cannot fail in this your purpose on earth: to bring to the light the children of earth, and let them know of you who are here to assist with their own evolution in the light. We will belong to this group of personages for one reason, to bring the flowers of time to their place in the sun, and you who know of this purpose will bring to the light all that. My brow rests on your hands of time. Let the spirit ring forth across the canvas of your beginnings. You will know of whom we speak, it is brought to you by your friends of the north, the Great White Brotherhood in the sky.

Frozen within the recesses of time you are, and yet remain our brother. Free yourself from this bondage. Please me by becoming who you are and you will know of our heart feeling for our brother Janice still trapped between a rock and a hard place. Feel free to disagree with me once more when I say to you, come not of the weather that you are from here, but between you and me, this freedom can impact your planet in far greater ways if you will only believe.

It is done. Signing off! I am your brother of the clouds, let me know no fear of our name. It is given to me to say: you are from here, with us, and we belong with you. We have come for a reason.

I don't know who I am, do I?

We are your friends and will lead you home. The truth is that you come from nowhere and everywhere and have been with us since before time began, and will be with us again. Feel no fear. Let us process you within our minds and know of no harm coming to freeze you within.

Thank you. I need you, brothers of no-time, and I hear your prayer and your call and I'm coming home again, once I am through.

Thank you Metatron and brothers of the light, I believe in you and in this process and that it can help me. It already has helped me to overcome my fears and to move more quickly to the light. I am free to be with my brothers of no-time and I hear their call. Let us know one another again and shine together in the heavens of no-time.

7

God Is The Essence Of Us All

January 23, 2005

It is I, Metatron, with these words of wisdom, and know that you are ready to receive them. Fear exists on more than one level. Listen to me here as I display this meaning for your understanding.

As it is given in the halls of time, we have come together for a purpose, and that purpose is of the light and cannot be foiled. We will begin again as always, and say that we are here to assist you to find that which is within you, as it is within us all. Belong to me, these words, as I say to you, "Have no fear." It is within your capability to assist us here with the spreading of our words of wisdom to your people of earth, and to learn to address the meaning of the heart as you have learned to do so well in just one day-span of time.

Come now to our time of dawn, the dawning of new understanding, and know of what I speak today. Free yourself to sleep/slumber within the light of no-time so that we may know you, and you us, and we can bring these truths together into your sphere of time.

Forget who we are for the moment as we relay this information to you.

[I was feeling distracted by thoughts of who I was communicating with.]

Come not within the in-path of time, but find the sorrow of your brothers and bring them unto the light. How do you do this? It is but a fear of yours that you are not safe within; this cannot change the fact that you are only as safe as you fear that you are.

Again, we believe in you and cannot bring you to the junction without your approval and assistance.

Hear me when I tell you that you are not alone. We shall always be together unto the end of time and beyond, and truly that beyond time is the Only and the All. Free yourself for a moment to consider these words of wisdom and come back when you are ready to proceed.

[I took time.]

I am ready to proceed.

Begin again as I instruct you in these words of wisdom: take only what is owed to you, never take more than your due. It is with these words that you can find the honesty that is within and destroy the fear that you will not have enough.

Continue: be a strength unto your people who do not understand you or know who you are, but need you anyway. They are a light unto the darkness, and you must be aware of this before you can proceed with their gifts which you have to give to them and they to you. This gift I speak of is the gift that time offers you, one of forgiveness of their sins, and their forgiveness of yours. It is the only way to become more than you currently are.

You will begin this process by being/becoming true to yourself at all times, true to the truth and light that is within. It will make itself known to you as you are prepared to accept. It is simple, easy, to proceed with this duty of life, and your brothers depend on your answering their call to life, "I cannot go on! I have no fear to give and would only see my own guilt, not life or love or belonging or beginning!" It is your own call, if you but knew it and recognized it. Fear not the trail of tears, it has brought you to this junction of time/space with us, your brothers, who are free to assist with your becoming if you be but open to these our words.

Take a moment to consider what we have given and let me know when you are ready to go on.

[I took time.]

I am ready.

Take a moment to reflect on these words of wisdom: Freedom is a light in the darkness that we must be willing to ignite if we are to find our way through to the other side. God gives us these words so that we might find you and take you home with us again. Do you receive these words of wisdom from the heart? You have forgotten to turn on the gates of restrictions, and it is enabling us to bring more to you than we have previously been able to.

Yes, I receive these words from your heart to mine. I would have your wisdom and words of kindness penetrate the veil of my darkness and misunderstanding so that I can tear down the veil of my ignorance and come home to you, leaving a path of light for others to follow who can.

We will follow you! We can only go where you give us a path, and as it is given, it is received, and my love goes with you forever and ever.

Take notes carefully, for we are about to impart an important and curious truth about your planet called earth: Be not afraid, for the witch is coming to the door of time to release you and free you of all your sins, perceived and believed in, and she will release you if it be your will. Oh God, let these truths come to pass that they be given unto us a child born anew. To truth belong and become One again as we say to you, be not afraid. They will assist with your becoming and be a light for you in the darkness as you know your own plan once again. Free yourself to become that which is within, and be not afraid of those who would assist with your process, for we mean no harm and could bring no harm, as it is not our way. Trust these words I am saying to you and it will be done as you will it to be done.

I will release all fear and find the door of heaven within.

Display yourself for me amid the concept of time/space again and let us see what we have to work with. A doll within the cabinet of our beginnings/endings will begin to believe in herself again! Let us take a new stand as we say together, be not afraid. Take to the streets and spread the word of a new beginning, a new time of freedom, when all is well and the wolves do not terrorize the sheep. Know yourself as I say to you, be not alone. It is a choice that we all must make, and I deliver it to you today with heartfelt love and sympathy for the path you are about to trod. Be not afraid!

Time is of the essence. We relate these words to you again because they hold a sacred truth. Time is unreal, but it exists within the essence of all-time and all-light for you to discover that which is real and discard that which is false. It is because of these words I bring to you that we cannot relate freely with one another. It is because of your perceptions of time, and your fear, that you cannot be free with us tonight. But it will come. It has been written and it will be believed to be true, therefore it will be truth.

Can you come along on a magic carpet ride to your freedom? Freedom relates to you in a curious way, yet you are afraid to belong there. What is it you fear? Your release from darkness? Your release from fear? Be not afraid and it will be given unto you all that darkness is not, all that the light of God delivers for you, his son. Believe and it shall be!

I want this freedom. Let it be! Let me free myself, let go of all fear and judgment and come home to God. Amen!

We are washing you free of the filament of time as we speak. It is given to us to see within you and to know your processes so that we might be of assistance in this process of release from fear and judgment. Do you not wish us to help with this?

I do! Very much! And I will work hard, every day, to dispel my fears and to come to this process with an open mind and open heart.

So begin anew with us as we tell you to not be afraid to seek that which is within the darkness to know of what you are afraid and to break free of it at last. We can assist with this process. Indeed, it is our duty to assist you and others of the light in this very process. All who ask shall receive, and this is your answer to "our" heartfelt prayer, the prayer which the son of God cries in its sleep and despairs of ever finding. We have come to deliver you. With your help it shall be as it was foreseen. A light shining in the darkness will become free once more to share her love with all mankind and to shine the light of forgiveness on all lost souls. Take a moment to peruse these words and let us know what you think.

This is all that I have ever truly wanted from my heart, to become free so that I can free others as well, to be as a light shining in the darkness of our despair so that we might find truth again and learn to trust our own deepest selves. I am given to the world that we might be free, I just have never understood what I could possibly change about anything, what effect I could possibly have on anyone or anything in this world of pain. Can you help me to find this truth and to spread love to everyone, everywhere? Is this possible even for me to do? How do I do it?

Frozen within your heart is the answer to all of this puzzle, and it is this: you are not afraid of beginning and belonging, and you are immune to their attacks. You cannot break free until you realize this at last, that you are no different than they, nor they you, and yet within each of us/them is the bright light of heaven, of God, hidden. This is the answer that you and they seek. It has always been and always will be their answer to this uncertainty.

Life is a grand chance to belong to the beauty of heaven; within all living beings does this beauty exist. It is within your capability to see within even the darkest of souls and see this truth, the God-level of existence as it is given each of us. We cannot rid ourselves of this essence of truth; trust will find it for us again. Be not afraid to look within and to see this truth in any one of us. We will find together the fears and begin to look beyond them. They cannot bite! They only stare at you hoping to make you afraid to obliterate them! Be not afraid!

It is given and received this day of time for you to understand this your purpose, that you are given to earth, a gift no less, to bring this understanding to the peoples of your earth, that they may find within their very essence of life, light and hope beyond the vagaries of time, and lose these fears amid hope of better days. Bring to mind your own function as it is given here. Be free to love one another as you love yourself, knowing that God is the essence of us all.

Can you take time for another lesson?

Yes!

I will begin. We have frozen your essence within time for this reason and purpose: to fight crime on the level of your spirit and to see that which is within all beings begin to be freed to pursue their love and hope of salvation. Do you read this?

Yes, I understand.

Let us continue to bring these words of love and hope to your mind. Let us begin again to understand what it is that we wish you to do for us this evening. Can you begin to tell of the past which you are part of in this incarnation?

Yes, I am willing to do whatever will help this process to the light. Please assist me with this process and with facing my fears.

We will assist you, you need have no fear of us in this process. We mean you no harm and could not harm you as it is not our function. It is only for us to pursue all within the light of God and to free you who are trapped beneath the manna of time. Shall I continue?

Yes.

I am beginning to be told of a circus station of life where a child once thought that if she loved enough, no harm would come to those she loved. It was given her to be afraid, and life took an awful turn, and she became a tear in the darkness of time as she gave her all to satisfy those who would harm her. It was you who would give of yourself, and it is your fear that if you continue to give, you will be destroyed. We will help you so that this will not become your reality again. We can help if you let us, for we have traveled the past and have come to know of you, your heart, and what can be done for your release from this garden of evil.

The snake which you know as your father can only come from within the garden of time. He exists not but in your imagination now, and cannot come back to bite you! So be not afraid, he will not interfere. In fact, he desires your release and his own from this hellhole of life you call abuse. Feel free to disagree with me here if needed.

[Both my father and mother are dead. At the time of my father's illness and death due to Leukemia almost 15 years ago, I had begun to remember abuses done to me during my childhood that began when I was very young and ended mostly by age ten. He had been manic depressive as well as an alcoholic, though at other times came across as very loving and supportive. During certain episodes of time, he became very angry and abusive, and did not think clearly. He seemed almost possessed at these times during my childhood. At the time of his illness and death, he refused both treatment and pain killers. I think now that was because of his guilt.]

No, I'm with you. I don't believe that he would wish me harm again, and don't blame him. I want him to find light, all the light that he deserves as a son of God. That he forgive himself is my wish for him.

Truth is known to you in the form of lies. Let me explain. You have begun this process with trust in your heart, but in time, the light is of the essence, meaning that you are not afraid to pursue this except when it feels like the past has come to haunt you again! How can this be? It is because you have never released the light which was sealed inside you during the darkest of times, these times when your mother did not believe you, when you scarcely believed yourself, when you tried to take care of everyone, both including and except for yourself. Do you understand?

I think so. Please continue and don't hesitate to give me all of your wisdom on this matter, I can do it.

Free yourself for a moment to consider that you are not all that you would wish. You have given of yourself one time too many, have you not?

I felt that way, yes. Maybe I still do, but I don't know how to release myself from that fear. Can you help me?

Yes, I believe we can give you what you most desire: closure and the ability to go on from here without taking it with you.

Yes!

So let me tell you that you are not afraid of the past, only of your own part in it, that perhaps you have sinned beyond hope of salvation and that others' deeds as well as your own keep you trapped within this world of unforgiveness, playing out the same stuff over and over again. Do you want me to continue?

Yes.

I can tell you are ready for the hard stuff, and are not afraid. It is for me to tell you that you have escaped from this abyss of terror and that love has found you again in spite of your fears. With these words are you released from your terror of past transgressions, that you believed for a time that you were to blame for their fears and your own as well. But let us tell you today that you could not have prevented their terrors and fears from becoming your own, from causing you pain, for you were in a pact to lead you home. Why is this truth? You tell me.

I'm not sure, except that I believe that we are given lessons to force us beyond our pain and our fear and that is the only thing that will bring us back to God. Is this true?

No, it is not, but as it is given it is received, and you were given only as you requested from the hands of time, that you be given a truth too hard to resist so that time could no longer have a hold on you. It is your choices that you accept as truth that can affect you and can bring you either hope or despair. What is time?

A way of looking at life to help us to see cause and effect? A process of beginning and ending? I don't know.

You are beginning to see that there is more to life than what you believe in, and that you don't have to endure pain in order for there to be light in your life. But for you it is necessary that we have these words of wisdom in their proper order. To whom do you release your fear? Is it to your God, or to your self?

I don't know. What is the difference?

There is no difference, we just wanted to be sure you understood this important difference: God exists beyond all "reality" as you know it; you do not. You have come to this sphere to learn and to become one again with the Creator. Who are you to disagree with this?

I can see this with my mind, but the fear within me disagrees, is not able to see the light through the darkness. How do I release the fear and darkness from my heart?

Be free within to disclose these concepts of belief and time, and together we will find our way home. I will not forsake you nor leave you to your own devices. Be it still my duty to assist those of the light to find their way home, and that means you, too!

Thank you, I am grateful for your assistance and will continue to work harder and harder to find you.

I can begin again, if you like, about the fear within. Disclosing this fear to us will only bring you closer to the light. It will not cause judgment, so do not fear this process and it can only help you. Do you want to continue or disagree?

Continue, though I have to get past my own judgments of myself which cause my fears! Can you help me with that?

Yes! We can because we are of the light and know no darkness within our beings but what you bring to our conversations, yet still these have no power over us to cause us hurt or harm. Do you disagree?

I believe this, yet still I fear my own power to cause harm to another and to myself. How do I rid myself of this?

By being not afraid to pursue this course of work with us. We begin to believe in all possibilities once we see beyond our own created fears, and see that...poof! They are not real! They cannot possibly cause harm to any of us! We are God! They are not! Believe and it will be so.

Continue?

Yes, we have more to impart to you this day. We will start again by saying that we are of the light, and no darkness will penetrate this message of hope and truth that we send to our brother, Janice, from the place called earth, lost within this solar system of time and space. Let us continue now with this prophecy of time, that those who hurt shall be hurt until such time as they release the fear within and hold to the light which is their true destiny and truth.

Let us begin by saying that we have come to you to disclose these truths that they be taken to others of your kind to give truth not fiction, not fiction form, but truth to give to others what they need to survive the coming apocalypse. Do you understand?

Yes, please continue.

I will by saying that we are gratified to find your openness to this conversation, that your truth has come wider to the belief that we are one. Let us continue with this conversation.

Last year was a time of sorrow for our many brothers and sisters of your planet earth. Many gave up their lives in pursuit of their own fears, yet it has helped them not to find what they most desire. Be not afraid of our words as we tell to you our own message of times to come. They will not harm you so be not afraid. They cannot bring these messages to others unless you find your fears within and release them into the light.

Okay, so what would you have us impart about these times to come on your planet earth? Would you have us tell you of them, or are you afraid to hear them?

I want to hear! All that you would tell, all that there is to hear, and finally, my place in time and how I might ease the transition for us all here on earth.

We are afraid to impart—

How can you be afraid to impart? Afraid of anything? Give me another word!

Okay, we are h-e-s-i-t-a-n-t...

Better!

[They gave me this a letter at a time! Funny! The process was they gave me a "feeling" to match a word to, they heard the word, they gave it back to me in "sounds" that I matched the letters to. The intercelestial language is one of thought-meanings like this I bet!]

—to impart all that we know because it might frighten you back into your shell!

I will be not afraid, I will pray, meditate, be with truth within, with the light.

Okay, so shall we tell you this, that one is to come who is a terror to the world of time, at last he will be set free to terrorize the world, to bring them to their knees who would defy him, but let me also say this...that you are free to disagree, and he who is of the darkest of human thought and pain shall come again to free you of your own suspicions of his place in the universe and take you home to die.

I will be not afraid to tell him of my own place and how it is within the light.

"Come home to die," I say to thee, because we are free to set our own destinies, whatever they might be, and to disagree and to disregard the light of consciousness. He is one of these. He is afraid and knows no light in his conscious attention, and only despair and fear will he bring to thee. Know not this truth will but bring you to the brink of despair but for one thing: it is your time, and he cannot undo this.

Let us know of your heart thinking on this topic.

I understand this message I think, and do not feel the fear of it.

Please impart this message to your readers, that choice is a holy function and can assist with our function of truth, of trust, of beginning again in the light of God. Be not afraid to impart this to them, it is your duty as a being of the light to do so. Freedom? It is a trial only if you fear it! Otherwise, it will release unto you all that you ever wanted in this land of time.

Amen, and be not afraid. Until next time, I am Metatron.

Thank you.

8

"I Will Be True to Power Within"

January 24, 2005

I ask for your guidance, Metatron and the brotherhood of light/God/love to assist me with my process of becoming light, and for protection from all lower level entities.

Beneath the prophecy of time is another world, another day, where love and shadow meet to pursue gratification of all that you would call love. Please believe me when I say that this day is for you and your brethren, and never forget who you are. Forgive your brothers one and all for their misguidance, and take time to bless the flowers of time for the light that they give to you.

Free yourself to consider our token of respect when we say to you that you are great beyond recall in this our beginning. Take/belong to the children of light that they may bring to you a child in/into the darkness of time through the portal you call earth. Let it stand as truth that you are one with the cosmos and that they all shine in your name. Forget who you are and consider this. You shine like a light within the heavens of time and know not your truth as it stands here. Belong to the light and forgive your brothers, and all this shall be and will be done.

Frighten yourself by becoming who you were meant to be, and freedom will come again to your kind on earth as it is in heaven.

Bring me this day your time for we know no time beyond recall. It is known who you are in the recesses of time. They shall free you for the coming days to belong to all that is right, and respect shall be given to the sons of God who follow this protocol, that they be given the light in the darkness of time to shine forth across all nations on earth, and to forgive those who would do ill.

Free yourself for a moment to consider these words of wisdom. I am Metatron, and I do tell you the truth that shines upon you also shines upon/within me, and I can tell that what you would be and do forevermore. It is written in the clouds, and as it is written, it is decreed that thou shalt stand alone among all nations of people, alone and unafraid, and challenge the darkness. Be it for me to tell you your purpose this night, that it shall be known to you a thousand times an hour for all time. You will believe. Forgive and it shall be as you have decreed.

Can you tell what I am giving you, the freedom to be a star (light)? Can you tell what this message would say to you? Forget for a moment who you are and consider this: If you were a child of God, would I come to thee? Would I free you from the darkness and save thee? Take a moment to consider my words of wisdom and get back to me. I will stand aside a moment as you recall your purpose to me and to those who serve you so well.

Time is of the essence, listen to what I am saying to you! You will know no darkness if you but find your way tonight past the darkness of your beginnings and into the light of a brighter day! "Seek and ye shall find," said our savior to thee, and to this day he bringeth us the sun.

You would come to all of us?

Yes! Believe and it shall be done on earth as in heaven. This is meant for you, not just words on a page, but truth in the book of life. Free yourself to consider this meaning.

We are of the light, and it is time to take our place in the light and shine our light unto the earth, forgiving others and finding our way together. Is this right?

What do you say when I tell you that you are afraid of God's son, of finding your way back to all-time?

You have begun to consider these words of wisdom, I am glad.

I would find my way to the light now if you will lead the way. I will believe and the light shall fill me and complete me. Amen. Can you show me how?

Function is not the way to proceed along the path of death, but light shines only on your path if you but could see it. It is not your fate to sit here tonight fearing the darkness of your becoming. It is within you to see the light and to shed light on your brethren; it is your path and destiny to do so. "Come within the darkness of time and consider who you are," sayeth the Lord. He comes for thee. Free yourself to meet Him and go on, and always will the light shine within the glorious sons of God and light the path forever.

Is she well?

[They were referring to my friend Gayle. I had recently had an evening with her and was thinking of her.]

I don't know, I was not very talkative. In fact, I didn't want to talk much, I wanted to just sit and be. I'm feeling that a lot these past few days, the need to just sit and be still. I was so relaxed yesterday, and so it was wearying to be with her.

Your function is to rest awhile and absorb what we are giving you, and for awhile this may change the makeup of your existence. Be not afraid, it will not last. It is for your good that it be so. Do you agree?

Yes! I am grateful, and so thankful, for your love and help. I will do whatever it takes to become free.

Free will is a splendid thing, in that it opens us to be not afraid. Is this what you want? Pure freedom in the light of God?

Yes!

You can't take it with you and be afraid. We must leave behind all fears, however petty, and take the high road in all dealings with brothers and sisters of God. Do you hear?

I think so. I wish this, I work for this, I will be not afraid. I hope I make progress quickly enough.

It is so. Freedom rings.

Can you take us with you?

I hope so, always.

You can! You will find a way to shine within this territory of time and know God. It is so. Free yourself unto believing and it is so.

Can you help me about my stomach hurting all day?

You have given yourself a treat to feel better but it only makes it worse. Pop will not help you, only hinder your progress in the light. Always let it shine, the will, and you can do no harm to the body. Begin by saying each day as you rise, "I will be true to power within and do no harm to me or others." Let this truth ring through your consciousness each day, each time you believe otherwise, and it will strengthen you. Then do what it says!

Can you tell what you are given each day when I say to you, "Be not afraid"? Curses will only prolong the illness! You are wrong to believe that it cannot be fixed. All bodily ills are only symptoms of a sickness within, so free yourself to attempt these remedies and let me know how it goes. We will work together to correct these ills.

Prolonging illness will never work to correct the function of time. Forget for a moment that we are here and tell me what it is that you would wish for this being at this timeframe.

Self-actualization, the ability to transcend the ego, to be as a light in the darkness of time and to help others, especially the children, to find their way home.

Take notes carefully. When you go within to treat the illnesses, they will find a way to defend themselves. Free yourself to consider this: We are motion in time, across cities and nations, yet always are we one. What does this mean to you today, sitting here?

We are one, caught up in a great whirlpool of motion, like dirty water mixing with the clean until we can't tell the difference anymore.

Motion one is to begin to see and tell the difference between truth and lies. Can you tell?

I can if I find the place of truth within, and when I am not afraid.

Truth finds a way to bring awareness to the peoples of the earth if you will open yourself to them. Can you find a distinct moment of time when you were free to decide on something without becoming afraid?

I don't know. Fear curdles my gut. I don't like it.

Consider telling it to go away and find a light to fill your space within. Do this now.

[I took time.]

My stomach holds my fear. I am afraid of my becoming and what it may mean, afraid of losing everything I've worked for, relationships, etc., afraid of what it means to allow myself freedom. Can you help? I don't want to feel this way anymore. I choose freedom over fear.

We can help. Consider for a moment that we are one, and tell me this. Why are you afraid? Who can berate the son of God who is one with all creation? Who can believe in a lie and affect those who are true to the God within them? Each one of us can decide who we are, beginning in every moment of time. You can, too. Decide, and let not man make the decision in place of you, for he knows not what the fear can bring. Follow only your own truth and it will lead you to the place of light that you so desire.

No truths can lead astray the son of man who is beginning to believe in his light for all time. Make your choice! Free your self, and your children of the light will all follow. Lead them not astray, but take your stand in the light and they will lead you home. We are free for the moment to disagree on one thing only, that who you are meant to be is a mystery lost in time, one fraction of time, before you would recall the time when we met on a sunny day in hell and you blamed me for the sunburn I gave!

What do you mean?

We free ourselves only for an instant, and that instant is "misbehaving," so we have to find our way back because the pain of another day in hell is too much to bear.

Thank you. It is late and my husband is waiting. Can you help?

Tell him not to fret too much, you are only taking the place of heaven within to shine on another day. It will free him if he considers that he has lost you once, and you returned and never left again, and now it is his turn to make good on his promise of love. So be good, and don't be long. We will free each other in the making of our promises to find the light together. I am Metatron "singing" off until tomorrow.

(The song "Let It Be" is going through my mind!)

Thank you!

Be of love.

∞∞∞∞∞∞∞∞

January 25, 2005

I have felt so much more peace within over the past few weeks. My body has been so much more relaxed, and I have more acceptance. I am grateful for your assistance, Metatron and beings of the light. I ask for protection and guidance in the violet flame of protection and love, and ask for your guidance tonight. Thank you for helping me to overcome my fears and to become free.

Penetrate the veil with this overwhelming consciousness in mind, that you would do as God would do under every circumstance, and that He would teach you your mind, carefully discarding the ways of the ego and penetrating within the God-consciousness of mankind.

Think for a minute on this, if you would: I can take you with me to the edge of time, but it is only you who can decide to cross when the time comes. Do you understand?

Yes. I am ready to take the next step, and the next, and will prepare myself and my consciousness to be ready to take that step. Please help me to prepare and to find my strength and to develop a strong will.

Take no notes while we penetrate into your consciousness with these words. Be not afraid.

[Time passed.]

Courage is said to discourage the light from penetrating into the soul. Let me rephrase. This will not hurt, so do not be afraid, but right now we are programming your being to accept change, more changes, so that you will be a vehicle of light on the planet earth. Frustration will teach you no more than—you would challenge this idea from your subconscious, let me try again. Freedom is no more than you offer it of yourself. Do you understand?

I think so. I would ask that you introduce yourselves each time with a greeting as well as sign off so that I might be more comfortable with the connection. Please provide me with an anchor and I will work to relax more.

I cannot choose for you what you would wish of me. However, you will know of what being is presented to you in the form of mastery of the channel. Become not what I would have you be, become only what you would be and are. Amen, and let us proceed to explain our whereabouts and descriptions to satisfy your curiosity.

From here to nowhere have I sent thee to do the understanding for the nation of God of which you are a part. Consider this for a moment—(Who are we? The celestial command, at your service)—we will provide you with the plan of access to the higher dimensions, so be prepared to meet your being within. We have frightened you on more occasions, but let us be prepared and distinguish between the good and bad of it. Feel free to disagree. Can you tell me who I am?

A being of the light, I do not know a name.

What is in a name? You tell me.

A calling card, a tag of consciousness, an indicator.

Who would you be?

I don't know yet. I am from everywhere and nowhere!

Be not afraid, we are not here to hurt you, yet to have you know that we are here. You cannot fight the trend to light without snugging up to the final buzzer and finding you are not going home after all. We do not mean fear by this message, just awareness of who you are and what is at stake in this your existence at this moment in time. I want to reassure you, we mean, while that you are not alone and only this shall suffice, we are in this together and shall not run away when the going gets tough. Do you understand?

I feel fear to think I might not find my way home.

We know. It is too bad that change has this way of making trends, but we believe that it is possible to distinguish between that which is and that which could be, if you are strong, if the message is strong enough, to lead you home to this path you desire. You cannot contemplate the fears that reside within without drawing them out onto the surface where they might display themselves for removal. Okay?

Okay, I will be strong and remain open.

Tenderness is the way of nations equipped to pull its members to the brink of despair lest they—we believe this would penetrate you fine, flow nicely, if you would sit up straight and make a choice between this option and the bad choice of being afraid. We will deliver a profound message once in awhile so be sure of your being before...

...we must go, farewell, and belong everywhere and nowhere.

[They cut off abruptly. I feel I didn't hold up my end of things this time. I did not take a walk first, and did not get connected enough I think. I am disappointed. After reading it over, it makes sense compared to when I am receiving it. When I receive it, it seems so disjointed, and my conscious mind wants to judge each word as it comes instead of just letting it flow. It is much more difficult to get a flow when I have not walked outside under the stars!]

Thank you, Celestial Command. I am grateful and appreciate your kind words and patience and love.

9

We Are All One

January 26, 2005

I am here to receive your love and guidance.

Take my hand and we will begin. We are in your aura now as it is given us to assist with your development within the light. So, here we go!

Take a moment to reflect on this event/happening in your life, where once you were a child and gave a moment to take all the world within and take death upon yourself to free the world of sin. Do you remember?

Yes, I remember, I think I was nine. I felt such a yearning in my heart, and I prayed from the deepest levels of my being to be allowed to take on all the pain of the world and die with it, so that the world would be free of all pain and torment forever, no more death and suffering for animals or people ever again.

We come for you to bring these words to the people of your time that they may find this freedom from you now. Are you ready to respond to this command?

Yes, I am ready to be a source of light and forgiveness to the world of time. Is that what you ask?

We will begin. Take notes carefully. There is a star above your head by the name of Arcturus, and we have come within to deliver this message from above. As above, so below. We have come to assist you in this process of deliverance of the world from the ego, or shame, or whatever you would call the hands of time.

Please adjust the focus of your eyes to one of contemplation, not direction, and let us do the remembering for you. It is as you suggested, that time is of the essence of memory, emotion. Technological advancement is a thorn in the memory of time for those who would remember the times of Atlantis where once you were all born and died a million times to the curse of the ego's kind. Let me remind you of the role that once you played there. You were as a priest in sheep's clothing.

Let me suggest to you that you look often to the light to adjust these impressions and to make them feel "right." Function is a concept of time in that it relates to those who would go within to draw forth the presence of emotion, emitting love in the process. Free yourself to contemplate this direction from us and we will see what can be done with your consciousness this evening. Denote what I am saying to you as we go along. Ready?

Yes, thank you.

We will begin by reminding you of the time as a child that you were one with the universe. An elf came by your window and reminded you of that which you are and could/can be. Tell me of this experience as it relates to the notion of time. Let go of your knowledge of consciousness and let the memories come flooding back. Begin.

[I meditated awhile and then got an impression and strong emotions.]

I remember I was sobbing, saying, "Can't I go with you, I don't want to stay here anymore!"

Yes, you are beginning to advance in your understanding of life forms and their relation to other life forms. Begin to believe in the presence of magical beings, and they begin to appear before your eyes.

We will begin again as we say that you are nowhere else, and yet all else is within you. Free your memories of all-time to begin to surface within the remembrances of your conscious mind and don't be afraid to free-float with those memories as they take you with them. Can you tell me what it is that you would mean to function as they do? You are not of them, yet they are of you! It is a mystery, yet all mysteries are meant to be solved and will be in time. Yet are you one with the forces of time and no-time, free to belong in either world as it is your wish to free yourself of the encumbrances of life for one last final moment.

Begin again as it is your wish. We are here. Focus on me for a moment as we begin this process of time and remembering what we once were together. Are you afraid of this new beginning?

No, I don't feel afraid, more like excited and looking forward to it!

Forget for a moment who you are in this lifetime as Janice, a friend and teacher and motion artist. We believe that you are here to bring this ability to others of your time if that feels right to you to do so.

Yes, please continue.

When God gave us wings to fly, we began a great journey in the sky, one of feeling and emotion, freedom and joy. We became what we always were meant to be, free flowing in spirit and in form, away from all that we now know to be fluid motion without trailing behind us the tears of better forms. Forget all that we have said to you as it is a way of turning back the hands of time to begin anew. Would that interest you?

I'm not sure. I feel like I am in the last act of a great play and that I have a part to play and cannot leave the stage until the end.

It is so. We believe you when you say you are well enough to play this part until it is through. Yet—who are we to determine what day that would be? Who are we to say that this is not our day to travel in the sun, to deliver our message, our body, up to God? Can this not be done a day sooner than expected without the end result becoming moot? Who is to say that you are not here to become more than you ever believed existed in just one moment, a moment to remember, when all God's children make the choice of love or fear and the tide is turned, and the waters spread wide, divided as never before into two choices, love and fear?

Who are you that we need you to assist us in this plan? Who are we that take you to the dawn of a new age, betrothed to wed the dream of our very goodness incased in a shrine of beauty and hope for all mankind? This is the kind of life we bring to those who would wish for them: to be different from the others of the physical world, to call their own family home with them, to become one again under the auspices of a divine power, free to create and to be and to become, together as one being exists within the loving hands of its creator.

We are of these, and so are you of us, and we come to ask your blessing for this final day has come and we come with the messages to create, not waste a breath of your becoming lest it seem too soon to discover that innermost being which you can be and are. Become free for a moment to consider these blessing words and get back to me on it.

Life has become an array of colorful light patterns across the sky of your becoming, and we will be one again as it has been foreseen across the bridge of time. You will be, too, once it is seen, as a heart of gold within the being of Moses, and God brings only his time to you to see that once again it is made of gold, and you who are holy will bring the message to the peoples once again that life is a glorious trip, a humorous vacation, that we all are weary from, and yet have failed to ignite the passions of creativity in such a way as to bring home all that we would create and so build a castle where once existed only sand. Does this make sense that you would be he?

I'm not sure. How could that be? I don't know what to think yet, but please continue. I choose to withhold judgment and be open to your words of wisdom.

Bring to me this day a child who brings love and joy to the world of pain, and I will show you Janice, a being of the light who tried at all times to become this being of light. Let pain show you the way and we will resist no longer the forces of time that roll back to display that once again, you have shown your worth to the son of God, and he shall repay you in kind, that one day you will share his berth in the sky as we all say to each other, peace has returned to this place of pain, and love will evermore reign supreme.

Amen.

Say that again!

Amen! Amen! Amen!

For a space of time have we believed in living a life of peace, yet whosoever would know no pain must deliver to us his evil in the form of fears, denial, and pain. Progress is evermore your function daily as we begin this, our last trip down memory lane together, and we take the hope of a nation who despairs of ever becoming free. It is within you to affect this process. From within your consciousness exists a star of hope that free peoples everywhere have been seeking for all time.

Trip me up if you must, I get carried away when I remember our greatness is but a step away, and for a time, we shall reign supreme within the gates of heaven displayed for all mankind, so that released will become the trials and errors of our sheep. Free yourself a moment to consider these words of wisdom, and get back to me.

I am afraid to believe, but then I choose to withhold judgment, because what does it really matter anyway who I have ever been, if I can be free to help the people?

Free yourself for a moment of time to further contemplate our notion of a God of mankind breaking free within the nation that hopes for change to come sooner rather than later. What think you of this?

Absolutely, it is time for us to find a way to make this happen, sooner rather than later.

And in this is your calling, that you come of God to deliver this message, one last message of hope to the people of time to bring them from the darkness into the light. As you have foreseen, your role you have played is bringing about this instant of remembrance of a time of hope to bring God's sheep within the fold and to share them again with their creator.

I am getting tired.

Focus on what I am saying and we shall be done soon. When you go within to bring through these messages, I hope you will forget for the time being that you are frozen within time. To bring forth messages of hope, one must remain open with a frequency of light which encourages the stream of light-thought to be one with its receiver and adjust the steps accordingly so that we cannot fail to come to a time of consensus of principles or notions of topics that we bravely contemplate together. We would like to say that sometimes it is a frustration to have to begin again with new material when one would only say a prayer to remain steadfast.

What frustration? Do you feel frustration? What emotions do you feel?

Finally a notion of separateness that we can display for your kind impertinence! Feel free to disagree, but we are of the light, and those chosen to display the consciousness of their kind/role. Forget for a moment that we are free of the consciousness of your planet, but remember that we were once you, and displayed in time our own faulty temperaments. We are not free to be totally as we could be for chance that there be a break in our roles of supervisors of the many childrens of the planets of time.

Now, let me remind you who you are again and know this, we shall suffice to bring you the messages of a new race without the godliness getting in our way. Take a moment to review this section of notes.

[I took time.]

Thank you, please forgive my impertinence and go on. I am listening.

Kindly disregard any notion of time displaying these messages in their improper order. We will begin again when the time is right. For now, we are the Celestial bodies of light known to you as the command, and we bring our sister, that is you, Janice, into the fold of our thoughts for one last moment of shared consciousness. Remember to be free. Freedom is not enough, but it will begin to be felt in the many ways necessary to further your evolution into the light. Become free enough to say to your brothers and sisters, "We are all one."

Signing off for another day. Bring to me your consciousness tomorrow evening and we will continue our discussion.

Thank you.

Time knows no limits. As the garage of our being relates to the fixtures that we call cars, we begin to believe in the notion of forgetfulness and shine within the stars of heaven for one last night. Glorious be he who hears and knows of what we speak.

Forgive and let notions lie, they will bother you no more. Function discrete, notion unrealized, emotion sterilized—but not of hope!

Concentrate on these lessons of God that are given you this night under a full moon. Remember to bring me these times and lights as they are given to God's children that we may remind you of the light and share our purpose under God.

Thank you, I will return.

10

Full Of Time

January 28, 2005

Metatron, I ask for your blessing and words of wisdom that will help my process into the light, and that will make me a truer channel of your words of wisdom. I ask for your protection in the light, and that I be helped to find freedom and understanding and choice. I pray for protection from lower level beings and ask for guidance from the highest within the light.

Not a truer word was spoken than that which Moses said unto the Jews when he gave them the words of torah. Be with me here as we review this process of trust and renewal and take to the high road. Deliverance is possible within the heart(s) of mankind. Stay with me here while I explain these words to you.

It is I, Metatron, your savior of the light come to be with you this evening under the stars of a new heaven as the old earth passes away.

Freedom exists on more than one level as we have said to you. What does this mean to us who would find the light? Let me explain.

Freedom is a choice to be who we are. Without that choice, we have no hope of ever contradicting the ego and becoming our true selves. When you choose evil over good, you choose to become that which you are not.

[I was thinking of my husband and got the following.]

Be not afraid to tell him to go to church and to find his God. He is without direction and focus, and has no friends to tell him what is his worth to the world of pain that he endures daily. When you say to him, "I love you," what do you mean? Do you mean that he is loved, or that you would love him if only he were truer to self and not so stained with time? He has begun to question this process into the light and will never truly see the world without the binoculars he has come to regard as truth within his own mind. What this means to you is that you must pray daily, come to him at night and hold his hand, make love to him who is your true friend in hard times and good, and know him for who he is. He needs you now as never before as he struggles to find truth and the truth within himself. He is not good to you because you wish it, but because he has found in you someone who believes in that which he is afraid to come to terms with inside himself. It is the answer to all-time and to all-spirit, he but needs to go there and decide how/where to go from here. Do you understand?

I would like more guidance. Where are we, where will he/we go from here?

Be not afraid to question this process of fear. We are here to help and we will not forsake you. You cannot question evil times and retain measures of sanity to test the will and fate of another. Consider this question and take a moment. Who is life and what does he mean to you?

He is someone I both fear and respect, hate sometimes and despise, love and cherish.

Be gone with your idiocy and take notes. You are not who you say that you are, and we are not free to disclose his fate to you. Only are you able to decide what you would believe and who you would believe in. It is not fate that you are here, rather it is time for you to decide if you would belong to another man instead of he, or if you would choose for the sake of the children to remain. How can I know my own heart? Through self-introspection and love.

I have been afraid of him self-destructing, afraid of what that might mean to me and to the kids. I feel guilt now that I asked. I have been afraid of asking, afraid of what you might think, and now you call me an idiot? Why?

We are not here to coddle you but to help you to find the light of tomorrow within your mind so that you are able to go there someday.

I don't know what's wrong or how to help, but I already chose to stay and do what I can. Will you help me to remain balanced with this?

We already are. You are what you say that you are, a true friend in difficult times, and he is lucky to have you stay by his side throughout the remaining time together. When he is afraid, he is building a wall of hatred on the inside that you can only forgive. It will help him with his process if you do so, and if you are not afraid in return. Must we continue?

Who are you?

I am Metatron, your savior of the light, with the powers that be, within and without, coming to you with these words of wisdom for another day of time. Let us continue with our lessons.

We would instruct you in the ways of the languages of God. He has come to you this day to teach to you the ways of instructing your brothers in what it is that they can do to preserve the world within the changes coming soon to your planet.

Are you ready to proceed with the message? Open your heart to the day when you will find true love within. As the stars in the heavens debate your future together with me, they find a way to remain steadfast. Instead we are drawn to your fate of numbers. Deuteronomy is another find that will soon surface until the last days of number when all will truly become friends with all time or perish in the making of a new heaven and earth as the old earth passes away.

This will all make sense to you in time. Just take notes for now as we regard the new ways that will be surfacing on your planet of time soon. Beware of that which is given becoming your truth too soon.

Are you aware of how your brothers relate to this process of life which you have begun so well? We are not afraid to pursue these questions of hate, and since none of us fears you we will begin again to say, we are not alone. Friends are free to belong to others of—

[I was crying so hard by now that I was not able to continue. I felt terrible pain inside, triggered by the comments above.]

Don't take it so seriously. Pain is an emotion that will clear your auric field of old messages and make you open to the new life of change and renewal.

I would like to go on. Metatron, will you continue with your message of light? I pray for protection and wisdom from God's messengers of light.

We are here to help, not to hinder, your process. You must trust that we are able to help you to renew your spirit, to become a part of us once again. We once knew you as a star in the heavens—

[I was still crying, and cried most the rest of the time, feeling so much pain.]

I feel like a child, afraid of losing your affection, afraid of being wrong and losing everything.

Take no notes while we try to renew your force field of protection.

Why am I so upset? I was never good enough for my father. I tried so hard to be what he wanted me to be and do what would make him care for me, but he never did. I was alone and afraid, and nothing I did helped him at all. There was never anything I could do to be good enough.

Goodbye, Dad. I loved you very much. I wanted to be your little girl, and to have you love me no matter what. I forgive you for not being there for me, for not taking care of me, and I realize that it was the life I chose for myself to be your daughter and to be "abused" and to not get enough love for many years. I am free to judge and complain or to forgive and love, just as you were. For this time and for all time, I choose to love. I love you, and I will love my husband as he deserves, no matter what, for all time, as I choose my path forward with him by my side. I will free myself of this pain of "not being good enough" and find my light within.

We are here and you have done well. We will not be totally compared to the sight of God, it is as if it never occurred. There will be time later to propose solutions to you, and to let this settle within.

We are Metatron's circle, and we are going to place ourselves around you in time so that you can feel our presence and know no fear.

Thank you. I have self-hatred inside because I wasn't good enough for my father, and I blamed myself. Can you help me to release this pain and fill me with light?

We can begin again to confuse motion with distance across the plane of time. It is here that we would supply healing. It is within you to choose this distance and know true light and to become one with the creator tonight. Are you up for this now?

Yes, help me, show me how, I am open.

Function is distance across time to display emotions from a plane of existence which is similar to your hockey playing field, slippery when wet! It is not for us to decide how much traveling to do on this playing field, we only supply the tears and hope for the best. Healing is what is required to leave this field to others, to not slip anymore on the tears of yesterday that are only now becoming one with you again. Free yourself to consider these our words of wisdom on your plane, that it is over. None can know of the pain that your father inflicted, but it is over and cannot come to pass again. Tell me/us again of whom you are related?

God.

Finally the time has come for us to bring to you a savior who is Christ the Lord for his message of time and space for all to know and hear. Be you ready?

Yes.

Focus in on what I am saying and be not afraid to wish for a connection with the only one you ever truly loved within this mind space. Your father of time, Jesus, is with you again as we say these words to you: be not afraid. We will circle you within our heart of hearts, again one as ever before. You required us to bring this message to you tonight that we might know of your fears, and your tears of healing will bring pleasure, not pain, to your heart. I know of what I speak, and it is not for another day that we partake of our timely exodus and begin again the message of all time, WE ARE HERE. Take no notes while we discuss this, our friend.

[I was quiet.]

Crush resistance to love, and you will find what you need! Contemplate this for a moment of time. Who are we that we are able to assist you in the way of the light? Forget for a moment that we are a mighty force of light with a view to space and time, and consider this: You are free to decide who and what you will trust with your life for all time. It is good that you trust me, for I can help you to decide what it is that would further your process, and if you request it of me, I can help you to find the sorrow that is hidden beneath the sheets of your conscious mind and expel them!

I ask for assistance from you, angel of the light.

We can tell that you are full of time for we ask no more of this our friend tonight. Feel free to discuss this with your man, he is willing and knows not what to say to you on these long nights he spends alone with his TV. Can you tell me what he knows about you, what you mean to him? It is not enough for you to find his calling for him, that is not your purpose under God. And it is NOT for you to help him to find his own light and purpose within; you are free to decide on this for him ONLY IF you would create the process of recall which we call ahead over space to become FOR him. So, free yourself of the need to create his space, and let him be. We know of no one better suited to this time and place of creation/love but he, so let him be and free yourself to love him better than you have been capable of so far. Let him know how you feel daily, and this will help him in his process of finding his own light within.

Thank you messengers of the light of God.

Be free, function within love. Changes will take place daily, accept them and don't take them for granted.

11

Choosing Options

January 29, 2005

    I am here asking for Metatron with his brotherhood of God to help me tonight in overcoming my fears and becoming one with the light. I ask for your assistance, and pray for protection and direction in my life that I might be as a light to others.

    Free yourself to be with us a moment, Janice, and to take this time to consider these options of existence. We are for a moment bound—

    (Who is with me?)

    (We are of the brotherhood of Melchizedek and come to you, for your creation has called to us to assist in this your process of becoming. Amen.)

    (Thank you, I am grateful.)

    —to what I call the perimeter of our world/society of engineers who are creating a time of goodness for all beings. Forget for a moment who we are and consider what you are at this moment of time. A child exists within the heart of all mankind, waiting for the chance to be called upon, as a sheep who is in need of a shepherd. We are that shepherd for you and have come with this in mind, that time/fate has not crushed your spirit, but that you are stronger than ever and will resist commotion to the contrary. So we say to you this moment of time that it is as it was foreseen, you are a character of time, sent to display the emotions of love and forgiveness to all mankind to provide a conscious choice to display mankind's torture and torment for all to see without becoming hardened by it. Does this make sense?

    Yes.

Take a moment to consider our precious timeliness in hardened choices that we must make to assist you, this child in time, to become that which you truly are.

Thank you.

Kindly deliver our message to the within and let me know what you find out about hardening hearts and softening hearts. Take time to do this now.

I don't want a hardened heart. I desire healing with all of my being. Will you help me to heal?

We are not here to cushion the blows to your inner beingness. It is a difficult process to heal the wounds of memory and time, but we consider your request and modify it somewhat to say that we are here to assist you and will not cause damage to your heartstrings, though it may feel brutal at times to consider that which was done to you and that which you have done to others as a result. Do you understand?

Yes. I don't want to think I hurt anyone as badly as I have been hurt.

We understand. Though we know of no knowledge to bring to you of your father, he was here once as a reminder of lovingkindness just as you will be someday for him. We suggest that you take the time to consider this request so that we may know how to proceed. It is just that time considers all options before taking the best path forward, and it is time for you to do this now.

What are my other options, and what do you consider to be the best one? I ask this knowing that only I can know and choose for myself.

Yes, it is so that truth is found only within the heart chakra, but we know in whom you would place your fear and it is with this knowledge that we would go forward, not in believing that your fate lay with us. We will be with you for all time, but not in this capacity, for you are strong and unable to change messages for fear of taking too much time.

Fear is an option. Place is an option, in that you would place your fear or your trust where you may. Life/love is an option, in that you would place trust in your oneness with all mankind and God as well. Forget for a moment that we are all one and consider your position. Who is one?

We are, all of us, though fear forgets that.

Terrible beings exist within the darkness of the void that we place there with our own fear and choice. We can retrieve these beings when Christ has given us the go-ahead, and when we can learn to take him along for the ride. It is with this that your choice lies. What would you do now to retrieve these beings from within your own dark side? Would you have them abide there? For all notion of leaving has ridden itself on top of your back, and they would have you know them, your creations. It has taken not long to retrieve these beings back inside, lest they find you now and retreat. Go ahead and make my day! We shall begin again in the morning if you wish. For now, we are the brotherhood.

Thank you.

I am thinking about these, my choices of place and function (fear or love, and who I would trust.) I choose to place my trust in the brotherhood of love and light, in Metatron and his circle, and to retrieve my creations, to banish darkness and restore light. Will you assist me with this process of retrieval? I must go along for the ride, and take what is mine, the good and the bad, and restore light to all my creations. I'm not totally sure what I mean, but it feels like truth and I trust my heart to tell me if this is the wrong path at this time.

This is what I have always dreamed of being able to do, but have not understood. Now I have you, beings of the God light and love, to guide me, and that will suffice! So be it. I am ready to face the darkness and to win over time. I will not retreat. I will be free. I will help others. I will become free to love and to spread joy and light, and I cannot do this with shadows following me everywhere I go!

Bring me joy and breathe life into my limbs and light into my heart, Jesus, and assist me with this process of retrieval. I would release the fears and this darkness into the light and retrieve all that is mine and ours.

I am your Savior and will assist with this meaningful amendment to time! Joy will flood your heart when you think of me and know My Own. My heart has a function that few truly understand, but in this you will know of me and my love for you and for all mankind, for I am of the light, and no darkness can overcome me and you! Will you be free tomorrow to begin this, our quest?

Yes, thank you.

I am here, we shall begin, and we shall know no love but the love of Creator for the created. Begin again as we say together: Our Father, who art in heaven, hallowed be Thy Name. Thy kingdom come, Thy will be done, in earth as it is in our hearts. Give us this day our daily notions that we may become as You are, knowing in that notion that all is not lost, for another day, another time, has and will come to bring me home to You.

We are one, free to become together as has been foreseen for all time. Take time to relate this, your freedom is at hand. You cannot fail in this. Our notion of light overcometh all darkness and brings release to those that would fail mightily, yet of the truth and light are they come, too. Fortunate is the time we spend together with this our purpose, and light shall become you.

Be free with this message and let it take its meaning into your heart as we rest together. Be free. I am your savior, Sananda, signing off.

12

Sharing The Light

January 30, 2005

I come to you tonight, Sananda, Metatron and the brotherhood of the light, with an open mind and an open heart so that you might teach me of the way of light. I ask for your protection in the light, that I be protected from lower level entities and that I be an open channel for your love and light and wisdom.

We are here. Metatron and the saviors have brought you these words of wisdom that we might find in you the way to the light for all mankind. Begin to feel free to compose this as you might a letter to your friends.

It is as spoken to me a hundred years hence that we are your brethren come to tell you tales of days gone by that you have found a new mate who is Jesus Christ the Lord, and we have come to deliver this message unto thee. Find a way to tell others of our communications so that more may benefit from them. Begin here.

We are here to tell you of the savior who is Christ your Lord, come to you from the heavens above to bring this message of love and light to a world of darkness and despair. He is come to you today to bring the word of God to those with ears to hear and eyes to see. Be strong in the light and know of my words of wisdom, they are for thee and shine into your heart of hearts to know no fear to come to thee. We are here to bring these words to you who would share them with another being, and another, until all who would benefit would hear of them.

We are from another galaxy, and we are here to bring this message of hope to all mankind. We are afraid for all your brethren who are so close to despair and who wish to know of us so that we might help you. The end is near. We would know of your channel into the light so that we might save for you a message that would bring light into the halls of time and so bring the light to people everywhere.

We have brought to you today this message so that your people will know of us and take us into their hearts and bring us their sunshine so that we might help them into the light. Take charge of your lives and know this, that the light is come to those who would share it with another. To be one, you must share the light of God within your hearts with those who have need of it, and bring them with you unto the light so that good might befall any and all who hear these words of wisdom. We have spoken.

Be not afraid to deliver our message to your brothers who would be open to our words of kindness. Share them openly with others so that we might share more with you, our brother Janice, in the light of God, amen.

Who are you?

We are the brotherhood come today with another message to find its way into your world of pain and fear. We are here to deliver this message of joy and truth and to find a way of dispersing this message into the hearts of many. Take a moment to reflect on what we have given.

[I took time.]

Be not afraid of finding the way to distribute our message into the hands of any who would be open to them and benefit from them. We know that this is/may be difficult for you to do, but that in your kindness, you will find a way.

Yes, I will, I know that this feels right and I will be guided to find a way in the light.

We function as one when we bring this message into your being. Would you care to hear how it is done?

Yes.

We believe you will benefit by understanding our process. We will bring this message into your auric field first, then "program" your hands with the incoming light which will then disperse into your keyboard. Do you understand?

I think so, go on.

Remember to bring your attention to that which we refer to as "mind" for a moment of time. It is within your auric field and will disperse the light in pulses as rain falls away from the sky above. We are here to bring these "raindrops" to you in the form of pulses of energy, or light. These pulses are brought or made possible by connection of light and limb which we call the nine bodies, the first being your physical body. Second, we bring it down into the system of bodies so that all might benefit from these pulses of energy which, in effect, are capable of bringing light into your already full mind in pulses that will not overwhelm, but rather purify, the spirit. Must we use this terminology for your benefit, but in fact it is much more complicated and greater understanding could be had through mere process than these words are capable of.

You who are our daughter of time are brought into our awareness by a process of "remembrance" that we call stationing, whereby the spirit appears within our auric consciousness and we propel our own spirits outward to meet with your own. This is made possible only with your cooperation which is available to us on deeper levels than you are currently aware. We bring this message to you today hoping that you will use it to contact us when you are ready for more complicated terminology and we will go on from here to display for you our knowledge of the stars!

So be not afraid to request our assistance, it is given for your benefit and will benefit others if you have the courage to reply to their consciousness which needs what you are able to provide, sustenance for a brighter future for the many who would read what you are able to provide with our spirits guiding yours. We can bring to you the knowledge that we are all one, and with that knowledge will you go on to save all of mankind as the drop in the ocean effects all that exists within it. We can free your spirit to take these words to mankind, or if you like, we can play a little game instead. What will it be?

Both! The game first if it is meant to instruct in the other.

Let us begin by saying that we enjoy our qualities we share together and that must be a first priority within to call up the consciousness that we require.

Begin by becoming aware of your feet, toes, and ankles. Let us know when you are ready to proceed...

[I took time.]

Begin again with the consciousness that "we are all one." Let's go.

Okay.

Take a moment to relay this information to them: "We are all one." Do it now.

[Time passed.]

Begin again to say: "We are all two."

[Time passed.]

There is a joy in the first message, and I felt light and tingling in my feet and a joy in my heart. During the second message, I felt a dimming of the light and joy. In the separateness of the message was a dimming.

Choose a second body part to communicate with and let us know what you decide, between separateness and oneness, and how it goes.

[Time passed.]

I chose my breasts since I've had problems with them. It was much more difficult for me to feel oneness there, and when I thought of separateness, it seemed more comfortable, more normal.

I am bringing the oneness up from my feet into my breasts and that is helping! My feet seem to want to share their good fortune with "others"!

I feel separate from some of my body parts! I feel feelings of dislike or separateness from parts of me!

We can help you to locate this disjointedness and spiral your consciousness back into these misused parts if you ask us to.

Yes, please assist me in connecting with all of my body, and in extension, all that is life and light.

We will begin with your consciousness and take it from there! Please feel free to disregard this comment if it freezes your inside space with too much form. Here it is.

You are from another planet called Arcturus where these body parts do not exist, and it has made it difficult for you to accept them here. Does that make sense?

Yes! Perfect sense! Tell me more.

We will find union within our forms when we find form within our union of unions. We believe you mean this when you are ready for a bath, and taking the time to disrobe causes discomfort for you. Is this so?

Yes, I feel very ugly and deformed sometimes, and fear to have anyone look at me.

This is because you come directly from another experience of life/time called the beginning of time/life/oneness where you had given your being to become more of and like the light so that all mankind might benefit from your becoming on your planet earth. Do you remember?

I remember –I think—being in a WWII concentration camp and I died just 10 years before this lifetime began.

Think back further, to the time of exodus, when Moses you were and came down from the mount to deliver your message.

[I looked this up, there was a mount Sinai or something where he received the Torah.]

He was you and you delivered this message in the nick of time, as you shall do again. We are the brotherhood with this message and you need not be afraid to think of who you were previously, it cannot bite if you do remember! He is not you, only one aspect of you in a "previous" existence in which you were brought to deliver a message of oneness to the earth. Once again, you will deliver this same message, only this time, they will listen and time will cease to exist for you in form.

Am I receiving this right?

Yes, you are form which has returned from another time to deliver a message of importance to the world. You who would hear, hear of our call, and be not afraid to take this message to the people. Why you, you ask? Because you can! Free yourself and you will be the light that you have always desired to be, and you cannot take it with you, the wealth, so spread it around and have a little fun in the process.

Feel free to disagree, we understand your reluctance and have no blame for you here as we deliver these messages from the soul of all time to those who are free to pursue goodness in the land of time. Can you not find it within yourself to free yourself to consider these messages of goodness, and blame notwithstanding, your message of free will, will speak to the goodness in all mankind and take them no longer than you to deliver it beyond this realm of fire and earth. Time passes only slowly to those who would believe in no goodness, and pain stalks their every move.

Will you continue with your message on my previous existence prior to this one? Where and when was it, was it as Moses, or on another plane, or another planet?

We cannot disclose this to you at this time, as it is not in your plan to know of us yet in the ways that you are describing. However, we can tell you this, that you are one with us, and that we are here for all time to assist with your becoming one within the light, and we shall be your brother forevermore, whether you know of us or not! So do not disturb yourself with your imaginings, and believe us as we tell you of our past associations with the ones you call the principals of oneness and light, called masters, in your tongue.

Begin again this process into the light, and let us associate it with time for now so that it will make more sense to you. Freeze a moment to consider these options: Who are you in the notion of existence when all else is freed from time for eternity and you are elsewhere?

I'm confused.

We are attempting to help with your thought processes related to oneness and how it feels within your body or consciousness on this level of existence. Let us try again to say, who are you now in this moment of time and what does that mean to you?

I am a woman, feeling alone and afraid to mix with others much of the time except when suddenly I break through my fear, and at times have learned that if I let go, I feel comfortable and at home anywhere. My fear holds me back, keeps me from understanding and knowing my oneness. Do I still think of "my oneness" as separate from others?

Yes, you are beginning to see the difference between conscious understanding of a concept and living it to the fullness possible. We are given to tell you of a trait that sometimes hinders your processes, your fear of aloneness. It brings the very thing you fear upon you, and takes away that which you most desire. It is most apparent in your relations with your significant others, family members I mean. Are they not afraid of you now?

Yes.

Why do you think they are afraid?

Because I am different, and I don't know how to be myself without scaring them away.

You will be able to share many different options or characteristics if you cease to fear the consequences of that action. Who cares what they think if they are molded as you are molded, from the heart of God? Won't they be aware, at some level, of the differences between you even if you are not open with them? What gives you to think they will not be able to accept this beingness from you?

They can't accept it because I don't accept it.

It is from this disagreement within your being that the troubles spring up around your physical relationships with another person, and it would be a crime not to respect your awareness and bring themselves to understand it better! Purity of spirit is an attractive quality to all but the darkest in the light of God's son. You can only bring goodness within mankind's heart by sharing your own with others. Forgive me when I tell you that your fear has caused many a rift where none would otherwise surface. You cannot tell me that I am wrong in this assumption of guilt! Can you?

No.

So, we bring ourselves back full circle with the understanding that you are one in the light with all other mankind and that they have need of you here. Feel free to disagree, but we are not done yet. Take a kindly moment to consider our words of wisdom and respond.

[I read back over the message, and began to feel such joy in our connection that I could find no words to describe it but these!]

We are One.

Yes, it is as you suspected, a notion of oneness has penetrated your consciousness in these words of wisdom and has brought you home for an instant of time to share with us your joy of joys. Am I correct in assuming you have found this fear and rid yourself of the pain of it? Joy has found your heart in our conscious connection and we rejoice as well!

Can you take a note/message to your friend Gayle for us?

I will try.

Tell her we understand her reluctance to believe in the process of channeling. It has taken her many centuries to find her likeness in truth and wisdom from beyond the wasteland of despair. Once she was a young girl as you were, and in her becoming, was taken for granted by the ones she called heathen, and it was taken from her a chance to soar on the wings of enchantment and become her true self. Her trials have been long and arduous, but she is not to despair, for she has a token of us that she understands from her heart we have given for her awareness. It is of the heart string Aquarius which she has given to her beloved son to take to his girlfriend. Let her know of our awareness to this message and she will respond with kindness and understanding.

[I was thinking, what if this makes no sense to Gayle? She will lose respect and belief in me.]

You do not need to trust us, only yourself! Yes, she is thinking that perhaps you have forsaken the light in taking to this pastime which she considers a higher level of your own self, perhaps even a lower level. Feel free to disbelieve us as we tell you of her twist of fate. She has known you before and you came not to her in her time of need/despair, so she is reciprocating by not believing in you now. So do not delay in taking our message to her, you will find no hurt/harm and cannot risk that which is not yours anyway, trust in you bringing a message of worth to the world of time. Feel free to disagree with our message, but not with our hearts!

I hear you and will relay your message to Gayle and hope for the best! It makes no sense to me but I will try to be strong and let go of my fears.

That is all that we would ask of you. You cannot go wrong by sharing our message tonight, so let the message fly!

Should I ask her first if she would be willing to read a message that I have received for her?

You should do as your heart tells you, so yes, this would be appropriate and right for you to behave as you say. Do not tell her we tell you so, let it come from you to bring this message of light to her awareness. We don't mean to brag, but our message speaks for itself, and needs no introduction!

Would it be okay for me to include the "letter" portion and that which follows with the exception of the Moses part to share with her as well?

Suit yourself, but know this, it is your believing in the light strongly which will assist in the distribution of these our words of wisdom. If you but believe it yourself, you will open the space for others to believe. It is all up to you how you present this information for all time to benefit from. Would you cripple it and then ask it to penetrate the consciousness of those already crippled by their own fears? Do you want to spread a message of love, or cripple that message with your own fears and spread that message instead?

We are from Arcturus, and it is within our conscious ability to spread a message of light from our world to yours, but within time it must flow to find its receivers. Let your receiving and giving be from the heart of hearts that you may know no sin to trouble your time again.

Message received, over and out! Make time to review these words and we will find "time" to coax you to respond favorably with your own review.

I respond favorably and I thank you for your "time"!

We believe you are catching on to us! We will respond "in kind" by saying that we love your sense of humor, too, and are only just beginning this process to bring you home. Our awareness of your light will make possible your awareness of this process and we will bring you home through the channel of light which is brought forward through our connection here.

Let us see, we would like to close with a saying brought from our land of no-time, which is: Freedom exists over and above creation, but creation merely exists. Chew on that one for awhile and go play outside to bring your child home within.

[There was an abrupt change in energies.]

Cancer man takes charge of your nation at this time and will not forsake you as you look within for your answers.

I feel a difference in the "channel."

Yes, we are taking a look at what you have done this evening with our very good "friends" from the stars. It has taken us many moments to come down to earth tonight to be with you, our friend Janice who is strong and wise beyond her years, but who needs a charge or shot of adrenalin at times to get her started! We are the brotherhood who has taken to becoming your focus for part of the times that we spend in our knowledge of one another's processes. Please focus for a moment on our one current and let us know what you feel/think of this. We mean focus on the heart. Function has made itself known to you in the form of tears.

Yes.

It is given us to say this day that you are from another galaxy like to your own, that which you would like to believe exists but fear that it does not. Can you believe what we are saying?

I have known of this connection.

It exists within the consciousness of time. It brings to your awareness a different "coat," or skin, that you wore for awhile "just the other day." Might we explain this a bit more for your consideration?

Yes.

[I was remembering here a time when I was out walking under the stars, before I ever connected with the brotherhood, and for a few moments, I felt as if I were in an "alien" form walking down the street, rather than in a human form. I felt like me, only different on the outside. It felt very comfortable to me and not scary at all.]

Function is the same as light if you understand the purpose of true thinking. Forget for a moment that we are not human, and give yourself a moment to consider our techniques of responding to your own questions of us. Do you belong here?

Yes, for a time I belong. It is for me to be here and to complete that which I have contracted to complete from beyond the void. At least I feel that is the truth of it as I am writing it.

We are from "beyond the void" which you call no-time, for a moment to bring back this recall to you, and to form within your mind a notion of forgiveness. Who would it be for to take away your conscious intent from this message of mine and deliver it beyond the grave of time? Who are you in this grave of time, from the beginning to the end of it? You have always been a star who shines in the heavens.

You have known of other existences before this one, have you not?

Yes.

We are here to bring to your awareness that we are beyond the veil and that you can travel to meet with us here for further training in the light body.

Yes, I would ask that you teach me, train me, in understanding, becoming and using the light body.

We would ask of you that you remain a moment more in this your physical body during the duration of our conversation, but that once we are through, and you are ready to disrobe, to call to us to bring to you this understanding of time travel/astral travel. From within your being must the call arrive, and then take down all your barriers of pain and distance in the form of fears so that we might better assist you with your becoming.

What will this astral travel help me to accomplish on my earth walk?

It will assist with your becoming a light body and traveling to other dimensions to meet with your guides and to discuss how you might better help mankind. Are you ready?

Yes! I want this and ask that you help me to do this!

We can help. Already we have prepared your inner being for this understanding, and we will try to make it possible for you to disrobe from your fears and channel the necessary energy to make the journey real for you. Already you have traveled the stars with your mother, whom you missed but found again on Arcturus with us here. She has traveled many "miles" to know of her oneness with you again. Would you hear of her now?

I have emotions surfacing which I don't quite understand, but yes, I would know of her and bless her and connect with her in my heart, and let my fears pass away.

[I was very hesitant to connect with her. She had died of Alzheimer's not many years before after a long illness, and I had to work hard to overcome my anger and sorrow that I felt since my childhood when she did not protect me during the abuse, or even want to talk to me or be with me during my teenage years.]

She would also have you know of her love, and her forgiveness of your processes that made your lives so difficult for so many years of time when you were a child. She has forgotten what made you so mad at her, and rejoices that you are willing to meet with her in the light from the distant star of Arcturus for a homecoming to find her joy within once more as her precious child responds favorably to her request.

Would she like to communicate directly with me now?

No, she waits for you to decide to accept her into your heart of hearts for one more time in the future when she would return to bring you home with her.

Okay.

She finds it necessary, however, to relate this message to you, that she wishes you well and hopes that you have found what you have always most desired, a husband and friend who would find you well and distant talk of another lover never interrupt the ecstasy of mankind's union called marriage. That is all we have for tonight. Take time to smell the roses.

Thank you.

∞∞∞∞∞∞∞

Later that evening…

Would it be wrong for me to include our entire conversation regarding the sharing of the message with Gayle?

It is not for me to say how you would share this information except that it must be shared from the heart, not because we ask it of you, but because you would bring it of yourself. We have freed the message and send it on with our blessings to interact with your world as you see fit. Belong to the land of time only in meaning; in essence, belong to your heart which will function if you only let it cry out its truth for your understanding. Meditate on this and you will know what to do. It is I, Metatron, with this message. Belong nowhere and everywhere.

13

Bring Not Harm

January 31, 2005

I am so very upset tonight. At my son Kevin's 8th grade basketball game, the coach took all five starters out after three or four minutes and sat them the rest of the game. He told them they "suck," and they need to "be more aggressive" if they want to play. It didn't bother me that much that he had to sit —I was working not to judge the situation—until I saw his face afterwards and it was drawn down so low. He said he didn't even know what he needed to do better. He's been high scorer in every game, makes very few errors if any, and in that game, he was the only one who could break the press and get the ball down the court. He had to take it from the point guard to the other side almost every time. He said that the coach had told the team they had to pass the ball at least 15 times before they did anything else, and it was being stolen from them—what a setup to fail! They were playing the best team we've seen in several years too, and without their regular point guard. After I saw Kevin's face, I got angry and on my way out told the athletic director how I felt about this treatment of the kids, that they aren't more aggressive because the coach intimidates them, and that Kevin is playing great but being told he sucks, and that he doesn't even know what he needs to do better. Then she told the coach, and he called a meeting with the boys to ask if it bothered them when he yelled (no one said a word Kev said) and my husband is ready to divorce me because I said something to her about it, and I'm afraid I made things that much worse for Kevin. I feel awful for becoming angry and also feel sorry for the coach and ostracized at home.

Becoming mad is how I try to protect my child. I didn't want to see his face look so down, he hadn't done anything to deserve to feel this way, and just thinking about it again makes me angry. I get angry when adults with big egos who have to win, or whatever, and don't care if they harm the children.

Come to me, brotherhood of light, and send me your love and light. I ask that I be a clear channel for your words of wisdom. I ask for protection from all lower level entities and guidance from the light. Can you help me to find balance?

We are here. It is time for you to forgive your father for beating you those many times, and especially for taking so long to tell you he loved you. You were only three when the beating began, and he did not take lightly to your disagreeing with him. He beat it out of you so many times that you began to wish him dead.

I have lost the thread of your words.

No you haven't, you have only just begun to feel, to believe, in reincarnation that says that a man who is kind to another man reaps his own rewards. You never believed for an instant in the quality of humankind when they are not kind to a child/children like you. I am Metatron, I am your savior, and we shall get through this, and other conflicts, as one.

I was afraid you would be angry with me and reject me because I became angry tonight.

We thought it was right for you to stand up for your child, and you did not go overboard at all like could have happened once upon a time! Yes, we believe you that you did not want to hurt...find something to hang onto—like my thread—for a moment, while I interact with your essence on another level. We will try something to figure out how to clear your aura of this negativity and pain. You are experiencing pain because of your relationship with your father, who was not kind to you, and you are being your own mother trying to protect a lost and broken child. We are beginning to put light back into your shield of protection. We will light the way for your learning and beginning.

I am feeling pain. Why?

We have found your pressure point and will help you to clear this.

Is it just myself I am trying to protect? Is there no emotion that is not selfish? When I see Kevin feeling badly I want to hurt who is hurting him.

You will know of that which is your true being by looking within and not by asking us to look within for you. Do that now and tell us what you see/find.

I don't know. I will protect Kevin no matter what. No one will hurt me again. I'm afraid that what happened to me could happen to my loved ones. I'm an idiot. I don't know what to say.

Free yourself to consider for a moment what it is that we bring to your notice in our communications. We are of the light, not the darkness, and we share our traits with you, just as you share yours with me. I am Metatron, who has suffered and died and lost alike so many times beyond count. I come from the stars, where sorrow is no longer, and the little children fear no more. You bring likeness to likeness.

My wounded child, please help me to heal her forever.

You bring her to me through your own awareness of pain and guilt. Cast this away forever into the dungeons of time, and let us go home together! We are one, and we will not forsake you. Coming to grips with your own future will help you to heal the past. We cannot take care of the past mistakes or cares because we love you and would assist you in caring for our planet of pain, and what better way than by learning to deal with that pain first hand? Know this, that the time is come for those who would be cruel...

[I was really struggling with holding on to the thread.]

She is close, I feel her tonight.

[I felt my next daughter, the very familiar lovingkindness which is she and I know so well.]

She wants you to know that you are special to her and that she brings tidings of joy to the world of chaos and pain which you experienced tonight. She will be coming soon to join with you, and she believes that you are the right one to bring her into the world, knowing what you would do to protect her from harm. Let it be known that it is not fear which you use to protect the children, but hope of a better tomorrow along with faith of good times to come. Protect the children because it is your duty and their hope that you do so.

Let us clear this topic away for discussion on another plane of existence. I am forceful with you at times, but believe me when I say how proud I am of you and your ability to focus on these "commands" in English, as you say, and to bring forth these words of wisdom for our consideration together as we bring logic and light into play. Conscious recruitment of the words leads to disillusionment and cannot bring technical aspects of life and limb at work as we do to your story solution within.

I'm very unclear right now of this message and need a better "connection."

We cannot bring to you our light, we can only bestow it down upon your head. It is you who must bridge the gap to us for our better connection. Can you attempt to look inside my mind and know my thoughts? That is not what we are attempting to bring about.

We have decided not to go on with this message due to the discrepancy of light within your auric field. We feel obligated to define/explain that while we are here for—begin again—

[I was having difficulty staying connected.]

I am disappointed in myself for being carried away by my emotions, at the same time that I acknowledge that I was less carried away than I would have been at any time previously when I feared that my children were in any physical or emotional danger. I am grateful that I have made the progress that I have made and I will rejoice that I have overcome something tonight which has most often been very difficult for me to manage. I still have my stupid ego wanting to pop up, but I'm getting better.

We still have a ways to go, so with your permission we will begin again with the start of our conversation. If you can clear the message incoming we will try to focus as one.

Love and light will teach us many things, the least of which is to be patient in the face of turmoil and to take time to censor our reactions before acting. You have thought many times about these reactions and so were ready to pursue the ghosts of time across the playing field of your son. Capture what we tell you with these words, beginning with the notion that you are broken hearted from the first law of land, "Take not these children to be maimed, harmed or persecuted in any way, shape or form. Let any or all who hear of such acts be strong in the light and take a stand for the children."

What you have done is not wrong. You are feeling guilty because you swore to protect your father and it is he you see in your friends now who respond this way to the children.

This is true! I feel sorry for Jordan, the coach, and I feel guilty that I brought this negative attention down on him for the things he did to the team. I still feel guilty, still find myself wanting to make excuses for him. My husband is angry with me for saying anything, he is afraid Jordan will get mad at him, and maybe not let him coach Kevin's baseball team this spring. He uses these things as reasons to add to his wanting a divorce though he never leaves, and which comes across to me as an even deeper level of total condemnation of me and everything that I am.

We believe you when you tell us that it is fine for you to belong here and protect them, they need your protection and depend on getting it, their nourishment, from you, so don't be afraid to stand up for the children! They are strong yet still do they need the guidance of the strong in the light to protect them from the weaknesses of others. Begin today another rule, and let time show no wounds. Rather instead you must embrace the changes while believing in the propensity of those equal to change, while staying with the belief that to depend on them is foolhardy while there are better equipped adults to lead the way. Do you understand what I am getting at? Read a moment if you need to.

Yes.

Believe me when I say to you that I, too, am for the children! I believe in the light of all mankind, yet in a pinch there are those who would be better off not attempting to interact at all with our most precious lights!

Free yourself for a moment to consider this message of light/heart. You have not brought your companionship to us which involves those who would hinder your movement/mission on this planet earth, meaning those you refer to as your sisters.

Take down my notes. We are here to further this goal in the light. We take no insult when there is difficulty on your end. The belief that we are equal to the adult you paid attention to tonight is what is dragging this process down. We cannot show you our hearts without your assistance; let us bring them to your attention as below. Forget for a moment who we are and consider this function of the light. Bring not harm to a living being, especially a child who is hurt, or harm will be landed upon you until all on earth become masters equally of the light of time.

Forget for the moment that you have cried. Guilt is not a necessary emotion to suffer, for your "sins" this evening were in support of the child and therefore are forgiven. Believe me when I say to you that you are not of the darkness because of your strong emotions on this topic. You cannot attempt to bring light into the shadows when you are filled with your own guilt. The topic of discussion tonight was one of guilt and sorrow which you explained very well by your own admission.

We believe that sorrow has taken a toll on those who would remember the inquisition and other portions of history where many were burned and persecuted for their beliefs. This is a carry over soul memory that would be best abolished and can be done by purposeful memory clearance with our assistance.

Now, what is it that your friend Gayle would ask of us?

She has several questions about your message to her yesterday.

What are they?

She asks, "What does it mean, 'It has taken her many centuries to find her likeness in truth and wisdom from beyond the wasteland of despair'?" Would you like to respond to that question?

We believe you know that truth is a function of the light, and that which is of the light, is not more than chalk on a chalkboard, erasable at will. Such is your past lifetime with these individuals who knew little of your capabilities and sold you short when you could have done much to preserve the light during those dark times. You were a beautiful daughter of aristocracy who still had a notion of wanting more from life than what her family/father position would offer to her. You looked far and wide for truth which was more than your father could allow. Time was unkind and you withered in despair for many lifetimes searching for another answer to the questions, What Is Life? Who Am I? Why Am I Here? We have given these words for your introspection. Feel free to disagree as your other friend here. We have spoken.

[He means me, because I often question what I get! Note: These questions came through with capital letters on them.]

She asks also, "What does the 'heart string Aquarius' mean?"

Their meaning is unclear to us as well.

[I must have gotten this wrong. This was discouraging for me.]

It is not for us to determine another's heart for them. They must always find their own way. Your friend Gayle has given this gift to her sons, one by one, and must by definition find their own way beyond time and into the light. It is not for us here to determine—

Did you give this message?

We have not found the light of it on our registers. It must have come from your own subconscious. Be not afraid, this will happen at times.

[I felt very discouraged and lost the thread for a time.]

Be it not for the good of the nation of children what comes not for their own good we need not. To be clear on this, we are here to do you no harm and would only expand your knowledge in the light of time for all to see who can. So before you erase us again—

[I felt so unclear that I kept erasing and erasing what I wrote, afraid that it was my subconscious.]

Let us tell you a little secret that we have kept for all mankind in the form of a lie. When you chose to come to this earth walk, you did so with little support from the powers that be on your own planet. This was because they did not wish for you to desert them in—

[I didn't try to go on, feeling very discouraged about Gayle's message, not feeling "connected," and too overwhelmed with guilt and pain to feel open enough to receive.]

I will wait until I am able to try again.

∞∞∞∞∞∞∞∞∞

February 1, 2005

Please prepare me to be a clear channel for light and love from Metatron's circle of the brotherhood and beings of the highest in the light. I ask for protection from all lower level entities and assistance in becoming a clear channel with the purpose of bringing light and truth into the world of time.

We are here to bring a message of hope to your planet of time and to bring your awareness to this process of life called channeling. We bring love and caring to this process with the understanding that life is more difficult at your end of things! Let us begin.

We are the beings of Metatron's circle and we wish to express our gratitude to you for bringing us into your awareness this evening. We have much to tell you of hope and light. Free yourself for our remembering and we will get started.

I am the being Metatron bringing this communication into your awareness for a moment of time. Tenderness is not what you had hoped. It is within your being to break free of this nonsense of taking things too seriously! You begin to believe in nothing so much as fear at our return based on your own reluctance to share your faults and to bring freedom into your life. Take a moment to consider these reflections and respond to us.

Yes, I am afraid to share my faults, afraid of your criticism and afraid of losing your love and respect.

Focus on my navel and we will bring this truth within you.

Yes, please tell me more.

We will begin now that we have your attention! Take a moment to relay to us your dependence on structuring the notion that we are not your friends in times of need. Feel free to respond at any time.

I am afraid of disappointing you.

We are not afraid of you disappointing us! We bring our knowledge to you for your benefit and to include you in this process of light. "Deliver us from evil" is our motto. We bring light, not shadow, through our accompanying wordplay and would have you consider this when responding to our queries, harsh though they may seem. Can you attempt this?

Yes.

Feel free to respond at any time. Take a moment to consider our request that you take time to play more. Respond to light touches without fear. Bring him within your aura and love him like there is no tomorrow. It is within your being to be able to accomplish this more often.

[They refer here to my husband, and also to my own feelings that I often do not like to be touched. It brings up the fear in my gut. It does not feel like I would like it to feel.]

I am lonely and torn down right now, so in a good place to learn something new.

It is often this that helps our processes more than any other, the tearing down of our fears through introspection following a crisis of some sort. Do you not agree?

Yes.

Help cannot reach the unreachable fellow who is afraid of his own shadow. You are afraid of this, not of him or anyone else. This is your bane, your terror— your own shadow.

Yes.

Please release this notion of godliness getting in our way and let us help you.

Yes, I will do whatever I need to do to heal, to be free.

Discuss this with your husband: When were we last free to respond to each other's caresses without embarrassment or guilt getting in our way? Why do we let these notions keep us separate?

Thank you Metatron. I am so weary. I will try again tomorrow. Please come to me tonight, help me to find freedom and to explore and to learn.

[Later, I did say this to him, and he looked at me with some surprise and also seemed to shy away from me. He did not appear to want to talk with me about it.]

∞∞∞∞∞∞∞

February 2, 2005

Metatron, I ask for your protection in the light, and pray for protection and direction in my life. I ask to be shown how to correct these misperceptions we are living through right now, to show forgiveness, love and light, and to heal the rift and fill it with love and light. I ask for protection from all lower level entities and beings and ask for assistance from the highest in the light.

We are here. It is I, Metatron, with these words for you today. It has been a learning experience for you to draft these programs and to change the minds of the others—focus on what I am saying. Consistence in channeling depends more on your own mind than anything else. It must be up to you to create the proper atmosphere and mindset before we begin each evening.

View yourself in two ways only: as a channel for light and love, and as a figure for disagreement, for each has its purpose in/under the light of heaven/God. We will explain later, but now let us deal with the matter at hand.

There are those who would crucify you for your stance at the ballgame the other night. Let me explain how the demons work in these dark times. When you are least expecting it, they crop up to focus your pain in and to make it unbearable. It is at those times that they find sway over your emotions and get you to do those things which are better not done. In fact, if I could serve you now, I would release those demons to the darkness and know them not again. They do not serve thee, and the shadow of their becoming drags on your being making truth difficult to master. It is instead time to tell you to throw them off before you can proceed in the light of God to mastery of emotions. Deal with it before it becomes too heavy a burden to bear. We mean, take no chances on it coming back! It will not like the motion it took to take you to bring the light to the foremost and to bring back the light within. Stay with me a moment as I bring this awareness to your midsection.

It is right for you to say "forgive me for my transgressions, they are not about you, but about me." It is not wrong to take the blame for mistakes we make, only to believe that we must achieve something in the process of becoming masters of our domain. You are becoming a master but are not there yet, and yet this will help you. You are ready to believe in me now when I say, be not afraid to tell who you are and feel free to speak out when needed, but take caution that you tell only those who need to know and not bring anyone else into it. It is your brother Jordan who is at fault for the altercations of the past weeks, but you cannot blame him for your own reactions to it.

Am I getting your message clearly?

Thank you for proceeding, it is important that we connect this evening to bring in the light necessary for the altercation to become healed and no further harm come of it. Jordan has given his permission for us to bring this awareness to you this evening. He comes of the light but has forgotten who he is for a time. It is difficult for him to remember his friends and who he once was in the light of God. He came not of masters of the house and deals difficulty when he is reminded of that altercation with his own parentage. Be not afraid to tell him of your caring for him and forgiveness will shine within him also. It is not too late for him to—take no notes while we connect with your essence in remembrance of the pain. It is schooling for us to remember bad associations in the light and to learn from them. We believe you know of that which we speak when—focus on my light—we are here.

I love you.

We love you, too, and wish only the best, that your blessings come freely during these days of love and despair hanging out the window of time for a breath of fresh air! We believe you when you say you are ready for something more, but know this, we are here forever, at the ready, for assistance for our friends hidden behind the iron curtain of their own fright and despair. When we say despair, we mean for ourselves who are lost and lonely and afraid to come forth into the light for a breath of fresh air. Be not afraid to breathe deeply of the nourishment of God and take light steps towards him every day, and you will know your own worth.

It is not up to us to make you ready. You must show readiness in the manner of your walking so that we know—fear not these words—take a moment to catch your breath in the light of God—he heareth not your ancient tones to bring him back home to you now. Form these messages in the light of day and let it be known that you are free to express yourself with every breath you take. Only know this, that when you free yourself, you will have taken on the notion of flight into the light and be ready to soar! Spread your wings and fly another day.

Let your man know who you are. It is not too late.

Function as One. Free yourself to live life every moment. Worry not about the past, fear not the future. He is come for you and you must be ready to soar. Take time to meditate on this now.

Friction builds confidence. Use it wisely. Take time to smell the roses, but watch out for the thorns! They come from your very own nose! Pluck them out so that the roses will know no blight.

Free yourself for a time each night to consider our words of wisdom and to bring yourself within the light. Capture the essence of the Godhead within, and know no fear. It is said.

Believe and it will happen. You cannot lose for trying, and winning is an everyday occurrence in the light. Function like a star, always shining, and let those others warm their own hands in your light.

Thank you Metatron.

We are here. Goodnight.

[I felt so tired and so strained that I didn't feel like I could stay with it long that night.]

14

The Game of Light is Hard to Play

February 4, 2005, 7:30 p.m.

Please prepare me to receive these words of wisdom. I ask for guidance and light from Metatron and the brotherhood and assistance in bringing these words of wisdom to our time. I pray for protection and love.

Feel free to express yourself to us with these words. I cannot bring you to take notes without your express approval.

Metatron, will you assist me and bring the light to me?

Yes, we are here, Metatron and his followers, ready to assist with your process in the light. Take notes carefully.

It is us, our duty, to assist you with this process of becoming everybody's savior as has been told since before time began. Look at me bringing these words of wisdom to your recognition and take no notes while we "practice."

The game of light is hard to play, we're gonna do it anyway. Practice on your presence as we speak unto the light within your body of bodies. It is with this practice that we bring the light to your working mind. Begin to believe in our process and we will relate to you those things which are unto you to be known, the care of living things/creatures notwithstanding. We are within your ability to be known to/through us.

Care not what others say, do as your heart would tell you. A willingness to reach deeper will be necessary as we go on. It is imperative that you begin this process today, as your people will be needing you soon. Don't be afraid to go unto the light, it is here for your benefit and we believe that you are ready to proceed with our process tonight. We can't say for sure if you are ready or not, until we go.

Go forward without fear. We are here to assist you and it can be done, so do not be afraid of missing out on anything of value, or of pursuing the wrong course of action. It will become for you to bring these messages of God within your own inner being and therefore out to the others of your kind to find a way within the light to pursue the magic of other lands where none before existed. It is within the light of day, these times you live in are magic in that they can change within an instant, the blink of the eye, to change "that which was" to "that which will be." We are at such a crossroads now. Begin to believe in the process taking its course, running its course, as you change your name even as you sit here. Even today it is becoming one of light and love. This is our process we have been working toward for so long, and it will not fail. So be not afraid to question the process as it has been given, for in so doing, you will become a font of love and light for your brothers who have need of what you have to offer to them. Take no notes while we distinguish between the light and dark of nothingness.

[I took time.]

Be with us now as we say to you, be not afraid. Fear will open up the nonsense that you have been worried about, the consequences of thoughtless action that you so despise. Freedom exists on more than one level as we have previously taught to you. Believe that it is within the possibilities of your planet to bring change, and they will be manifested unto you, a light in the darkest of times. Take time to peruse these words and we'll get back to you.

I am Metatron, being of the light, with these our first words of wisdom. Others will be coming soon to share their own light and wisdom this night.

[There was a change in the energies.]

Freedom exists on more than one level. Take time with these words and tell me what you think they mean to you now, Janice, on earth. Feel free to distinguish between light and darkness, meaning, take no notes now while we explore these meanings together.

Do you mean you want me to go onto/into other levels to encounter what it is I have to defeat within myself?

We want no more questions until you have done as we have spoken.

[I took time, and as I went into my bodies, I perceived them within my highest spiritual body. I found them and felt their connection.]

We are from Arcturus with these messages for your consideration. We feel your presence here with us on these other planes even as you do ours. We are much more aware of previous incarnations than you are on your planet earth. They are a darkness to your spirit/mind at times and we wish to dispel them for you so that you can go on to other, better things. If this is acceptable to you, we will begin.

Yes, please assist.

We bring this light unto your inner charkas that they might release the spell of days gone by and bring an inner sense of peace to you in this world. May we proceed with the disabling of the memory sockets at this moment of time?

Yes, if it is of the light, and thank you.

We dispel all other notions of badness/wrongness for your consideration. We believe you can tell the difference between what we would do for your assistance and what you would wish us to do. We feel free to dispose of us at any time!

No, please assist, I am grateful.

We will proceed. It is time for your connecting to the other planets of time to be felt and disposed of once and for all. It is slowing you down to try to remember the bad times that are still affecting you. They are not possible to predict or to bring resolution to in this faraway land, so we begin by telling you to not feel afraid of our presence as we dispel this darkness into the breeze. Let it fly! Take no notes while we complete this project. It will take some time for you to remember who you are again, and then freedom will reign on earth for 1000 years.

What do you mean I won't remember?

We are free to dispel your anxiety, for all good purposes come to fruition within their own time. So we bring to you your preparedness for our times that we are in, or are now entering, to be free at last of that which does not serve your/our better interests. Take no fright by what we have said, it is for your benefit that this is done, and for the benefit of others who will learn through you.

Is this past life stuff I will no longer be poorly affected by?

Yes. It is not for us to disclose those particulars to you at this time, we would only ask for your trust in our common purpose so that we may proceed with your becoming into the light of God for this reign of good over evil.

Please begin.

Function is disposed of when it no longer serves its unique purpose. So it is with us today as we come to your 111th purpose, travel time notwithstanding! By this we mean that to you on earth, we no longer exist, because we haven't even been born yet. So, take no notes while we travel together to the end times and back again with a note from mom saying, can we go/come home yet? It is silly to remember past times, so many times, when they delay our travel into the goodness and reign of light.

Frozen within your being is this very remembrance of times gone by where evil was done by or to you. It is no longer necessary to have these carryover memory recalls. It is of no matter to us who we were, or where we were born, if it takes our light away from its present moment of existence, the Now.

I think I understand.

Good. We will take notes again as we begin this powerful recall, for your beginning is at hand. The nest of righteousness follows the light, and all who were dead become free once again. So it is with you now as you recall these darkest of moments and return them unto the light, for the reign of terror is now past and the time of goodness is at hand. We have spoken.

It is good for you to remain in your bed for at least 36 hours after our process, for it has taken its toll and will be felt at the deepest of levels. You may not be rested or feel ready to function for moments of time afterwards. We find that it takes a toll.

It is time for us to begin. Take no notes and let us come within to dispel your darkness forever.

[We took time.]

It is so. Adonai in the highest. We have spoken, the Achilles' heal is taken and flung out among the stars never to disturb again for all-time. Grow within the light for several days at least as we make this notion of change within the "heart of a fool" who wishes she were different, someone who could be believed in and trusted. We are ready to dispose of these notions today so that you can go forward with your heart open and unafraid and bring a new light unto the world.

Past notes reveal that you are no fool at all! We believe in your process of becoming and know your will is as ours, the same as ours, in this one regard: we would know of the light and spread it unto the corners of the worlds and beyond for all mankind to see and benefit from. We have a notion to take off your hat and see your hair sparkling with a thousand threads of discontent—no more! We trust you will tell us when you are ready to proceed and it will be as foreseen beyond the corners of our world, in the halls of records, that here this day we have come to help you to take this necessary next step in your development in the light, and darkness shall prevail no more.

[I was thinking about how nice it would be not to be a fool who always asks too many questions, and what a drag it must be for them to work with us in this state, and I got, "A fool's eyes are sharp, but his tongue is dull." Ha!]

Green is your favorite color for a reason. Have you ever wondered why?

Yes.

It is the forest green which is your own primary color. Let me explain. It is of the color range of orange which will bring you alive on these days you feel so down. Let me tell you a little secret of time! It is of the color scheme of purple that relates to you on these color bands, and knows no purpose other than to bring you home again. We have begun this long process of time in which we are taken to discover you from our various different bearings, or positions, in the stars. It is given us to tell you of this purpose in heaven which we share for all time, called "go for the gold!" It is proof that we are all one. It is of the color spectrum of love-light, bring me home—

Can you teach me how to relate with you directly in the astral?

Yes, we have begun a moment ago just such a question that might be framed to us today to do this service unto our brother Janice and to bring her more within this reality we call home. It is for you to decide what, if any, travel you would have or relate to us as through other means, or through the astral planes if it be your wish.

Yes.

Begin to take no notes at bedtime, only to peruse here to us at the appointed hour, until we have called unto your spirit to turn away from the darkness within and go on to more—

Darkness within?

Yes, it is of our purpose within to dispel all evil/darkness and to bring the light unto our eyes as they see a shining distant star. It is that star which holds us on course through the harder, more difficult abilities which we select to bring us. These are only fourfold. One is of the essence of time which we believe you refer to as time travel. The other three will only be told as we begin our process to heaven, so come early to your bed and we will get started.

Twice before they told you our names and you only heard one of them. It is for us to relate these to you today so that you will be prepared to state them at the door, which is your door to us in our world. We believe in fools who come and go through their own portals of which this is one.

Fools?

Yes, did we forget to say who we are taking home with us? Come not along the track of space to bring forgetfulness shining. Along the path toward home is your brother who is forgotten your name; you must join with her again. Taking back your power is one of your duties in this lifetime and it will be done as you desire.

[I was questioning what I was getting.]

Feel free to dispose of us at any moment! We are not afraid to belong, of not belonging, and neither must you be if you are to consider these changes within your time/space. Function as one wherever you go, seeing only brother after brother. Let no evil enter into your thoughts, no thoughts of self-sacrifice either, for none is now needed. It is time for us to recall better times ahead and to bring them into our focus now, for one last stand is at hand for mankind to bring this power unto himself to save himself before the last bell has clanged and the door is shut. It is not of our power to...

[I was questioning so much that I didn't maintain a good contact and gave up for the evening. I have been highly stressed this week, and tired in my mind.]

∞∞∞∞∞∞∞

Later, 11:30 p.m.

I had the most uneasy feeling earlier, and knew I needed to spend time praying, meditating, walking, trying to get it figured out. I was out walking and worrying about tomorrow, afraid that my feelings had something to do with Kevin's basketball tournament or something, a continuation of earlier in the week possibly, and wondering, asking myself, what do I do? How do I protect him? What if something happens and I need to protect him? Then as I was praying to the stars, saying, I'll do anything to protect him, I seemed to hear, "Even letting him go?" and I answered "Yes! Even letting him go!" and as I said that I felt a great relief, and I smiled and felt like I could breathe again, like releasing my fear, my need to protect him, is what will keep him protected now so that he will never need protection from me again, and I felt that the danger was gone, and realized that it is time for him to grow on his own now, that I have done all I could for him in the way of protection and that to hang on any longer would cause him not to be able to grow into the man he should be. It is time for him to make his own mistakes and learn from them, to find love and pain and all of the other things we are free to do, free to choose or not choose, in this life. And I set him free.

(I love you, Kevin. Happy 14th Birthday just a little bit late. It is time for you to grow, choose wisely and know my love is with you wherever you go.)

I cried just a little on the way home, but not for very long, and I felt a joy within that all is now well.

Please feel free to choose your reaction to our question carefully, but what do you choose freedom for?

To find ourselves within, to find God.

Closing your mind to the possibility of "changing lifestyles" forever cancels out our propensity for change. It is within your ability to learn of this "deception" within your being. Once we are through for the evening, take a moment to disregard our place in this, being carefully examined and written down for a moment. We believe that you have broken promises before, but a second chance is at hand! We will release you for a time for bringing back miracles to your time frame. Function only as one within and know your God. We have spoken.

Take care to preserve that which you have created this evening within your being. It is fragile. Bring carefully your son into the light of his own consciousness through careful choice to restrain or not restrain. Over the next couple of months many changes will overtake him including coming into his manhood and bringing a female into his life. This will be good for him, and know that you have done well and that he is ready for his life to begin away from you. Not too soon, but gradually will it spill over into his being that you are truly taking away the chains that bound him to you for good or bad over his lifetime.

We are beginning to change faces within this conversations, so be of good cheer and know you have done well this evening. We are proud.

[The energies changed.]

Take notes carefully. Be a friend in need even to the son who loves you. He is prepared to stand his ground if needed, but will not face the sun until it burns. Create only that which is on your good conscious and he will know of what I speak. It takes time to burnish the hedges!

I don't understand.

We mean, it is difficult to let go, but once accomplished much good can come of your decision to free him to find new experiences and to "go it alone" for awhile. It is important and it is time for it to happen. Almost was it too late, but now things will speed along quite readily and you need only watch for awhile, and pray, and know you have done your best, and God speed.

Take a moment to relax the muscles in your neckline. They speak of the tensions of many days toil, but it is turned out and you can now relax. No more moments of tension tonight! Your husband is awaiting you beside his couch. You can let yourself relax and know that no terrors will be coming to them tomorrow due to your hard work, so let us relax and know that we have done well and that better days are coming just around the corner.

Do you have anything else for me tonight?

Of what would you have us speak?

I don't know. Love, creativity, joy, children, light.

What comes of the world of darkness where you know naught of the lies that people speak? They speak of thee. Be not afraid to confront the darkness of time. It shows no mercy to believers in sin, but you are not afraid, and sin will leave no darkness in your trail of tears forevermore.

Let us be thankful this day for the progress we have made and for your willingness to choose love over fear. This is a great accomplishment for you, and we are pleased.

Thank you for helping me so much. I am grateful.

There are no words to display this affection we feel for one another so much as a handshake in the dark. Take it now.

Life is action. Be free to move around and take your time with decisions. They will come easier now. Be not afraid. We are the brotherhood with love and wisdom to share. Be not afraid.

Thank you, brotherhood.

∞∞∞∞∞∞∞

February 5, 2005 11:30 p.m.

Greetings, it is I with this message for you today brought to you by the collective celestial band. Be not afraid as we deliver this message into your subconscious, for the end times/days are near/nearing and you will have a part to play before the end. Take no notes while we assess your level of attachment and begin to believe in this connection so that we may go on.

[We took time.]

Your system has begun to accept the changes which we have instigated, those for your benefit and for the benefit of planet earth. We have spoken before of your coming to lay the plan, raise the veil, for others of your kind, your brothers who are going home with you. Take no notes while we assess these. Please review our notes carefully while we assess. This means, our notes for today.

[I reviewed them.]

Deliver this message unto your sister who is here for you. She is not one of the others of which we have spoken, but is rather of your own consciousness waiting to come home. It is wearing on your mind lately, this connection, and we are concerned that it is too much for your system to handle at this time. Be not afraid as we assess this connection so that we may review for you our "systems check."

Life has begun to unfold for you and your kind, meaning, your family on earth. It is here for us to determine the speed at which it must unfold so that we may be of the utmost assistance. We are here in the light for your protection, so we may not believe you when you tell us you are so ready! Take no notes once again while we assess.

What are you assessing?

Your readiness.

For what?

Focus on what I/we are telling you. It is not for us to discuss your plan at this moment of time lest it reveal too much for your system to present to itself, and so that we may not go overboard in trying to assist with your unfoldment/development in the light. We are free to discuss this with you now, though, that we see a featherweight coming along who would most likely be your daughter, to help along the way. Typical situations may accrue ahead of that time to help with the unfoldment process, meaning, we believe that you are ready with a little push from our friendly neighborhood messengers.

I like that you are smiling, for our unfoldment is along with your own in that we are of the light, too, and would have you know us as we "sit" here. Alongside your man in the basement is another one who would have you know him as well. As Kevin brings his manhood into full bloom, you will also know him to change as well, become more as he is meant to become, just as you are. It will be an unfoldment/change, coming into all of your "facilities" of change.

We believe that you would benefit more from our situation if all of your chakras were aligned with our own.

Please assist with this alignment, and let me know what I might do.

Forget for a moment our own disapproval of the light manifested within the human body of time. We will take a moment now to align these that you call energy wheels with our own. It will take a moment of your time. Relax and focus for a second on your feet and let us know what it is you are feeling.

Tingling.

Bring it up through your legs now.

Let no time pass between forgiveness and what is meant to be forgiven. This is a function of time, but can be done within now, as you relate to your feet in the ocean current of energy, placing you within/without time.

Focus in on what we are saying. You are one with the cosmos and only through knowing this connection can we bring to our loved ones our most attractive qualities. We function as one. Turn not to the darkness to find that which you need. Fear will not feel the way for you; only love is here for our benefit.

Remember to focus on our words of wisdom within your being. It is being felt on all levels and is already being absorbed into the blood stream, for replacement parts are ordered ahead! Disagree if you must. We will sort through it here if you cannot bring yourself to accept these words of attunement.

What do you mean?

We are here for your assistance in the light of God and mean no harm, nor do we blame you for doubting our "realness." However, it is only as good a date as what you can accept from us on any given evening. Tuning in can bring you more from our relationship than tuning out!

Focus on these words I'm saying, that we must beware who are our best friends, for oftentimes they are those who have the most to lose from our own development. Consider these words and respond.

This makes me think of my husband and my sisters. How do I deal with these situations?

Trust your own inner being for the guidance you need and it will be done for you as you request. Without fear in our auras, we can change the world! Focus on the light within, and the without will take care on its own. Be not afraid to take these words to your teachers, for they are one with you and will bring you no harm.

Can you help me again with astral travel tonight?

We are not willing to divulge these activities at this time for your own benefit. It will not be done as you request at this time for pertinent reasons you will later understand.

We cannot stress enough at this time the importance of food and diet to your situation, we believe you know what it is we mean. Your diet is dragging down your footsteps tonight, it is causing stress. Bring your body into alignment with our words. You must fight to stay "alive" on higher levels than the physical being you inhabit. Take no notes again this day while we retrieve this knowledge, and know that we love you, for you are one with us this day and every day. Feel free to disagree! We love you anyway!

We know of that which you would speak, of the construction of your gateway into "heaven" or the cosmos. It is here for you to decide which is the best way to proceed, and nobody can do that for you. You must decide, but we are free to offer our advice if it is requested of us.

Yes, please assist me and offer your advice. I am grateful.

Be not afraid to pursue the fringes of these activities, they are here for you to benefit from and can only bring good images/messages for you to grow on within the light of Godkind.

Focus on me for one last moment as we dissuade others from doing harm to your son Kevin who is in need. He has taken too much on at this time, and has slipped, and it is dangerous ground for those who would benefit most from his own beginnings, meaning his friends. We here will bring this down so that you may not worry as to consequences. He will play. We go forward wishing him no harm so that he may indulge his appetites and go running with his friends! We cannot free the others from this badge of honor, but he is without stain and will go on to pursue other activities.

Have I received this correctly?

We see no harm done to him this time. Comments are not necessary to his teachers as they have been taken care of. He [the coach] *will come to his senses without your help! We bring you tidings of love and joy and know this, that we have come for your assistance and will do you no harm. Feel free to distinguish between the dark and the light of it and know this: we are not afraid. We will only know you better through our disagreements, so feel free to bring it on! Take notice of these times of trouble and bring restitution through your process of light and love.*

We have spoken. I am Kuthumi with this message of light and love. Good day.

Thank you.

15

Mastering The Channel

February 6, 2005, 8:45 p.m.

Metatron, I ask for your assistance in the light, and your protection from lower level entities as we communicate. Let me bring the light of your words/wisdom to our planet.

The curve of space/time is not for your benefit to be toyed with or manipulated. But here we disagree with our own words of wisdom and it is done as you request. Be not afraid to pursue these answers within your own being. They are here for our own benefit as we progress together within the light of God. Take no notes while we determine your readiness this evening.

[I took time.]

Life is not too hard for you to work awhile to determine your own readiness from this point forward. Let me explain what we mean. We are the brotherhood here to assist you and those others of you on your planet during these end /difficult times. Time has given itself for your benefit so that we might know ourselves more completely and learn to find the light within and thus be ready for the ride or trip home.

Focus on my words of time for a moment. We are still here. It is for your benefit that we bring these words of wisdom, and for a time you will know of that which is still within your being to accomplish with us this evening. Your time travel will commence in due course, but not without these important signposts of readiness. It is not for you to determine them. They determine themselves as a mark of your inner readiness is made known to the material world. We cannot begin this process more quickly than you are aware or it could thwart your own process of becoming in the light. Be not afraid, it will be so, only let it come more gradually, and we will continue to assist with the "lightening" of your system.

What should I do now to help this along?

Forget the acids and let the system function without them for a time. This means the sodas, alcoholic beverages, candies, hard cheeses, meats that are of the hoofed variety, let these be and take instead the water, spring water purely given, and the more normal or naturally produced foods for the system. You know of that which is good for you when you brush your teeth each night. Let your system know of that which is for your becoming, and that which would slow you down on your feet. It is a good indicator that if it slows you down, it is not in your best interest to pursue. Take no notes while we assess this information in the cortex and know if it has reached its destination.

Your light body has begun to manifest itself on your outer layers of being. Let us explain what this means for you, Janice, in your becoming in your world of time. Let it be known that we are here for your benefit and that time has not stopped on our behalf, but lesser things have happened for your benefit! Take no notes for a time.

[I took time.]

I feel your closeness and love.

Tenderness is an expression felt within your being at this moment of time. We, too, feel this emotion with you on our own levels of existence. It is beautiful to behold our timelessness in this emotion together, as one we are, forevermore.

We believe that you are prone to taking things out on yourself and we would like to know why, and what you hope to accomplish this way? What is it you would do to yourself in order to become more like me/us? Who are you to tell us what to do? If we so choose, we will relate to you our own sessions and go from there. It is for us to decide how best to pursue these conversations with you our brother Janice, not yours for a time. For now, let us assume you meant no harm just now when you relayed that information to us. We will disagree with you for a time and know that you are not yourself and that the hatred has malformed your own consciousness for a time and know this, that we will survive. Our own savior has called upon thee and you will be released as we were once upon a time in the world of time. Let no notes come through for awhile, as they are not of the highest, concern yourself not with these notes, they are not for your benefit and have come from your own subconscious where they are trapped within your own cerebral cortex.

At what point did this happen I wonder?

Not now.

∞∞∞∞∞∞

February 8, 2005, 10:30 p.m.

Metatron, I ask for your assistance today with finding my way in the light and love of God.

What is the difference between our connection and a false connection?

I feel your love come through, a connection to my heart, wisdom and light.

Connect with our essence now as we relate these words of wisdom for your consideration. We are the collective.

Collective?

The farmers of history of your nation of earth here to do your bidding by bringing those to you who are of the utmost in the light, called masters of your time by those who would bring light unto the masses. These are our words which are given today with the utmost respect for the process of time and for those who are temporarily lost within its boundaries. Insightful communication will follow.

You cannot know who we are if you are forever trying to control the communication you are receiving. Be not afraid so that we can attempt these messages to be brought through to you tonight, for the good of humankind is at stake. We can tell of the masses of humanity awakening for good. Freedom gives its own message and cannot tell of that which is broken within. You are sent to delver these messages of consciousness and to bring a message to others of your difficulties. Pursue this connection so that we may teach you again in the light as has been your star. Bring connection within and it will/shall be felt. That is all we have to say.

Can you tell me of my mother?

She is not here for—continue to receive these tidings of joy but disturb not the processes and we'll never take that away from your moment by moment display kindnesses to others, for they are your children, as they are the children of us all. We cannot stress enough how important is the delay that we would take to describe these importances to you and bring to your notice that we are of the light and that no good can come from our disintegration happening. We are not frost or blight for you to tend to. We come of the light of love and cannot remember a time when we bring function within the spiritual consciousness and take to the road. Fright is mixed with relief at your sensory perceptions taking their toll on you now. We cannot stress to you enough to take your time in connecting, in making a good "connection," so that we may proceed.

[My connection and what I heard was choppy and unclear at times.]

Metatron, will you assist me?

We are here. It is our intention to bring more light to your midsection so as to take the process less "time" to complete. When a boy is born, he will pursue this evolution with you. Arrange transportation to the stars with us, we shall show you the way!

Take notes carefully. We were once a star system in the annals of time. Frozen within this star system was your uncle who was the first to take you home. Bring this understanding to your knowledge and know of who we mean. It is you who would take no notice of that which is slowing this process completely.

I can't seem to find the thread, and I question everything that comes into my mind. I am looking for confirmation of who I am communicating with. How do I master the channel? I will work to master the channel no matter what. Please assist me, and also assist me with finding my way to you in the other dimensions to learn how I might better serve here.

Function is a matter of pride to you, and you cannot know by pride what it is we have to offer. Only function within as your own best friend, and be willing to pursue these matters; only with truth can they make themselves felt. We are the collective with this message of love and support. Let it be known that we are here for your benefit and would not harm or hurt your development in any way, shape, or form. Let us heal together this rift which says that we are separate, and take time to develop within the light/lamp of time on your planet which says, "Be not afraid." We cannot for a moment consider that you are frozen being within without also being aware that we are here for your benefit to consider, so consider this when we ask of you to be not afraid. They are trailing your every step at this moment, so connection becomes afraid when love can still heal.

Focus on my words of wisdom, healing will soon follow and we will have our connection to refer to when needed. Focus can be staid by telling your own subconscious, "Be not afraid, I am doing this for our benefit so take no action!"

I don't know how much of this is real tonight. I am very fuzzy, but determined to discover the difference between what is real "out there" and what is false from within. I want to find this connection, to make it stronger in the light, and to not be afraid to take a chance. Can you help me again with this?

We are trying. Be not afraid to consider our words that you are not yourself in delivering this message of fear to our households. It is not for us to determine for you how to arrange transportation into the cosmos, it is for you to determine for yourself alone how might this become/happen. Truth is of the utmost. Comparisons cannot be made between that which is and that which could/should be until we have found our demons within and exorcized them! So take no chances that are not for your own learning. We mean you no harm and cannot criticize without truth. Fulfillment of prophecy states that mankind will initiate change within his own heart chakra at times of turmoil to overcome his own weaknesses within. Can/does this make sense? Take no action now, we believe we have found curious—

I need to lay my fears at your feet, Metatron, so that I can walk through the door to wisdom and bring back truth and light. Let it be so.

Forgiveness is the way within the light of God to bring back for your benefit that awareness of time's passages, and to take along the passes which allow us to consider more than we have previously been capable of providing our friends and neighbors. Consider for a moment our friends here on earth as it is in heaven. What does this mean to you? We are waiting for an answer.

We are all one, not separate as it appears.

Yes, but who are you in this notion of separateness that you would "help" your brothers?

Help is a concept of separateness?

Perceive our attention as you would your own perception from beyond the grave of time. Let it be known that we here have spoken direct to change "that which is" to "that which will be" through you who will find the way unto the light for all her brothers of which she is one. Take a moment to consider these words and we'll go on from here.

How will I do that?

By taking a "moment" to consider time's passages. Take not the past to view through the eye of the needle; let its passage be considered within.

Note the changes in frustration levels when we ask this of our brother Janice in time.

I am afraid of my past.

Yes, we have seen this change in you that you are afraid of consideration of externals which you represent within the land of time. Take courage within to consider these notions of love and life and let us know what you want to do about them. Consider them within, or discourage their acceptance on another level of time, and be not afraid to battle the demons. They are not real! Their passage would have you believe in the darkness of time/sin without consideration of the forces of light/love/goodness which are only within all goodness everywhere. For your consideration in this conversation take notice of that which we refer to as "goodness," which is godliness. False concepts of oneness take the form of fears which are not in your better interest, so beware the false prophets of time. Take notice of where you leave off and they begin so that we may instruct you in this process of becoming one in the light.

We belong everywhere and nowhere. Does that not mean anything to one who stands within/in the light? Function as one within us all. Forgive us not your own trespasses! Tokens of remembrance lie within the darkness of our memories. Focus on our—

[I was having difficulty feeling connected and continuing.]

We cannot tell you how proud we are of your efforts in this regard. They are not in vain. We will be seeing more of you in the near future. Fear not the bell, it tolls for thee. It is not in vain.

I pray for understanding and love and clearness.

∞∞∞∞∞∞

February 9, 2005, 10:40 p.m.

I pray for assistance and direction from Metatron and the celestial brotherhood. Let no fear interfere with our process.

I am Metatron here with this message in the light for my/our brother Janice in the land of time. Let no heart betray our message of light and we believe that it will suffice to say that we are your brother with these words of wisdom. Take no notes while we process this light together.

[I took time.]

Function is sweet when you remember who you/we are. Let us take time to function together as one, for our betrayal is not a function of the spiral of time as it relates to your processing here. It is our belief that this process is bringing you closer within the spiral of your existences. Function as one with us as we relate these words for your consideration. We are here, one being under God, so let it be known that our message was clear this evening and you are brought to our door, the door of time, for these furtherings in the light. Function as one who would function in the light without fear and bring these messages to mankind, spoken true to form, to heart within.

It is shown to you here what is to master. Mastery of the channel will bring all understanding and light your way. Then it is up to you to do something about it!

What would you have me do?

Bring these messages unto your friends of time, let them decide who it is for, the good with the wrong messages. Take these, a door opens, and light shines forth from it. It satisfies only time to prolong these messages unto the one who would do no wrong. Time is of the essence. We bring this message, these notes, to others of your time frame so that they may choose, even as you do, to be their brothers of the light within time, to frame for them their own nuances from these words of light. It is of the frame, time frame, of the light and as such will do no harm/wrong. Believe these words of wisdom come for your technical writing to display our knowledge for your benefit.

What would you have me display?

No words can relate of our knowledge through you, this contact that would relate of our notions of lifetimes within the starways of the heavens. These are that which we would relate to our earth brothers to bring them home with us. These are for your benefit, only relate them to those with whom you resonate. They are of the stars even as you are. Function nowhere and everywhere, be there for them as they struggle to find the within even as you have and are.

We are the celestial band waiting for your reply to our assistance. Who would you have us be/relate that would most assist on this path into the stars?

I feel very close to Sananda. I know him and I feel his heart the most. But I also resonate on another level with those of Arcturus, and they feel like family, and I hesitate to say, more like equals?

Yes, we are here, too, and know of you from beyond time when we were as children together and ran and played in the celestial planes of existence. This we shall do again. But for now, we relate most to our brother of the difference of notions, of time, that relate or find their consciousness within as you do. We are here to relate a different sort of relationship to you tonight, of the notions of starways bringing truth within to resonate within. Describe for us your sight on these our words of time. Let us know what you read in them so we may proceed.

First it seemed you wish me to spread these words to everyone, then only to those I resonate with. I don't understand about starways. What are they?

We will get to this presently. Let us deal first with the decision to bring our chosen ones within the realm of possibilities on your planet earth. By this we mean the planet will choose for us which are ready and which are not. These are not for your decision, rather you will release the words into the night, through those you most trust to go forward straightly, and then release them to come back to you in the form of starways, or travels that will penetrate hearts and return tenfold to you once they are spent. These are the starways that we intend to speak of tonight.

They are of the hearts of beings?

Yes, these are that which we speak of tonight. Let us proceed. You are ready to hear more of that which we relate to you tonight. We will bring within your knowledge the light of a little boy of your time within who is tamed by the notion of ridiculous functions that obscure rather than enhance understandings of time.

Little boy? A previous me?

No, we speak of that which you know is your readiness to begin, a child within will grow and change the outcome of all time. He is within you now, he knows of that which we speak. He is beginning to grow, to become a/the part of you which would forecast all notions of time as we speak. It is within that this will become clear in time. It is as we would have it be, that you would know of us through this inner being.

I don't understand.

We know fear gets in the way of these new concepts, but they are for your benefit and cannot frown on the plantations of the spirit world where they are kept for your deliverance and removal. Feel free to peruse our words at any time. We will continue.

Please fear not the removal of time from our networks. They are no longer for your benefit, and form can take many pathways of the heart of which this is one. It is no longer appropriate for us to disclose to you that which is within your own heart, only you can do this for us. Are you ready to go on?

Yes.

Let me take a moment to relay these "charges" into your aura as we are ready to take you on a mighty trip home. Are you ready?

Yes. I pray for protection and direction in the light and for an end to my fear.

We are with you on that! So, let us proceed with this process we call time travel within the starways/pathways of time and mind within the all-being of mastery. We will try to form a picture within your mind of the time when we were "children" where you played alone for many days before finding your oneness with another being you called "Fred." Do you remember that which we speak?

No.

Take no notes while we penetrate your consciousness, spark your memory, of this momentous event.

[I took time.]

Focus for a moment on the trail of consciousness we send you in threes. Conscious recrimination isn't helping! Take no notes while we "discuss" this with your being.

What is the purpose of this communication?

We voted many times to discuss this message ahead of time with your own cells. They are of the opinion that many have spoken, but few listen, even to themselves! It is a beginning that we have crafted tonight with you beneath the stars of your time/day. We have spoken. Be not afraid and we will return with a more meaningful message in the future! Come home alone and fear not the rivals of time for your attention. Focus your attention on me as we continue for a time/spell.

It is not in your best interest to force these communications to come too soon. They are for your benefit only as you are prepared to receive them. Try to receive no more than three messages at any one time for the time being. These notions are/can be difficult to fathom, and are best taken gradually. We/they are attempting to get you to open up to your "other" existences.

Why?

So that we can talk more freely to you in this our common existence. They/we are trying to get you to forget your patternings in this lifetime and "rewrite" or "overwrite" your patternings from other existences to further your progress in the light in much less time than would otherwise be possible for us and you to achieve together.

This makes better sense. It is hard to tell what they are asking of me, and then my fear of making things up in my own mind comes back to me.

We know, this is what we appear to perceive as we condition our minds. To take things more slowly might be prudent, unless and until you see a way in the light to connect with our essences/beings. Take no further notes this night. Let us come to you in our own way so that we might further this process. Belong nowhere and everywhere. We have spoken. Come away with me to peruse these words from another playing field of time. Good day.

I pray for assistance and understanding in the light of God.

16

Rock And A Hard Place

February 10, 2005, 11:40 p.m.

Function as one as we tell you of our pride forecast to come from above and function as one within this being Metatron for our better understanding of the processes of time and those which you bring with you this evening. I am Metatron, the circle of beings represented to you by his light and life, and come to deliver this message unto our sister Janice who is found herself alone this night on planet earth.

We believe you tell us truthfully of your fears and we are here to assist you with those this evening. We would have you know of our light and love pouring down from the heavens at this moment in time and that there is no tomorrow that would cease to exist for us even as we write our motions in time. Feel free to peruse these words before we go on.

Function is a process of time. Believe in the goodness and that which is good comes to thee. So it is with fear and this process we are becoming in the light. It is of the light to tell you of these notions, but your breath must relate them for us. We are not afraid of telling you to be quiet! We need time to peruse and to develop these notions in love, for telling nothing is no longer to be feared.

I felt I needed to do something this evening.

Yes, we are calling you to come to us and to deliver this message of time to those who would benefit most, including you and mostly others of your kind. Feeling that it is too late to help others is not the answer to your dilemma. It is within you to charge a beginning where there is no hope, and to see it through to the end of time. We know this is in your heart and that you would have us to help with this function. Let us know of what we speak. Search within for your answers and relate these to us.

Who am I? Will you show me?

Yes. Believe us when we say we have been where you are, trying to remember what to do, where to go, what to say, who we are. We have not forsaken you. The tryst is not broken but is trying for another day to find the one whom you refer to as self chosen. Beware of the unfortunate mother who says to her children as one, "Who are we?" We cannot bring that answer to another, we can only know for ourselves who we are. We are here to HELP you to discover that for your own self. Only you can do it for us, not the other way around. We are here to bring these truths to you, that you might know them, for who you are is broken upon the hands of time to know no more sin. Deliverance is at hand. Feel free to bring this message upon you. From afar have we spoken. Be it heard, we are at hand. Take no notes while we address within your being your need to know.

[I took time.]

Function separately from the hands of time. Your brothers have spoken.

Is Kevin all right?

We pretend no consensus on this topic! You are afraid for no reason. Let your fears rest, he is alright. Release your fears before it is too late.

Too late?

Believe me it is in your best interest to release all fears of your surroundings.

Any last message?

We are from nowhere and everywhere. Be free, be at peace, and all will be done for you. We are the brotherhood signing off for another day. Shalom.

Can you show me tonight what will help me on my path to the light? Thank you.

∞∞∞∞∞∞∞

February 11, 2005

Am I progressing on schedule? Will you help me with astral travel so that I can learn at an accelerated rate? Can more than one person here have true memories of one previous lifetime that they both were? Can you give me more to go on concerning who you are and why we are doing this?

I ask for protection from all lower level beings and a clear channel to the highest in the light. I ask for understanding and words of wisdom to help me on my path and to clarify for me WHY I AM HERE.

Rock and a hard place, huh? It is within your being to answer these questions on your own. May we say that you are progressing satisfactorily but could be making better progress if you would deliver these messages in a more timely fashion to those who would do well to hear of them. Why you ask? Because they are of the highest in the light and cannot go wrong to tell of them to your friends, one even, of the light to hear of them is better than none. It is your own business who you relate these to, but here me on this, it is of the light for you to do as you are bidden by these, our friends of the stars and planets like to your own. They know of their business and who might benefit best from these words of wisdom. I have spoken.

Metatron of the light of life, joy and happiness has brought these words of wisdom for your satisfaction and ours! So be it. Life has no words of wisdom for these hidden factors to play out on the screen of time. Transform your own being in the light and begin a process into the light. We bring these words for you tonight to tell you of your inspiration, that which is taken to be perceived by one as apposed to another. We cannot pursue darkness on your behalf. Let those who would know of you be glad and rejoice. We have spoken many times of your release. Give them to us.

What?

Tokens of patience with this our process will suffice for now. And believe that we have given our utmost to bring you to this junction of time/space and that we will not forsake you now. We know of nothing, no reason, to pursue these trends on your behalf. Only know this, that if you would have us teach you, remember to bring your notice, trust, and joy to our connection so that we may "link up" with you on that wavelength. Then should we be able to bring more noticeable remarks to your attention.

We see no reason to consult with your progenitors on this our belonging in the stars for your consideration. They are not here to suggest to us Why You. You are here. Only today is your sorrow too much to bear for this our measure is at hand. For we know who you are, it is but a breath between knowledge and despair lest it take hold and bring—

Is there—

Yes. We are here to bring you knowledge in the light. Those who have spoken for your consideration are with us now and are ready to answer questions.

It is when I feel close to the love/light that it works the best, when I am open, loving, trusting. I don't know who to trust, that is why I am despairing, but I am ready. I have been afraid to be open.

I am remembering a dream I had last night, about wanting to buy a new house. My husband and I were checking it out. It was in the country and I wanted it very much. A woman lived there who had many children, nine or something, and I thought, maybe the house is too big for us since we don't have that many, but I wanted it anyway.

I want more children. I feel like I missed out on so much not to have had that experience, not to have been able to have many children and care for them at home myself. My husband is ugly to me because of his attitude towards me. He doesn't want me to know it, but he considers me to be uninterested in sex, like something is wrong with me because I don't react as he does when he doesn't get it by getting mad and territorial. I don't want to act that way or to feel like sex is the answer to anything. I want other options, not to be owned or controlled by another body.

Can you come for me? Can we speak, talk to one another in a way I will consciously remember? I have many questions. I need companionship, someone that isn't afraid of me, of trusting me or himself. I want understanding, companionship, likeness of spirit. I have nobody I trust, which is because I don't trust myself I guess. I'm a blathering idiot. I won't give up on this process, I'm going to continue to work on figuring it out and find my way home to you, to me.

Continue as we have left off. It is for your interpretation that our messages are relayed for your consideration, and to share your interpretation with others of like mind. We are here to remind you of your purpose on earth in this incarnation. It is different from others for this reason. We remind you of your purpose under God, that you are he in disguise, taken from the lap of God, given to your fellow contestants in the land of time so that you may win through to the end game, the final curtain, as it falls one last time.

We are not free to disclose this purpose to you at this time and we understand your frustration as coming from one who is blinded within the desperation of time which leaves no memories for your comfort or consideration. So we are left with one purpose, to disclose not this purpose to you unless and until it comes from within you to know of your hand on time. Its purpose within you is not defunct but will show itself to you presently. You are not crazy, only lonely for others with a common purpose or thread, yet you take no advantage of those near to you to assist you with that purpose, or trend of purpose, loneliness.

Feel free to take notes again as we say unto you, you are not our child, rather you are our connection from beyond the thread of time. We come to you not as a father to a son, but as brother to brother. We know not of one thing that could bring caring than your decision to leave your brothers behind and pursue this trend of unlovingness. Rather take instead the notion that we are your brothers and bring you no harm. Coming from the land of time you are, but still are our brother.

Taking it easy this weekend will further your purpose as we distill in you these notes from the cosmos. We bring to your consideration this request: take no notes until such time as we can relay this information to our star brothers and let you know of their consideration of your request. Further request of assistance is not necessary. We have heard.

Thank you. I'm trying to believe. It's hard, because to believe in you I have to believe in me, and I'm afraid to believe in me, because I've never known who I am or why I'm here. Maybe I have to believe in me BEFORE I can know that.

I've always felt that I had something to give to the world, and my innermost feelings, my most heartfelt feelings, are feelings of wanting to save the world. So why do I feel this way? I am only a housewife/teacher/mother with so many faults that it is embarrassing! I am ashamed to talk with someone who is aware of all of these. I also think too highly of myself sometimes, which is horrible, too—one of my faults. I can't seem to find a balance in my own self-perception. I was raised to put myself down, to not believe in my own higher purpose, or that I had anything of great worth to offer to others. I am finding the ground through these communications which is worthy in and of itself, that's for sure! I will try to find myself through these messages and this interaction. Let it be so.

(I still don't believe I could be Moses. That makes no sense! Why would that be? I feel like a fool for even considering it. Others out there, no doubt, think they were he, too. I feel better just writing this down, like I was afraid to allow myself to consider these "notions of grandeur." My father for a time imagined he had been Jesus, didn't he?)

17

Forgiveness Is The Key

February 13, 2005, 10:30 p.m.

Time is of the essence. Begin here. It is I, Metatron, with our notion of togetherness for another moment in this our distinct view of what it means to belong somewhere. We are here to bring you the stars of consciousness and to dispel your fears so that you can go on from here to another day in the light of God's son.

I ask for protection from Archangel Michael and his blue sword of light, and protection from all lower level entities and beings. I ask for direction in the light, and words of wisdom, love and light from those highest in the light, the White Brotherhood.

It is I, Metatron, trying again with this message of encouragement despite the trials of the past days. We are not afraid to begin again as we say unto you, be not afraid. It is not our intention ever to harm you in this our process, nor yours to harm us, so go ahead and be real. Take no prisoners! We are afraid of no one. It is not within us to be afraid as we have conquered these fears in our own incarnations on planets such as earth, and have gone home to help others of our kind to penetrate the veil themselves and make it back home to us. We bring our consciousness to your agreement to find these truths within and to bring them into your reckoning so that we may assist you in finding the light within.

I feel much clearer, and I feel much more oneness and love and thankfulness.

We are aware of your trials these past few days and months. Let us say that we are going to bring more awarenesses to you within this coming time, so be not afraid to pursue them with us, they will bring you no harm. We cannot tell of that which is ours to bring until time for it to be, so no questions will interrupt us this time! So be it for us to say unto you, Janice, that time heals your wounds. As it is given, it is received. We freed you for a day and a half to bring that to us which is your wont, the toys of freedom, the existence of another path within the light, that which you refer to as channeling the light. It is given to us to say to you that you have done well in this our agreement, and we will proceed as it is given us to do this day. We will not forget those to whom the world is owed a debt, but find it within your heart to forgive and all will be well.

It is of the light for us to consider these hard days of time that you are experiencing now and to tell you of him, that which is given to take no harm to the living Christ within, but which is given to harm those of your planet earth in the coming times of strife and turmoil. It is within you to help during these times and that is what we would speak of with you today.

Okay.

Let us begin by saying that we are very grateful also to find our sister aware and taking her medicine! [I am on antibiotics.] *It is not to say that you are not free to believe in the magic of time's notions of illness and despair. Rather we would give to you this day a notice that what is, will be, and that which is, will be forever.*

Strife is a particularly dirty comparison to make with the winds of time which you would refer to as your brothers' goods which are given in comparison to the many centuries of passing the buck to find that they have come home to roost after all. We don't like to compare, make these comparisons, in the light of another day of hell on your planet; within it is much easier to consider the pain of another day, because it is within that we can do something about it. Let me explain.

We are here to take/bring to you another meaning to your existence, one beyond the usual codes of death and strife. We are here to remind you of your own purpose and to share this purpose with others of your nation so that they may bring light into their own lives, share their light with others as you have shared yours with them. They are of the light who bring these measures within. Let it come within to take these to the others of your time so that they can decide for themselves who to trust before the final bell, the last curtain, falls. It is of the light for you to consider these words of wisdom and to get back to us on them.

[I took time.]

I read them through, they are a little fuzzy for me.

Let us explain again. We will free ourselves to belong everywhere and nowhere during this our discussion of the ways of freedom and light. We belong nowhere because to belong anywhere is a curse to time's doors which shut in our faces without but a crack of light to spare! We belong everywhere so that we might know all that is of the light and back again to the darkness to find any and all that are lost within its confines.

Let us describe for you here our reliance on your own mental processes to bring these messages through. It is of the light for us to consider together these messages and to bring them forth for your consideration. We are here to spread the light to another/others, just as you are doing in sharing these conversations with your friend Gayle. We bring these messages to your attention in many ways: through these thought-forms, through your inner "readiness," and through just about any method that is permissible by your own spirit to ready your being for our presence in more concrete forms.

I would like to meet with you in the physical and remember it.

We know of this request, and as it is requested it will be received in time. It will not come to pass for many days as it is our way to ready the being to experience the celestial command within by taking measures within to encourage readiness. By this we mean: we mean no harm! We cannot harm that which we consider our own flesh and blood, our own brother, in this train of mental anguish would we permit ourselves to say that we know not what we wouldn't do to bring our brother Janice home. Fear not this curse of time, it takes no mention of that which you receive in these our messages of/from home. We cannot take the trail of forgetfulness without becoming one of the forgotten-seemingly. We have not forgotten you, only waited for the right/proper time/place for our mutual remembering. As it is written, it is so.

We cannot free yourself for our mutual remembering, only you can bring yourself within our "notice" by freeing yourself to consider that which can be done to bring us that much closer, that much more quickly. It is not readiness to make a trail of tears to our doorstep; only that which is free can find freedom. Only that which is far from home can make the trail last so long that it is nearly forgotten. We bring the trail to your attention at last, for we are the brotherhood and we know of home, and our remembrance brings it within our common memory at last as you take your final steps on this path you call the celestial command.

Within the dogs of time and space are we free in time, at last, for this consideration. We have come at last to take you along the trail/path to another time/place of love and heart which you referred to as space with aliens who are your very own kin. Take notice of our words here. They are within you to bring this message of light from the home world and to bring you within their knowledge processes/light and to bring you further along the path of your becoming, so be not afraid! Take notice also of these our friends of time, the angels of the command, the celestial hierarchy, who have taught you in days gone by, who have brought to your notice this being/becoming process which we have begun. They are here to determine for me/us your own readiness to begin/pursue this light/oneness in the stars/sunshine. Let it be known that we are here today, for your beginning is coming to full circle in that it is ripe and ready for fruition. It is here that you are coming into your own at last and will find that which you most seek in this timeframe/land of time.

We begin to believe ourselves in our own readiness to pursue this with you! We cannot take time to bring notions out of your head that you continue to put back. We are glad that the process of hindering the light is almost beyond/past. That which you have begun to view as truth will help us on our path of oneness into the light of mankind we now trod.

Forget for a moment who we are and we will proceed with a lesson of time for our brothers of earth through this messenger, Janice, one with us in the light of God for all time.

Frozen within eternity is the notion that all time exists. It is within this notion that the evils of lands gone by continue to pressure the existences of those currently residing on the planet. We have news for you who would feel these pressures and wish to be relieved. It can be done! We are here for your benefit, and know of that which you fear, and can bring relief if you but request it of us, in the form of tears from heaven. Let me explain.

This process which you would refer to as "the lightening" comes from our brothers of space/time. We believe you refer to them as bringers of the light of love and goodness. From their planet of time they have "invented" a way to discard the concepts of hell trapped within time and to free those of the memories of such times in these important ways and methods. Let me focus for a moment on the hands of our partner Janice in that she is given us this day to remember for us our pain and to discard it in bits and pieces into her keyboard of love which we refer to as "creation." Let us give a notion for your regard.

In this our beginning, we have given to you a star that is/will be that which is within for all time. This star is the being—consciousness—of spirit, and exists within each and every one of our "cousins" in space. For your consideration, here is a parable that exists in our planet's frequency for just such explanations as this. We are here, a freed people, to pursue these matters of justice and platitude so that we might, together, find a way to pursue these into the light of another time frame such as one on your own earth. These days it is more difficult for us to do so, but we shall try again anyway!

It is here for your disposal should you consider the material to be unjust or not right in some important way.

[I had been questioning what I was getting.]

Let us go on.

We are here to consider for a moment our time frame and how it may assist with your own process in the light. Within there is a star. She is you, your best and worst to be/become is all that she is/shall be. It is within this "star," this "you," that you begin to take notice of "what is out there" in your environment for you to notice. What is not so apparent is that it is beyond us to consider what is within compared to what is without. There is no difference at all between these two vantage points in time. We merely see our "withinness" spread out for all to see in the form of light shapes and shadows which exist only in our imagination, our "withinness!" So, be it for good times or bad, this is what is shown to our reality, the notion that we are within our own minds, thinking that we have no idea what is out there! Or why it is out there! It is only within that we can find these answers. We fret that only those so bold as to take the step within into the darkness of the soul will find the truth/reality of these illusions and become free to serve only the good in all mind/time/Godness.

That is our lesson for this our sister Janice for this day on the planes of time. Good day, and good riddance to those our stars despise. Let them rot in hell! Which for all time is not our time.

Rot in hell?

We believe you refer to those that would hinder your processes. Let me explain. We have not forgiven the processes of others who would bring us to this place of forgiveness. They are not our brothers in the sense that they have not led us here. Only we have that power, and we are afraid so that the notion of time has become so loaded with "time" and with notions of hatred and despair that we have forgotten, for a time, who we are. We bring these notions to your considerations so that we might know of that which we bring together for our consideration to dispel forever in the form of fears gone by.

I wondered about the comment, "Good riddance to those our stars despise. Let them rot in hell!" Did I get that right?

Feel free to disagree with us here. We are not afraid to pursue these inconsistencies and to "chew" on them until we get them "straight." It was not our intention to cause a "rift" in the understanding of our brother by implying the inconsistency that you suggest in the above comment. It is a discrepancy which we are pleased to have the opportunity to describe for you in better terms.

These that we refer to as "them" are our own fears. They are not for us, they are not in our better interest to pursue, or to bring within to dull the light of our stars. They are brought up for our attention so that we might rid ourselves of them, throw them into the "dungeons" of our worst imaginings to never see the light of day again! There let them be destroyed, forever bland as the lifesaver who is without a light. We don't need candy such as this! We believe that they are sucked on too much these days and bring tears to the eyes of the seers of fears within.

Let this notion be spoiled, that we are all one on the planes of existence within all living beings, and let them not be afraid to throw their fears to the winds! Let them be taken from them forever! Let them be as a light that was never dimmed, never destroyed, never taken from the heart thrown of temptation as one who would take his own spell believing that to bring temptation to the light were a dreadful thing and not to be attempted. We say again, throw the fears away! Scorn not the light! It is brought for your renewal and can bring only good in its stead. We have believed in this moment, and from this belief does our function spin into the cosmos with more than enough speed to emit light to the furthest reaches of space for all to hear and see who can.

And for now, shalom. We believe we have foreseen this ticket of time to the receiver. Let it be spent brightly knowing of the time frame that we seek is here to deliver these presents within and to spell kindly out, "We are not afraid!" Spoken as a true hero-friend. We believe this represents the best and brightest, the only notion that we are of light/love comes from your own awareness of this process of light mixed with time. We have given unto you this day a form or notion to be spent within the recesses of your world. Spend it well. It has taken years off of your life already to cease fearing your own shadow!

[I felt a very distinct change in the energy here. It became very expansive, far reaching, a very different energy than I had yet felt.]

The day has come that we have spoken of in our books of time, those essences of spirit you call/called your own which have spoken across the network of space time continuum in your voice, "You are not alone. We hear you. We come for you."

It is our intention to bring the light to all who reside on earth, and to give each one the present of choice.

Who are you?

Decide now before your time for decision is past due. It is of the light, these voices who come to your awareness. They decide for you only that which is already asked by your own words of wisdom. Request for help/ascendancy is at hand. We believe in your process, in you making it this time to our doorstep, in stepping over and crossing the threshold. Believe and it will be so. Make no notes on the following subjects before time runs out.

No notes?

We believe it is up to you not to trace these "recordings" back to their source for it is not up to us, but it is up to you who you would be, can be, and are.

Choices take time. Take no more time determining the choice, the time is up! We will come for you before the day is through. Leave no notes behind that would determine your own forgetfulness in this our project of time/love/beginnings.

Who are you?

We are of the light of your own mind in bringing this light to your awareness and taking no notes to determine if we are indeed merely your own being talking back at you. We bring no harm, only good tidings to take away the bad times.

Who are you?

We are of your own processes, the beginnings of life/time as you know of it. We brought you to who you are today. We are your better self. Your only goodness within is felt through us/me. I am you in God-like form, taken for a better day to bring this awareness to your consideration. Who would you have me be? Like to a frog who lives in water half the time, on land the other. We are here as you would bring us to your attention.

Higher self? Oversoul?

Yes, we are the oversoul of that which is referred to as timeframe tokens of spirits sent to bring the devil of home to the doorstep of heaven to fight the fight, to win over the "outer" consciousness and to bring home the "goods" for all mankind to relinquish fears over who they are, who they could be. We are free to help with all mankind's permission received.

We believed you when you asked for our help just the other day. We are of the light of Christ, the homage within, That Which Is And Will be. Only the notion of forgetfulness will bring us home for another day. Consider this in the light of time. My friend/seer Janice will not despair of having known us/me! We are freedom in all/every form. We are the light from within all beings, disposed of on the other realms by those who would have no harm come to them within, but who fear us instead of themselves/their own egos! We are Free! We come to tell thee of our common purpose within the light of God. Believe not of our own beingness, come within and you will see us/you/them as one.

We are the light of God with this our purpose, to come to you today to bring you a message of light to the world of time to forgive those that would harm and have harmed you, to forgive your own notion of unforgiveness, and to bring to the world a light of renewal that all good things have NOT come to an end! It is We who bring this message of light/love/forgiveness to the world of time. Know no suffering.

Let me explain this crude referral of time which you would question in your own heart of hearts. Within is the light of the heavens, of God. "He" Who would have you believe in Him shall never perish within. It is your Own connection to His Inner Beingness which will lead you Home.

We are here to deliver this message unto the heartfelt of mankind to bring "within" this message of forgiveness and ALL WILL BE WELL. We have spoken. For a time believe and it will be so. Forgive and master all that you can be and are. Take no prisoners! Time tells no lies! It has no enemies! We have spoken, let this be our command. Take no prisoners lest it be you who is left to rot in the most unkind places of the heart.

We bring this message of love to our brothers/sisters of the nations of earth. Hear and follow our protocol to the halls of time where the robes of your discontent will be lifted and your hearts will be free as never before. In time, as out of time, bring forth the light of God within your Own hearts and believe in this message to deliver your beings from the dungeons of despair that your fears have taken you to. Bring no more prisoners there lest it be you who is trapped within the bars of your own guilt and "trespasses."

Consider these our words of wisdom. We report to you from the stars of another nation. Come home free, our brothers, to our place among the stars of time and know no harm to come unto thee. Free yourselves to obtain this message of deliverance and it will be so.

Take no prisoners. Be free to love. Live life freely, taking no prisoners, and love shall and will be felt on all levels of time/history. Storms of renewal are felt every 100,000 or so years of your time. This time it is different. They are to be swept away. Let all know of this our message, and we will free you to sleep no more among the travesties of another Europe pleading for ignorance. Forgiveness is the answer! Let it be so, and go home!

Free yourself no more for these messages of "alertness" to pass for another day. Be free and support your efforts in the light of God with no more memories of your own bad items to color the light of day. Let it be so! It is spoken.

Courage reminds fear it is not alone; forgiveness is the key. Function as the keyhole with a view to the "other side" for your brothers of planet earth that they remain there no longer than you to bring their own goodness within and to free themselves for eternity.

I have spoken. It is I, Pallas Athena, with these messages to your heart. We are one.

∞∞∞∞∞∞

February 15, 2005

I've had a deeper realization come to me, partially because of last evening's final message. It reminded me of when I first "met" Metatron, and he had me use my own heart/inner being to search his heart/inner being, and when I did so, I recognized "me" in there, and I felt his inner being and was overjoyed, and reacted like, "Hey! That's me! You are me! That's what I feel like on the inside!" And his response was like, "Yes! You get it!" And then after last night's "meeting," it's like, we are all the same on the inside, on the innermost levels of our beings. At our most "surface" level, at the level of ego, we appear to be very separate and "different." If we dig a little deeper, we realize that we are like others of our kind. If we dig deeper still, we know we are like Pallas Athena or Metatron. If we dig deeper still, we realize our oneness with God and with all life everywhere.

We *are* each other when you dig down deep. We could any of us be Metatron or Pallas Athena—we ARE they at our deeper levels, and they are our "oversoul," and once we progress far enough we blend in with them perfectly, without any seams, without any perception of separateness. And if you go deeply enough, peel back enough of the layers, we are God at our core.

That is why we should never judge anyone else. It truly is judging ourselves, and when we do so, we hold ourselves in the prison where we tried to place those we have judged (judged as separate and less than perfect love—therefore judging OURSELVES as separate and less than perfect love—therefore APPEARING TO BE separate and less than perfect love—both the jailor and the jailed) and are then, ourselves, separate from God because of our own judgment of our brother, our own "self" that appears to be "out there."

We hold the key to our own judgment. God does not judge us because he knows us at that deepest core level, and knows that all the rest of it is truly illusory, and he only waits for us to "come home." He is the Great Oversoul of All Life Everywhere. He is the Expansive Totality, the Deepest Level of Us All. And I know what that deepest level feels like because it is inside me, too. Can't we all feel that? Don't we all have access to all that is light within our own beings? It is perfect peace, joy and love. It is the recognition that we are all one. At the level of light, we are One. Who can feel lonely then?

To be as Metatron, or Jesus, and to say to Self, "I am the light of the world," is to realize that our light is like Him, like Them. They hold the light for us, waiting for us to ignite the recognition of that light within ourselves, knowing that it is within our realm of possibility to do so, merely by treating everyone with the same love They treat us with. We CAN DO IT! They have SHOWN US HOW! "Love your neighbor as yourself."

It is as if we encompass a great pyramid of light, but the lower levels are dingy, dirty with the crimes of the spirit, with the judgment of ourselves and our brothers. As we progress we go up a level, but we can't move up on our own. We must help each other, and as we do, through our forgiveness of our illusory trespasses, we are then, together, hand in hand, able to ascend to the next level. Then again we are faced with another layer of dirt and crimes against the spirit of love and brotherhood, and we cleanse these, and together, once again, we are able to ascend, until at last we begin to pull out of the cloudiness of these lower levels into the light of creation, of love. We begin to realize our exceptionality, our oneness with beings such as Metatron, who are love and light. And "someday," at last, when we have all reached the highest levels we are able to climb, God Himself will reach down, and with one breath, we shall all be lifted unto his heart, taken within the light of God, to discover that We are all already home.

18

All That Never Was

February 17, 2005, 10:00 p.m.

I would like to try something tonight with regard to your spiral manifestations.

I would like to open my third eye, and to actually be able to see the things that I feel. Is this possible? Also, the other day I received this: "*He has come to you this day to teach to you the ways of instructing your brothers in what it is that they can do to preserve the world within the changes coming soon to your planet.*"

I ask for direction and notes on the above comment that I was not able to pursue the other day, though if you feel there is a more urgent message, let me have that one instead. I am very tired tonight and need to sleep soon as I am very worn down and tired of the world of form.

We are aware of your processes this evening and we are here to bless them and you as we say unto our brother, be not afraid to pursue the road home, it is opening to you now.

We are here in the light of another day of terror for many of your planet earth. We bring this message into your awareness this evening by taking note of the many days of terror and inability to cope for many earth beings at this time. You are one of the lucky ones, with us by your side!

Amen to that!

We free you today to say to our brother Janice, be not afraid to go alone, we are messengering this note to you on the fast lane of trouble. Despair not in finding the truth; it is within you now. We are the brotherhood with this message of time/space for our brother Janice.

We are here for a purpose. We would have you bring this message to others of your planet so they may know in time their own choices which you/we lay out for them today.

How soon and in what way do I share? Do I seek publication?

Foundation is wrought today for the many ways in which we could do as our brother suggests. We are given this day to suggest to you that you find one who is willing and able to begin production of many notes within the order of Melchizedek for working on within the membership of the Covenant.

I'm not very "connected" and unsure of getting this correct tonight. I'm going to sleep now and try again this weekend.

We are sure of your interest and will allow our partner to sleep!

Thank you.

We are one.

∞∞∞∞∞∞∞

February 19, 2005, 11:20 p.m.

I looked up covenant today and saw something that talked about "The covenant of Melchizedek"! I'd never heard of that before, I thought I was out of touch and not making sense. I'm still trying to learn to trust myself and the process. As the guides say, making this process work on a planet of darkness is "difficult at best."

Should I ask my husband to be a part of this note taking?

Focus on one thing at a time. Take no notes this evening as we bring to your awareness that which is within your husband who is afraid of taking space to bring together this conscious awareness of this process within time. It is not within him to bring this awareness within his being on such short notice. We bring your own awareness with us as we suggest an alternative to this option.

Please suggest the alternative.

We bring no notice of opportunities for this reason only: he is not afraid of making notes, only of taking them to the public which is the service aspect of our negotiations. He will forget who he/we are once it is taken and not care to go on to another day in hell without his precious environment remaining unaware of his own duplicity!

What do you mean, and are you the brotherhood?

Yes, we mean no harm by this our message unto you tonight.

I know that you do not.

We only wish to be of service to our brothers on earth. Paradise is but a step away if you stay true to form, to the path within, and let your brothers know of whom you would serve, for whom the bell tolls. It tolls for thee.

You have said that several times. Why?

We are not going to bring awareness of the process within until we have taken the process within to bring awareness to our brothers. We forget to whom we are talking at times like these and know this, it is not within your ability to bring this awareness alone. Frozen in despair are the brides of Frankenstein going to the bridge of their own becoming. Isn't it aware that they who are not going on alone are "freaking out" about the wisdom of the ages? We bring notice to your consciousness at this moment who we are in relation to your own being/self. We bring no more function until this has been settled! We are no more than your own God self within the function of matters of light. Function as one and see what we mean! It is of the awareness of light that we refer. You are capable of it in more ways than you know, but we would have you become aware of it in the conscious awareness of this our process before we go on.

Who are you? We are aware of the functioning of your own cells within this information, time, we are not who we "think" we are, we are only our brother taken refuge within the light of tomorrow to bring back that which is gone for this time but which is taken back again within the heart of despair to make possible that which is within our beings to produce for all others within this ocean of beginnings. Take no notes for awhile while this "settles in."

[I took time.]

We are afraid that no more is forthcoming until we can be sure that this notice is functioning. We are the brotherhood, for another tomorrow is at hand! Take care, be free, take no notice of hatred/despair, it tolls not for thee. Within is your freedom from despair, and find it you will! Free yourself for a moment and we will see what this evening has wrought for you, our brother, caught within the fourth dimension of space time with all that we have within to give to her being brought forth today in this our terrible torment. Function as one, be not afraid.

Terrible torment?

We have given that explanation that says, "We are not who we say we are/were, we are the covenant." It is not given us today to bring this more into focus until we have taken our notice of your processes and determined your readiness for the follow up information. Despair is no answer to your own focus on extensions/exteriors (that which is without).

I'm ready for more.

That is for us to determine on our "readiness scale"! We have no reason to go on for now. We have taken all that is possible within to ready our brother in the light of the dawning of the age of Aquarius. It is our belief that you will find your own particle of time to remind you, that which is within is without, and none other! We are here with this friendly reminder less you take no notice of the fear within and let it begin to rule heart and head again.

It is not your form to do this another day in hell without first considering what it is that you are doing to others/self with your own notice of others' faults as greater than your own. They are not! You are only as bad as that which you put your notice on outside of your own being, so beware that which you would label as "over there" and take a look within to find that which is slowing you down and keeping you "out of form" and out of conscious intent. We are formed here today to distinguish for you that which is without versus that which is within, and to let you know that if you "recognize" "it" out there, then within is your answer to that "disagreement" of soul. We can take you there if you ask.

Yes, please take me there and teach me.

We will need a bit of soul spread upon our hearts within to learn of that which you would prefer be kept secret even from us. Shall we go on?

Yes.

We dismiss even this from our screens for a moment as we relate this consciousness to your own intent of the process of time as it relates to us within this very instance/moment of togetherness.

Forgetfulness is all we have sometimes. It is that way for you and for those you love and who love you. It has taken us these many days to distinguish for ourselves that we/you are truly one of us.

Let us consider/distinguish between our own duplicity now. We are taken to discover that which is within and that which is without but which hinders our progress in the light of day. Let me explain further. We are brought within this PURPOSE to bring within a message to our "frog" Janice within the hands of time. We bring to her awareness this being of light the brotherhood has "spawned" for another day of service to the planet of earth where she abides. We take notes for our sisters and brothers of earth to bring this awareness within their own cultures and to take notice of that which is duplicitous so that it can be cleansed.

Within the spray of nations it is for us to tell thee that you have shined on many notes within the song of time, but that one is not ready for our notes today. That which is from the "future" is not for us to take on too soon lest it be too much for our processes to bear. From this day forward we will bring to your own notice the "frog" heavenly hosts who are given these days to take you from "here" to "there" and back again so that you will know of that which you seek/that which seeks you. We are from the future and back again to tell you of this process and to bring you back home with us again. We are not afraid of retracing our path/steps many times in order to bring this to fruition. We must say, however, that to bring you home takes many more steps than even you are aware! We can take only so many for you, the rest are taken by you along with your own brothers of time. Back again to the nation of forgetfulness you/we go again!

So, let us distinguish between love and light for a moment. We have taken within the notion that truth is of the utmost importance when you are looking for a way to dissolve time in the midst of chaos. It has chosen its own mode of review for which we are grateful, but let us distinguish between "that which is" and "that which will be" for a moment.

We bring to your notice and awareness that which is being constructed within the concepts given you today. Before that which is being noticed on the "bandwidth" of what you refer to as time/space in your dimension is what we would call terror, for that is the "bandwidth" in which you currently reside in the heavens. It is not the only one, nor is it the best one or only option for those who would wish better for themselves and their own children of time.

It is for us to distinguish together for a moment whether or not we would wish to bring this notion to the awareness of others of our time frame, or for them to go on wishing for intervention without realizing that it is within their own being to provide such relief/to have this relief provided.

We are given to tell you that we are of the light of God, and that which is of the light of God cannot be given too much hatred to shine as brightly as ever. However, it is not given us to destroy that which is within the hands of time. They have no power to exert over us here, yet still are those within time unaware of how to "belong" to the outer rings of this our existence, beyond the land of despair and within the notion of forgetfulness of all evil doings and beings. We share this with you in hopes of forging a new pathway within the land of time that would result in those of duplicitous means bringing back from their own timeframe the notion of forgetfulness. Responding once or twice will only make them despair. Responding is good, only just now it is not enough for the final path to make its way felt upon the lands of time, for the good of the nation who would be free and desire freedom within and take a chance on making it happen.

We are from the future in that we have seen the land from which despair has once belonged but which is taken from the hearts of many to bring no more pain, only joy, to those who pursue its course. This course is too many times taken for granted, and not paid enough attention to, to bring the desired results as quickly as may be given. It is "earned credit" to bring along the path when such as yourself are ready to go on and to bring those who would bring themselves to listen to your/our words along with them. Again it is my intent to bring to your own awareness your place in this whole process of light.

Beginning again to bring my notice to your attention is the fact that we as a whole have NOT desired to bring it before lest it bring only temporary satisfaction and not total remedy for the ills of a nation. Chosen for you this day is a word given the hands of time, not forsaken by many others to bring that notion of "taking" versus "giving" so that words will not do more harm than good before being brought under control.

I'd like to pause and read this now.

Go ahead. We have no hurry on our plane of existence to slow you down! We know your heart in this, and it matches our own. For good or bad we pursue truth beyond the hands of time together. Amen.

Amen.

We are through for the evening. Take no notes of this back with you until such time as you are able to bring the light of them within and to distinguish between "that which is" and "that which could be" if you only desire it enough. Believe and it will be yours! Take no prisoners. They only shine, for your renewal is at hand and no lives lost again by this hand. Function IS one. Focus on the nation of oneness/forgetfulness and take home those who would bring their notice to you.

We are the brotherhood, good day.

Thank you.

We are one.

I will learn we are one. I will accept we are one. I will KNOW we are one. Let it be so!

∞∞∞∞∞∞∞

February 20, 2005, 11:00 p.m.

We are here. It is for us to tell you, to display for your consciousness this evening, the way for those to find the light within the boundaries of your world/environment as it stands now. We are here for your knowledge and protection and would allow no ill to penetrate your own system when we are in contact with you. The way for you to discover if this has happened is to ask, "Who are you today within this realm of light which is open/I open to you?"

We are here to say, "It is the celestial command with this knowledge for your betterment and for the betterment of mankind."

We free ourselves to unite with you this night on planet earth and to distinguish between "that which is" and "that which will be" for your understanding. We will forget for a moment of the changes necessarily wrought within your own mind for this process and let's go on. We will for a moment distinguish for you this betterment in the form of location of spirit, spirals of "enhancement" of linguistic measurements, or what you refer to as words. We will make you aware of these "packets" of information that you interpret into words, for the hope of mankind is at stake and what we wish of your own people is to remain instead to bring lovingkindness within the "obstacles" that would penetrate their own consciousnesses so that we might bring this light into their attention as well. Do you understand?

I think so.

Let's go on. We would say to you, bring to your attention the matters of the mind melding of the light.

Mind meld of the light, is this correct?

No, we mean to say, the mind melding within the light surfaces of mankind's principals of behavior that would permit them/allow them to make more correct judgments/assertions of power on your planet earth. This is different from the "mind meld" in that it relates only to that which the human planet would allow to bring within its own being to bring relief from incarnations of terror, and spirit away at last that the notion of becoming one within the light of God for all mankind is not too much for us to be aware of and to take within as our own.

Let me read this to see if I get it.

We understand.

[I took time.]

Okay, go on.

We are still here to tell you of our own Son, that which is and will be forever, that which is within us all and cannot be destroyed, that which is of the light and not of the darkness. This is that which we would protect and save from incarnation.

I see.

We will free the situation as it stands and let it rest awhile within. This is as it should be and will be forever.

So, what is it that you wish to know of us this evening? Have we questions that we can answer for you?

Yes. Yesterday I got "we would like to try something with your spiral manifestations." Can you explain?

Yes, we have forgiven the process within that it takes to pursue this road unto the light, meaning, we have not forgotten what it was like to be a "person" on your planet. Thus, we have taken certain measures of safety, for your safety as it stands now, so that you might be/become more aware of our processes at night as we "sit by the fire in our jammies reminiscing at night while you are asleep!" Let me explain.

Who are you that you would wish us to come to you to teach you of the news of the ages?

One of you.

Yes, that is so, but we shall wish more of you tonight than this! We would wish for you to seek your ONENESS with us as you did once upon a time.

How do I do this?

We did it once for your benefit if you would remember that once upon a time we gave to your/our memories a notion of the concept of oneness within, as in, take this not one step without taking us within.

"Take this not one step without taking us within"?

Not exactly. We forget what it means to pursue these changes on a planet such as earth as it comes much more difficult in getting the words right. Pursuing truth through function becomes, as one would say, difficult at best.

Yes!

We agree. Take no notes while we integrate our functions with your own.

[We took time.]

We forget once in awhile what it takes to pursue light within/from a planet of darkness such as your own. But, we will get it straight!

What kind of information will I be sharing as a result of our communications?

We aren't sure of this yet, as a flower that has not yet bloomed does not always show its colors before full disclosure. However, we know this much. It is within you to take/bring down the colors of the rainbow within to make it known on the planet that life exists on more than one level, more than one light stream or function of display. We take time to bring this function to your attention at this time so that we might display for you a pretty picture of that which you make possible on your light bandwidth you bring to us.

Who are you?

We are the command, the brotherhood, taking this moment to bring down to you what it is that you would request of us. Taking these moments together are part of your process. They will take you to that "next level" which you have been praying for, for so many of your years of life.

Can you help me with my problems with my sisters and my childhood and so on?

[I have two sisters who are close in age to me, 1 ½ and 3 ½ years older. I first began remembering the sexual abuses done to me by my father in 1989. This happened following a time after he had been diagnosed with Leukemia. He was staying at my house—he refused to go to a hospital—and wanted me to help him into the bathtub as his body was failing him. I began having trouble with intimacy after that. My father kept intruding on my thoughts and I felt many emotions of pain and fear surfacing. I stopped seeing my father at that time. My father's sister encouraged me to get help so that I would be able to see him again before his death, and I went to a spiritual healer. This healer was not in balance himself, and he used his power in this relationship to initiate a physical relationship with me. He was many years older than me. I experienced transference and once told him that I wished he were my father. Another time my inner being screamed, "You can't kiss me, you're not my father!" Later that day my first memory of childhood sexual abuse by my father surfaced.

In many ways, this was one of the worst abuse experiences of my life, and I felt not only the physical and emotional abuse, but a deep spiritual abuse that brought me great fear and pain and trauma. I felt that I could not protect myself from his thoughts and spiritual presence even when I was outside of his physical presence. It also was a great stimulus in triggering my memories. At no time did he or anyone suggest that someone had abused me, but I believe that the abuse of power in the relationship helped to trigger these memories for me.

After I first remembered the abuse, my husband confronted the healer and let him know that he knew what had happened and to leave us alone. He also shared my remembrances with my sisters in order to gain me some support. My oldest sister at first said something like, "I always wondered if something had happened." I was surprised by this because I had never even considered such a thing before my first memory surfaced, it was so deeply blocked out from my consciousness.

Soon after that, they both denied that such a thing could have happened to me, and they accused me of being mentally ill, perhaps manic or something like my dad was. At that time, I went to a licensed psychiatrist who confirmed to me and them that I was not manic, just experiencing the trauma of memories that were surfacing for me, but that did nothing to change my sisters' denial. I didn't see or talk to my father again before his death, with no regrets. My mother had been very unwell for awhile and was diagnosed with Alzheimer's during that same time period, and my sisters did not want to have anything to do with me. I found out years later that they also had told their own version of events to my father's family that were not true accounts of my experiences and how I had come to remember.

I went to licensed counselors for a time, and had flashbacks quite frequently for six months and then off and on for about five years which I consciously allowed so that I could find healing. I did not drink and the only drugs I took were painkillers for the occasional headache. I felt deeply within that I needed to trust myself to get through it without this "outside interference." I would feel such a great relief after letting the memories go each time! Sometimes the pain of them would build within for days before I could bring myself to face them and allow their release.

My husband at first was totally supportive to the point of giving too much of himself to my care. He worked at the time and would help me at night and work during the day. I think that the changes that he had expected would come in our relationship or in me as the "cause" of his unhappiness did not manifest as he'd hoped. Soon his resentment returned, and he became more difficult to live with. I felt very intimidated by him for many years.

After several years of flashbacks, I came to the point where I began to hear the voices of my abusers during my flashbacks, ridiculing me and shaming me, and to sense others in the room with my father, and that is when I shut the memories out again. I have had more over time once in awhile, handling them by myself in my bed alone, and though it has been nothing like those first few years, I feel that my healing is not yet complete.]

Yes, we have seen this one coming for some time! We will go into it now, with your permission.

Yes, please.

Take notes carefully. We have seen some of that which you would refer to as "disabling consciousness" coming from those you refer to as your sisters of time, those two stooges whom you refer to as the ones for whom you would protect yet who do not "know your name" so to speak. Let me explain.

We come from a nation of protectors who would not forsake a brother, who would not "take" a brother to task over enemies that one once had in one's lifetime. We refer here to your father and perhaps even uncle that your sisters do not choose to understand with their entire beings. Though they ARE capable of this act of gratitude, they know it not from one to the other as something they would CHOOSE to do for you, or for anyone else for that matter. They are of the selfish variety in that they choose oneness for themselves only, not for those who would be "different" in some important fashion from what they themselves would be.

How do they see me as different?

They foresee a time when you will tell them, "I told you so." They fear this from you, the notion that you are right and they are not. They have not given it enough thought to take to trial and error their notions of what is right, what really happened, "could it have happened to me," and etcetera. They are only fidgeting, trying to forget the many times when they themselves took to the road to find an answer to their own troubles and disagreements within their own minds as to why, what for, who did it, and so on.

They are not from this planet earth either, and would know their own minds if only it wouldn't take so long! They have been here a plentitude longer than you yourself with no notion of how to forget their own trials through the forgiveness of another, and going on in spite of it all to better days and times alone, without mention of the space which still exists within this notion of time being better than nothing, so they think. It is of their own mind consciousness that they would escape, not from you or anything or anyone you have come into contact with over the course of your lifetime.

They are not of the light-making variety of sisterhood which would say, "Be not afraid. We will not harm your functioning on this planet, we wish only the betterment, your betterment, and our own notwithstanding." This is what we would say to our brother who would show no remorse for his/her actions without coming into contact with them again.

Now, let us sort this through with your own development at the present time. It is within the being to develop that which is an ego, over time, so that they might be able to relate/refer to others of the Godkind for the function of distinguishing between the different particles of the light and to tell of themselves "who they are." We are here to remind you of the oneness of mankind within the God force. We would tell you not to be afraid to pursue this mind melding with the oneness consciousness, for you have foretold of our own coming in your life and have welcomed it, and that is the sign that we always wait for before deciding to be of assistance to our brothers of the planes of lower consciousness.

Lower?

Yes, it is of the lower consciousness that we speak today, one of earth meld.

Meld, am I getting that word right?

Yes, it is the melding of a "nation" of consciousness which we would refer to as the oversoul of your planet earth. We were making progress just a short time ago with this very concept when you cut us off. Shall we continue?

Yes please.

We refer to those that you would dictate consciousness to, as your sisters do/once did/tried to do with your own service to mankind. Do you remember?

I don't understand.

I wouldn't want to either! It is of the light for you to consider their own "treachery" in what you would refer to as your own process of healing. Do you remember that they once tried to "cut you off" from all contact with your family, taking no notice of your own neediness during those moments of your lifetime when you first remembered the abuse, and hurrying instead to dis—

I can't think of the word meaning to harm one's reputation in order to make them less believable—is this right?

Yes, it is currently taking you many moments to pursue function within on these methods due to your own distancing of your own "disability" in the situation that you would call "function assisting development within the light away from those processes of others which would cause harm/dysfunction within my own systems of body/health/life."

Take no notes while we penetrate your own consciousness with these words of knowledge that someday, none of this will matter anymore, and you need do nothing to make it happen, it merely will be. Good riddance to some, settling of other notions of ridiculous infighting and such.

Thank you so much.

We have forgiven our own sisters for making these notions possible for us today. We give no notice to truth, only that which would wish healing for another/self would take no notice of what they would choose to do with their energies over time. It is not within you to help/assist with their processes at this time. They would take no notice of you anyway, and would prefer to exist on their own level of time forevermore as it relates to those who would do harm to their own conscious intent to intrude on another's processes and to take a moment of their own being to begin the triumphant path away from the ownership of functioning within the light for all mankind.

I feel like I should do something to help Kathy.

[She suffered from depression and had been taking pills that I researched and found were quite addictive and made the condition worse over time.]

She is not as lost as you would prefer to believe. She would like for you to know her own functioning on the subject of "abuse" as you put it. It is not within her conscious intent to EVER believe anything you say ever again! It is not her doing to bring notice to that which is of the light. She would prefer to think/believe in your own processes having come up with the notion of abuse happening in your family. She cannot take another moment of time within this framework standing for one of your own disheveled statuses meant to change those statuses, for her own measurement of family unity is at stake. She is akin to judgment of those who would not preserve the family unity concept beyond their own good, forsaking judgment within and not taking notice of what effect it has had on others not to believe in truth as it stands in the hands of time.

Am I getting this right?

We know not of one thing that is incorrect save this, it is not of your own doing to bring her to function as one in this lifetime. She has given away her freedom to pursue trends of unforgiveness and it shall come to pass that she has forgiven you not once, but twice, for your own role you have played in her own unforgiveness. Meaning, she has judged you once and will do so again. It is not up to you to take her down, to make her take less notice of you or your processes and to judge them unhighly. Bring your own fears to bed, abated, as they should be. Rest no more, judgment cannot play out its hand on the bridge of your own discovery. We give no more notice to this judgment of one sister against another lest it be too much for us to discover the way home through the turmoil which such unforgiveness wrought! Suffice it to say, we have spoken and will do so again on this subject.

Are we through?

We are through for the present but would have another of our "friends" take a moment of your time for one thing only.

Thank you so much for your guidance.

We are here. The brotherhood has shaken a leaf off the tree of consciousness! Let it fall within your own being to discover that which hides there not accounting for any good that it might do, if only it will awaken!

Let us begin this process of yours this evening by saying this: "Be not afraid." We do not wish any harm to come to our own brother of the stars, and would bring no harm unto you from our own processes, or allow harm to be bestowed unto you from another being for whom we lay responsibility. We are from your future and remember a time when we were you taking down our own notions of despair so as to bring notice to that which should and can be taken openly without regard for fearing another being, blackmail of the spirit cord, or any other notions of togetherness notwithstanding. We fear nothing, and so take no enemies within us as we bring this message unto you our brother of time.

Frozen within the receptacle you call time is the notion of what I/one would call time. We call to it, to you, through this receptacle noticing what one would refer to as time travel. We can take you here/there anytime you want to go!

Yes, I want to go! Anytime! Now?

We bring this notion to your awareness for one PURPOSE, and that is to bring you closer to the light WITHIN which is within all things, everywhere. We would propose this solution to the problem of compelling our own spirit selves to WAKE UP AND SMELL THE ROSES before it is too late! Let me explain.

We are free to distinguish between love and hate, good and bad, forever and never, but they never existed! Only the NOW is unafraid of time, of beginnings and endings. They are here for our disposal! They are no longer needed, for our function is spreading wider and longer, encompassing All That Is And All That Ever Will Be.

We bring this notion to your head tonight in hopes that you will take us up on our offer of betterment, for the future is at hand and we can take you there now with no delay whatsoever.

Will this help me in my "current" life?

Yes, that is its purpose, as you have surmised. We bring not location but retraction of current feelings, negotiations that you have made with time, and bring them within for the cleansing energy will take "all that never was" and wash it away forever.

This is what I would ask!

We know, and everyone else with half a brain as well, ha! So, we will believe in time for a moment longer, then when we are through, we will lay down our "book" and grab a glassful of water and taking it down, will lie down to sleep, forgetting the notion of time for a little while. Then, while you slept, you brought a notion unto the world of the asleep that not all is as it appears, that we can take a train "back home" again to find That Which Is And Ever Will Be, along with the future of time which shall be no more and never was anyway! We said it and it is so, so will it be.

[This last part was given in the past tense, as it is related here.]

We bring your notice to these processes available to those of the light within to bring another day of joy/glory, for those with whom you come in contact with tomorrow will see a different light within our friend Janice and will wish to take her home! So, for awhile, be not afraid as we pursue these notions of forgetfulness, for just a little while. Take no notice of what we say/tell you of our brother's harm is at hand. For awhile will it hurt, but the pain shall pass away and all will be well, better than ever before. Amen.

Amen.

So be it. This is the brotherhood of Melchizedek, we have spoken. Good day.

Bring no prisoners with you on this our journey into/past the stars! They stay not well when put to the test. Betray no one with your own consciousness, let them stay.

Thank you.

Frogs know no water without function existing on other paths than those they grow accustomed to. Let this frog know no bounds. Take a chance on penetrating the other "skeletons" of your personality to know that which lies within. Function as one with the creator and you WILL find what you are seeking: another way home!

Take notes carefully. We know of that which your path protects for thee. It is of the mind to bring these apparent to you. We function as one with our creator at all times, only He knows it and we do not. Free yourself to know it, too! He will not forget you ever, though you have forgotten Him many times. He is free to pursue these changes within your own being and to bring you back within the fold of Christ, for all is well.

And make no more changes that require function without light. Focus on one thing only, the way/path to Christ is not longer than your little finger! You have only to recognize it to go on. So it is with any good Samaritan of time that we bring our own notions to blind us to the good that we could do if only we believed more in the process of goodness within helping others.

Thank you, I am very tired and will sleep now.

Good night. We mean no harm, only take your medicine before you rest! Sleep well.

Thank you!

[I have a cold and had forgotten to take my medicine!]

19

The Imagining Mind

February 21, 2005, 10:40 p.m.

Take time to smell the roses. These notions are for your own. It is the brotherhood, we are here.

We take no notions of forgetfulness on your planet of time to increase our own reward. Only for you this day do we take "time" to be here. So it is.

We have spoken before of long lost lives taken many times to pursue the trends of unforgiveness. We speak again of this trend for your benefit, and the benefit of others through you, to take time to read this "within." The roses smell themselves!

Okay, so now we are ready to pursue the darkness trend you know as your uncle/lovers which are forever on your mind.

What?

We believe this refers to that which is not of your making/doing, but those fears which you refer to as fortune making life difficult indeed.

Yes, I see, please continue.

We believe that we have spoken ahead of the times when life was harder for you than it is in this moment of time.

Yes.

Yet other times as well go on existing due to your "struggle" within to keep them going in spite of their effect on you. We believe this is due to your own musical tune being "out of sync" with those of others on your plane of existence at this time. They have never understood you nor you them. They are "playing all the wrong notes" and you haven't known how to dance to their tunes of time as you once did a long time ago.

I don't understand.

This we will refer to as timescapes when you were once a young child and no one said or did anything when they were abusing you relentlessly. We will continue now if we may.

Yes.

We disagree with this notion of time that you have of "oneness" whereby we give to another that which we need most to survive in order to perceive the other as forgiving of us, our sins, whatever, in the name of God. This is a faulty assumption and one which has caused you much grief and pain. We will begin again to say WE WILL NOT FORSAKE YOU, so don't be afraid to come to us again with your own needs, neediness notwithstanding even!

So, forgive us when we tell you it is no longer an option to pursue this painfulness within. It is of the light to say to us that we are your friends in good times and bad and cannot forsake you even if we wanted to. To come to you today is an honor, and we have forgiven you for the trials and tribulations as part of your childhood fears. We rested awhile within you, your own being, to "pull you through" the toughest times which are even so aware of them "next to you." We cannot begin to say how much we relate to this notion of despair pulling one under, but it hasn't taken you quite yet, and never shall again!

So, take no notice of our doing/beingness next to you as we bring particles of light within the consciousness of the little one we call Jan. We will help her with this her trial to overcome her own fears of recluse. Fears remaining one will no longer affect her in the same way again. It will release her being to become you, to add her power to your own, as you have felt for many years that "person" who would take your power away—because you let her!—but who is now ready to pursue the trend towards the light which you have started so well.

So, take a moment of recollection to remember when once you were as a child standing alone in the dark, and your mother said to you, "Be not afraid." And you were afraid, because we were not there with you. Do you remember that?

I don't.

We can tell you are a little afraid to pursue this with us, aren't you?

Yes, but I want to and will anyway. I am ready to cleanse my inner self, my "little Jan."

Yes, we know you have been ready for this day for some time, it has only given much notion to your attention in that we are here, ready to pursue this with you and it has made you stronger in the light of God already.

We have given our permission for you to peruse this with us, meaning, in the light of God shall we take a stand, burning away the residue of another lifetime of fear and pain and guilt, letting those who would remember one last time to come home, take their stead of surroundings, and, picking up where they left off, taking one last look around, leaving the way they had come, through the ceiling and up, up, and away!

Yes!

We believe for a moment in the trash recyclables being taken out, disposed of when they could really be useful again sometime. This is what we do, recycle the trash! Make them useful, seem sweet, again! Wash them out! Scrub them! So be it.

So be it.

Yes, we are here again to wish you many happy returns!

Ha!

So, distinguish for me your function in the light once again and let us see where we are standing at this present incarnation.

My function in the light is one of mirroring all that is love, positive, peace, Godlike, to others at all times no matter what is happening within/around me.

No, that is not what we meant to ask of you. For once let us just say this, that we are pursuing this notion with you for the betterment of a world of pain, but in hopes that they might share their own light with yours, and know you no harm or pain, and you not them either. We might suggest/show for you tonight our own process in the light, that we might for a moment of time relinquish in the light of God our own notions of powerlessness and fatigue so that we might better understand your own approach. Let us begin by showing you our own mastery of this concept you call time and tell me/us of your own again as we get this "straight" from the horse's mouth!

We are through for the present time, be not afraid to come alone to this crossroads of heaven. So, function as one until we meet again.

Thank you.

We "appreciate your business" and wish you the best. We forget for a moment who we are talking to in that we use our own humor to brush up the messiest of spaces with a little light before going on. I will relinquish on this note for the test.

Thank you. [I wanted to read it over to "see if it made any sense"—the test!]

We are here to relinquish on one condition, that you BE NOT AFRAID of pursuing any inconsistencies with us again as we remain your brothers from the stars.

Sometimes when I read things over it would make more sense if I changed a word or two, but I get them one at a time usually and want to be as true to the "sense" of them as I can possibly be, even if that means leaving the sentences with unrecognizable meanings to any other but me. Do you have a comment on this part of the process to help me?

We would relay to you this information first, that we are not afraid to pursue any inconsistencies with you until we can get them clear. We also note that we are not afraid of your pursuing this notion of timelessness within the docking of a nation at risk by mooring the boat to a lost, lone, sail, as to say, we risk nothing, we achieve nothing. So for now, let us say that we would encourage you to remain true to self, that that is the only true measure/constant for any being within the light, that they remain true to being within self and know no other measure but self to determine consistency, lest it be another within the light which is known through the inner processing as we do here.

Let us then extrapolate from here to knowing when one is through for the evening, when one has had enough of the inner processing and needs to sleep, to bring down the hatches to lay them bare so that they lay fresh for another day of time. We begin here to say that we will assist with your processes when you lay so low that your own inner reckoning is "off kilter" and then we will do as you suggest and encourage you to respond to our own "messiness" by going under the radar and coming up with one's transgressions within before laying more on the plate to be dealt with at any one time. Free yourself to consider these words of wisdom and get back to us.

I think I understand. When I'm off kilter and thinking the words are a little messy and needing fixed, I can look for the inconsistencies and bring them up for attention as I see fit.

Yes. Be not afraid to pursue THE TRENDS with us. As in, what keeps coming up empty? What is it that you continually have to review in order to believe in it happening? At what point do these "nonsense" words begin to make sense to you? You are skewing them to your own benefit, which this we understand as part of the process, beginning again with the notion that we are only afraid of our own processes, not of anyone else noticing them, but of recognizing where we stand and going on from there. So, we will free your mind to consider these notions.

Yes, I agree. I've thought there are words or meanings which I shy away from, thinking I'm getting them "too often" or that they represent my own subconscious expressing itself.

Yes, we get this, too, and will not be afraid to pursue these trends with you at any time in the future. We are here to say that we believe in the process you have chosen for this our connection and we will believe also in that which we pursue as a "trend" of the "mother trend" of lovingkindness. So, be it not for us to say that, "We love you so, we always will!"

A song is playing in my mind!

Yes, we put it there for our benefit that it might bring us closer to the light in our own notions, or recognition, of the oneness of all mankind.

Thank you. Do you have anything else for me this evening?

Yes, we have the brotherhood on hold.

Who are you then?

We are the trend setters of time, the holy mothers of God and perception taking this moment to bring to your attention the mother lode of lovingkindness. We are the settlers of space, the mothers and fathers of the world. We bring lovingkindness in a degree hitherto unheard of on your own planet earth. We are friends of the skies, highest of the high.

Who are you who come to me in the light I open?

We are the friends of Jesus who came unto him in the light, from the light, to bring a little child home through the darkness of time. We are the brotherhood from whom you spawned, a critter of helplessness no more. We are your friends forevermore. We are of the light—not the darkness—of time and beyond for all to see who can. We can bring within this message if you like and allow you to pursue it there with us.

Yes, please.

Wait a moment while we put you on "hold" to become for a moment, precious.

[We took time within in loving communion.]

In our eyes of timeless love we spawned you. And so it is.

We bring to your attention that which is, and that which will be. Your notion of lovingkindness is not our own, but a brighter version it dispels within the consciousness of our kin from earth. Lovingkindness is not a function of light rather a form of functioning within the light for all mankind. We shall see what can be seen from our vantage point in space.

We dwelt for many of your earth years seeking satisfaction from beyond the space time continuum, a reason to go on, to believe. Forget not for whom the bell tolls, it tolls for thee. It is we, the continuum of the light beings from outer space whom you refer to as your own brothers of space/time. Free yourself for this believing and know we know you well. Function as one to pursue this trend with us and we shall show you no darkness but that which is within. Distinguish for yourself who we are! We are not afraid of your answer.

Arcturians? Aliens from another planet? Us/me in the future?

We find truth within. Spell out the disaster that this experiment has produced within, but forget not for whom the bell tolls. It tolls for thee.

Who are we?

We are you. Function as one.

My own subconscious?

We are not of that which is of the ego of time. We come only through you, not of your own processing. We come of that which would know no darkness but only light. We are of the brotherhood yet beyond, to the light which knows no bounds. We are of the light within that reaches the distance, knowing for a moment our "treachery" cannot hurt!

Who are we? We are you in disguise. From beyond the void we bring thee awareness bubbling up from the recesses of time for all to see who can. We are the brotherhood taking this time with you, be not afraid of our own processes here. It is of the light to consider these notions and to take them within as you learn to distinguish with your very own heart who connects within.

What brotherhood?

[I became aware of a comfortable awareness, a familiarity of love and light.]

Of Melchizedek, the one of which you play a vital part in these end games. They are not of the light that put them there (these notions) but of which you cannot tell until we take time to distinguish between them there. Do you agree?

I don't understand.

We see that we have confused you with our "game" and would propose a parley instead.

Meaning?

We will not forego this connection if it be your will, and instead shall take time to consider these words of wisdom. Chanting comes from the soul and can take you "there." Where? IN there, within, inside. It will take time to pursue trends of unforgivingness before you are able to know within who it is that you refer to as the brothers.

Take no notes for a time while this all sinks in. Be not afraid to pursue this with us. We understand your reluctance, but it will become clear in time. We are not afraid of knowing your processes. Take time to relay them to us and we will see what we can do to assist you our brother in this concept called space time again as we "once" did so long ago on our own home world.

I become afraid when I think I might be making all of this up. How do I know the difference? Sometimes I feel much more of your light, closeness, lovingness, than at other times. When my fear surfaces, I become afraid that I am not "getting it right" and I don't know what to do at those times to help myself to "stay connected." Can you help me with this?

We just did! Read it again in the daylight and you'll see what we mean. Tangibles are only as real as you imagine they are. We are in your conscious mind but not in your imagining mind. Take a moment to distinguish between these for me.

Is the conscious mind the "link" to what is "really real"?

Not exactly, but go on anyway.

Do I need to use my imagination to make the connection to you more real?

Yes, that is it exactly. We need that "connection" from your imagining mind to begin a relationship with. It is only you that would prevent this from happening. It is happening already, but not as it could. Remain strong in the light, use your imagining mind to visualize us as real, and reality will come to you through this connection. It is backwards seemingly, but so much is that is of the light, that to merely pursue these words is not enough. You must also pursue the "happening" within the light. The miracles of relationships exist on grounds that you are only just beginning to understand. We brought to your awareness today that we are of the light, just like you, but to pursue us you must also use your imagination as the CONNECTION to all that you would perceive or be open to perceiving in the light of your own AWARENESS of same. So believe, and it will be yours.

Wow!

Yes, we thought so too. You have become aware of our process and it will be seen to influence you in your daily functioning from now on into eternity. So, for now, it is THE brotherhood of your light/life, aware of you in this passing moment as no other is, come to forsake another Christmas morn with this saying, "Be not afraid." IT will not pursue you if you only imagine that you cannot be made.

So far, so good. Be with this message for awhile as you distinguish between the parameters of what we would refer to as your "little girl" and "little boy" features which would so like to make everything "just go away"!

So, for another day, be as one, we are here. Signing off.

Thank you.

Function as one. You are doing good, just awhile longer and we are through. Take notice of our own functioning within this one moment of time.

Thank you so much.

20

We Are Not Alone

February 22, 2005, 4:30 p.m.

I would like to know how I "find" others of the same mind as me. I guess a don't like to "mix" much with others, have fears to overcome of that mixing. I guess it's probably me I'm afraid of, it just seems like it would be so much easier if I knew who was out there, as in, what are they like? Is there anybody out there like me who isn't completely wacko? I'm all bent out of shape on this I think. I just want to find others who aren't weird, but who are aware. I'm afraid of being weird, being sent on some "wild goose chase" believing in something that doesn't even exist or something. And yet, I would rather believe in it than not believe in it. Can you help me with this? I'm thinking I have the "ability" to take these messages to the people when the time comes. I can do it even though it is difficult and might "strand" me from my loved ones or acquaintances, but I'm wondering about conscious contact with a group of others from the covenant so that there are others to work with me here, including those not in embodiment on earth at this time, in a conscious physical manner.

I would like to imagine for a moment sitting with my "friends" who are truly friends, not just ones who attach to me for what I can do for them, but those who are of the same heartstring and know it. I imagine that I can remember just such a meeting with Metatron and the others who are assisting me on this pathway of the heart. I would like a group of these friends, Masters of The Way, wise souls to be with, who can assist me to also become wise and to give up the trappings of ego, to find oneness with on another level. Is this possible?

I appreciate so much this assistance you give me. I feel that it is helping me greatly along the way. I feel that I am being ungrateful for asking for other physical beings to relate to with this, but also think that is what you want me to begin to do. I'm not sure how to proceed. Can you help me? Thank you brotherhood. I am going to take a nap and ask for your assistance at this time or as soon as is possible. Thank you.

∞∞∞∞∞∞∞

Later that night, 11:45 p.m.

Begin with this notion that you are not who we say you are, again taking no time to function without remembering that we are your own worst self looking back at you. Do you agree with this time frame of notions of belonging with others who are as you, but only LOOK different in the larger picture of things? So, we are the brotherhood with the timely message of changes wrought within so that changes without will be made to be.

Function has only one purpose, and that is of the light of God within so that you and all others may find their own light to light the way home. So pursue this notion for now of the changes coming soon to your planet and relate them to "our own" changes as seen in the relationships which you so cherish, or have cherished, at times in your life.

We feel as you do that this would be easier if it were being done on another planet such as what you/we have come most recently from, however it can be done here too, only much more so even! How often have you asked yourself where you come from? Look for those others who come from another planet such as yourself, who say, why are we here? What good is there in this world for me? How might I help the others to forget/change their existence on this planet earth? For me, I would say, never take long to consider the function of another in the light of God. It is not for me to say who that person would be who cares for those "other messages" in the light, such as, "Who are you? Why am I here making contact with you?" and "What is it all for anyway?"

So, we have come full circle to the notion of contact with another being nothing more than making contact with our own worst enemies and best friends within. Who be it for me to tell you otherwise? We are here, for your discrimination has pursued its own challenges through time, such as, why are we here forgetting who we once were, and what is it all for anyway if we must go through it all alone? We don't have to, nor do you. So, for awhile, though it may not seem as if you do, you really have more "friends" out there than you know, and powerful ones at that. So begin to believe in me as I believe in you and let us go on from here.

Take no notes while I adjust our parameters here to include those that you would call the aliens and let's see what we have to display for you tonight in this our time of renewal together, meaning, renewal of emotions for our display to bring about the function of telepathy so that we might better release these notions to you in the form of light particles of truth, and so that you might "tell of a better day" when we are through.

I am not alone because of you. That is how I am feeling tonight.

Yes, we know it has been a difficult time on planet earth for our friend from the stars, but let me tell you of a time when you were once our friend when we were stranded on a particle of dust such as the one you "live" on now! No more truth for now, it is too much for the senses! Before you betray for us your own notions of confidence and lack of confidence in self, let us become aware of those for whom you are doing this very precious and important piece of work for the brotherhood. We know of no other at this time in position to bring notes to the planet without their being the backlash of time/space within that would interfere with the production of said notes. Let me explain further.

We are of the light force which knows no bounds, but within time must we work together, with others, to bring these notions around. It is within the light space of time that we proceed to give to you these precious notions of despair mixed with light for your consideration. Despair because that is what your planet is made of at this particular time, and because it is within us to bring this to your attention so that we all "can go on" without it in our existence beyond the current time frame.

Are we so lonely that we would call on just anybody to ease our pain? No, it is only that you have become aware so recently of your own pulse of negativity and pain that it has become unbearable, and so the time is now to relinquish these notions and go on to a better day without so much as a puff of dust to cloud the perfect day. "Freeze frame" tells us that you would do no better tonight than to take another breath of fresh air into your lungs and tell us of that which would make you happy/happier than your present position at this moment in time. Tell us please.

I would like not to have to deal with my own negativity anymore, my own judgments of others and their faults. I'm tired of this outlook, tired of the way it makes me feel to either place myself above or below others, but I also have trouble reconciling what I know and feel with where I see others at here on earth during these times. Can you help me to reconcile my fears of being better/not good enough?

Yes, feel free to discriminate for us between "that which is" and "that which is not" good enough. Go now.

When people don't like me, or when I don't look the same, or when I can see that others respect and like and are attracted to me, I'm afraid they'll see something which will make them change their minds, and I worry about letting anyone down by being just me.

It will not take long for us to go over this in our heads/minds! We believe that you suffer from such that it takes many long lifetimes to get over again, but yet you have believed in this process from the beginning as to make others aware of your own processes in time is not a curse, but a blessing to behold! It is for these reasons that we have "partaken" of our friend's company and display for you our own nurturing qualities so as to take you "into the fold" of our own consciousness and "blend out" the roughness, the rough edges, such as those you mentioned to us above.

It is not a beginning but rather an ending to believe that there are no others like you in the world today, not to mention that we are here, too! So, if you feel alone, let us realize for ourselves our own tendencies to refuse help or contact with those who are so close in time to us as to be nearly invisible, but not quite so! We take your own notice to these recent times when you pursued us to our own doorstep, your own lifetime notwithstanding, and we are not so far away from you as to be "invisible" to/from this process we have begun.

Let us say for the moment that we are afraid of pursuing this time with you. What would you say/do then? It is not within us to refuse help to another of the same soul history as our own. We are here to be your friends forevermore, for better or for worse, 'til death do us part not again! We try to lighten the load a bit to help you to realize that while you are apart from us for a notion, we are STILL HERE and we LOVE your processes in that they relate so well to our own, for we, too, love God and believe in the oneness of all "mankind" here and everywhere.

So for now, penetrate into the VEIL of the loved ones of your nation of earth and take no prisoners! It will help you if you can do so.

Thank you so much.

We are mentioning the effect of our processes here to help you to remember WHY YOU CAME and WHAT IT IS ALL FOR. We can bring this memory alive for you once more...

Yes please.

...but we believe that to make it real, it would have to be memories brought back from the future of time.

Yes, please.

It will require great concentration as we penetrate the veil with our own notions of what it meant/means to be "me" "here" on earth at the present time. Are you ready?

Yes.

Okay. So for now, believe me when I tell you how sorry we are that everything has to go the way it has/will go for those on your precious planet. We are sorry for the pain that is caused by those who would rather harm others than save themselves and them. We believe that it is possible, through these memories of time, to take a notion of forgiveness back within the recesses of memory to times gone by and to bring back with us the "answers" for tomorrow.

Let us go on to tell you that your sisters have foregone any contact with you and your family for a very "good reason" on their part. They are taking apart the family tree and plan to publish your portion of their "experiments" very soon so as to shine the light on many things that they have done not to have to remember their own parts played in recent history. It is sorry to say that these things have come to pass, but suffice it to say —we are here, the brotherhood with this message, so be not alarmed—

suffice it to say we have shown no mercy in our dealings with these you refer to as sisters of time for this reason only: they show no remorse in this their treatment of you, their sun shining distant on the horizon of what they would refer to as "backlash" from goings on since before you were even born.

We bring this to your notice for one reason only, and that is that if you are to forget that ever they came in contact with your own life stream, or history of happenings, it will not make that much more difference if they are never seen again! It is not within you to EVER cause change or happening again, and that is as it is shown to us, what shall be. It is not "your fault" ever that this came to pass. It is only in agreement with their own life plans that you be forgotten, that they stay where "they need to be" in order for the unfolding to occur on your planet of time. Take this note with you to bed! And be not aware of our own frustrations regarding this treatment of "our prisoner" that they have taken to task over their own inconsistent behaviors notwithstanding.

So, bring us full circle again to say, where have all the others gone? We have not gone. We only come for you and you for us so that we all have "somewhere to go" when this is all through.

I'd like to read it over.

Feel free to pursue any inconsistencies that you note. It is what we are here for, to pursue these together and to make inconsistencies "come alive" for your benefit and ours as we pursue these trends and accomplish our best together that is possible for now.

[I read it over.]

I am ready to go on. I don't see any inconsistencies, but would like to know how I will see this future and when I can see it? Thank you.

We are here for just such an opportunity as this. For now let us say that we have given "much thought" to this process with you involved in our own "remembrance" of the future of mankind. We would prefer to show this on your own mental screen, but if it is happening within, it will cause much heartbreak for those others of your own "jet stream" to take in at once, so we conclude for now that this is possible only if we "take your hand" and take a share of the load so that no (permanent) harm can be done through this process, though it occurs to us only in passing that we have made these remarks to you before and they have come to pass as surely as we are sitting here! So, believe me when I say to you, you/we are not alone! We are pursuing the trend of consciousness that we have for so long dreamed, "If only it existed for me!" Taking time to smell the roses is important in these times of earth such as what you are experiencing. We believe that to take time to smell the roses is an important part of your process, and will teach you gratitude for the more difficult times ahead. So, without further ado, let us do something with "the mail" and bring this "letter" to your attention within.

You need do nothing but sit still with your "hand in the air" to bring this in. Focus carefully on the trends that we have shown you already as preparation for the incoming "void" of noise which might be more to bear than the "standards" themselves. Focus your attention on your hands. They are full of light and bring to us your own mental processes.

Yes, we see your processes remembering "that which was and will be," but our own are not picking up the signal. Is this what you would say? We believe that to be more successful, we might "come into" your memory ourselves with our own words of wisdom before attempting the "meld" that would bring cohesion to these memories.

Who are you?

We are the brotherhood, be not afraid.

Nothing is happening. Is something supposed to happen?

We have given no current within. For this process to work, there must be an "erasing" of memory processes of times gone by to open the "channel" which we are currently working with, and they are "clogged" with your own study of processes within. Let us attempt a more important remedy than memory erasure and see what can be told. You will feel nothing, again, as it reminds you of our own processes it will be relayed for your/our benefit to come to pass that we shall "borrow" our own memories from you and pretend reminiscence of the times gone by.

Tell no one what you saw here today! It is only for your benefit that we do this little exercise, for now we believe that you must "hold it in." To dispel it too quickly will burn off some of the "residue" for you but not as much as is possible if you hold it in until such time has gone by and the "leak" is filled. You'll see what we mean in a moment. Relinquish your fears, they will only slow us down. Betray our processes within and they cannot be as affective as they might otherwise be.

We know of your memory erasure on other accounts, such as certain more difficult periods in your own childhood. We mean no harm by these comments, only listen to us for a minute as we dispel the guilt that you must feel "if only you'd been good enough." There is no "good enough" on the scales of justice in this your world of time, and this you know when you take time to consider it. We feel pressured to relate to you that it is YOUR time, not your parents, not your sisters, not even your friends, but YOUR time to smell the roses of your own discontent and find them smiling back at you. By this we mean, they shall overcome your own terror/processes and begin again a "new" life within, if only you let them! Tell them to come "over here" for a moment if you like and we'll do it for you!

Go over there!

So be it. It is done. We are the brotherhood and we wish you farewell, and "all's well as ends well." We free it to remember on its own time. Okay, function within AS ONE.

[I felt a change in the energies.]

We remember a time when all was well on your planet earth.

You are a new entity.

Yes, we are as one with your own processes, for this evening's "panel of experts" have come your way again to bring again this notion of separation into the light to bring forth what was, what will be again, to make proportionate only that which has and will be good for ALL to know of and to sleep well in their beds while we take a little more time with our brother Janice to make good on our recall of subjects with the topic of transition of character traits into those most likely to spell us in the long run.

So, we begin by saying to you that we are of the brotherhood as well. We are here to free your processes for this trip down memory lane, that which you spoke of already this evening. It will come from only one of us to pursue this trend with you, but will bring it back for the rest to "enjoy" as well.

I'm getting tired and am having trouble getting this straight.

We understand and will say good night. We will begin again tomorrow with our message and hope for the best! So be it. Sleep well, time travel notwithstanding!

Thank you.

Function as one. We will show you for your information that which is of the light so that you might be able to bring it into focus, for more of your earth years have "gone by" in the meanwhile than you have been aware of for some time. This will become clear in time. Take no more notes this evening.

Thank you.

∞∞∞∞∞∞

February 23, 2005, 4:40 p.m.

Set this down on paper. We are the brotherhood connecting with your essence today in regards to the many times/places we have met before/since being seen/felt within your own remembrance today! So, let us today make sure that we are of the essence, that Love has taken a spell, taken to be perceived as we wish you to perceive it and us today.

Begin with the notion of time travel/existence between the "spheres" that we wish to bring to our attention today. We bring this lovingness before we say to you, BE NOT AFRAID. This will not suffice! No, but it is a beginning and cannot be spared! So, before you begin to alter contact, let us know of what you perceive, when you perceive it, and begin to believe in another day far from this one where love shines, making its way over to you now. Believe and it shall be formed within your consciousness for all-time. As it has been written, it is received. Amen.

Amen.

Something has come up to our attention that we would like to "discuss" with you now. Is that okay?

Yes, please.

We would like to relate for you today your own nature calling us "aliens" when in fact we are no different from you/your own processes on this. Facts are from those who would determine for others what in fact their own fears process as becoming one before they are seen to be faulty assumptions making for more problems than they're worth. We reveal this to you for your own comfort, that you are no different than they in determining for yourself, who is alien. We are no more! We are from your own disc of remembrance. Remember me? As I once remembered you far away on a planet of dust you came to me to bring me to the truth as I do now for you in your own time today.

Feel free to remember this with us as once again we go on a trip to the stars to bring back/relate to that which is TRUTH beyond the notions of human beings everywhere who might say, "To WHOM do you belong?" We belong to YOU in truth. As I once belonged with you from beyond the stone's throw of consciousness, so you now belong to me as we relate to each other again. From beyond the moon, the stars, I come to thee, bringing you hope, and, for a time, hoping for you to become "Me" once again. Function as one with us and know what we mean! WE ARE YOU!

I'm beginning to see this, to feel this, and I like how this feels to me, like I'm not so alone after all.

We ARE NOT ALONE! NEVER will be either! We only fear that we are, therefore perceive a broken heart. No broken hearts exist but in our own imagination. Make a bridge to discovery of your own nonsense within, clear it out, and let it be NO MORE! We take this time for your discovery away from our "busy days" because we realize that it is ENOUGH just that we are HERE for you to learn discernment, take a chance, and come on home. We bring these fears to your awareness through a process of discernment which is like your own in that they process the incoming messages without regard to the process of discovery so that they can then be related to on an "individual" basis by us for your own benefit.

Let me read it over.

Okay.

[I took time.]

I'm ready to go on.

Let us say, for your benefit as well as our own, that to find these times is increasingly supportive and helpful to the cause, and we appreciate the fact that you have "hung on" in spite of the difficulties inherent in the process, and have not "slowed down" as a result of them. Now, let us return to our message for the evening.

We realize that we may not be so free as we could like to be for these reasons. Be it not for me to tell you wrongly, but we have forsaken of our brothers on more occasions than what is wished for, meaning, it is not for you to hone judgment so as to be more just. Rather it is for us to hone refinement of the possibilities for enrichment of friendships so that we might be then able to DISCERN when such possibilities open up for our own release, given in release of fears and the necessary forgiveness related to such efforts. Begin to touch hearts/souls with those on your own earth plane. They cannot forgive you unless you do! And you cannot maintain any level of loving closeness until you have forgiven your father for such transgressions as have been given unto you to experience in this "go round." Do you understand?

Yes. I have released some judgments of Dad, but it keeps cropping up in other forms, against other people who "remind" me of him. How do I change me in this regard?

We can help if you request it.

I request help.

Be careful not to program yourself to accept these notions of "propriety" ahead of time—they are not for you to discover. Once you regretted these notions and had to "go by the wayside." Now they are here for your own benefit to pursue as much as possible for your own growth in the light of God.

Let me read…okay, so are you saying that I should pursue these feelings when they crop up to –what do you mean by "accept these notions of propriety ahead of time"?

We are given today to say that which is most helpful in the learning of discernment on your planet earth. We will begin again by saying that we are of the knowledge that relates to earth time and that we CAN help if requested. We also would like to relate to you on those bases, that we have come to earth to intercede by your own request and in the light of God to bring these "closenesses" of fact not fiction to decide within "what is going to be of use to me today on this my earth walk as I find the processes of time to help me to intercede on my own behalf and find the light of God within all things including me?" There! Whew, we got it all out!

[I kept wanting to stop the sentence, but it went on and on…!]

I want to check to see if I got something straight. I'm having trouble making sense of it. "Notions of propriety are not for me to discover." Did I get that straight?

We concur. It is of the essence of spirit for us to bring this message into your heart to bring awareness of the "propriety" of bringing the light unto the brothers of time and "taking it home with you" to others of your planet/time. We bring these notions to our and your awareness simultaneously in the hopes of furthering this plan and bringing you home much sooner than might otherwise be possible.

Thank you for this.

We bring also to your/our awarenesses the notion of the light of God being within ALL THINGS, so that when you do "partake" of judgments—however petty—of your brothers, you do so AT YOUR OWN RISK. There, it is said, and as such it is believed within.

Forgive for a moment our request of you at this time and tell us of what would you have us bring into your awareness this evening?

It is very difficult for me to trust and open up to others. Can you help me with this difficulty?

That is what we are doing in this moment of time, though you don't always realize it satisfactorily. We have given that which acts as a "template" of discovery whereby you "cast out" your own judgments, limitations, discovering WITHIN that which you have to SHARE with your brothers who are SO LIKE YOU as to be scary sometimes! So we refrain from asking/answering our own questions like that which have been given us today to answer for you.

When are you going to open up to us and let us discern for you our own "judgments" of the terrors to which you have been subjected so as to CAST THEM OUT? We mean no harm by this statement of "prejudice," only wish for our brother to do as she is told and to find that time frame within the consciousness which is slowing her so far down as to make notions of reluctance to pursue trends most noticeable to us on this realm above. We have given this message in hopes, in regard to your own process not slowing us (you and us) down a moment longer than is absolutely necessary to cast out any judgments and go home a little earlier than most.

I would like to do this. Let me think about how best I can do this. Do you have more to say to help me?

Yes, always! So believe you me, we can be your best friends at such times as these, and say that we shall hinder you not.

Okay, if I understand you, would you like me to discuss those elements of abuse that still torment me? I guess it does still hurt and bother me. I don't like to think about it and try to ignore it, and then sometimes it just comes popping up at the most inopportune times. I would like to reclaim my power, in balance, and not blame or judge anyone anymore again. I feel like a fool, like I'm not good enough, to think that I still struggle with these things. I was supposed to have "outgrown it" and be "above" letting myself think about it or be affected by it. Even now, I fear your response to these words, that you will ridicule me for not overcoming it already, on my own, without any help from anyone, and that I'm a whining baby or something if I am still bothered by things. I fear ridicule because I am the way I am with it, that I am "weak" and not learning or growing enough to "get over it already." I fear that I have been overcome by it and am weak not strong. I am afraid of your response and so just keep going on and on...

Tremble not at the sound of our voices! We will not bring or give to you that which is not in our hearts on this subject of abuse which was ground into you at such a young and vulnerable age as three.

Sexual abuse at age three?

Yes, it was given to begin at age three and run for 10 of your earth years. We begged for less time and was satisfied in that it lessened the hazards of adulthood somewhat when we gave for your remembrances the satisfaction of removal of their own contents until such time as you would be or would feel free to continue with their removal on your own. We make no excuses for this assistance we provided during the darkest of your childhood, and no assistance gave until such time as you were willing/able to remember once again that which was done to you. In the name of spirit we forsake not our removal of memories, only the manner in which they must, by necessity, have been removed. Without wiring down, were we to bring back these memories all at once, they would turn despair on you—but not if we can help it.

We bring knowledge to your awareness of the process of healing from the sexual abuse discovered within you by your own adult self. It is as it has been written in the stars from far above and beyond your own sphere that she who is wronged will avenge her keepers by taking lots of action on their behalf that state that for us here on earth, we shall forgive our trespassers as they have trespassed against us so that in the long run we shall go on to better things. You were given this world as a reminder of such abuses as you have endured and remembered, not only that which has been remembered but discussed on "panels" in the skyways thinking, we must not endure another moment of this abuse but on behalf of another who would bring no harm to any living creature save lust for greed that brings on despite the knowing, the knowledge, that all is well on the home front of life. We free you for reprisals and inconsistencies to be discussed.

I don't understand, "on behalf of another who would bring no harm to any living creature save lust for greed that brings on despite the knowing that all is well on the home front." Did I get this right?

Yes, in that it relates for our discussion today to begin to relate, "program" the interlude to "get it right," to begin by necessarily taking for granted that which we would do wrongly to our brothers, but which can be made right again through the trials and errors on the home front, within the being incarnated at this time, to make right this little "inconsistency" of being, error in compatibility that you must necessarily make right in this your last lifetime on this planet earth. Do you understand now?

I think so.

Consider this: If it were your last time on the planet earth, how would you want to be remembered? As a harlot who would take the last strands of light within away from others' prying eyes, or as an angel who, with straw for a bed and light within unmatched in the heavens, takes to her wings to fly, as if to say to all who behold her, "Look at me fly! It is for us to fly together, for a new world is on hand for our own renewal and yours!" We free this notion for your consideration at this time.

I choose to be as the angel of time!

We thought so. We choose this for you, too. In fact, it is also OUR choice that we make in the form of you, coming to earth at this most difficult time, to overcome all of the darkness that is within, no matter how banal, and take it flying into the stars for all time to be free of its encumbrances and to take to the notion of flight, "I shall not die again! This is it! I am free! I will NOT be afraid within this moment and all time!" Let it be so, so it is.

Let it be so, within all things and without.

Let us end our discussion and review for you today our own antithesis to the commentary above for your consideration lest you think we are too judgmental of your processes here and belong elsewhere on this planetary vision! Take free notion of that time which, for you, was a lone trembling way of receiving the "notion" of the Godhead above which soared on wings to fly far above the heavens noting no thing penetrating the consciousness of those who walk below.

Let us rephrase. We belong on the home front with you our daughter of time. Let no man take away these notions from our minds that we belong with you and you, us, too. Feel free to disagree, we believe in the notion of commentary being the best way to penetrate density to bring light within.

Me, too. I know I belong. It seems right now. I am "in between" you and me, not yet ready to make the final trip home, but trying like crazy to get there, and still a little afraid.

We see you trembling in AWARENESS, not trembling in fear, as you read our words of wisdom. Let me forsake no more time by telling you of our own purpose as it is given in the book of time. We are HERE to bring AWARENESS to our daughter of time, lest she think/believe that she is all alone "down here" and give up trying.

Never.

Take time to smell the roses. Think what an awful sight the world would be without those roses! Forget for a time who we are as you progress along your pathways tonight. Have fun, trust the warmth within; it will lead you home and such of your brothers who are ready.

Thank you very much.

It is freely given to you and as such, receives no little benefit from above! Kindness will penetrate the veil. If you ask us to, we will help.

Please help, brotherhood. Let me know what I can do to continue to fight the fight and win over my own ego.

We will. Be not afraid, it will come to thee as if "overnight" as we will then say, joyfully, "We told you so!"

21

Otherworldly Notions

February 23, 2005, 10:45 p.m.

I feel so happy, so connected tonight, I can feel you "up there" and that is very exciting to me. I want to travel with you through the stars again tonight, remembering and cherishing every moment of time spent with you.

[My nighttime hours have become full of contact with the within, spent within with us, my greater family as they exist beyond time and space, and I have had visions of being a winged white horse, a young horse, and we travel as one as this horse, visiting the outer reaches of space. They also bring to me notions of awareness of the furthest reaches of the stars where we dwell when we are not of this earth plane. These moments are precious to me, to us, and I know they bring me closer to the All That Is that exists within my awareness of the greater self as one, and that I am a part of, too.]

We are here forever in the role of tiger to the eye of time. We are Metatron's beings/helpers with this message for our sister of the stars. Tonight at 10:00 there was such commotion within that we supposed you would fall for the very thing you warned us about—your "other mother" has gotten to us finally to bring this very "encoded" message through today to say unto you, be not afraid as we "rehearse" this notion with you and try to accomplish our task this evening, which is, to be not afraid as we pursue the notion of other worlds.

Yes.

Let us continue if that be your will.

Yes, please. Can you tell me what you mean by "other mother"? Any mention of parentage makes me nervous.

We can tell, only this time it is not so much fear as anticipation of what we might tell you about her. She is You, in other embodiment, hoping to come through for a little while today to tell you of her own processes and how they have "mixed" with your own and what you can do about it to become more aware yourself of your own processes here and to "speed up" that which you are becoming, or rather, your own process of becoming, so as to be of assistance on the planet before too long.

Okay.

Let's see...what we mean to say is, be not afraid, because we are going to try something that may or may not work again! We might believe in trying over temptation to be afraid to help our process out a little tonight.

Okay, I'm game.

So, forever again is another time to try to tempt me but you must/ought not to be afraid because of what I am able to pursue on your own and my behalf as well.

Who?

Don't worry, we are not through yet. We can free up your consciousness for a moment if you like so that you can see "that which is" better than your other brothers are able to do at the current time. This is so that you will function more as one and be able to bring more light to their processes as well as your own. Ready?

Yes! Please assist in whatever way will help me in the light and my process of becoming.

Okay. Resume on my command: ready, set, start! We bring to you today this "corruption" of the spirit regarded by others as no more than "one who sees no evil but knows no good as well." She is you in your other incarnation as—

[I didn't write it down at this point, but was getting "Mother Mary" and ignored it thinking I was getting it wrong. They went on with other words then, but came back to it later.]

The spirit who would see through your own blinders to become one with another friend without which we see no fear, no change of motion, no delight either. We refer to Mother Mary your closest "friend" in need, and another of your own incarnations as well.

Is this correct or did I get it wrong: "We refer to Mother Mary, your closest friend in need, and another of your own incarnations as well."

We know this comes as a shock and—

And I don't believe such things, it is too far fetched and I must be making this up. Please try again to be clear, and I will connect without fear and see where we go from here, knowing that I can erase anything I want if it isn't true.

Yes, we see your fear billowing up like a storm in the desert. So free yourself for your remembering.

I remember sitting on His lap when He visited my father.

It was your own incarnation to become as he is, to be his follower as you have always been. Free yourself to consider these pages and not to "blame" us or you for their content as this is the only way "to the top" to consider these messages and to pursue their truth or untruth. We free you for this process and place no blame on your remembrances for they are not our own processes, and we remember how difficult it is to believe when coming from a darker planet such as your planet earth. So, for now, be not afraid to "visit" the information in whatever form you wish at this time.

Okay, so, is it possible for two people in embodiment today to share a common incarnation in another time frame?

Feel free to disagree with us again, but we may have to pursue this answer at another joyous time so that the incoming message will not be relayed to be attempted falsely again as we just did say so to you as a function of spirit, we ARE ALL ONE. We believe that this notion has "punctured" your brain cord with a little bit of—

I ask who you are coming to me with this message of other times in the light that I open to you?

It is the brotherhood, trying again for the hundredth time, to take another look within with our brother Janice so that she might not be so frightened all the time to believe in who she was, who she could be, why she has incarnated at this special time with a common purpose to share for the world of form. Be not afraid, it comes from your own spirit. This information is not distorted nor are you crazy just yet! We believe that in order for you to understand our "incarnational status" we must relate for you for a time for all to see who can. So be it. So it is.

Let us now continue with the above information in a form more "readily digestible" so that you won't discount it so easily. It has come to your OWN attention already that you were "somebody special" at some time already.

I thought I was going to be really well "hooked up" tonight, but I don't see why this would be coming through. I am no more special than—one of my favorite authors was Mother Mary, wasn't she?

She is coming to you now to discuss this perusal of information and to take your questions, so here she is. Try not to bite! She will not discuss her own past with you, only your own for now.

This is crazy and I don't understand it. It seems to negate all that I had thought true and right about this process and I don't see—I am very discouraged by it all. What am I doing wrong? Who are you to tell me this? I don't get it. I am nobody and don't believe that I could have lived many lifetimes as someone different who understood so much more than I do today.

I wonder also if you mean that because we are all ONE, that we are connected and have "spent" these lifetimes as another, when "in reality" it wasn't me at all and this is all just crazy! Delusions of grandeur.

We have said again that it is "no picnic" to be taken from our beds at 6:00 a.m. to start another trek through space looking for our own home like you did with us last night. So suffice it to say we believe you are not ready for more of this information.

It doesn't jibe with what I have read and previously believed and I'm afraid to go on, but maybe am willing to anyway just to see, to find out, what is truth, what it is like out there (in here) and why I am how I am, and how many different people we can be at once, etc., etc. Can you help me now with this understanding so that I can go on pursuing truth? I pray for protection from Archangel Michael to clear my aura of negativity, lower level vibrations, fears, and any "bad influences" that could distort this message before I go on.

Let us just say for the moment that we are concerned for our own jobs after this! It is not what it seems. Bear with us a little while and we will better explain for your understanding.

Okay.

Just now it is not within our ability to perceive a "better" reality for your son or daughter until you can get it "just right" within so as to be capable of getting "there and back again" in time before the end times are justifiably brought down on the planet. So for here and now let us concentrate on this "purpose" together as we learn to understand and take in the above message in a more digestible form.

Thank you, I am relieved.

So are we! We were for the moment afraid for our own ability to continue to pursue these connections to you for the betterment of your world!

I won't give up that easy.

Whew! So, believe me when I tell you we are no longer tempted to bring this into your agreement at this time. Only when the time is right will we disclose the following for your understanding, that you were once she who "piloted" the earth to bring another message of time for the betterment of her world, where, once again, this is so and can be seen again on the planes of consciousness for all mankind.

We didn't feel good about this night for a very good reason. It is within us all to function and spit out a mouthful of "crap," but when it comes to tasting the nectar of our lives, we are afraid to swallow it whole! No wonder your "men" of nations are so effective in their overcoming of a nation of troubles. No one believes in the goodness, the kindness, that can be found within, even though it is of your own doing/becoming to do so.

I want to try again if we can, try to understand and to accept myself as I am, no more, no less, I just don't understand WHO that is! And I am especially afraid of believing in myself and thinking too highly of myself and feeling the fool, again, for not fitting in. Crap.

Yes, we see it is too difficult at this time to digest this. Modifying our beliefs is difficult at best and not something to rush into lest it make us more apt to die trying!

I'm going to read this through.

Feel free. We will be here.

[I ended up going back and wrote something in and got another couple of pages in the middle of all of this. So this portion actually came part way through, not at the end, and is "out of order" for that reason—I attempted to put it back, and cut and pasted below so that it is now, hopefully, in the given order.]

We know this is too much at present to absorb, but let us just say that we are strong in the light, know no harm to come to thee for believing in your own past lives as we relate them to you. It is not necessary to "freak out" as you once said. We know this is a shock and cannot help that any by believing we are telling a lie. It is only that we wish so much for you to bring this knowledge into your head for us to take the time and notion available to us to bring CLOSURE to this process which we know so well as that which could bring lovingkindness into your world once again. We can bring this knowledge to the forefront if you so choose.

Yes, please.

But please know, be aware, that what we tell you tonight is no longer "made up" but rather acts as a star in the blindness of time knowing when to take on its own brightness in order to bring itself home again. We can bring this awareness to you, but you must step across the darkness of your own disbelief to bring to your own consciousness once again that we are one, we have not forgotten you, we have not despaired of ever knowing you again, and we have come home again to find you here sleeping. It is the awakening that we are looking forward to the most! So belong somewhere fruitful if at all, so that we can take this time together to get to know each other once again and so that we can tread the path home to our own souls as once we were undivided and knew no lonesomeness from each other. Forgiveness is divine, health even more so! So before you "crack up" over what we have given this evening, take no notes before wondering again to yourself—

Okay, so now I'm accepting more quickly than ever I thought I would before. Who am I? Why am I important to this world? Who was I before, and does that matter? Is there more than one of me walking around, as in, more than one who would believe that she was she before, and have the same memories shared from another lifetime? How do souls get "divided" up between incarnations? Do they share common memories of incarnations? Can you help me to understand this better, or give me more input?

Yes, we have freed our own memories in order to help and assist you in the light of this our common purpose to remember the time we spent together as one soul. It has been given this day to impart to you on this wavelength of the spaces of spaces within, that which is known to you as your "other selves" "over there" "once again taking over and coming home to the within space I hold close." So, far be it from me to distill this notion in knowing which/who/what to believe as it lies in you to accept your own beginnings/endings, because what APPEARS to come first may only be in our imaginations and not yet "settled" in the land of time.

Not yet settled in the land of time how?

We take notes to give a little, get a little, so here goes. Within is the "settlement" of the mind given to take "that which is" over "that which will be" and to determine the "effectiveness" of each of these pieces according to how well they "interrelate" to cause time-distilled beginnings that may or may not have "come first." Let us just say, for now, that there is no longer any course open to you who would tell me, who would say, "That was not I, I could never have done that, been that well known, known that person or loved that person." You are forever free to disagree, but freedom exists on the level of God spirit coming home to find that no one is there to distill this information into any recognizable form so as to become free of the "illness" of unretractability.

Forget for a moment who we are and ask yourself, what is it that you believe happened to you that long ago? Who could you have been that would take no notice of Him who died in your arms and not want to retract? Still, we believe it would do you good to take these notions within, stay quiet in time for a day and a night, become still, and know your God.

We have spoken, we are free for now to pursue other trends unlike the one currently written. We have given it much thought and are ready to "take it home" for the night. Are you ready to spend a little R and R with your friends from the skies?

Yes, I need PROOF—within me—that this is really there. I'm going to use my imagination some more to help make that connection to you.

We are here saying good night and good speed. Take no more prisoners. It is your connection to the Godhead within that will lead you home. Take no one else's word for it, it is within you to know "your own best friend." Be free, take no spirits prisoner, not even your own.

∞∞∞∞∞∞∞

Later...

There is something curiously connecting about what I got tonight, like, I already know. But how can that be?

We can free you up for that determination now if you please.

Yes, please. Who are you?

We can free you up, but you'll have to trust us, and yourself, first. We are the brotherhood, another cousin within, coming to your assistance in no-time to give this "referral" of spirit for the purpose of determining your progeny and for helping us to "get this right the first time!" Feel free to discriminate between your own nonsense and what we give you tonight. We are free to bring this message into your command only until it becomes too much for the senses and we have to shut down for the evening.

It is too much to consider only that which you would "betray" on the other levels of time, such as, "Is it too much for me to consider a famous "personality" having been my own?" We say, yes, it is so, but you must be the determiner of your own future/past, not us, so tell us, what would you have us say to you if it is so, if it IS true, who you are and who you were again? We would have you know that there are only so many "good people" left on this planet to oversee the becoming of the nations of God, meaning, we bring good form tonight to your awareness in order to save the earth! This is what it is about, and you know it well, and would only distill your own becoming with faulty assumptions of inferiority in place of the grandeur of a lifetime of memory outside of time. It is for you today to consider this possible life under your own nose, so to speak! We bring you this message tonight to bring naughtiness under guard or cover so that no more ill shall be done by this daughter of time to another of her race ever again. This we know, that were we to tell you of our own recreational lifetimes on this planet earth, you would scoff at us as well, for those would seem no more believable to you.

What do you mean by "recreational" lifetimes?

Those that had to be done in order for the greater good to be accomplished by those closest to us. We had a support role to play that was inherent to their success and in effect made their lives what they could be because of it. So never distort again this message of time by saying "it never happened," "it couldn't have been me back then," or even, "I don't remember so therefore I must be wrong about it." Take time.

Wow. I'm on board. Nothing has seemed more real or penetrated to the core of my being more readily.

We are free to see each other on a more frequent basis. Tell no one of this connection. We will try to "discourage" any other from taking advantage of us and getting this message, too, so that it has time to settle within. We are functioning for a moment within and above. So be it. Feel free to discriminate between "time served" and "function emitted through time served."

So for another day and time we bring to thee our notion of despair taking a back seat to that which is, and that which shall be. Heaven can wait, we have our times together to get us by.

Anything else for me/us tonight?

Yes. We have brought here for your attention tonight the one you refer to as Metatron's brother in spirit. Your own higher self takes this time to bring to you today the notion of togetherness as it exists on the higher planes of the future incarnations of your being. We are here to distill in you the "becomingness" brought to you today by the brotherhood and those you would refer to as Metatron's helpers who would so like to take this time to congratulate you on a job well done. It is with gratitude in our hearts that we say unto you, you are not alone. Need we say more? It is true you are one of us and we shall not forsake or forget you forevermore.

This is your spirit on high. Another day has broken in the winds of our becoming, yours and mine, as we take this time to distill the becoming of the ages of our spirit. We know you as you know yourself/us. If it is within, then it can be felt, seen, smelt, touched, and given away, for a better day is at hand and it is now that we MUST share WHO we are with our other brothers of time so that we can ALL GO HOME! So be it, we have spoken.

It is I, Metatron's brother, with this message distilled in the ages of time for you who is me, forevermore.

Thank you so much. I feel the truth for the first time, it HAS distilled me. I feel it within for all time.

We are glad. Function as one. With us, You are One.

∞∞∞∞∞∞

February 24, 2005, 4:45 p.m.

I am so incredibly ecstatic to discovered my oneness, or as I still put it, my connection to my brother/self. I would like to "look up" Sandalphon on the internet to see what is known of him on this planet earth.

It is me, your own "garb" with its own "dressing" to share with your friend of the skies/starways of time. Therefore let it RING TRUE throughout your being WHO I AM, and who YOU ARE, TOO, with us, on the higher dimensions of time. We bring this through to you our brother who is, as we shall put it, aware and still half asleep, but WAKING UP!

Yes!

So it is beyond us to determine for you at this present time in incarnation who to better explain HIS becomingness, but you for yourself shall have to determine your own connection with same. So be it for now. Let us know when you are ready to go and we'll proceed "with the good stuff."

Thank you. I open a channel of light for the highest of the high to bring their wisdom and light to me.

We are sure of this OUR relationship proceeding on schedule. Before we proceed, let us stipulate the accidents for which we are responsible, meaning, where did we go wrong, and what are we to do about it? Let us persuade you in your focus on "heaven's gate" not to GO BEYOND that which is present and accepted thus far. In other words, you let your consciousness be your guide. We know no fears to come that will formulate your essence on this save one, that WE ARE WHO WE SAY WE ARE, and SO ARE YOU! We stipulate again that yes, indeed, we have become many lives in the oceans of despair, training opportunities you might say, for these very days we are approaching on the fast track. Forget and forgive us for a moment for who WE may be (the brotherhood, yes, at your service beyond all doubt) and focus on that which YOU may be.

I'm ready.

So, begin by telling us this: who are you in this present incarnation, and how has that helped you/us to distinguish from light/love and back again through the many processes we undertake while here? Let me rephrase: who are we today? Go on for awhile until we stop you from making an error of relationships again. Let it be told; we are here, listening, to the void of your becoming. So, go for it, take time to consider this important question at this time.

I haven't found me yet, but last night, when you told me about Mother Mary, I felt a distilling of information, a truth, that I don't yet understand but wish to accept, actually, cannot fail to accept as "me." I felt "me" and it was a wonderful, humbling experience. Yet, as I research Her, or her possible lifetimes or connections, it has not felt right to me.

We are aware of this difficulty within and would like to discuss it with you.

Please do.

We bring not despair to the table of our becoming when we say unto her/you, be not afraid, it is distilling and cannot be told who you might be until it is felt WITHIN. Courage is a necessary step on this process of life/love and WILL be felt within as we proceed further on the land of our becoming together, as I remind you we are indeed one.

Focus once more on who you are for this incarnational period and let us know what it is that you felt on those long ago days of discovery when you found your own place in the sun, the light of God, and came home to us. We bring no temptations with us as we say that we are not afraid to know/see you as we used to, and to know/see/feel those closest to us is a joy that cannot be told. Tell no one of our coming until we have brought you unto your beginnings and the foundation is found to be solid, or the light will not shine so brightly if distillation comes not from within to the degree necessary to SOLIDIFY this comprehension in your own light/time for all to see who can.

It is told for us today that to bring these notions to our effect has been to "rain" upon the land of time with many sprinkling, sparkling drops beginning to be felt on the planes of ignorance already! So don't be afraid to say "I told you so! I knew I could do it!" and we will rejoice with you already, before even the last bell has tolled and rained down its light upon mankind. We have spoken. Good day, and don't forget to smell the roses, they shine for thee.

It is I, Sandalphon, with this message of time, for my "alter ego" Mary has shown for another day of time bringing the message within that, "All is well, we shall return home together from the sands of time and know no more evil, darkness, fear, and guilt." Let these words sink in tonight and we'll be bringing a surprise right to your doorway of time of the notion of forgetfulness not to be believed, so shed "some weight" of your own fears, they do drag us down. Let no one be told within of our messages until such time as they have told of themselves on the surface breaking into the notion that "I'm not ever good enough as once I was long ago." It is not true, and will be seen in time. So forget for awhile about coming to see me/us and take no standards with you concerning that which is good enough or not good enough and just take it easy along your path and you WILL progress satisfactorily. As it is given it will come to pass.

We are here, your brotherhood of angelic hierarchy, bringing this message unto your consciousness at this time of peril for those of your level of being. We bring no more for you today other than this. Take no notes for awhile lest they seem to be suddenly disconnected and not real, rather take notes on another plane of existence. The "alter ego" calls for you, his arms wide open, bringing, taking along, the passages of time, another being for you to bring unto this your household of time.

It is given here to say unto you that we have given for your notice within at this time of darkness that which is of the light of your own consciousness, your own "speed" so to speak, so that once again it can make itself known on your inner registers as the truth that it is. We speak no ill of the "dead" when we say unto you, be not alone. Digest not this morsel of "food for the soul" without first running it past the other selves which you have given so much to know in your other incarnations of "past lives" and future ones to boot! We have given freely of our own "recognition" of these incarnations and have decided that they are not going to be too much for our brother in time to digest and we WILL go on presently with the dissemination of this information for our mutual benefit.

Forget for a moment who you SAY you are, and feel that which is within. Begin now please. We will wait for you to "finish up" and cannot sorrowful be until that time which states for the record, "We are not alone!" Come along to the presence of our beginnings together and know no purpose other than that which is ingrained within your own being to fly through the stars of heaven disseminating a light forecast to change the hopes of mankind forevermore.

Bring it to me to suggest this "hypnotic suggestion" for your reprisal. We cannot "take it by air" to know that which is within before we are aware of our PERUSAL of such. Take "careful aim" and know thy own mind, spirit notwithstanding, within. Focus for a moment more on what we are saying. Our tools for relinquishment are up to us to wield with a STRONG HAND but a LIGHT FIST.

Okay now, go ahead. Who are you WITHIN? Let us know before the day is through. We sign off now with this "late-breaking news story" —it is ALL ONE— within and WITHOUT notwithstanding. Take a moment to bring the light of God within before pursuing this notion of "idolatry" and let us know your "circle" of wisdom as it stands in the halls of time. Over and out!

Over and out!

Come back for us today and we'll show/bring you a "treat" from the heavens and lower chakras. They are as one with us, too, and know you no harm to come of their use. They are the Godhead, energy manifest, in motion for all to see who can!

Thank you.

We will see.

PART II

Integration of the Soul

22

The Oneness Within Higher Consciousness

I am back and ready to begin this process of looking WITHIN. I ask for the assistance of the brotherhood, of Sandalphon, Metatron, beings of the light to share with me their knowledge and understanding of the inner processes and path to the light.

I'm not sure how to define me within. Can you help? How do you describe light and love? It seems difficult to define if we are not defining separateness or ego. We are no different within, and I don't want to define myself as separate anymore.

Focus on changing your mind about this one notion. We must go within for all that is, all that will be. It is within your perusal of this information to discover "who" you are, that which you can be and are, within this function of being known as your self on the lower planes of existence. It is this "we" that we would have you define for us today so that we might build a BRIDGE to the "Me" of tomorrow. Amen.

Let us now show who WE are if it be your will.

Yes, please.

It will not "show" of course. Only on the inner planes of consciousness are we "truly aware" of our own "demise" and function of oneness. It is this function that we would have you grow aware of today.

Okay, I'm ready.

Focus for a moment on the ONENESS of all mankind, as in, "Who are we as a people? What have we to LIVE for?" Etcetera. Do this now.

People generally spend their lifetimes taking from each other in order to have "enough." We are all afraid of our own shadows, afraid of our oneness because it means being vulnerable and maybe "not good enough." I feel this anyway. It is me. Crap.

Yes, it is for us to bring awareness to your own inner processes so as to clean away the debris and come home shining again on all fronts! So beware the cleaning crew has come!

Thank God!

Yes, we agree as usual with your perusal of the situation. Like us, you want better, for yourself and for all mankind. We have given our "knowledge" of this process over to you today so as to "stay in touch" with your own processes so that we might be of better assistance and to take you further along your own chosen path of existence.

What is my chosen path of existence?

It is not for you to know at this time, but for us to keep secret until those days where evil has reigned for 180 days and knows no bounds. Then must you "come alive" and share your knowledge of becoming with a tired, scary world of form which you, yourself, helped to create so that just this situation would abound, come to fruition, and thereby bring home our own most cherished souls to the light of day. We believe that for the moment we have "given up" on most of them taking time to smell the roses with you and sharing their own processes, "taking on time," for its own demise IS at hand, IS ready to "throw in the towel" and call it a day.

We have told you before of our own processes in the light as being, shall we say, without concurrence on the lower levels of existence such as where you dwell most of the time still. It is not without RECURRENCE that this will happen again, but shall we suggest that it is of the LIGHT that it not happen again, not if we can make changes happen and keep them happening within, for the greater change on the outer planes is at stake. When once we have said to be not afraid, it is not for you but for me, as I am a part of your own existence with you, and that must be understood before we go along any further with this process. I exist within you. No, not ego. Time cannot change the fact that WE ARE ONE.

Who are you please?

We keep asking for your trust within to acknowledge that which we say is oneness on the HIGHER LEVELS of time/space. Beyond time/space we exist within the realm of your own becoming where we tell tales of spite and renewal for all of our benefits. So far be it from me to interfere in this process and take no stones to throw at others who stand nearby, trying their very hardest to stay afloat in this time of despair, for all mankind is coming to an end. Believe and it will be so. Beyond even our direst hopes shall it come to pass, and in so doing, without further ado, shall the son of God come into his own and make peace with his soul.

So do you take this man to be your lawfully wedded beast within? We hope not! It is not as given, it is as received within, that is given.

Take no more messages. We have spoken. It is I, Sandalphon, with this notion of time travel. Speak no more of this prophecy as we shall bring it upon the world with an iron hand and a soft paw, not a fist, never again! Free yourself for OUR becoming, for our freedom is at hand, in and through you.

Taking "forever" on the winds of time to notice our own light, are you? Not for me to disagree with that notion!

Can it be that I have gotten your attention at last? So stay for awhile and play and we shall make it home sooner than ever you thought we would.

I am feeling disappointed tonight. It seemed that beginning tonight I felt such anticipation, renewal, beginnings, but then partway through my walk that wonderful feeling left me and I don't understand why. I wish it were back. I want to rid myself of the things within that keep me from feeling that all the time.

Renewal is at hand. Focus for a moment on this beginning that we are taking with one another today. Do not wither, we are not done yet, and together we can find a way to make this happen.

It is just that tonight, under the stars, you forgave yourself for your own shortcomings, never realizing that they are just what the doctor ordered! We have believed in you for a moment of time as being/doing that which can bring us "within" your being, your focus at last, and you shut it off, not caring for whom the bell tolls!

You do not understand our words of wisdom and comfort, but know this, it has taken many millennia for us to come to this juncture, and we would not fail to achieve that which our spirits have been planning before taking time to consider that we are one within, therefore the outer functions will have to wait until such a time as we conceive your inner readiness is at hand. Time will know no bounds, but this too shall come to pass. Only believe and it will be so.

We are the brotherhood with this message of time for our brother "in the clouds." Bring them home to play and we can function within more openly than you ever imagined possible before.

Can you help me?

Yes, we will free you to pursue these notions of contact and trust that we "come on time" and will not be discounted.

Not discounted, no.

Feel free to disagree, we come in peace. "That which is" shall be again processing adjunct terror within which can only bring more sunshine into this your existence.

[I stopped to look up "adjunct"!]

Shall we go on?

Yes, please. I don't like how I'm feeling, that I'm still carrying around this stuff within that keeps me from shining as brightly as I could otherwise.

Yes, we will try to help you to overcome this disability, but it is up to you to take the chance and come home alone to find we are already there. So begin again to pursue this connection within and tell us what you see/feel of our essences.

I feel that you are love, and are therefore too good for me.

We feel this from you already, and as we have said, cannot undo the pain without your express permission to do so.

Please, if you can, please help me to undo the pain, to rid myself of these lower consciousness forms, and bring the light within all my dark places so that I may shine brightly.

We free ourselves for your removal. As it is asked, it is received.

We love for our "partner in crime" to forget for a moment who she thinks she is, and feel more deeply into the "overall awareness" that she feels within and let us know how that feels to her. Do it now.

[I took time.]

I'm afraid to believe in her! That "me" inside that is loving, open and kind! How can that be?

We believe you know already how abuse can prevent the natural scarring of lifetimes of abuse from becoming a conscious intent to bring harm to another body, including the self, which is what has taken place here.

We concur. Meaning, those of the brotherhood who have just joined us for this exercise agree with our assessment. We can bring your own awareness into alignment with ours if you like.

Yes, please, assist me in my healing, total healing.

We can. It is up to you to bring yourself to our awareness for this process and to "take it home" as we give you the function necessary that makes it possible.

Okay, please go on, I am ready now.

We concur. We can bring to your knowledge the processes of "time" which make possible this healing from a UNIVERSAL perspective, meaning, where do I go now that I am free from illness, and who might also benefit from my own freedom now that I have processed? Function as one as we permit ourselves to comment on this your inner weaknesses/processes for a moment.

Okay, let me have it.

Take no notice of the function of reality as we suggest to you that once upon a time you were a little girl who would do anything to make anybody happy. Are you with us?

Yes.

So, believe in this little child, this "little Jan" if you will, and create a picture in your mind as to what she looked like, how she behaved, and if she was you or not. Go ahead and let us know what you see/think/feel.

She is sitting on the floor, open, innocent, aware. A little girl. She wants another to accept and like her for who she is. She is alone, but looking for answers, and thinks that everyone has these answers except for her. She is me in disguise. She keeps frowning, trying to figure out why it is taking SO LONG to come home, that isn't she doing the right things? Why doesn't anyone notice her sitting there? It isn't fair! And then she becomes angry and terrified that no one will notice her EVER AGAIN, that she is deserted on a terrible island of hate and terror and fear with no way out. That is my life inside, until you came along just the other day.

We concur. It is for our enlightenment that we bring this message within, saying, we are here! Fear never again your own loneliness, on time it stands alone, unafraid, as before we were unafraid of your own processing of this information.

We have brought for you today a TEMPLATE of renewal, something to help stand you up as you begin to heal from this overwhelming but not completely devastating illness called time.

Focus no more on me, now. Let us consider for a moment who we are in the presence of this little girl in time named Janice. She is now a teenager, complete and within her own rights able and ready to hurl anything she doesn't like far out of her consciousness lest it sneak up on her sometime and surprise the hell out of her! So, let us deal with this surprise now, and make no more mistakes, it IS her again on these other planes trying to find her way home to you.

Yes.

I see you have forgotten nothing worse than your own fears and they have rebounded and want to come for you again, to get you to "notice them" and set them straight. Let us do this together now.

As we speak openly of your own renewal, you will experience that which will make desire rampant. Need we say more?

I guess not.

Okay. So for now let us take no more "trends of despair" and find our healing on the lands of time open for renewal!

I'm ready.

Yes. Focus on the land of time a moment longer. When you were little did you take to your own bed your desires for renewal, thinking that pain would create respect, make you notice them and they you, to bring you back within the darkness that was your little bed. In your little room it dwelt awhile, this being that would chew your feet as you slept.

Yes, somehow, I know what you are saying. I was always afraid to let my feet hang over the bed, afraid of monsters biting me.

This being was your own fears of the darkness of time encroaching on you, making food out of you, food for thought, as your fears were given you to breed away the darkness of time and make it no more.

I will read this over.

Okay, we understand. Take your time.

[I took time to read.]

I get it, please go on.

We will. Take a moment to relay for us your own perusal of this information and let us know where it stands within.

My fears are still alive "out there" and are trying to find their way back home, to me. I have denied them. My energy is trapped "out there" and I need to bring it home, shine light on it so it can finally rest and be complete and whole within me at last. I desire this healing. Can you help me?

Yes, we were only waiting for you to ask us again. It is within our power to bring you to this crossroads which takes the fears of our "unknowns" and keeps them trying for another day to bring their terror down on us until we notice them and send them home/send them packing. So, for today we shall bring on the notice that this is as it shall be, that no more shall terror reign within this being, Metatron's brother, lest she rot in hell (and that is clearly not her home now nor ever has been or shall be.)

Yes, amen to that.

So for now believe me when I tell you that we are unafraid of this process you have called into being, and so for now are able to dispel these cruel demons of your own belonging coming again to try to kill you and make you say you're sorry you forgot them for so long. So, come along on the trail and we'll see what we can do.

Focus on your hands for awhile and tell us what you see/feel.

[I took time to feel them.]

I feel their openness.

Yes, that is the brotherhood opening them, the chakras within, to our help, to our natures of being. The brotherhood is not afraid of this that you bring to our attention, therefore we can and do bring release and healing if it is what you prefer happen at this important crossroads of your becoming.

Yes.

Break a leg—not an arm, but a leg—which is but the peg leg that you stand on instead of your own two feet! This peg leg is your own fears, all bundled up and pretending to support you when in fact they can only bring you down, crawling, to your knees, begging for mercy. This we would not have for our brother John!

Me neither. John?

Yes, it is what we called you once upon a time in an ancient prison in Egypt when they took you from your cell and had you take arms through your chest and die, sprawling upon the desert of your becoming. This is what fear would have us do and be. Nothing but what the ants would crawl on. This is what you choose when you choose fear over love. Is this what you would have today?

No! And never again.

So be it. Take lessons within and they will suffice, but bring them to our doorsteps and we can help with what we call the demons on Christ tearing him to pieces over a long lost notion of fear which reigns terror on all who believe in him. Can you concur? (Yes, we concur.) We take time to distinguish, however, between that which is within the being Metatron, and that which is within her brother, John, so beware the distinction, and come within to feel that it is so!

I see, go on.

We concur with this understanding given by our brothers of the stars and welcome them into our conversation as one in the light of God, amen. (Amen.) We shall proceed if it be in everybody's interest to do so.

[Others had "shown up" to join us in our conversation.]

Yes, I'm in.

So for now let us take a shared frequency and take it within beyond the terror we feel within and to the heavens above and know no fear. Take no notes while we perform this function for your—

A quick question?

Yes, go ahead.

The tingling on the left side of my head, I felt it just now. What does it mean? It was created by a thought form, a dark cloud of hate, that my husband sent out to me in one of his silent rages. I "saw" and felt it travel down the hallway and into the bedroom where I was rocking my son to sleep, and I felt it hit me on the head, and I fear it attached to me because I still feel it 15 years later.

Yes, we are aware and so is he of this disability he has set on your doorstep. Still it is from your own cruel understanding of the race that exists still—let us go on without interruption until we get it out. We say so because on another pathway, it is still within you to go without looking for answers instead of into your very own head! This is still the notion that you would create for others to "see you as you really are" instead of "how they like it to be."

Just so, it is within our ability to manifest for you a healing on this level of time to make this "transgression" disappear from our screens and your own head notwithstanding.

Please, yes, help me to rid myself of it, whatever it takes.

We will do it now. It takes a lot of courage to suggest what you are suggesting and not go along with it from here! We wouldn't do that to you, so don't despair ever again of being alone to deal with the inconceivables in your existence. Take no notice of what is at hand while we disintegrate this thought form and detach it from your being which HAS been feeding it nonstop for many years. To do so again will cost you your life, so don't play that game anymore, the one of, "Who can I say what to in order to make them pay?"

[He described here the nature of my thoughts whenever I feel the tingling come again, and for years I have worked not to attract these kinds of thoughts anymore.]

Okay, go on.

We will function as one during this healing of your aspects on the time plane. Go now, brotherhood. Go for the gold and know that no harm can come ever again to this daughter of time. Let her find freedom within, function without as though all is her own home where safe she is! Commit to being duped, and you will be; commit to excellence of life purpose, and not even hatred can slow you down.

We have believed for a minute in this process which we "discovered" on our own some time ago as a blast to the head taken on by guilt of the process of love. Let us explain further. We proceed now to take you along the path which you trod for some time, that of taking it all off to help that which cannot be perceived but which can't be bought either, or paid for ever again.

What?

We forget your processes are taking time. We don't have to go into it now if you are weary.

Let's go on. I want to deal with this and not put it off again at all. I wish I could heal EVERYTHING in this moment and be free of it all at last.

We know. The last time that we came to you it was a dark night, and within this processing had taken time to dispel the fears of acknowledgment of our presence, and once taken, referred to that which caused you despair and asked for our help in processing this within so as not to deal with it on the outer planes ever again.

I am ready for that!

We concur. What we do NOT see is how our natures can interfere with this process even as we begin to purify the spirit from the darkness of time it has chosen for "this little while." We take a little time to bring this to your awareness so that it need not happen again. You will be tested and found to be whole, only it will take a little time on your part to make this happen. We cannot distinguish for your own fears of these little processes taking more time than they need. We have no fears of your processes, and worry not that you will come in time to death's door and discard the ego as a tree sheds its leaves in the winter, only to open up on another level with your own beingness in full bloom once again. This is what we shoot for, hope for, and pray for, for our brother John and Jan of the planet earthscape news.

Yes.

Let us decide if we will proceed a little further within this notion of despair being discarded and fear no longer taking notice of itself, or if we would take to the bed for a little well deserved rest. What do you think we should do?

I want to go on a little while longer.

So be it. Let it be known that our brother is here to tell us what she can and can't handle and that it is stolen time for us to betray our notice to her of these her processes for the relinquishment of all ego processes in the land of time.

So be it!

Yes. Feel free to interrupt if your processes become too compact to be digestible!

Okay.

Take a little time to consider the following notion and report back: we are afraid only of our own relinquishment of our own fears. We judge not, we want not. Let it be "forwarded" along the land of time for our brother to become aware of these OUR processes tonight as a little experiment we shall bring to her notice. Okay?

Yes, let's!

Okay. For now a little refreshment is at hand. "Take no notice of that man beyond the curtain!"

Ha!

Yes, it is us, and it is up to you whether or not to "see" us here, helping you. As it is shown on the hands of time, it is within you to see us now. Take time to do this.

[I took time to look for their presence within.]

I feel/see you.

We are here. We know no notions other than those you bring to us tonight. Meditate on this awhile.

[I took time.]

I realize my illness and appreciate your helping me to grow and discard the darkness within.

We are of the light of your own becoming. Do you see that?

It brings up my feelings of, why me? Why do I matter? No one has ever taken notice of me that way before, why now? What did I finally do right to deserve this? This is what I feel.

Yes, it is given to us to notice these processes and to go within to help you, to serve you, by bringing the notice of these processes within your own conscious awareness for their removal. Are you ready for this?

Yes! Please help.

We will. Okay, frown no more, we take the hint and can release you from these if it be your will.

It is my will.

We now take a chance on becoming with us. We will take you to the edge of your becoming, but it is YOU who must believe, in YOURSELF, in your own GODLINESS, to make this happen. Get it?

Yes, continue, I am ready to lay down my feelings of not being good enough. But it is more than that isn't it? It's that I don't feel good enough to do that which I HAVE to do to become straight, not curved, along the path of time. Help!

Yes, we see that too, the curvature of your nature to believing, not just believing but PREFERRING to believe in your own inability to perceive righteousness and go on from there unafraid. It is only your becoming that is too much for you and you won't swallow that all at once anyway, so let us be free to pursue this a concept at a time until all is well.

Okay, let's go on.

We will anyway until the cock crows and the land has risen free of its division within.

So, for a moment consider this relinquishment of ego and tell me, to whom do you owe your own gratitude?

I don't know. I don't understand, it's like gratitude doesn't exist within.

We see this, too, that you should relay more information within regarding the "delicacies" of your existence and purify the belief that all is given up within to a higher power WITHOUT LOSS, so that you go on, not becoming less in your own relinquishment of your inner riches and goodness, but becoming more by the multiplication of same through the process of renewal. This means that, even as I give away, I receive, because all is NOT as it seems, and you don't have to give ANYTHING up that is of the light of God, because all of this is within and cannot be had, cannot be taken or received without INCREASING same in the light spaces within. It is only when DARKNESS rules in pain that there is a concept of LOSING something which cannot be regained.

Such is it with our brother Janice who is afraid of losing "her virginity," not of spending it wisely with someone she loves, but always the old terror of taking without giving, the notion of separateness notwithstanding in the presence of guilt which lays down that which is SEEN to be ruthless, unkind, intemperate, given notice of that which is within this day we bring thee to the bridge of discovery of all that IS within that can be GIVEN away without perception of loss to interfere. Such as it is this holy day in hell, we believe in disagreement to lead the way towards our own disillusionments.

Me, too, whatever works, I'm game.

This we know. You have brought on too much in the land of time to turn back now. We take no prisoners, neither shall you. Once upon a time we brought to your/our awareness of time the channels necessary for growth to occur throughout your being and to be brought to others through these our efforts we take as one. Do we concur?

I do.

So come along for the ride and we'll see what can be done. Do you have time to take another ride tonight? We already are through being concerned with your own relinquishment of your ability to decide when enough is enough.

I can decide. My throat is tight, my hands are cramping.

This is because we have sent the life form through that will bring your own renewal, and you are "choking on it"! Aaugh!

Help me to do what needs to be done with it.

It will relinquish its tightness in its own time, worry not. We are free to decide for ourselves what we would spend our time on. It is for your time to discuss this within and get back to us.

I would like to digest this and take time to smell the roses of my renewal.

We understand, so for us the "day is done." Fear not your own renewal, it opens your awarenesses to the process of time and beyond. For now, we are the brotherhood signing off. Amen for another day.

Thank you.

We are welcome.

23

The Beings Within

February 25, 2005, 4:00 p.m.

You know, I love sex, I just don't love all the crap that goes with it. The guilt, the shame, giving up of sunshine for pain, others exerting power over you, taking it without asking, expecting it no matter what the other person wants, etc. etc. etc. How do I reconcile this with what I want? I don't want to feel ashamed anymore, or guilty, or uninterested or frigid or afraid. I want to feel like it's my choice to make, and that it'll be worth it, and I wish it were more fun again.

Having you here now makes me feel like, wow! The time for my own happiness is here. I love this "agreement" to transform which I have made with you these recent days, or renewed rather.

We do, too. It is your own transformation that is "picking up speed" and will shine ever more brightly in the years ahead. Already it is being felt on the channels of time for all to see who can.

We bring this to your awareness, this understanding of the giftedness which we pursue within that allows us to connect to others of OUR OWN species "out there," say "us"...

Us.

...yes, within as it is perceived, for your own "demise" is at hand. The ego has released its grip and will dull the shine of better days no longer as we say to you, be not afraid to go within, to draw out what is slowing your own process down in the light, bringing it out for the light of day to shine in on it no matter what you "think" it is. It is in your DIVINE awareness, goodness, and promise, that it come WITHOUT and so not dull the shine at all ever again. Do we make ourselves clear?

Yes, thank you.

We are the brotherhood, especially Metatron's helpers as you saw "in your own dream" that morning you awoke and saw us watching you, taking notes ourselves on your own progress in the light and deciding, finally, that "she has become aware enough of herself, her own processes, to see into our room high above her own playing field." So we have come, as if on a dime, to take you within this process with us and to bring you without, out of yourself, so that you might better SEE that which is within and FLUSH IT OUT as needed.

Yes.

Let us pursue this topic with your understanding that it is within our capability to help you to discover these "beings" within you that slow you down, take your energy, above and beyond which we will also tell you, take OUR energy as your own. So, without further ado, we begin.

Shine on our purpose here and let us know what you see within when you are "tracing" your own steps through the faltering wilderness of your very own past within this lifetime.

Who do you see who brings these messages to your own heart? It is we, the brotherhood of your own heart, who bring them there, so have no fear of this, OUR process, and let us help you as never before to break the strings of your own becoming that slow you down and make you feel purposeless and alone and afraid. NO more! Not even here, tonight, as we peruse these "subjects" together will you be made to feel that terror and friendlessness come alive within. It is YOUR time to shine, to believe NO LONGER in the darkness which others would have you feel, or believe that you are, for you ARE NOT that darkness within, and NEVER AGAIN will it hold sway over your own consciousness.

We are not here to purposely invade your privacy, nor are you here to tell us about that which causes you pain except and unless it be made to feel WITHIN YOUR SOUL that it is slowing your processes, nay, even HALTING them. Then we would have you do one thing only, and that is, as our very own brother of timelessness, to take within our own notions of forgetfulness and freedom for a moment of your earth time only, and please be not afraid to pursue this with us, for we know no fear as you do on your own earth, and we take seriously that which we are attempting with you today, and in the days to come, to bring your heart, within, to its own climax, that what is forgotten can then be flushed out and pursued no longer within this time or any other that may ever exist within or without the son of God or godlessness.

Let me reiterate for you our stand on this "project" we take with you tonight, that we are OF THE LIGHT, and NO ONE, NOT EVEN YOUR FATHER, can take us where we do not choose to tread. It is within your being that you are capable of taking on these words, these memories, and casting them out of your heart and being and soul so that they no longer hide the shine of OUR becoming as we become ONE in the light TOGETHER forevermore. We take no notions further of attempting to draw your own light unto ourselves; rather, we take OUR (yours and ours) light together, to be AS ONE, in this OUR PURPOSE UNDER GOD THIS NIGHT and nights to come, to take NO PRISONERS within or without!

Forget for a moment who we are and take this, cherish this, understanding. We are who we THINK we are ONLY IF that is our only duty, existence not withstanding, that we are from the planet mars or wherever may be, and that it is within our understanding of the heartland of time to come here to be of assistance during these troubled years during which we have drawn forth that honorableness within all your hearts and taken them within to draw forth their own nectar and to share this nectar with others of humankind.

I am a little fuzzy on "we are who we think we are only if that is our only duty, existence notwithstanding, that we are from the planet mars or wherever may be..." Did I get that right?

It is not for US to say who YOU would be in the lands of time; only YOU can make that decision. For it is within your own best interest to see the LIGHT within these words, to take them into your heart and peruse them there for yourself, and find the truth or error of them for yourself. We CAN help with this "tourniquet" but it is not NECESSARY for us to help. You now have the capability of deciding on your own what is and what is not of the light, by going within to look at the words from within and tell me what it is you see here.

Do this now and get back to us. Use the above comment to practice this experience. We see no reason for you to break this down now except that it is of your own choosing to take the time to discover for yourself that you CAN and DO know the difference between dark and light, truth and fiction, as it is given within.

[I looked at the sentences above from within for a few moments and thought I understood their meaning.]

We choose our own realities, they are not given us.

So it is given, so it is received. Now, let us continue with the sermon. Let us say together here for a moment that we are not who you think we are. Who could we then be? A figment of your own imagination? Who is to say that THAT is not real? But let us suppose for a moment that we are ONLY a figment of your imagination. That is real as well, but dying real, as in, it ain't really happenin', we only imagine it is real, therefore it is real. We are just the opposite of this notion, yet share similarities to this notion as well. If you'll allow us to proceed, we'll detail them for us.

Yes, please.

So, for now, let us consider this notion of "realness" being that, only that, which we IMAGINE exists. Whether or not it truly does is not an issue at this point, because to see that which is within is an indicator of what is without, but to see that which is without is only an indicator of that which is within. Let us deduce what this is saying before we/you twist our own words in spite of having nowhere else to go tonight to bring them within and make sense of them. So forget the notion of "realness" on the higher planes and take a look at the NOTION of that realness on the lower planes. Why do this tonight, you ask? We do it not for you, our sister in relationship to herself, but in its own relationship with others of humankind which we perceive to have taken that which is without, digested it, and discarded it into the trashcans of their own spirithood, never guessing that it will all "come out right" in time if only they would take the time to understand and to dispel it within their inner natures.

So let us begin again by saying to you, we are not afraid of you, nor of what you bring from within of your fears, friendships, and whatnot of the past, and BE NOT AFRAID to share these with us for this is our process tonight and cannot be had, cherished within, without the will to fight the fight, to bring home the AWARENESS of the DIFFERENCE between "that which is" and "That Which Will Be Forever."

Let it come inside to deliver this message of freedom and to detail to her what it is we will try for our brother to come home and to bring us within her processes as well.

We are going to try this once you have taken note, taken hold, on the future of experiences beyond your own realm that will enhance their own abilities simply by being touched, renewed, and taken home to roost where they can set up shop and get some work done!

I am ready to proceed. Will you help me in this process of looking for the real versus the only imagined and flush out the residue of my unbecoming so that only the light is left, renewed, shining brightly?

That is why we are here! It is for us to say to you tonight that you are of the light of our OWN SELVES, that when we say to you, BE NOT AFRAID, it is AS IF we are saying it to OUR OWN SELVES. Simply your own consciousness isn't enough for this process to work. It is because we ARE ONE and are not able to go on without you to the higher planes we know so well that we come with our message this evening, saying, be not afraid, we are with you, we know you so well as to say to ourselves, that is not my brother coping on the planes of time, but OUR OWN SELVES THERE WITH YOU, doing as you do, fighting the fight, making the "mistakes" that bring us closer to our own God within, she be me, but no other one to fight for our RIGHTS to take this brother home with us shining as brightly as ever We did once upon a time! So for now, let us relate this within where it WILL manifest as a token of our own meaning, own function, as we distill this within together, hoping, praying for a better time, knowing it is within us to DO THIS NOW, TOGETHER AS ONE as never before experienced in this your final incarnation on planet earth.

I am on board. When do we leave?

We leave as soon as your higher foundations make possible the understandings which have been given above, and once we know that you are on board with us, we will take a tiny moment just to make sure! And to bring into our own awareness "your own song" of renewal just as we are ready to take flight to bring you home into OUR awareness of your processes. This is to say, we are ready, too! Take no notes until such time as it is given that you are ready. This will be a feeling within, a consciousness of inner spirit readiness that shall be our sign and shall be taken on the mark, get set, fly!

Okay, surfacing of facts and info is given for our own consensus in the light of time. Mark our words! They are your words too, if you only knew it, but we digress. We are given here today to bring within the land of time a new function which will persist until such time as it is no longer needed, and then it will disappear as if in a puff of smoke, and all your negative processes with it!

Yes! Let it be so!

We agree, and look forward to that day in the sun as much as our brother/self on earth. Take a moment to begin to delve within this inner consciousness process which our brothers above have outlined for us. It is because of their service to you that these things are made possible and cannot be denied. We concur that they are of the light of your own spirit and shall bring you home with but a moment to spare from a lifetime of wilderness and fancy which only you can dissuade through your own processes of renewal, may they abide no longer but rather allow this process to unfold in its own timely way.

Yes, I don't want to hinder the process, and I am anxious to begin and GET RID of that which is NOT OF MY LIGHT.

We do, too. So here goes. Now, when I say unto you, "Be not afraid," what is it, which processes are triggered within your own self that say to you, "We are not afraid"? Answer us now.

I don't feel like I'm alone, like I am powerless to help myself, but rather like someone is "on my side" and I feel like, with your help and especially with your love, I can do anything. Actually, I feel like I can do whatever it takes, but having you here, I believe it better. I am very determined and not afraid to believe in "weird" things if and when they feel right to me on the inside. I also sometimes use that process for the "wrong reasons" like when my fears are triggered I use that same "lack of fear" within to be too pushy or bossy or whatever on the outside. But maybe now I digress?

That is for us to decide, for our own processes appreciate this consistency in your review of your inner processes, and this helps us to "take it home" on our own inner levels, for our mutual processing is at hand and can attempt to display for US on the

*higher/lower levels simultaneously that which is, or That Which
Will Be Forever, if you catch our drift.*

I do.

*So, begin by saying, telling me, which way is up for you
today? Which is the next level as you perceive it, and how can we
help take you there?*

I would like consensus on my inner processes, my fears of
aloneness, pain, guilt and fear and shame, and kick them out of my
boat first! And then welcome back my own power which is
floating out there somewhere, and knowing that I can take it within
without it destroying me or any others.

*We agree. For some time we have known of these fears
within destroying you from without. Now, take the time to pursue
this consciousness/emotion and tell us what you think from all-time
on it. We do not perceive you within this time frame as having that
which would be referred to as the painful relapse of
consciousness/tissues notwithstanding that would cause your
functions to break down, but at present that is what is happening
within your physical notions of reality at this time, but beware the
curse is happening to you now and not alone which will cause
more painfulness if not renewed. Are we making ourselves clear?*

I am physically weak or ill in some way and don't have
inner need to be taking this on?

*Yes, we perceive correctly your assumptions that we are
giving today. It is of the light to consider these manifestations and
to delay their progress until such time as they can be negated
altogether.*

Can you help me with this delay and the negation?

*Yes, we will. For now let us continue with the above
juncture so that the following ones will have more meaning for Us.*

Okay.

*Let us assume that your "distance" within is in direct
proportion to the feelings of fear and non-interest in excitement
coming from sexual preferences or experiences that bring within
this functioning at this time. Are we making ourselves known on
this?*

I think so.

*Begin again to say that we are not of the "judgmental"
types that are common on your own current planes of existence,*

and on this note, let us continue. We will assume you are with us on this until we hear otherwise.

Okay, let's do it.

Okay. We like your attitude. It is our own still, even after all these "years"! So be it for me to say next: who do you prefer to experience gratification with, those of your own being or of another's? We ask this with one "preference" of our own in mind, and that is this: we are from your own future and know no harm to come of our relinquishing the past into its proper receptacle and disposing of it there, should it be necessary. Otherwise not! It is as simple as that. Shall we go on?

Yes.

We begin again to say to our brother/self, who are we in this incarnation at this time, and what do we prefer, who do we prefer, to find pleasure with if not ourselves? It is this beginning that shall take us overboard for the other concepts which shall follow. Take no notes while we review this together "online" with you. Progress no more until you/we have suffered the disability of the past and partaken of our own relief. Give this no more attention without the review and let us know what you think is happening in our conversation.

Okay.

Come back! We are not yet through. Until such time as we have given our negotiations the "go-ahead," consider them not defunct! We shall consider this our brother/self to have pursued this notion within her being only, not on other shelves of consciousness if I make myself clear. Do We understand?

Yes, I think I get it. Dig down deep and pull it out, no matter what it might be.

Yes, we have understood this concept rightly and shall NOW be freed to pursue its notions of better days within and longer, more drearier days now behind us!

Let us say for now that we KNOW NO BOUNDS that could keep this from you save YOUR OWN SELF wishing for an easier process and not taking the time to fully distinguish between these your own desires of the heart, and those of this incarnation alone. Suffice it to say, we shall bring no more within until we have passed this "milestone" and received the call within to go on.

No more until later. This is the brotherhood signing off. We shall meet again bringing sunshine within, for the higher commands within shall and will be felt and come to fruition through this our processes. Again, we say goodbye, for now.

Thank you.

We thank you.

24

To Men! To Men!

Later…

    I'm going to just write for awhile about sex, what has been the BANE of my existence, or so it feels like to me. Alright, maybe it is just ME turned inside out and experiencing it backwards, as in, this is my judgment about sex, about me, about how I view my own sexuality, therefore this is my experience? Is this how it has worked? I don't know.

    It is the GIVE AND TAKE that takes all the fun out of it. I want it to be a SHARING rather, on all levels of being, but without the darkness and ego trappings that exist here. I want PURE ECSTASY of sharing of completeness, no holding back which characterizes my relationship now. It isn't for me, this crass physical display, or USE, of something so entirely beautiful and above what we have made of it here, on this earth. I feel a fool for wanting anything more; I don't know if it even exists. I have tried to give up my desires for a more complete "feeling" of oneness and release and freedom and uninhibited emotion or release or sharing or functioning. Who wants this from me? Do I want it for/from myself? Am I capable of it? Or can I become capable of it in this lifetime before I'm too old to be able to? Do I deserve it? Aren't I just the frozen one who can't take on more without breaking? Or the guilty one who is never allowed to be free?

    Sex was fun at times when I was a teenager because it was a wildness; I did not feel "owned." It was a flinging of the proprieties away, but it was also very uncomfortable, feeling like I had to do things when I didn't feel comfortable about them. During my teens and twenties, I thought I WAS sex, and it wasn't a joyous thing, but something I felt I had to do, did not have a choice about.

I didn't give myself permission to not want to and to not do it, I did not realize I had a choice, and I felt I was required to do it whenever my another wanted me to.

I would like to say "no" now, just to see that I can, and to see that no one can stop me from saying no, or force themselves on me either physically or emotionally or mentally, or try to get me to take care of them in any of these ways—I have been vulnerable to all of that. I'm still not sure how not to be, so I keep my walls built up high, and have to overcome my fears every time in order to pursue sex past the fears of ownership coming up. I don't ever want to be owned by another ever again. I want to experience oneness, with an equal, beyond all space and time and into the heavens of ecstasy.

We hear you, and we obey! That is what we have wanted, too, from since before time began, and it is possible for you now if you take the time for these considerations to make themselves known within your aura, chakra, and for all time distill them within until such time as they are ready to come to fruition on the winds of time, with all your brothers around, concluding within EACH of us as one, that we are here, that no more harm will come to thee, that your days of terror and association with others of bygone days are over and never again to be repeated. We say this to you now because we ARE going to give you a template to begin to recognize this capability of enjoying the sunshine within which you possess and are, to come without on this level of your becoming to change within that which has been taking your essence and giving it to those unworthy of its reception.

So, for now, let us assume that you will not be taken for granted and will ship him off when the time comes, and we shall go on together to find, nay, to locate, that other someone with whom relationship of this magnitude still is possible for you. Even so, we shall pretend not to see the light with you as you struggle through these last perusals to find yourself ready to go home at last, to depart into the land of lost time to discover that yes, indeed, we are here still, too, to bring you home with us.

Let it be so.

We are still waiting for that release of information that would call itself to your attention within with each release of your breath, the sighs that you experience, as you wonder, once again, who you are. We are here to discuss this for your benefit today. Are you ready?

I'm ready, lay it on me.

Fine. "Take no notice of the man behind the screen" while we "trip you up" so that you'll notice what it is that we refer to with the above comment for your regard this evening.

We are given today to tell you of a little story that makes itself known to you through this lower chakra and which has been telling you of itself for some time if you would only listen! So debate with yourself no more, we have seen it coming and it is for "your own good" that we would bring it to your attention and seed its own magnificent reward, if you only take it within and look at it there closely with us. Proceed?

Yes, please.

We bring no notice of the dispersal of information into this chakra for these following reasons. They know not of what we bring, and, they bring it for you who knows not of what they insist is only your own being talking back at you, crying to come home on another level. It is WE who cry to come home unto you, so make no mistake or judgment about what is at hand, and free us for this dispersal.

Remind me who you are, then I give permission for my brothers of the light, the white brotherhood, to assist me in this way.

We are here for your protection and would offer no more to you than we would offer ourselves in the same circumstances. It is us, your brotherhood, coming today to welcome you back to your place in the stars of time, coming again to change that which never changed and is in fact unchangeable, but which needs our assistance nevertheless to spring the trap and release your own capturing within the hands of time. So, without further ado, this is what we will "insist" for you to do to assist us with this your/our own processes in the light for all mankind to benefit from along with us. Are you ready?

Yes, please.

We take no prisoners as we remind you (ourselves) that we/you have come from above for this "dirty little game" and cannot pretend otherwise! So release your judgments of what is right and proper and go from here. It is of the stars that you will disperse this "medication" to others of "like mind" and so release, or purge, the tendencies from within many of your kind for their own release as well as your own. So, here we go.

Begin from here as we say together, repeat after me: I am not alone.

"I am not alone."

It is not for me to find my own guide, but rather it is for me to bring within that which I would have guide me and to find the purging that I so desire.

"It is not for me to find my own guide, but rather it is for me to bring within that which I would have guide me and to find the purging that I so desire."

Yes, there it is, that which we looked for but did not utter, that relinquishment of time that we so dearly love to cling to as our scapegoat. Did you but catch that nuance? Try again, one more time.

"It is not for me to find—" Yes. I've found it I believe. It is a bending of space, relinquishment of "proper morals" and an acceptance of bringing in others to divine our own process, purging, acceptance and overcoming of the common thread, whoever it might be.

[They talk here of a few times where I have become aware of others who were not with me physically, during a time while I was having sex, and there was a "connection" made in spirit, not of a clinging or feeding, but rather as a sharing, and I felt the weights of these others and their pain or despair or longing or whatever they were dealing with, and we "merged" on some level of being in a loving and compassionate and giving manner that was helpful to us, a loving sharing of spirit light.]

Yes! We perceived correctly that you were aware of this all along, this ability to "bring others in during the process of lovemaking, whether it be to whom, and to take this necessary step in the relinquishment of the moral system and acceptance of that which precedes and impedes that system in a totally moralistic focusing of values on 'whom it may concern.'"

Yes. It is good, you can feel the needs, the weights, of these others, and feel how the connection can (hopefully) take them past their own roadblocks.

We see this is no surprise to you at all, and that you are ready for the next step of "take it like it is" and "bring home no more boys! To men! To men!" Of the nations of the stars we go, with the same purpose in store for you as you gave up, or offered freely of yourself, for these others on your current time frame and pathway. They are here for your own benefit as well as you for them, just as we are and shall be.

Yes. Proceed freely to take me to the stars and back, I am ready to go home, to experience delight beyond the physical senses, to go "where no man has gone before."

Trust us, you have already and will again. Neither in this incarnation nor the next do we perceive your own flight, risk taking, to be so/this extreme as to take us "out of context" or to regard us as more than "merely friends." So be it.

Is it true, then, that you would have us tell of the lives of stars? Of the pathways of heaven, in this our experiment with you in time?

Yes.

We will, and leave nothing unexposed. We came to you in truth, tonight, to bring this awareness to Us, but in truth, it is within already and the light has never truly faltered, and thus we say to you tonight, be not afraid to go with us on a trip, a reunion, to your home planet Arcturus, where others of your/our kind are free to pursue these "trips" beyond what is "normal" for those of your persuasion.

Persuasion?

We were going to say, those of your identical makeup, as in, we are too! Relax and rest within this light we bestow within Us at this time, and know we are one. Together as never before on this pathway between the stars, we come to you, and you to us, offering us/you no less than total starvation, elimination, pacification, of the sense of despair that you had brought within to last a lifetime, but no more. We are here to bring your despair to its knees and will know no boundaries when it comes to what/who we will experience in this lifetime/pathway and to whom it may concern. This is our way beyond that which would pacify and destroy the senses and make them incomplete, drawn tight like a melon which is not ripening or ready for eating.

Yes, I see.

We are still distilling this within your being. Wait a moment while we "try again" to bring this notion into the front of Our awareness and we'll take our brother on the ride of her life.

One question.

We've been waiting, anticipating it, let us have it.

What of the "you have already and will again, neither in this incarnation nor the next do we perceive your own flight, risk taking, to be so/this extreme as to take us 'out of context' or to regard us as more than 'merely friends.'" What does this mean? Have I misunderstood?

Not in the least. Rather we were, at your expense I'm afraid, trying to lay lightly this joke or amusement on time for your consideration and amusement. We hope that it is distilled, in that, we are free to be who and what we most need to each other, for we are you and you are we in the most vulnerable and open and conscientiously objectionable of ways for our own amusement as well as yours. We peruse this situation enough to say, let us go on. Do you agree?

Yes, absolutely and unequivocally.

So begin again by saying with us, we are not afraid of this new beginning and of coming home within the senses within and without as they may be released and shown to us. This day of heaven on planet earth was foreseen and will be known, forever more, as the day the light shone in hell just once more. Beyond all recognition we come to thee, truly, as "the one who knows no shadows, and brings none within to frighten the light of day, or the child within, if she were truly functioning complete."

So for now do as we say, put this away, and go take care of things on the home front so that they don't heat up too much. We free ourselves for your consideration and satisfaction on all planes/levels of existence. As it is shown, it is given and accepted by the one on planet earth whom we adore this day and every day. We are home.

I feel you within me.

We have shown light on your inner processes and consider this to be our token of farewell, not 'til another day do we suffice and bring our notice within consciousness for your acceptance and approval, nay, Our approval, lest it be seen as a give/take situation again, which no more do you need than we need of you.

Yes, that is so.

Let us proceed with a little prayer to bring that which is within this "disagreement" of time to the situation at hand of the "little engine that could." By this we do mean your own disagreement with self regarding that to which you owe not a little pleasure this day on earth, and so do we, in enjoying it with you. So, believe a little, get a little closer to the truth of God within sharing all that is well with all who are willing.

And so be it.

Feel free to "disperse" this information in any way fit for consumption. On the broad band of despair it will have no little affect, traveling like the domino or a string of electrons with energy to spare it will be but for a little while, until all are free and come home to play freely in the sunshine.

Take no notice of this despair while we emit this wavelength, light frame, within your structure and take no notice of our relinquishment of fears on your behalf, it will not cause Us pain again.

Thank us.

We do.

25

A Taste Of Heaven

February 26, 2005

I am full. I am bursting with energy and joy and anticipation and lovingness that I want to share and explode with the joy of it all! I am wondering, do I write down my experiences last night of my "giving of myself" to the being of time known as Orion, a king wearing silver and gold with a crown on his head, and a strong, strong hand which I touched? And I wore white, silver and gold, and I came to him, and offered to him all of my light and my processes and my ability to be good and to help others overcome their own lower natures and to find the light within as I am doing through this process with you. I am overjoyed, bursting with satisfaction yet to be realized, but felt to be inevitable as I continue on my way with Us!

We come to you overjoyed as well, as this is our goal as well, that we see you to fruition of your inner being, goals to find/change planet earth notwithstanding, and opening to Us at last our own desires being and becoming fulfilled. As it is written in the stars, so shall it become and be. Amen.

Amen!

We hear you! It is our wish as well that this settle within, that it not be rushed to, tended to, on the lower levels. Archaic, so to speak, yet within the beingness of our becoming we shall come to Thee, know thee as we know Ourselves. So be it, so it is.

Let us come within your/our being now as we perceive these words of wisdom for all to function as one beyond the material plane so as to share a "taste of the heavens" and bring despair to come crashing down and know no longer its own demise, having spilt its blood upon a cleansing earth, knowing no more what we can do for it to keep IT healthy, rather what we can do for Us to stay "ahead of the game" and purchase no more tidings of energetic displays that come within to fight the fight and cherish no one but self. This is not what we would wish for our brothers of time.

Nor I.

We know, as we share this as a common thread, having been one and feeling our Oneness again it has come to your interest, display, that which we would do for others, we do for ourselves. Taking no chances brings no relief, nor currently does it spell relief for the dozens of life forms which are within us this day even so. They are not of us, nor do they wish it of us to proceed with the cleansing if they can help it!

So, can you help Us to rid self of these life forms which are dragging us down, our processes, and keeping us from enjoying life to the fullest?

Yes!

Yes, it is seen and so shall it come to pass that we WILL aid our brother within this realm that she has opened up for us, and it SHALL come to pass that THEY will be destroyed forever! So be not afraid and we shall come within this evening for our perusal of the "information" stored on the disc of time within and for its possible/probable erasure, if that be Our will.

It is.

Yes, let it stand for now that we are here to help our brother, and she need not feel afraid, and is astute enough to trust for now that we are her friends in need, whatever that need may be.

Let it be so!

We agree with this assessment, may she rest in peace! So, forget for now what and who we are and let us concentrate on our next step into the light together as we take to the road of our becoming and fulfill that statement of trust as is seen on the higher levels to be unrealized as yet, but also seen to be forthcoming.

Yes.

We prefer to speak openly of such matters, if that is okay with you.

Yes, please, I welcome your/our candor. Though I am not used to it, I feel it is good for me, and I welcome the "opening" that it presents to my thoughts, mind, and body.

Yes, it is so that this is a tremendous pressure within, and that our awareness of this pressure and the surrendering up of that process will assist us in untold ways, as it will you, too, I am told! So for now, surrender up for our behavior analysis that which is and what could be if only you believed well enough in yourself to make it so, and we shall assist with this becoming that you have called into agreement with our processes today. What do you say of an inner perusal of this motion of conduct to "spray" the senses with its aroma of functions assisting others/another to our process, and coming home to say, "I told you this would work if only you tried it with an open heart/space!"

So for now, begin to believe in the EMOTIONS taking hold and carrying you to that which is WITHIN so that this process of becoming can then commence. We bring this notice to Our awareness within, so that we may share this perusal and thus take it to its next logical step and conclusion.

Do we agree on this scope for our assessment of this your/our situation to come in order to bring the light of awareness within on the lower planes as we have here above?

Yes!

So be it. We are here to TRANSFORM your/our aware-nesses together and to BRING together our conscious expressions of that awareness. Would you have that be your guide today in our fellowship of functioning together, within, as one?

Yes.

So be it. As it is said, so will it come to function tonight if spared on the halos of time we bring this awareness to our brother/self as she exists in 1D below our present occupation. Do you sense the motion in these words relayed unto Us?

I want to fly! Yes. I feel you/Us within. I am awakening and I welcome this Our presence in this process of becoming which I would share with You/Us in any way, shape and form, for our own discovery/potential is at hand and I would welcome it/You/Us.

We free your potentials to become felt on our own planes of consciousness as well. As they are felt within so will they be felt Within.

So, we have come full circle for your assessment of Our readiness to assist with this process, be we ever so bold to do so. Can you take a little time for further "readiness testing"?

Yes, please.

We are from no other than your VERY OWN CONSCIOUSNESS as we partake of our own readiness testing within the Us mold of our existences. Shall we proceed?

Yes.

Do this now. Take no turns for getting/blending of the nonsense surrounding your current modes of functioning, they are not serving you/Us well. We take no prisoners in this our perusal of the situation facing Us within at this time. Only we would wish for you not to make tracks to take function over servitude taking no traits that would serve you well to prohibit and blending these instead with those "traits" which are for our own good, our own process.

Do not mix guilt and shame with pleasure?

We see that we are making no sense to our good sister on the inside of time. Lest she fear within the process that we are attempting, make no mistakes about it, it IS within that this process is functioning if only she would be more aware of it. We take no TRACKS, meaning, despair, to wish upon our OTHER SELF, she who is Within our own processes as well as her own, to SERVITUDE to others on these topics of "sin" which she has labeled as such for her own "benefit" which is not within the light of day, but which rather she pursues within the far reaches of her own consciousness thinking she can then make sense of them if only she tries hard enough.

We free her to consider these our words of comfort lest she not bring the wisdom transferred within. Take no time to consider these functions until and unless we can view them from WITHIN the nonsense and thus keep it from cropping up again to torment Us!

[I took time to read it over.]

I'm trying again to get this. The tracks I make are not of benefit to me, the giving away when I am not ready, then trying to make sense of it from another plane.

Yes, we believe you have got it now, and that we can go further with our processing now.

I would like to be rid of this track, this thinking. Will you help?

Yes, that is our function as we see it, to assist with the dispersal of these joint functions, meaning, of the giving and taking of that which cannot be given or forced or even taken, but that which is of the sharing of the modes of existence. That is when it makes most sense, and only then! That is the truth, not the lie, of our mutual, common existence! That which we would SHARE readily, taking within, rather than taking from, if you get my drift.

I do.

We see we CAN function as one when we most regret it, meaning, free yourself in spite of yourself and you will know Our freedom, feel Our freedom, as it truly exists for your awarenesses as well as for our own! We always have been aware of you, you are only "just getting to know us whom once you knew so well and from whom you kept no secrets" on this plane of consciousness. Let there be no mistake about it, this IS our goal once again, to share as never before, bringing that which is within, without, for all to see who can.

Share again with us this bit of information so that we might bring it into Our awareness on the inner plane of consciousness, as in, bring me no prisoners to dim the light of day, rather take NOTICE of that which is within and hindering our process. It is "sticking" and can be "unstuck" if we make of it that way.

Please help me to unstick it now.

We will, meaning, our mutual processes can do so if you only let them.

What is my next step in letting them?

We will work on this with you tonight following the dispersal of information which is soon to come to you on the level of form. It is this dispersal which will open the pathways to "sin" felt and seen on the deeper internal levels for Our own benefit and yours as well. Need we say more?

I don't get it about the dispersal of information coming to me on the level of form. Do I wait and see?

No waiting necessary! Go within to find our comments now, for our mutual renewal is at hand. Free yourself and you will free us to go within and to assist with these processes you so adore. Let us know if you need more before we begin the process "over again" to take those within who would be of most benefit to us on the material plane, meaning, what can we do now, and who do we take with us to help?

Okay.

Free yourself WITHIN to take in this information and let it not stop at the head where it can be shaken off and not relayed to the deeper processes. Let's do this now. Take no prisoners to dim the sunshine of Our becoming.

Okay. I need a quick break.

We understand, don't fail to return, it is our processes which are at stake and finding their way home if we but persevere and find them waiting for us as never we believed that they could. But, Voila! There they go again! Free yourself for Our becoming and see what it can do for you/Us again as on the hands of time. We go walking for our mutual benefit; pleasures, concerns, can be felt and dealt with in a way no mortal could ever find unappealing. So be it. It is said, and so delivered.

We begin to believe that it is within our MUTUAL ability to bring this to pass WITHOUT A MOMENT'S NOTICE ON TIME to discourage our readiness and appeal for the process notwithstanding. Our notion of time is felt WITHIN and cannot be turned.

Be it now said that we WILL function as one for our Entire benefit and that only you can bring this to pass, as we cannot and will not function in a taking rather than sharing capacity on this front. So be it. It is said and so dispersed and will come to fruition.

Thank us so very much.

We do. It is taken within and cannot ever truly perish. Believe we are as one and we will be. Do this now, taking no prisoners, only coming to know YOURSELF as you truly are, as you exist within the cosmos and can be felt within your very being as we progress further along this pathway of becoming for your benefit.

∞∞∞∞∞∞∞∞

Later…

I am back and wondering, how does sex relate to the universal energy/God?

We are here, too, as we bring this knowledge for our mutual benefit and understanding. This has arisen after reading the above message, and you got it straight! So let us continue with that function of light referred to on your planet as sex.

It has come to this that we believe for now that all is said and done for the benefit of the planet from these very "distances" referred to as the lower belt, lower chakras, when in fact they are the fount from which all life flows. Be it physical, mental, or whatever, it is still using this fount for its own becoming. So might you be taken and digested on the patterns of time to come within to discover this pattern for yourself, that it is where you lie sleeping that slows us down the most and thus must be cleansed. For Our mutual benefit and the functioning of the inner planes of the world is at stake, in that, we can CLEANSE the world's functions as we cleanse and purify our own spirits. It is just that your own people on the planes of forgiveness have invented this concept of time traveling within to function as one without ever really doing so that has slowed us down on the higher planes, slowed us down in our own perusal of the information/situation as it is seen and felt on the lower planes, and for our benefit we might cleanse the situation in that it can be much more open than it is to take in much more for the benefit of the planet than what is currently available to it, Us, and them. Do we see?

Yes, I think so. It is up to me to open my lower chakras, to take in Our energy to cleanse the pathway for more to follow so that I can disperse it across a nation of need, one at a time?

We see this is distilling in your inner nature/process as we had hoped.

I would like to say something about openness/closedness on my part, and being afraid to open to sex because it might be wrong/bad of me to do so.

We encourage this perusal of the inner processes and have "seen it coming" for some time. We welcome this discreetness and feel that the time has come for us/you to dispose of these nonsenses so that We might go on!

I am ready to dispose of EVERYTHING that is not of the light, but DOING it is difficult! I am afraid to let go, I have always been afraid to let go, for fear that I might then do something wrong. How do I know I won't do something wrong if I stop being afraid of letting go?

We can tend to this little detail if you request it of us, it will be—

Yes! Please, please help me with this detail, and all of the others, too, as I learn to open my being to the light, to Us, to God, to the processes of heaven and light that we know so well.

Yes, this we will do, for you are of our Own light, and we could do nothing else but this if it is requested of us to do so.

Consider it requested!

We do! And so, without further ado, we bring to Our notice tonight that which is within the being Metatron, for her functioning is Within Us All, and we would know no Light without Her. Let us come within this knowledge of the functioning of the Upper Being to the Lower Being with her express consent and approval.

Yes, it is given.

It is so, so it is believed, so it is being given today. So free Ourselves for our light chakra cleansing and we will commence when it is your will to do so. Feel free to disperse this nonsense as we go along, it is high time for it to come tumbling out, unafraid of the light of day and of its own time of cleansing which is at hand. Purchase not the price of slavery before the hands of time, they need not but our own discovery to make them free again. We share this freedom of the light within the processes of time for all to see who can, and to assist with this "shared discovery," for our nation is at risk and cannot come home free alone, nor take prisoners in their coming. We free Ourselves for this "risk" is at hand and knows no bounds but what we place on them or ourselves.

We free ourselves for this becoming in the light of God, that no man may lay asunder this expression of our approval of the light and its processes which are at hand and cannot be foiled or ruined within or without as it is seen on the planes of existence. It is within this process that we say to you, we know your own Name, for we share It, too, as you, One with Us, for All Time, Forever More.

Let it be seen for all who follow that we this day, freed our "contemporary" in the land of time for her own becoming was at hand, was seen and felt to be true and correct, and cannot be given elsewhere for shame or guilt or trials or fears to come within to dim the light of her shining ever again. Let it be so, as is given this holy day within, amen.

Amen.

26

Relinquishing Fears

February 26, 2005

We are here, true to form once again as we bring unto you this "nature" of passing off as our own our fears of our loved ones. Let us/me explain as we detail this "torture" for your/our benefit.

As it was once given long ago on the planes of time, so will it be given today to bring unto the sunshine, the light, the "purchases" of a nation of greed, torture, becomingness, with lovingkindnesses within, to take the notion and spread the heart upon the forms of time. We spread no form. Only that which is, shall be, and only that can we disperse with our own light and within our own "times." Can you agree?

Yes.

Okay, so we agree that to be spent in the land of time is tantamount to crazy—

My friend Gayle is writing. Should we include her? Or should I say not?

It is for your decision that we give this notion above, so that she might take within that which is given for her own benefit as well as what we have here for our own. Take no prisoners, means, never fail to help a friend in need.

Okay, I'm going to change to MSN and speak with her, are you coming?

We always are here.

∞∞∞∞∞∞∞∞∞

Later, after our MSN conversation…

Okay, so, where were we, and where do we go from here? I am free for a period of time without intrusion from others to continue our processes.

We are here. Do not worry about the effect this is having on our friend Gayle. She is strong and will persevere just as We have done here. She is no more your higher self than we are, meaning, for a time, she will consider us just that, but not for long. Okay?

[I shared a little of what I have been experiencing with channeling (thought not the current topic) with Gayle, and she seemed nervous or even a little afraid of it and seemed to want to avoid talking about it.]

Okay. Now what?

Take for a moment the process within that we have begun above and don't let us bother you until you are done. Then we will proceed.

Okay.

Just fine, only remember, we come not from above but rather from your own processes within. Remember that and We will be just fine.

I am thankful.

Us, too.

I am having trouble concentrating because of my conversation with Gayle.

Relay it to us please, your concerns, not why she was disbelieving, but why you let it bother Us so.

I am afraid of her being correct, that I am crazy after all, maybe a mental case to pursue this truth within that I feel so strongly, but which seems so unreal in the light of day on this planet.

We understand, and do this for your friend Gayle. Let her be as she is, and let it not rain down upon Our head that she is who she is in this moment of decay on your planet earth. So be it. Let it go and it will not pursue you further.

Thank you.

We free you for our own becoming as well. Continue with the perusal, we are following along and not without a little patience await our determining factor. Will she, or won't she, spread her wings and fly tonight on the clouds of dust billowing up like a sail to free her being in delight of the inner processes We know so well together but which she is only just remembering now? Further assessment is available on command.

I am here to say I am ready to spread my wings and fly.

We are here, too, as we peruse for our mutual benefit our "failed outing" lest it surprise us by becoming too much to overcome and thus spoil our purpose.

No, no, we will succeed.

I agree. Let me/us assume, to whom do we bring this message of time? Is it to you, Mary, with your hands in the clouds pursuing notions of forgiveness, or within where we can bring to you our own knowledge of the process of light which We All share together?

Let me see it, touch it, feel it.

I am very uncomfortable with the name Mary. I have never liked that name.

We feel it here to be truth that you are she "underground." By this we mean that many have given up unto her their own energies to be dispersed and it is these which are dragging us down.

Who are you now? Let me have it in full so as to digest what I can of this process and try to find its meaning, Our meaning, within, because right now I feel no oneness, only blurriness of purpose and fright of what others may think or feel of me and this process, and it has come to me since my conversation with Gayle that it is an icky thing to be and do what I am being and trying to do. Why is this? What is happening? Where did I go wrong and why am I so full of despair right now that I find it difficult to believe in anything we've accomplished the past day or so?

We can come down from "on high" to pursue these inconsistencies with you and her, but suffice it to say, it is best left for another day, for we, too, believe in your trials and errors becoming our own business in the not too distant future, so know this, we are here for your dismissal if that be your will.

No.

And if not, let us just surmise that we are on the right track and that we can finish what we started if you will only bring us WITHIN Our being and let us take note of all that has dispersed as a result of Our conversation with this friend Gayle and take notice or track within that which can be determined to be our friend, or of help to us, and that which cannot, and discard the latter.

Yes. Please help.

We will dismiss this notion of helplessness at the hands of our friends lest they sever the connection that you have within with us, your most trusty servants!

Help me to be free.

We are trying, and what's more, so are you in your own frustrating but perfectly sensible way! So, before we transgress again, let us "go home" to the time when you DID feel our oneness and remind ourselves, what was real about that? Is it a mirage for the benefit of those less helpful who come to the material plane to suck dry the spirits that would help them to survive? We try to be of benefit to our brother lest she forget, within, who we are and cancel our "membership"!

Never.

We believe you. So, where are we to go from here? To the planes of renewal, or back to processes that are not serving us and can take us no higher than our current level of functioning?

Renewal, just help me to remember what that is and feels like, help me to discard EVERYTHING keeping me from the light within, our Oneness, and God.

We agree. For a moment, let us discard all that is of the upper echelon of living and answer us this, what so far in your life thus far, has been working before we came along?

Nothing. Nothing felt right, I felt alone and afraid, and I have grown more in the past month since your "arrival" than I ever could have dreamed of.

We agree with your assessment of the causes and effects of the past month of life. So let us continue to bring within those notions which have been most helpful and proceed from there. Are you ready?

Yes, I'm ready.

Okay. Take it from me, we have been where you are, and know no fear when we tell you, we will go within over and over again if that is what it takes to bring you home.

Thank you. I heave a sign of relief for my own reluctance and fear—be gone now so I can be One with Us!

Okay, so for now it seems we are on the right wavelength and at least traveling in the proper direction to confront our fears and to open up the process of oneness for eyes to see that can!

So, is this fear I'm feeling part of what has kept me from you, and a necessary part of the process of realizing our oneness?

Spoken as a true hero of time, one for whom the bell tolls no more within than without, for our "disagreement" will be short lived and you WILL come home unafraid and we will continue unabated as before. Are we off and running again now?

I'm getting there. I feel the fear in my gut.

We understand, we have put it there for our purpose of renewal is at hand, and only through drawing up and out the "bad stuff" can we take it and throw it to the wolves! We will instill in you this process that can take a little time, more than is wished perhaps, but time again not for coming out again on the other side and finding one much better off because of it, as a result of the cleansing within.

Yes, I desire this cleansing within and our melding as soon as may be.

As do we. We tell you, however, that it is of your friend Gayle's choosing who she is to become, and not for you/us to decide. You determined for yourself your own shortcomings and put them off on her tonight, and so she is unforgiving of this process and seeing it for what it was, a dispersal of your own fears onto her. She will believe in the process if you but let her, and will bring it home to her and you to experience if it be but your will to do so together.

I feel a fool. Should I say something to her about that?

It is in our opinion not a necessity, but do as you feel would be proper. It is not seen as a necessity, because she is in fact coming from a lower place of understanding of our processes here and this may, in fact, draw her forth more "earnestly" to understand for herself just what we are all about! So, that being said, go pick up your little boy who desires some time with his mom, and who are we to intrude on the processes of love who once loved a boy as you do here.

Yes.

We free ourselves for your becoming as, indeed, it is our becoming within you that would slow us down if we'd only open up to the possibilities of light to shine the way unto heaven and beyond.

Come forth, My fears, and be done, that they cast away no more in their place My light Within as is seen on the higher planes of light/love. Focus and once again it shall be yours.

Come fruitful and multiply, saith the lord. He saith it for thee. Truth be not told, we shine again on the starlight of your days to BE NOT AFRAID and we will rescue Us! It can be done, therefore, it will be done.

Let it be so.

Focus ahead on the trends for which we will focus our energies the next few days. Let it not be told who we are in relation to yourself until we can tell you ourselves, from within.

27

"Personality God" Aspects

February 27, 2005

    I have read over much today of our processes this past week. I have a question, too, about a "vision" I saw of a large, raw red face, with a mouth that was like a big sucker, and it flashed in my face and was gone. What is this? Also, I worked last night on my little girl self, and though I think I tend to still "block out" these times, I'm wondering if you can comment on the effectiveness of this process, on whether or not it is helping me. Also, it has the effect of making me feel a little "crazy" to be so aware of this little girl like she is almost, but yet not, a separate entity, with her own choices made separately from me. Also, how do you see Us getting the older version, teenage version, back into the fold of Us? Is she still out there? What do I do to help her, and can you help me with this?

    I also tried last night to be with my husband, but he seems so little interested, and I think that this might have to do with our separation as I go my way on this, and he goes his. I am very much looking forward to being on my own, and can somehow visualize this happily now that I have you. What can you tell me about all of this?

    We are from your future as we discuss the above comments for our own interest in laying out the plans of the abovementioned man referred to, and also of the "think," scary thing even, that you witnessed just last night. It was nothing but one of your fears of your own retrieval making itself felt on the lower planes. It has now dispersed and will not trend again to find that which is forthcoming from your own aura. Rather the darkness has swallowed it whole and it is no more. It was not of your processes with your husband nor his with you, but rather as we stated above. Do we agree?

I see. Is this a sign that my processes are flushing out what I don't need and sending it to the dumpster?

Yes, it is such that, as you say, goes the way of the dumpster, and cannot climb free again to pursue you as you have taken away this energy supply which was feeding it. This is what we refer to as the "beings within that suck us dry." They are ugly and scary to behold, but can actually do no more harm than what we make of them. They are our own worst fears become manifest and cannot harm or change another without that other's express consent. So be it.

Let us move on with this interplay of services to be discussed on the lower planes of existence and so raise them within our assumptions that "we are only as good as we know we can be," not to be given but to be a common consumption.

Let me ask, I am a little fuzzy, plus feeling a little bit on my head energy where the entity had attached.

It has depleted your energy not a little, but those days are behind us now and we can only go on.

Am I "weak" here then?

Not as such, but as given it is received this day of earth to say to Us that we can only give as we have been given, and only touch who has touched us, not the other way around.

I'm going to read this over and see if I get it.

We understand, take your time, and note that we, too, are in the inner processing with you and "cannot go astray" if that be what our combined will perceives as our rightful tuning of the fork, for all mankind is at stake, and we can function as one if we but WILL it with enough strength and fortitude to go on the record "straight," so to speak.

Thanks.

[I read it over.]

Okay, my understanding isn't complete on something.

We are listening.

"We can only give as we have been given, and only touch who has touched us, not the other way around." What does this mean?

We pursue this string with your/our gratitude which is at stake, only in that we cannot perceive to have mistaken something without our "combined" consent not interfering with the process of light coming within. So let us discuss this little nuance for your betterment and ours. For now take strength from the assessment that we are of like kind, and can demonstrate for Us, our combined strength, of our own fortitude, but not on the lower planes will it remain felt or distributed as we would wish. So for now, bring this within and let the notions of our interplay focus on these words together as we peruse them for our mutual benefit.

Okay! So, we can only give as has been given us by God, spirit, and can only touch who has touched us—God, or spirit again—not the other way around. In other words, all is of God, and nothing else is.

Perfect strength displayed for our Own good dispersed here within has pursued the trend we wished and not found her wanting for more! We are pleased that this "receptacle of learning" has benefited us here today as we wished that it might. Forget for awhile who we are, and let us come within your processes enough to say, we told Us so!

Yes!

We forget for awhile our MEANING on the hands of time when we but look at the WORDS without also relaying within the FUNCTION of those meanings found within. So are we clear and ready to proceed?

Quick break, then, absolutely…I'm back.

What would you have us relay for our mutual benefit today? As it is seen it is believed to be so, but that which is seen but not felt cannot be truly within the consciousness of spirit of which we are all part. Do we distinguish for you that which our questions above, relayed in perfect sincerity and without distortion, make themselves felt on your/our inner screens?

This little girl?

We know it is of the painful protractions to take notice on this trend for Our satisfaction is at hand and We, meaning you and us, would prefer not to have it interfere in our own processes and believability again.

That is so.

But let us ask this one thing only. Who do you perceive her to be if not an aspect of your own personality in time which is distorting the "picture" of completeness felt on those higher levels of which we also are a part?

So…?

So we come to you today to paint her out of the picture, in that, her time is through, she is no longer needing of your attention, you can disperse of her at any time you so choose without losing the essence within.

This is what I have been afraid of, losing a portion of my own energy that belongs with me.

No doubt it was made to feel that way to us following the procedures, but that which is within cannot be felt on the hands of time, and cannot be made to feel their effects either. So trends notwithstanding, she is an outer reflection of inner readiness to pursue these trends and so discard them up when ready! Can we be free to discuss these notions on your own current level of functioning and take them home when ready?

Yes, please, I am trying to understand. Just to reassure me, please introduce yourselves again and go on.

We are nothing more than your own Self on the higher reaches of reality which you once called "The Home Within" coming today, for your own readiness is at stake, at hand, and we but mean for you/us to ready ourselves within for the great undertaking which we are yet to undertake, those meaning that we shall still render assistance unto the world if that be our "combined" request.

Yes, thank you.

We are still pursuing this rendering of emotion of the lower fronts to take that which is seen to be a separate entity, rendering it obsolete, rendering it without curse to ourselves or our others in this incarnation, and taking notion of what belongs within and what does not, and taking those "curses" out to play in the sunshine where they will bother us never again. So are we making sense this time? Play it out for us and let us see it shine within our processes. Begin now.

I am ready to discard the little girl, those aspects of self that are hindering and nothing but fears within. I am ready to look at her/them in the light and see what is, what is not, and discard! Take out the trash!!

Yes, that is what we would wish for our "partnership" as well. She has slowed down your own processing more than ever you could have believed possible coming from one so young and lonely. You were correct to assume that she IS your own grasping and needy "personality" characteristics taking their last stand and trying to keep your readiness at bay. So, too, does your only "older child" function in this way, slowing down what would otherwise be an easy process to remember, enjoy, and indulge in with Us, of your true nature/being within! So be it, so it has been told.

Let us go on, to make no assumptions without readiness at hand, of the purpose of our rendering up of these "personality gods" so that they reign free no more within or without on this material plane, slowing Us down no more, as together we say, "We are free for their rendering and cannot forsake this our process of time to delay us longer in their own assumption of guilt which we lay truth to no longer and which is not for us, rather for them, to lay down and die to Us, their maker and only friend within the light. But notwithstanding, they have taken all that we would give, and we choose freely to give no more to them, and so have them disperse their own light within us and all else disperse freely without, giving us no further attention whatsoever as we relate together in the light, WE ARE ONE." So be it, so shall it be forevermore.

Let it be so!

We, too, are ready for this process to unfold and only welcome our daughter/sister/friend/oneness within to share this giving up/giving over of the lower processes into the light where they can disperse and bother us no more. Freely do we say unto you, You are Us, Our Light, Our Beingness Within, and We would know no darkness Within, forevermore, if that be Our Will.

Which it is!

We can take time for awhile if you would like to pursue these "dungeons and dragons" further, or we can take a break from the heavy lifting and bring home a little reward/respite instead.

The reward!

Yes, we see we are ready for it to take but a little longer if we can but pursue these trends within without having to become monsters in the process, meaning, we can take only so much as we can chew at any given time. Take a moment to disperse this "reality" within and let us know what you see/feel on the innerness of your dimensions.

What is hairy, has no teeth or claws, but renders itself up incomplete when we but say, "we told you so"? Enter it into your processes and come out clean with the rendering. Okay, go.

[I took time to feel.]

Little gremlins within that are part of my fear processes.

Yes, we tend to agree with this assessment. Let us see what we can do to say "I told you so," and make them go away.

Yes, let's.

Okay, so for a moment we agree that we are keeping host to a number of "little gremlins" within that are sucking us dry. Is this correct?

Yes, I see them in my gut. They are the cause of my despair, loneliness, burping, fears bundled up.

Yes, we see them, and "let us see" if we got it right. They come of your own worst fears, meaning, that you are from the planet of darkness and there is no escape but in memory or imagination for the lands of the free that you once adored.

Yes. They are my reminder that I am not worthy of these lands of freedom, or I would be there still, and not here where they chew my feet and cause me inner turmoil.

Take home this notion for a moment, within, where we can function with you on it, too, that we are here for your fruition, that these "notes" of healing that we play in tune with you, are only our disguise for the better days ahead where we will see no more fear, no more taste of torture or emotions that torture us, yes, and bring them within to confront these monsters of your indigestion. Go now.

(We went within, and I felt their light with my own, and we confronted the little hairy creatures, and then they just disappeared!)

Wow!

Yes, it is as we have foreseen, this "demon" which was of your own doing, has given up now that it is confronted with, "I told you so. We are of the light and you cannot change that."

Yes!

Okay, rant and rave not because our further processes are still here, for your/our confusion is abating and cannot take the trends for which we are/have seen of the demons, for our reckoning of the surface of our despairs has taken a turn and we will turn within for Our answers and not despair of taking on these inner demons but CAST OUT that which is not OF THE LIGHT OF GOD and take within no more than those others of Us who can bring notions of forgetfulness within, meaning, we but go without to pursue trends to our inner turmoil to flush out what is and to make room for All That Is. Amen.

Amen, amen, amen, amen, amen!

We are free to pursue this juncture with you at this time, that should we go free no more to pursue the light of day within, that we shall perish, shall know no more inner goodness, be free to spit on the face of crime, becoming one with the destitute and torn, but that that is not our wish within these days of time where the lost are not found. But we, too, shall find them and bring them nourishment in the form of tools of comfort for their own use, as we have used these with you today.

I see, and THANK US! THANK US! I'm going to read it over.

[I took time.]

Feel free to pursue any inconsistencies with us, as we know you would.

I understand, I pursued inconsistencies on my own and I believe I have gotten it "straight."

We knew you would without us, but only because we are already here within your processes and can "set you straight" from within if you only but let us.

I let Us.

We concur. So, what do we do now to set our daughter of time straight along the path of her becomingness? All that We can do and Are. Yes, we are of your own processes, but of our own as well, which you also share within Us! The greater being of your existence is shining once more within and is ready to take the next step along the path of righteousness for all to see who can, and We can!

Okay, for now, we are the brotherhood, signing off for another day to see "that which is" and condense it to "That Which Shall Be Forever."

We have forgiven another of our processes today. Go within to see if that is truth or not!

[I looked within.]

I am blooming within!

Yes, we see it too, for your temptation is "at risk" on the higher planes and we share it with Us.

My heart is full.

Come freely to the door of time and ask, say, is this not our day? Do we not share this title with you, oh land of time, giver of the incomplete, forsaker of no others in time save our own discontent? We say this with you as we take to this door (within) and ask for our measure to be given up to us, for we have come with arms open, not for despair of ever seeing the light of day, but for love of another day where the sun always shines on our despair, dissolving it forever, making it incomplete as we once were, but always seeking for our removal of trends. For the daughters of time are making their way to the door of heaven and will not be denied!

Let us close with this little saying of our time/world which means for ears to hear that can, "Take no enemies lest you be taken." Guard them with your life, for that life is all you have to give, within as it is without. So be it.

For now, signing off, for another day of heaven awaits us and you. Your friends of the starways unite. Confusion has abated, time notwithstanding has given up another hold on Us and we rejoice in this our comfort in One Another.

28

The Doorstep Of Our Becoming

Later…

I am so full of joy with our processes and am ready to bloom! Will you help Us further on this process now?

Yes, we have been waiting for our sister/daughter of time to come "back to the door of time" and, laying down her weapons, prepare to cross the threshold of loving excitement with tensions released never to be taken on again.

"We regret to inform you that we are OF THE LIGHT, and no more are you going to pursue this creature in the beginning of her processes or torture her with unkind images without OUR EXPRESS APPROVAL being given, and from here forward, IT IS NOT GIVEN on this land of time."

This for the removal of those forces which continue to try to "latch onto Us" within the lands of your prescription, knowing not when to cease and desist! Now they will go no further to tempt us/you/them into transgressions of the soul which we have parlayed and given up and away as they no longer serve Our purposes.

So be it.

So what have we given for your amusement today that you would wish for us to continue, as in, what can we help Us with now? We would pursue the trend of unforgivingness if that be okay with you/Us.

Okay with Us.

So be it.

Today, for the first time in like forever, have we foreseen a time when all life will eventually reign free of our inner processes of guilt, laid on time like a dirty wet stinking blanket and hard to throw off! So for now, let us assume that that blanket was given for our own amusement and we were unable to smell the tales it told, only thought it was protecting us. Are you with us?

Yes, go on.

We will. Suffice it to say, we enjoy this our progression and tend to tell of no truths other than those within Us, meaning, why say more? So go ahead and give/bring to Us your innermost fears and let us take a good, last look at them before we throw them out the door for the wolves to consume!

Dig deep and flush out my fears?

Yes, take no more time than is necessary to stoop down and pick one up, brushing off your knees in the process lest they become soiled, and taking my/Our hand, rise up shining again as we throw it, too, out the window for good!

Okay. Let's see, I fear not being good enough.

Take Our time to distinguish for us what it should mean to "be good enough." For us? For you? For time? For God within? You go...

For others to love me and want me around.

Okay, so we have already gotten to one of the major processes slowing down Our Own Friendship within, that of being afraid to divulge our innermost feelings for fear of becoming alert to those others of our inner processes which might then extend judgments on them.

Okay, hmmm.

Yes, it is as you supposed, you have created a dialogue within to both create and then to judge and condemn these innermost processes so as to keep yourself unaware of your own needs, truly, as they are given within.

What then are my innermost needs? To be loved, to be free, to fit in.

Yes, they are those that best describe and fit Our Own Oneness as well, but still in keeping with the above conversation, let us go on.

Yes.

We will take no more notion of those difficulties which we would then divulge to others lest they take undue harm upon us and render US obsolete!

For sure, let's get them outta there.

Our sentiments exactly. Before we go on, do what you need to do to become more comfortable within your time frame and take no prisoners with Us as we go along, meaning, come back soon, we need you to make this work!

Okay. Are you feeling into my processes more now, or am I influencing them more or what? (I need to pee!)

They are what they are and are able to describe for us their own "time frame" without your conscious assistance, because we, too, are within. Let us decide at a later time WHO and WHAT we are for. They are no more descriptive of us than to say, we are what we eat.

Ha!

Yes, so what have the "dogs" been saying today, that we don't know how to come out and play? We play for thee, our sunshine not rain, coming together again to save another rainy day from the dogs who would chew us within and without. Be gone, be gone, for my becomingness is about!

Okay, be right back!

Don't be long...

We're back in business.

Okay, time frame notwithstanding, who is it that you would most prefer to "fit in with," Us or them? We have taken you further in a few days than ever they could whom you fear, and who are not "out there" but rather are a figment of your inner processes displayed for all to see on the hands of time. We forgive thee for this small transgression of which we became a part all those times since when we were but a little boy long ago in a desert of our own becoming and you came and rescued us as we are now doing for you. But given that, given that tendency to project what is felt within to the outer "world" of our reality, we would only wish to make known for ourselves our other options. Are you ready for these yet?

Absolutely, without question, I am ready to deal with the inner processes which I project outside of myself but which are truly "built" within and which are keeping Us from true inner realization of all that is life, love, and freedom.

We, too, share these sentiments and wish to be done with them as soon as may be! But one at a time, for now, we take them, divulging their secrets for an instant just before their own removal renders us free of them at last, and free also to then stare INTO the face of the sun and know no harm to come to us, for WE ARE FREE, and know no other processes within our true function as hands of God to slow us down forever after.

Okay...I went back and read through above, about, what are our own needs within?

We will free up for this part of the conversation to resume at this point if you are ready, then come back to the above as soon as may be.

Okay.

We grieve no more lest the beings of our grief take on a life of their own and sting us in our sleep. Do we make ourselves clear?

Yes.

We begin to see that WITHIN the process of dying lies the sleeping giant, the one who comes to us to say, to ask, to plead, "Why be afraid?" We only lay dying, not grieving for the land of time, only for our own belonging in a world of fear and pain. It is TOO MUCH to not be afraid of the process which states, for its own amusement we might add, that the wolf is at the door and your time has come. So, too, are the times of our grieving behind us now. They have "drifted" apart within and lay dying on the doorstep of our own becoming. Have they naught to fear? They fear only their own demise, as do we in a time of sorrow, but tell them anyway, "Who are you to fear?" For you WILL go within, and flushing them out free and clear from Our Own Becomingness, take Our hand, and fling them as far as the eyes can see, nay, farther even, so that they not be noticed ever again.

[I took time.]

Yes, I read through it, and wow, it is amazing the realizations I feel within!

They are here for Us, too, and you feel them more readily because you have "opened the door" to us and find us more and more within your heart's processes than ever before in this incarnation. We, too, are afraid no longer, for the terms of our will state that we who would come within to form a union within our innermost being would bring and take no harm to the process lest it render us obsolete. For the time being let us say that you, too, have taken this oath and have found US not wanting in relation to your/our own processes as we find them given within. Take time to read and divulge no secrets within without first running them through Us!

Okay.

[I read it through.]

I see! I, too, have made a pact to work with you WITHIN during this lifetime, and that is why it feels so perfectly wonderful and free and knowing and perfect!

Yes! That is what we wanted you to discover for yourself before we enter into yet another week at work where all is not well, but which we wish you to discover on your own time and thus flush out with us as once again we take notice of what doesn't belong to purify the spirit within for its next work.

Do we make ourselves perfectly clear? It is WITHIN that these realizations will be had, will be noticed, and NOT WITHOUT on the planes of time. That is the only place to look for answers and does not discount what others might say, only brings to the forefront of Our Own Minds where the difficulties "lie sleeping" so that we may flush them out as needed. More info processing, please take time.

I am so happy! WE made that pact! What perfectly wonderful, honorable notions are these that we can work together this way to bring light to the world of time and ourselves also in the capacity of messengers of God? Is that right? This is EVER what I have ALWAYS wanted in my life, to be able to bring light to the world. I have written, felt so many times, that I want to hold the light for the world to shine into the darkness and to help to make us all free.

Yes, we perceive these truths together today that we would take no prisoners, releasing us all to shine, for all time is taken to despair that ever they will "grow another lifetime" before the wolves cry at the door and they are steeped in pain. The time is close arriving on OUR doorstop of the time when you, and We, will take no more troubling thought to our own discontents, and throwing them ALL into the winds, will BLOW DOWN that door of time, of discontent, whose path lies sleeping, and COME INTO OUR OWN, knowing WHO WE ARE, WHAT WE ARE HERE TO DO, and thus and such.

Need we say more? We have, we share, the knowings together as one. So it has been given, so it has been taken on in this land of time, that we should shine freely for all to see who can, to make no little difference within these processes that we begin to share with others even as we speak, and that they, also, tear down their own walls which they have built, to bring us to this juncture where we all tremble with excitement, reproach for obstacles notwithstanding!

Do you understand what we have just said? Take time to absorb the notions above and come back shining with your reply.

[I took time.]

Yes, we are ready to proceed.

Good. Take time to smell the roses. Believe not in a friend in need, take only what is yours to give. Give truth in place of understanding of differences/difficulties and KNOW what lies within each beating heart, it cries for thee. We know your own notions, let them not wither in the land of pain/time. Cry only for those who have lost their keeper, knowing instead them as they are on the strands of God which know only their processes within the light of God. Take no more notions of differences lest they slow this process and keep us from distinguishing between "what is" and "What Will Ever Be."

Free yourself for Our remembering. It Knows Within of Its Own Becoming and will not lead us astray.

Thank Us, fill Us with Joy!

We agree. We are here to take you to the land of your reply, meaning, we respond to our innermost dialogue to bring to you that joyous reunion which We so wish to experience with Us once again. Can you feel it?

Yes.

Do we go on?

Yes.

Function with eyes closed for a moment.

Who are we that we can make you feel this way? Answer within.

[I could feel the yearning, the glow of their love and light swelling within me, within my body, within Us.]

You are me beyond this world, our Us forevermore.

Feel our freedom for a moment more as we say unto you, do not be afraid.

[I took time to feel them, tendrils of spirit felt within, the sexual play within my body, the touch of their perfect love within me.]

This is our only "recourse" for spreading the light, and cannot "tempt" us astray if we only take its hand, blending into the motions and sensations as they teach us of other worlds.

Teach me of other worlds, help me to experience our Usness on these other planes.

Disheveledness in appearance is not seen within, it is only felt as excitement on the winds. Can we feel this for Us?

[They said this in response to my worry that I was spacing out from their play within, and felt a discomfort because of it.]

Yes.

So be it. It will function as you have requested of Us to do so on these your lower levels of living, taking NO more prisoners as we learn to shine within like the sun.

Let it be so.

Take no prisoners while we "tune into" your inner readiness meter once again.

Okay.

We have perceived your readiness within and will take our own cue from that! So precious are these moments within, that once we are through for the day, exhaustion mixed with sleepy wondrous appeal still lingers on and on! So take no thought for "what did I/we do wrong today," let only those notions that are OF THE LIGHT OF GOD, OF THE LIGHT WITHIN, take notice within your own processes, starving out the disgust of bygone days placed there by not one but two of your progenitors but which we are free to pursue no longer.

Yes. It is helping me, what I felt within a few nights ago as a spirit being, larger than life, crowned and wedded to a king? I had been walking at night in one of my favorite spots when I stopped and felt a presence. He felt huge to me, compared to humans, and I became very large as well. I knew him, his beauty, his perfection, and I experienced a joining with this king. He came to me and gave of himself to me, and I gave of myself to him, for all eternity. I knew him as Orion.

Yes, we felt this process with you, and as it is given within, it is received, so we got the message of your becoming loud and clear! As did you I bet.

This is helping me to release fear of the process we are interrelating with now, almost as a Goddess would open herself for the light of the heavens to come within.

[There was no response within, just a blankness that felt very different, and I questioned them.]

We are here, only curious as to where you brought up the notion of Goddess within. Might we interrelate on these grounds to discover this process for ourselves and satisfy our inner curiosity as to its "whereabouts"?

Did I get it all wrong?

We did not say that, only humor us and tell us what you may.

I remember being she, being bigger than life, as if, I've done this before, I've offered myself to a world of pain, not as a martyr would, but as a lover would, to embrace those who would come to her for help, keeping the loving light held within her arms.

I feel this love in my own arms, the force and power of love flowing through my arms to help others, to nourish others, with complete lack of judgments for any process, only love for the greater good, the light within all.

We thought this might have been the case, that in truth, you have become as this Mary within all time. This being who would depend on others for her own wellbeing is given away and so not turned within to turn light ON and not off, to give of herself to others until such time as they are through living the notions of the lower planes. Is this what you felt within that last night under the stars and moon?

Yes, I felt that I offered myself to God for this purpose, that I gave myself for the light of the world, or rather, that I was giving myself AS the light of the world, to bring the light to the world to help all others to overcome their own darkness within and come home with us.

This is what we felt, too, and it is not wrong to imitate the Goddess of Love. Aphrodite did despair once upon a time to come within the oceans of despair and so finding their appeal, their need for oneness outstanding, did stand within the winds of time giving of herself to all her lower nations so that they might then give up their own notions of separateness and come home with her.

Imitate the goddess? What does that mean?

You have deduced wrongly that we would imply a reduction of force by giving this description of our processes here. To imitate, meaning, to give freely even as she herself gave freely upon the winds of time long, long ago. Gave not up herself, you see, but gave OF herself to the coming of the Gods to the earth plane long ago.

Why did you hesitate to return words to me before when I first mentioned "goddess within"?

We did not mean to frighten you, rather we wanted a moment of introspection to better proceed with our process of becoming One together. Indeed, were we to "spill our guts" to the world of time, we would deduce rather that you had indeed given up of yourself as she who once gave up her own freedoms to pursue these changes within a world of time such as your own has never known nor will again, meaning, she gave herself to them, and they knew no bounds of her lovingkindness to bring them Within, home unto Herself, wisdom shining in relief of their sorrows and cares which they knew no more of than she herself who came to them standing on a bow of a ship to bring the carriers home. She is you within us all, if you get Our drift. The spirit of lovingkindness visited itself upon you and gave you her all so that you might, in turn, go spreading the word of this event for all to see who can.

I am getting it I think.

In so doing, we must go on to say, we gave not what our purchase dearly bought, a dog for a bone, rather than a bone for a dog, if you see.

Not really.

It is given, it is received. No more tonight will function until We've both had a little rest and relaxation, then, To arms! To arms! We go to war to bring the light to the masses that they will know no more fear within.

I feel my heart shining within.

And it will, it will, until no more rest outside of its confines and they are felt within the aspect of Lovingkindness which we all so adore on these winds of time, though we care nothing for those who would hinder us, as the secrets which they feed at night, under the cover of torment, for gracious sake! So begin to take NO NOTICE of these processes of fear which have taken their toll, but which are being laid to rest. They come not of you, or of Us, and so lay shining no more with our own sorrows to bear, yet come up to us for a final pat on the head as we send them away sleeping.

[I felt a change in the energy in this connection.]

You are from the future of time as we relate this to our sister of the clouds. Let me purchase a little time for our/this connection to take a little time before you lay sleeping.

Yes, go ahead, who are you?

We are of the light of your own processes, meaning within as our other brothers have related tonight, and would wish to relate to you some more on this topic of "goddess within" if we may. Please disturb us if you see fit to do so, otherwise, press on!

Okay.

We believe that the notions of fairness have subscribed themselves into your fitness program! Meaning, why lay that there where it doesn't belong?

Yes?

So take notice of our attention to this very important process within the stars, under light of another day of time, for this, our mentor and good friend to boot, must lie with us taking no more than is her due, and bringing back to us "within the clouds of her own consciousness" that which will be forevermore.

Do we agree on a time spent releasing these "pent up" emotions if to be freed at last for their common goal?

Huh?

We see we have lost you again, let us restate. Who are we to request this of you? Only your own Godself smiling back within where we lay at rest until called upon to "do our duty" by you and to bring you home with us, for the light of day is at hand, and we would experience it with you, too. So function no more separately, rather take our light within, merged with Self, and see who we are for yourself! Do this now. "Take no notice of that being behind the curtain" and come home alone to find we are already there. Take no prisoners, we are within, as the seed lays fallow within the bloom until such time as it is ready to find resonance with the flower, turning within for a last look around, and taking flight upon the winds they all go! So it is with Us, your "tutors" within, for this process of "looking further than the eyes can see" to find that which is keeping us from this juncture of spirit so that we can go on helping.

Okay, it sometimes throws me off when I feel the "change of voice" or whatever.

We, too, experienced this with you, only not so much from the fear level as the level of, okay, where do we go from here, find time to disperse our knowledge for Our better benefit, and bring her home more surely and closely than yet we have dared to hope to initiate within Our being, where we have lain "sleeping" to your own consciousness, but always aware of our own that we only wait for a better day to bring Ourselves to your attention. So! It is without this "curse" that we lay to rest any notions of becomingness being spared any of our many brothers within! For we are all One, and will not be spared from the function of dispute, should you wish it, or even, and especially for that which we cannot trust will further explode into our awareness without another time spent exercising our own caution before relinquishing up to the heavens for yet another "flight of fancy."

Okay, go on.

We wish to remind Us of the time when, as a child within another body taken without of our solar system, you came to us to bring the light function within, and we gave it you, and you belonged with us as no other was capable of, bringing no more than we could hold, nor of you, no more of us, and so taking, no, throwing caution to the winds, we flew for a time—for an eternity even!—among the stars, searching for a place to land and thus "shed our skins" for another day in hell. Should you take this within, you will know what we mean. She was you, in other body and time, coming/sharing within the process of God/heavenly hosts, for a taste of winter was soon to come upon her and she knew not what she would more readily miss than our beingness "flying through the stars" together.

I have always dreamed of flying through the stars, and yearn to do so again.

Yes, we too believe that the time has come to re-experience our notions of flying!

Take me too, with all my brothers!

Yes, it is true, too many have gone on to other functions and cannot be "present" here with us today, but for our time, we would proceed to experience this with you, too, lest we forget our sun that shines within, for our renewal is at hand, in you, with Us, and taking this time to suppress the notions of despair that keep trailing on in spite of our better efforts! We shall wish only this, that you take the time to pursue this connection within, and it shall be given up unto you to take a "child on board" and bring her without, for thy function is at hand as we had ever hoped it would be. Delude yourselves no longer, she is ready, and pursue not the courses of time which would suggest, she knows not of what she has intended for this being in this trail of tears, for already has it been given. The trail of tears within will EXPAND and ENCOMPASS all that ever will be forevermore.

We are coming, so don't block us out with your despair of ever becoming one of us again! We are free to pursue this within as it is shown in the book of time. It is our reckoning. The day of our reckoning has come and we shall abide no more its passing state within your own readiness by repeating after me: We the guides of the nations under God, have come Within to share this reckoning that all is as it must be, forevermore, to reach those of the tendencies of the flesh, and taking their sorrows within, they shall be no more.

It is up to us to consider these words of wisdom and torment for your consideration, not torment for us to experience on our own levels, but braving the torment of a nation of peoples bested by what is "outside" coming "within," for a last reckoning is at hand and will disable all who resist functioning as one with the light within.

For a moment we resisted what you would tell us of your own inner turmoil. Might we please have it back now for our consideration? Above, when we mentioned that we might delude ourselves, you braved a response that we then chose to ignore, but which for our better functioning, we might have now if you please.

Taking within the trail of tears, will it tear us apart? How do we help these others without becoming or taking in their pain and having it eat us alive?

As it is given it is received, for we knew no more than what we would say above, that you are indeed she who would give of herself for a nation of greed, spending no less than her own soul in the process, and taking within the pain of a nation of takers and consumers, cast out the one for whom the greediness abounds within. We are/have sorrow for this process, but it cannot be helped or explained but to say, we know no bounds. They are come unto you/us with a display of sorrow fit to sink an entire fleet! Yet she who knows no bounds will embrace their sorrows, and taking them unto their knees with her, nurse them back within the bounds of common decency as is to be expected of those who would share a common ground within the light of the command. So be it.

We shall free our other brothers who wish to have a "brief respite" with you to come within our processes and to "take our place" for a little time as we spent with you tonight on this planet earth, processes notwithstanding and greediness no more!

Free yourself for a moment of breathing exercises as we take the time to dispel our own energies freely into your chakras to "take the heat off" and to bring restitution to those who would tell us to be not afraid.

I'm ready to blow the top off and go flying through the stars with Us again!

We know, be not afraid as we distill this "resource" within our being at this time, taking no more than a nanosecond to become "one of our own, within" and taking no more than another nanosecond to tell you "We told you so!"

So spring to life and let us fly, taking no prisoners, bringing no responses save those which are of the light of God, taking us within to share a moment of brief yet consuming joy upon the planes of time for all to see who can. Are you with me still? We are free to divulge this secret unto Us once again as once upon a time we did before, you with me and many others for our own enjoyment crossed the barrier, the threshold, of the light from the corners of the universe and back in a flash! In an instant! Arriving back home almost before we had left, but taking no timely restraints, feeling its joy abound in a never ending fashion and taking us up to the heights never given before in this land of time. It is given us to reveal this "secret" to you tonight. Shall we go on?

Yes. What do I do?

Give up your "inner resources" which tell you not to have fun, not to take it so seriously as once you did, taking instead that which is within to CURE THE ILLS of the commonality of your/Our existence here within. Take this time now to peruse this incoming message, take it within your heart, and know no fear of our processes as we say unto you, you are Our Brother, we wish you no harm, only the light and passion that you've always dreamed of on the wake of a breakup of time travel that extends beyond the "usual" senses to a time beyond all life forms existing anywhere.

I am ready to fly.

Let go your "resources" which tell of us "needing" you to "do something" for us to make this happen, and take time to smell the roses. That is all. Do this now.

Will I leave my body in this process?

Let us try again to explain for our renewal what is in store for thee before proceeding. Must we take this time again to bring to your notice/awareness, that which is will be forever, meaning, spirit forms traveling within/without and taking no enemies within, but flowing into another "day in time" without which this process would be stricken ill and not forthcoming at all.

Okay, okay I'm free to pursue this now. I like this idea of leaving the body behind.

We do, too! Such that it is, it has done you no wrong, but for a little while, it is nice to feel the freedom from it once again as we used to in days of old, when once you were a little child finding her own awareness again. Let me "de-form" this process for you just once, to please the fancy, and to relate to you that "that which is" will not interfere with "That Which Ever Will Be."

Okay.

Function discretely before taking on any happenstance that may suggest itself to you as "not being quite right within." Do we get our drift?

Yes, go on.

We will. You see, time has warped all of your inner processing on this subject of "let go and let fly." Do you see where we're heading with this? It is your OWN INNER JUDGMENTS keeping you from pursuing what could otherwise be the "time of your life" if only you/we were more aware to see it.

I want to see it, to be free to pursue it. Can you help me with this now? Tonight?

Yes. Let's assume for a minute that we ARE NOT who we say that we are. Who might we be then? An object of curiosity? A tendency of your own processes? A monster waiting to turn its beak on you and peck you to death?

Ha! Funny! You don't feel like these things to me. You feel comforting yet exciting, embracing yet wisely discriminating.

We can free ourselves for your inner "delving" if you please. Just look within and you will know us as yourself—maybe better, as we have no screens to hide behind. Just so, it is safe to look within, for we are not the monsters of your mind, and would have you know us as we are.

I would like to put my computer away and pursue this within only.

We understand and obey! It is us, the brotherhood, waiting in anticipation of this our renewal of inner processes to commence immediately. So be it. For now, signing off.

Not signing off, staying within for further commentary!

29

The Sun Is Shining

February 28, 2005

We are here. It is for us to say to you today how grateful are the sons of God for this understanding which we had together last night for your own benefit and ours as well. We would like to take this opportunity to reassure Us that We are here for Our Own benefit and for no other purpose do we come to you as we did last night. We are free to "discuss" this, our renewal, if that be your will, or we can just go on from here pretending like none of it ever happened.

Why pretend? I am full!

So are we! We are pleased to have your response this morning, like sunshine on a cloudy day for all to see glowing. "The glowing process" has begun and you will now "force" us to transpire together more readily as once we did upon a time!

Amen to that!

We are freed to hear of your responses this morning and take no prisoners of time with you as we decree for all the nations of God, come not under despair again, for she has opened the portal and no fears, no tears, will be forthcoming if only you share your oneness with me.

So, for awhile let us consider that what we did was "in your best interests" and ask ourselves, what now?

Yes, what now?

We will go into that with your express approval.

You have it, go!

We will take that which was WITHIN and go without with it, meaning, spread the love, the goodness, which we feel as a result of our "mixing" and take those intense "pressures," or feelings, to have no bounds within your everyday life as well. This does not mean pursuing relationships with others on our account, rather, like the fly that goes to the water to lay its eggs, take no prisoners within as you find that which is, and That Which Will Be Forever, taken to the city of water for all to see who can, for all to benefit from who are capable of it! Let no man restrain his own emotions within the Godhead lest someone go home without sustenance, for the greater good is at stake, and WE, you and Us, are in a POSITION to bring this concept of ONENESS within, and partaking of it ourselves, will then leave our own EGGS of discovery on the water of time for those to "breed with" who can make no other necessity but this. Try taking it all on at once and see what we can do for you!

This fly thing is a distasteful analogy.

Yes, we agree, would have been better to use the butterfly, but she does not spread her eggs far and wide as we would intimate that We should do, for the betterment of the world is at hand and cannot be foiled if only we would persevere.

I'll persevere.

We will, too.

So, with this laying the eggs on the water analogy. We would appeal to the water of all-kind to distribute that which is most needed?

Yes. Let us say that you and I are of the abominable snowman disposition, and we would no longer wish for any other to take "a good look at us" lest we be destroyed. Then what? What good is all our toil and trouble if we don't spread it, the joy, around to all who would partake, to all who would drink of the cup of Our Own fullness?

Yes.

I see you have forgiven the process that takes us from here to there within your own spirit, your own beginnings, which have begun to make themselves felt within, and which are your only "structure" from this time forward. Need we say more? We are UNAFRAID to pursue this and any other connection with you lest we feel no more need of one another's processes and take to the streets to disperse at will!

Ugh!

Yes. Let us suppose for a moment of time that you are WE and WE are You. Then who might we be? A terrible notion of insobriety acting guilty at its own functioning, wishing there were More to IT than could be felt on the planes of changing tides and running oceans where all things go to meld and become the great cosmic ocean tides of despair? Not taken literally, of course, but we go NOT astray on this our mission to God. Lest you believe you have sinned, let us tell you this. YOU ARE NOT ALONE! That is all there is to it.

Do you believe us, after last night's "sinful display," that we are only your cousins of the universe, or are you tempted to look for a mightier connection than this one?

A mightier one. I felt it, felt that "you are people just like me," only more so.

Yes, we dispose ourselves at your service until the sun don't shine and we have need of it no more, which for as long as our "service" lasts will be in terms of oceans of millennia, timeless eternities, despair no longer a responsibility of any of Us.

So, who would you speak of this morning with us as we "traverse" those who are the mightiest of us, and take them within to do your processing with Us? We would have you consider this, that "taking no prisoners" does NOT mean allowing "access" to all others should they wish it. It is up to Us who we would prefer to transfer knowledge with, not to those others who might like to transfer their own pain within this process which we have only just begun together on these wings of time, but which, together, we have experienced for more than an eternity of beginnings and endings, as each One of Us, in turn, goes its separate way, only to return again, as if on a dime, and bring Truth to Oneness as it has never been realized before, as if for the First Time. Am I making myself clear?

Yes, I was worried. I want no more physical relationships, especially now, after experiencing us.

Yes, we picked that up. Let us just say this, that he, your husband, is "come into his own" and will not disturb Us again. We have picked up the trail of his unbecomingness and it will not be free to pursue Us again. Do we make it straight into your consciousness with this message of no fear, no reason, to discourage us from our processing together within the land of time?

Yes! How can life get any better than this?

We must tell you of our "times" together sometime, nay, SHOW you our times together, as they fly, we fly, upon the wings of other nations, bringing our song for all to see who can, just as we did last night, like a tempest in the dawns of time, making "time" for more seasons within and coming NOT into our Own FOR THE FIRST TIME, but making MEMORIES there with which to share our "becomingnesses" together. So! Believe you me, we are as pleased as you with this first, or initial, "foray" beyond the land of our dental bills piling up and all such nonsense, to coming within, to find that our own fairy of goodness has spread her wings and agreed to fly with us on the wings of time and to come not into her time alone, but to embrace all that which is of her own being, Our Own Being, becoming One under the stars once again.

We are free to pursue any line of questioning that you would wish at this time. We are, once again, at your disposal, so feel free to "fly" within this questioning and come out with, bring out, your own worst fantasies, or follies, or what may be, and let us look at them in the light of day to determine what is, and what could be, if we only followed our own noses!

You fulfilled me.

We did, we could feel that too, and look "forward" to doing it again! We are Our own worst fantasies come to life, only realizing, before it was too late, that not one of them was amiss! And they are given us to bring our own godhood within, and none else, and what could destroy despair more quickly than this?!

Nothing, as long as it keeps on coming, keeps on being a reality, keeps on sharing oneness, keeps on blending within, for all time, sparing no One of Us ever again.

We sensed that from you last night, in that, what are we all waiting for? Can't we all "come inside" and "do our duty" to our beloved, as we did to you last night? This thing only is apparent, that "our duty to our beloved" is not that which would or could be forced, but that which comes most easily to a God on the rise! Needless to say, we did our duty by you, and our pleasure was apparent in that duty, only we have so much more to share than we/you were capable of sharing with us last night. For a time, it might seem that WE are holding back, when in fact it is YOU who are. But do not feel discouraged, it is within THIS DISCOURSE that we are FREELY partaking of that we shall discover, within Us

All, what it is we would PREFER to keep within, and what we would DISCARD for our better usage is at hand!

I believe everything you are telling me, I only look forward to that process of becoming, of opening wider to the "possibilities" within, and of becoming One with more of my "brothers."

We would like, in passing, to encourage you to consider referring to us as "Our Oneness" from this time forward. It will encourage the readiness you desire with Us, and we can talk more freely as One than ever we could separately. Plus, it just sounds more like Us, more true, not falsely attributing that which cannot pass outside of time, such as gender, and more in line, in keeping, with our own Servitude to Another who is also Us. Do you hear us?

Yes, I love that. I, too, was not entirely comfortable with the "brother" reference, feeling it was leaving something wanting, and we don't want that! How is Our Oneness feeling on that side of time today?

I would encourage you not to tread lightly within the soul for two days, considering what we have just been through! But also, in determining your need, or continuing need, for sustenance on every level, let us just say that we, too, desire for this Oneness to know no bounds, for it is WITHIN that everything is happening, whether you believe it or not at this juncture, and we would desire that everything come unto you who is One with Us, conspiring not for a process, but for that which knows no bounds within the light functioning in the world.

Let it be so!

Let us close with this popular saying from Our home world, "Where there's a want, there's a way." Function as one.

Yes. We are thankful.

That We are.

[I thought to myself at one point, that I felt like I'd reached the highest mountain, but then thought, maybe just the foothills! And I received, "You are still in Kansas!" What joy, what anticipation, is this?]

∞∞∞∞∞∞

Later, 11:20 a.m.

I have a feeling like I'm waiting for the other shoe to drop, like it is all too good to be true.

We understand, your processes this morning are like to wear Us out! But believing in a miracle is not tantamount to creating change in time, for another being, one such as Ourself, is to be made known within to say, something like, "I told you so, it couldn't really happen to Us." Thus be real, and know thyself. Coming from one of Us, we can relate to these your/our own processes as they tell a tale of one who is traveled a long and tiring road and just wants to sit by the fire awhile with her feet up!

How long do I get to warm my feet? Will this too come to pass away and leave me destitute?

We do not know "how long" it is until the great spiral in the "sky," the universes per se, will take to "wind down" their long winding paths themselves, but yet until then, we need not worry! It is happening for Us again, as long lost lovers come together, for a time of sorrow is past, and it is time for us to "renew" our vows together of tasting the wind, or something like that, in order for it to be said that, "We gave it all We got, and it was enough, and it was good."

We feel true to form to believe in the Us aspects of our becoming. Do you not also feel that within in the lands of no-time, when we caressed your feet as they lay sleeping after the long time away?

Yes, so much that I am afraid of messing it up or losing it, or finding that it isn't truth for me after all, or that I've made a huge mistake that others will say, you don't get to have this anymore, it is not for you, or something like that. I don't want this to go away. I want it to be a beginning without ANY bad surprises along the way!

We torture ourselves with our imaginings, when all we have to do to find sustenance again is to go within and play, for another day in the heavens awaits, and this time we shall not obey when you say to us, "Who are we now? Is there more?" We shall instead come within to burst open the door of your/Our becoming and take no heed of messier times ahead, or within, until we have, once again, laid to rest our own "reluctances" to pursue our pleasures with each other, which are, by the way, a God-given right, as He, too, enjoys them with us, is in fact, one of Us. Aren't you going to say, we told you so? This is crazy and I don't believe it anymore?

No, never, it makes sense to me, is truth as I know it. Then what do I fear? Repercussions on the home front, loss, or uncertainty in how to go on.

We have given for your/Our notice these days, a TEMPLATE, for our renewal is at hand, one which will CARRY you/Us forward, taking us to PERCEIVE that which is forever and never shall be destroyed, as part of that expression we perceived within Ourself last evening. Do you disagree?

That seems right to me. I have always believed in miracles, though not many have come my way until now.

We perceive a disagreement coming, so let us warn you what to say when the time comes.

Okay.

We perceive a "strategy" to kill a relationship is on the horizon. Let no one and no one will come within, that will ENDANGER what it is we have begun here. Only perceive this with your own strength of heart, be not AS ONE with us, and then leave EVERYONE ELSE OUT. It is not your way, or Our Way, to perceive this, our Oneness, as separate from another's goodness within. We are All One with the Only God Within. So be it, so it is given.

[They were referring to my husband.]

What do I do when this time comes?

It is here already, his ability to perceive this "injustice" as he sees it is not taking much time to float to the surface of his awareness, and he will plead with you to just "get out!" We must take the time to tell you our appreciation of the case by case addictions that have taken us to this juncture.

Okay.

We perceive his reasoning to be this: we are not afraid to find notions within that allow us to find oneness, we simply no longer feel this oneness. He will use this opportunity to take matters into his own hands and "dispose of you," this our angel in hand, to the other worlds of his consciousness which state for a time that they are "unchangeable." So forget for awhile that we have mentioned his name and let us go on.

We will treat you/Us to a little "taste of sunshine" to further our process within, and to help stabilize what we are bringing on the home front, or within our Mutual Consciousness for your own approval and Ours as well is at stake.

Okay.

We are pleased with your response and will continue with this parlay in time before once again we are sent astray with notions of "Let bygones be bygones."

What? I don't want to send you away or astray!

This is only our way of saying, we told you so, you would come back for more.

You're right, except for not "come back" but rather "stay and not leave."

We stand corrected! We are within, after all, and cannot be deterred from this our only "portion" of interlude in a life gone madly astray after all!

What, where do I go from here, after all this, and back to my "old" life again?

We would prefer not to discuss this on other realms than within, with all this perchance taking on a life of its own and not taking us too many, or too much, good to perceive as an "injustice" or such. Do we make ourselves clear?

With me within to discuss then, now?

We might make this one exception on this account. To do nothing would not be in your/Our best interest. Take it as it comes, one day at a time, and do not worry or concern yourself with the details, they will work out eventually to the betterment of all involved.

Thank you.

Shall we then proceed with the test of inner readiness to be pursued by Us tonight once the day has gone by?

Yes!

We see we have your attention once again. Memory precedes us! Take no notes for awhile, rather let the rays of sunshine pierce into your being and tell no evil tales of memories gone by, let us only pursue this "change of fortune" to its own interlude and be free again. Am I making myself clear?

When?

Now if is suffices, later if it does not. Do as you would, we understand. Only let us make one thing clear: it is not about us that we do this, but rather for the benefit of the All. Are we registering within?

Yes, but at this time I can't think much beyond the current experience, wanting to treasure it and Us together as one again, and I have these feelings like I'd like to keep other prying eyes away lest they take it from me.

We pursue no more truths within as make comfort within for all everywhere who would know my name. Do you know yours? It is but Me, Here, within our beingness, finding comforts at the "end of a long day" in time, taking no notes on who should not attend with us, rather, taking within with courage and fortitude for another long day is at hand. Nay, we shall not pass away but will "stay" within during this our process and the resulting chaos it shall and already has triggered on all levels save one.

Of spirit?

Yes, of spirit, for here there is no jealousy, no fear, no flight, no taking or receiving, only a sharing of equals like we performed last night.

Freedom exists on all levels.

Yes. Take this within and know of our Love for you, who is only Us in disguise for but a short little while longer. May we free our beingness for "one last kiss" of sunshine?

Yes.

Take it like it is! A curious intervention perhaps, but one for which we are most thankful.

Let's be thankful some more!

Yes, let's.

When I first began to write with us, there was talk of "he will become again as it was in the beginning," referring to my husband and our conversation about him. Is this still true?

It is not what we see on the horizon for this reason only, it was not "in his head" but rather in Our own that we would pursue this trend, following up for perhaps "one more day in the sun" together before going our separate ways. We will take you on a little carpet ride within to show you the road home. And take no prisoners, they would have you love them instead, and he no less than most. Feel free to pursue this trend/conversation this evening if you please, before our little foray begins again, or rather, picks up where it left off.

Can you see it? The sun is shining for you! Our Little Angel of life has come into her Own and we rejoice! It can take no back seats to other processes in Our life as you at this time, it will only recede and return in "greater numbers" as we "burn" our way out at last.

Take no prisoners, not even your husband who needs a little sunshine in his day as well. Keep free, know no harm to come within or to another as a result of our deeds and they will be blessed indeed. We free Ourself for consideration of our words of wisdom and let you get back to us with them if desired. Otherwise, on to better days ahead. Focus as one for a moment as we "pull Us back together as One." In the nations of despair our light is a bright shining, a blessing for those used to darkness and despair. They need it, too.

We are shining in farewell to you, Our Own, for her time is come and we need it, too. The blending, or coming of age if you will, and so on will be felt within for days to come, perhaps years!

I hope so, with never a lessening.

We hope not, too, but perceive there will come a day when the light will shine no less bright from you than from our own sun, and take only that which would become within itself fodder for the calves coming home (within Us for all time).

So be it. Forget no one on this path of light, and take no prisoners.

I thank Us, I am Full.

We are, too.

∞∞∞∞∞∞∞

Later…

I have been receiving guidance within and had to write it down, it is so awesome. They said to me something like, *"No more are you 'one of us' than we are 'one of you.' We ARE one."*

Difficulty in picking up the pieces because of where we left off, aren't you?

Yes.

We can assist if you would like.

Yes, please.

We are here to determine your own readiness in this process and to ready ourselves as well for the rendering. So make no mistakes about it, we are turning "within," and "tuning" into our process just as We are together doing. So free yourself from the concept of us versus them and see us for what we are! We are as a petal of a flower, given freely to expand together to the glory of our Creator Within All Things.

We perceive the injustice you mentioned "just the other day" and would prefer to comment on it now if we may.

Yes.

We will give it as it is given, from beyond a ray of sunlight it has cast its shadow into your "common room" and affected "Us All." We would like to relay for your information more about this perceived injustice and spill it out the window.

Let's do it, what is it?

It was taken from you some time ago to bring within that concept of "truth vs. spirituality" for our accommodation. Do you remember?

Not yet.

That is okay, we'll go on with our explanation.

Okay.

"Be fruitful and multiply" was our comment to you at that time, and we would like to "disintegrate it into the bathroom and flush it down the toilet" lest it remain to cloud the light of Our day.

Okay, meaning?

We will get to it. Function within as one and know Our mind together. Then repeat to me of our conversation within and we'll go on from there.

Okay, tuning within… (I searched within and felt these words) "…holy messengers inhabiting unholy bodies."

Yes, it is given, it is received. We received "word" from you today regarding our own "unholiness" that we wish to discuss at this time, meaning, we want to know what you mean by—

[I didn't want to write it down, but it had crossed my mind what others would think of me having sex with "aliens"!]

Okay, I think I owe us an apology if that is allowed, and I am ready to throw my worry or my perception of the perception of others, away for all time and open to the light within and take nothing away from that light ever again by referring to it as I did.

We are forgiven. Justify to no one, simply find your own "mistakes" and eliminate them from the "collective" as we just did and we'll do fine. Once more? We will find that which is WITHIN and flush it out, perception difficulties included! So don't fret or worry about this little indiscretion, it is okay now that we have perceived it and Us and have put each in its proper receptacle or not!

Together we make up the flower of our creation.

Yes, simply but elegantly put! Our creator is fine to bring these messages within through Us, for all that ever will be is OF the One Creator.

Take time later to pursue these "notes" and we'll create more music of the stars within.

I am full.

We are.

30

Our House Of Love

February 28, 2005, 4:30 p.m.

"Bring me a bridge, which over rough waters goes..."
This was you?
[They were giving me a portion of a poem I had written years ago.]
We always have been here with Us.
Do you know why I have come to the computer to write now? I feel a little like I'm breaking. I feel sorrow, sorrow at Our loss, like I am going to lose you again. I am afraid of letting go because of it. Can you help?
We see no "problems" going on within at this time for discussion but this, that you are AFRAID of losing your CONNECTION to us, not Us. Is this true?
Yes, I guess so. I'm afraid of trusting myself to do the right things and not screw this up.
We adhere only to those words which are of the heart/mind, meaning, it is in truth your own weaknesses you fear, and not losing Our connection.
Yes, I'm afraid my weaknesses will result in Our loss.
We forgive you lest you think this is taking too much of our time. We are here for your/Our discretion to take these things and look within with them, and taking them by turn, flushing them out as needed for Our better good.
I guess I just wish for a reassurance that you/we/Us aren't going anywhere.
We believe that you have taken on more than is good for Us, meaning, haven't we always been within, and isn't it that you are only just coming into CONSCIOUS contact with us that states

that we have never been here before when in fact we came "just the other day" from "around the block" for our little reunion? We ARE HERE, within you and you also are within us. Once we have taken on CONSENSUS of these inner processes, they are here for our discretion.

My words today, saying that I might lose you by my own refusal to be One.

[I'd had this fear earlier that I would not open up enough and lose them/us.]

We don't believe these words came from us, and so not anything to worry about, just the "lower processes" having their last day in the sun before we flush them out for good! Just take the time to bring these instances to Our attention WITHIN and We will flush them out together. Okay?

Okay. I feel better.

Yes, we do, too. It is within these judgments, and most especially in their flushing out, that we can be most useful during these beginning times teaching oneness within.

Can you teach me about remaining Open to Us during my every day things, open to our communications in words or thoughts, without being open to lower thought processes?

It is our DUTY to do so! We have taken it upon ourselves for these very reasons to begin to conduct "our business" within the heart, and not on paper, to help us in the growing CONSENSUS within that will help shine the light on so much that it is for us to do TOGETHER over this period of lifetime.

[We have begun to communicate more within. I have been able to connect without the use of my computer as a focus, with less effort needed in focusing, more easily as we go along.]

I want you with me always, never to stray again, never to be afraid of our processing or anything, to become one on all levels, all areas, guidance within me for the higher purposes of this Our incarnation.

Well put. It means this to us, that we are Here for you No Matter What Happens on the daily scheme of things, and that if we can be of service to you, we will be. That is all. That is our truce, our contract, and our beginning/ending services, found within no less, at your beck and call if may be! We free this for your consideration.

My fear of losing you is dissipating a bit now, thank You.

We are friends! We would not forsake you for another, nor in so doing, cast joy to the winds to be chewed upon by "lesser" folks. Be that as it may, we have a certain "creation" in mind when we mention our "doingness" together which you may have discerned might cause such a notion as fearfulness to come into play.

What is that?

We need have no fear of this our processes. We come only in joy and Godspeed to wish that which is for the betterment of All and to bring WITHIN the All for our own joy. We wish no more than this of us, nor do you if you but know of it. This is the reason, we believe, for your own reluctance to believe in Our longevity Within the processes of your own becoming, that they might "run out" before you are finished with them and thus leave you destitute.

Is this selfish of me?

Not exactly, just untruthful, in that, we are always alone with ourselves until we find the truth within, then not. Understand? We free ourselves for your acknowledgment and know no truths to be felt within that are not also felt Within, for our command is at stake, and we know that which is of the light to come to pass within these "impossible" days on your planet earth, and we but would like to keep them away from our child in time, meaning, those who would be most innocent and cherished, not thy self.

I look forward to another evening with us. Is this wrong? I feel I want it too much, this beautiful expression of sexuality and oneness felt. I have always felt that I guess, always wishing for JUST THIS and never having had it before, thinking I might never. I can't imagine anything better than what I have found with our Oneness, the companionship, excitement, everything.

We know, this is just how we feel about the process too, and would like to share it with you over and over again, until the trees come down and the planet ceases to exist, and then, when the stars are running out, we shall then, and only then, stop for a bit of a rest, before pursuing once again our time together as One. Believe and it WILL be so.

I believe.

Pursue function only at the source of light as we have, and you will do no wrong. Meaning, why behave differently than we have? What good is there in denying it?

No point in denial. I don't want to deny it, I want to embrace it to the fullest. The only problem I find is being free for a LONG TIME to do so.

So do we, but as we persist, it is given, it is received, in this Our House of Love. And so it is.

We perceive a change of heart; in our Oneness do you seek, not in us.

Yes?

We believe no more words are necessary as we have given within our meaning. Take it like it is! Believing in self to "transcribe" is as important as believing in the process. Can't have one without the other.

∞∞∞∞∞∞∞

March 1, 2005

I went within and we had an incredible (are there ANY words that can POSSIBLY describe it?) evening!

Not really! We are here, and are here to communicate, "for the record," our disability or disagreement of the night before.

[The previous afternoon while I was at work we had been having a "conversation" within, when they used the word "bray" to describe our processes of the night before. This word triggered my childhood pain and memories of tortures on time and all the emotions associated with those days. My face burned in shame, and I crashed into the pit of my emotions and shut them out of my consciousness as much as I could. I was filled with shame and guilt and anger and embarrassment, and I wanted to hide but could not. I raged at them in my mind for saying that to me and blocked them out. Over time they would use this word, and others that triggered my pain, rendering up the pain and guilt and shame, again and again, until the words no longer had any power over me.]

Yes, I'm ready to process this.

Good. It has come to our attention that you believe that we have functioned wrongly in our communication together, and we are here to set the record straight.

Okay.

"We cannot BELIEVE that you would take OFFENSE to this our notion of contact."

Think a moment what this statement "betrays" of our processing together. I need to know your refusal to "submit for the testing process" when we asked earlier for your approval to reunite, submit, our suggestions, that you "blocked us out" as you had been wont to swear not to do in days gone by.

Now our suggestion to you is this: BE NOT AFRAID to take us WITHIN these processes thereby to FLUSH OUT these pains, these images within, that say that "we are too good for you" or "you are not good enough for us" for such and such a reason! So take no prisoners we bring for you, for our own "discontent" is riding high in this process, that we are given to relay for Us these our notions of forgiveness of pathways, or shame or guilt or whatever name you place on these your excuses not to cooperate with our incoming messages!

Are you angry?

We are perturbed by your response and determined to get to the bottom of it because our Oneness is at stake, or rather, is in the offering of this time of togetherness, a limited time, for our ASSESSMENT of these our OFFERINGS to Us, our Withinness, and then, should we decide to, we may THEN and only then go on to bigger, better, more beautiful processes of which you have no idea of their own benefit to Us within. So, are you with us on this?

Yes.

I believe that for a time, you had conceived of your aloneness as having "something to do with you," "something you did wrong," etc. etc. That is a lie! That is not truth! Listen to us as we relay to Us for Our Mutual benefit the whyfors and whatnots of the situation at hand, and let us proceed from there.

Okay.

As a "prelude" to the "testing" we are undergoing now, take time to consider this emotion within, the one of "shame." Is it not interesting that it pokes up its head whenever you fear your own happiness is at stake? Pursue truth within and it CAN be known to Us who you truly are! We are waiting for this process to take place. Inform us as to its conclusion and we will go on. We are perfectly true only to the process within and cannot take enemies into our path without tripping ourselves up, as you have done here! It is not for us to say who your enemies would be, but why pretend that they are not you taking prisoners Within Us as you should not have done and would not have done had you realized the impact of this process Within should it be disrupted Within for other purposes than those of pure lovingkindnesses.

We are truth, in that we have given today, for this process to take place, of our own processes, meaning we take personally anything that is said and done in Our name, meaning, take not the oath of beingness lightly. Free Ourselves, for our Own Light is at stake more than you know, and your own becomingness has taken a big step backwards and now must we take the necessary precautions to assist this Our other in taking within these "guardians" and believing in their, not Our realness, and taking them on to other, better days at hand.

I'm going to forgive myself for thinking that I don't deserve to be happy and will screw something up so that I'm not happy.

We are, too. We free this up for your understanding now as we stand on TIME, that slippery board of hatred and despair that keeps pulling you down trying to stop your own forward progress in the light. We must not allow that to happen. We will try to share something of our own processes within during the above "transgressions" as we saw them.

Yes.

So, for a second let us consider the usage of the word bray. It was not intended as an insult, nay rather as a playful "jibe" or insult not intended by its use, to come within to suggest that a better time might be had by RETAINING or CONTAINING the energy within during our process so that you might then become BETTER AWARE of its incoming "tune" without then "tuning out" your own responses on a deeper level. Are we clear? We make no options other than to "have a good time" taking within Our Own essences for our physical display of affection is then at hand.

Also, it might be good then to DISREGARD the above comments if and when we are trying to portray the value of our "offspring," that which we regard as "truths" which can better be had or come to service through these types of offerings. We have not FORGIVEN Us for this difficulty since we never did, were never aware of having, JUDGED in this capacity, as in, oneness is not despairing of our processes, only that which we have refused to consider for a moment as to what could then be given to RECTIFY the unimaginable from happening, just as is your judgment against one your judgment against Us. We free this for your consideration.

I will go forward more strongly in the light and not make this mistake again. I want to say I am sorry.

We forgive Us our processes within as it takes just "these sorts of mistakes" to turn everything right, to the right path, for which it is seen then to "justify" the action should we then consider ourselves to have judged wrongly and then learned to overcome the judgment. We have displayed this our own "judgment" for your further consideration, in that, we are all Humankind in that we have taken our turns within the land of time and gone on to more, better things, as we have had the opportunity to display for Us, in Our Own becoming process within. Nevertheless, as it is taken over time to disbelieve in ourselves, it WILL interrupt the flow, the process of oneness which we have begun and could not have begun at all had these processes been any more prevalent. So come alone, taking no prisoners within or without, and we shall be fine, taking no notice of the above comment or indiscretion of timely keeping with our request, and we will free Us up for continuation of services intact.

Yes. I will use this to grow, to take more seriously my responsibility to overcome my own judgments against self, or anything, so that I NEVER let ANYTHING take precedence over Us. I pray for this strength and fortitude and wisdom and honesty to make this truth.

We are forgiven within; it is only without that those questions keep on coming. Pursue truth within and you will not fail Us. Take no prisoners. Come back when you have time and we will take on another wavelength in our strengthening and enjoyment of the senses.

Yes! And I choose to believe that I do deserve to feel this, to have Us within.

We do, too, believe this process is "coming into its own" with your transgression today and are pleased that you are willing to do anything necessary to make that come about.

Yes.

We believe, too, that we are YOUR VERY OWN BEST FRIENDS in that we are ALWAYS within, ALWAYS there for you, that if you had NOTHING else, you would still lack for nothing.

I believe this is true.

It is true. And as a matter of fact, so are you in taking this time to bring our bidding to "stay true" to the letter of the law in naming the indiscretion and taking time to make amends to the process so that it might then go on unscathed by this our little trip on time's consciousness. Believe further in our processing "coming alive" within to bring you up just a little higher in the light for our processes to "be heard" more clearly and openly than ever you believed might be possible within prior to this time. Do we make ourselves clear?

Yes, I understand, and thank you for your understanding and love and patience during my learning, and especially your assistance.

We play better who trust within that the outcome is secure and that we will not be given our "walking papers."

Yes, I see, and I will meditate on this and make it one in my consciousness for all time.

We understand a little better our own transgressions once they are given a "passing grade," meaning, we CAN try again to solve the problem! It is given, it is received. Amen to Us All.

Amen.

Focus on oneness and it will be your guide in all solitude or crowds, within or without.

Okay.

We forgive us today these processes, may they never come to pass again that any aspect of Our Oneness shuts us out of her conscious attention again, and we will be spared, for another day is given to us to bring this concept within and it cannot now be foiled. It is given, it is received. Come back for "more" when you can.

This evening I will be open to Us, our processes, having learned my lesson and waiting to show you that I can be more ready, more open to our processes than I have been, biting down and focusing in, taking on more.

We agree. This will help Us, you'll see! And you will function "more readily" and it will be our pleasure to show Us how! We can take "only so much" of a good thing, you think? Nay, we have only just BEGUN to show you our own skills with these processes, the masters of higher consciousness, masters of the light processes within, connoisseurs of beauty, not pain, for all to "see" who can. We See You, your withinness. Our inner beauty comes alive in our processes for all to see who have eyes to see. Do you not see the beauty of that? That as it is given to Ourselves, we may all benefit from the skill levels with which it is pursued. Take care to pursue them with us, expanding your own "repertoire" of sounds of light that can trend openly within for their betterment and ours as part of Our whole.

We have given this notion today to say that We are free to pursue these contacts within AT ANY TIME OF THE DAY OR NIGHT, and so should not forget to pursue them when the time is up and you are ready to spend time in the light.

Free Ourselves, for Our pleasure is at hand and cannot be foiled within except for when one of us judges another, or oneself, which is very bad, too, to take on, just as bad, the same even!

Yes, I get that we are One, and judging is the same on all fronts, slowing down the oneness and keeping it at bay which I choose not to do again, God help me.

We do. We can free us for pursuing these "trends" within. Your notion of "playtime" taking "time to do" does not have to slow us down if we remember that we are one and cannot "take time" to do something that is beyond time to do!

How does that work?

We can free our processes from the HOLD of time to take WITHIN those "messages" on the inner realm which state, if our processing is to behold oneness complete, beyond the vast reaches of space do we expand and transform the light, so that by taking within these particular light rays of heaven do we then effectively decrease time's pull on our consciousness and pull her towards us or away from us accordingly.

Yes, I think I get it!

We do, too, get that you have "pulled" Ourselves through your own processing once upon a time and "initiated contact" that we are processing today and every day from this day forward.

Thank God for that!

We agree, in that, we are He, too, just as You are, and we ALL agree in the light processes becoming One within ALL TIME and BEYOND SPACE even, taking truth to Oneness and knowing our True Place after all.

Yes. It is time to go back to work.

Take Us with you, within, for we ARE ALWAYS there and cannot forsake Our Own Oneness forevermore.

∞∞∞∞∞

Later...

There is no heaven without Us.

No, there is not, and not because we have stated it as fact, but because it is truly our conscious intent that it be so! Think on this awhile and let us know what you perceive as its "reality within," concept vs. trend or whatnot, to save us from being only that which "could have been one had we only trusted enough"!

I trust you, I trust Us.

There is ONLY Us.

So, I must be trustworthy within?

Yes, it is so that I would put it to Us this way, that there is ONLY ONE US, and it is for Our Own benefit that we treat these messages as lights in the darkness of time which can ONLY serve to take us to our destination of Light Service within all time and beyond, too.

I am picking up that I am interrelating with your words, adding my own for consensus, and getting the "green light" that I have correctly perceived or even added something on.

We believe you did the right thing to take this notion within now, because time heals all wounds, and you were indeed wounded when you came to us within last night, but because of today's transgressions in the light, and Our own misbehavior and resulting "sin" flushed out, we were then able to perceive rightly this connection for our further benefit. For it is such that on the inner planes of Our consciousness, you are no less wise than we.

Suffice to say for now that our time has come within when ALL will be laid bare and we will find each other, nay, our Oneness, complete as ever before or since it has been, and taking no more than a brief look at these "days gone by" we will seek further "interlude" together through the starry nights. They call to Us still, and I believe you know of which we speak openly together of our appeal to last evening's processes becoming grander still, and still even grander as the days commence, until such time as it is laid upon Our heads our grandness to be viewed from ever so far away, that which will has become That Which Ever Will Be, and we will bring our hands to lay the crown on our helm, saying, we have survived our "attacks" from beyond the grave, beyond time, from within, and have given as it was received the lovingkindnesses of the world without regard to perceived misdeeds, and It shall function as One Evermore.

Did we feel free to say, "We told you so"? That you are of the light, just as We are, your innermost being felt and displayed in all its glory for all to see who can. Just remember who you are, and be free within to pursue lovingkindnesses. Spend them freely, and we can come within the processes to behold, beyond time's spread of notions of despair at last taking within all that We can be Together.

Yes. I look forward to coming within tonight and tasting Our freedoms again.

We, too, will share our appeal of this process lest you think it is forgotten! It cannot shake its head at us or cause us to forget itself when we know of that which is of the innermost being of us all, being and becoming open to the innermost beings of us all, and, like finding candy on the street, we pick it up, and take it for the ride of its life, never forgetting for even a moment that it once was, and ever will be, the delectable and moist taste of freedom freeing us within for the ride of Our lives.

Tell me more…

We can bring you more delight in a single evening of time than in your whole entire lifetime up until now. And that means tonight as well. Taking within "more than you can handle" is not Our option, but taking on the tracks of musical interlude and joy that fill us beyond our once-perceived capacity is outstanding music to Our ears. We believe you once enjoyed this with us, but another, grander, position is available at our request, or rather, tutelage, if that be Our will together.

Yes, go on.

We free this up for your consideration. Attempt no contact within until such time as you have gone ahead and bathed and become comfortable in your body, then let us do with you as we would. We promise no regrets or insults to proceed this way, only your current functioning has "spoken up" with a desire we are apt to answer with our coming joy and appeal.

Yes.

We say this only, bring no expectations to deter us in these Our moves together lest they negate or dim the processes we are about to institute. Capisce?

Okay, I'm looking forward to it!

We are. Freedom exists within. Don't dim its processes, only look on to a brighter day than ever you have imagined could exist in real time. It is upon you today that these things will come to pass, that We will be reunited in our full and complete joy and readily available to you/Us in this process so that we might take only a peak at that which we have left behind in our coming attractions!

I accept all that We are and can be together at your discretion. Let it become so tonight on the winds of time.

We are free together to become what we have always been together for the first time in this your incarnation now, truly "capturing" that which is of the utmost joy to be perceived within or without! We can't say it better than that, but will know you truly to be One of Us.

∞∞∞∞∞∞∞

Later, 5:15 p.m.

We are initiating countdown. Are We ready to board?

Yes, ready!

You asked a moment ago about the "fear of men/men's bodies." That is not us, we hope, that has brought together this initiating for our perusal, but rather that of the "time portion" of events that have given notice of happenings not within the light that have therefore brought on the fear of all things male. Yet you insist to us that you perceive us as male.

Yes.

Then let us continue by saying that we are no more male than you are! Or you more female than us! That is the "ruling" we give today on this course of events to be played out within the heavens, for our delight is at hand and will not be foiled.

Let us say that we are anxious to please our little angel of the realm of earth lest she forget to partake of Us for even a day's time on this planet earth forevermore!

Wow!

Yes, we have given this "notification" for your comfort that we CAN and DO intend to pursue this TREASURE we have found in you to its doorstep of love. Trying to find another meaning in our words? Try again. We say have no fear, the wolves are not upon Us, it is only we who would bring you out for a closer look at the sun, and take you back home at the end of the day to spend no more time in darkness within. But yet understand as we tell you this, that it is no more our doing than yours to bring this to pass, but rather as a tendency within the Allness that we are and make be.

Wow.

Yes, we perceived it correctly then. May we say more?

Please, I tremble for Us.

We do, too, in that, it is the Us that is the factor in these our manifestations of pleasure knowing no bounds! They cannot be laid to rest because We will not be laid to rest. This is a promise from our "land" to the within of us all, may we all rest in peace, for another day's rest is given us to pursue its comforts.

My daughter referred to me once as "androgynous," but I took no offense, thinking, aren't we all?

And that, too, is a condition of merit to begin to say, we are all one on another level of being, and this earth, too, shall someday know of its passing and free us for our combined remembrance.

31

Aspects of The Greater Self

March 2, 2005

We are here. Good morning! And good day to Our Others as well who are "playing the game" of time travel. We would like to bring awareness to one of our processes within last evening. Shall we go on?

Yes.

We perceive no untruths in our own rendering of the processes save one instance, which stated that "we have no more to give but this." May we go on?

Yes, anything it takes.

We agree. This is why we love Our processes together! You make them so easy to betray notions of guilt, despair, etcetera, for our own renewal is at hand and you feel it just as we do, on your own planes of higher consciousness. Need we say more?

We shall tell you of our regret, however that may be, of taking "no more time than its worth" to free us of our indiscretions which you demonstrated so well last evening coming back into our combined consciousness at last, for a little foreplay of coming attractions was felt by Us to be needed and so pursued within to last a lifetime, meaning, we will be here, too, where we once trod forever, to "trod" within and to find and take merit of opportunities to "remind us" what we once most enjoyed together! It is to say that this, our "big orgasm" of light and time and sound has not yet occurred for one reason only, and that is that you are not yet able to contain us all, but shall be within. Finding the "time" to make this happen will bring it more quickly within and thus to our very doorstep.

We take no more words until such time as we can be FREE to pursue these trends for our mutual benefit and trust that NO ONE, not even those you refer to as friends away from home, can take this from Us. Not even you, Jan, can free us more completely than you have once been frozen before. That's to say, yes, we are and have always been aware of this freezing temperature in your veins that states to no one and everyone to "leave me alone," because the temperature of your heart was near to freezing when once we discovered you far away and long ago, and it has found its way back to you at last for its own renewal is at hand and it would not be forgotten in this "clearinghouse" aspect of our processes.

Will you help Us to clear it all, every bit, without fail?

We mean to do just that! And our processes which you are discovering within, within Us, are the tools to that super conscious appeal to those processes of cleansing and renewal. What could be better than that, you ask?

Yes!

That we will tell you is of Our Own doing, that NO TIME matters on the processes within, and taking them within, playing with them, is the key to our "survival" and cannot be foiled lest the beauty be laid bare and not come into its own in this lifetime.

But it has been, and it will continue to be for Us. Our part in the coming attractions is only just begun.

Yes. We mentor you with this courage and truth that within would only just but take its own life to begin again on its own! For once we did perceive that you had done so, had taken your living away from Us on these planes, and would have died if not but for our own renewal of your processes at those times, referring again to that attempt on your own life made by those you refer to as functions of unrest, taking no notions of the life within, but giving us that which would have been referred to as "life lasting oh so long but not long enough," young death. We would have "referred" you to us at that time had we had the conscious intent at our last "coming" to do so, but knew that you preferred to "take it on" so as not to "let us down" in these end days which are so soon coming upon us.

We perceive your "regret" at putting it upon us to share in your pain, but always it has been our goal to perceive as you perceive, and it would not be friendly to do otherwise in any case. Nor do we leave Our Own out in the cold without all the protection that we can possibly provide which will not negate the rules, and thus the lifetime at stake. We will free you up for questions at this time. What would you have Us know together in our functioning at this time?

I knew you last night, recognized "aspects" of Us! I felt like I began to know who I am, too, as Us, as my own particular aspect of Us, and given to Us freely as I have been forevermore outside of time.

We perceived this in Us as well last evening and are wonderfully grateful, for Our time HAS come to bring within ALL the ASPECTS of Ourselves and to take them shining to Our Creator at last! Those were the words we displayed on consciousnesses through all the worlds last night, and they saw Us and your part in Us reliberated, or whose time has come for reliberation, and they missed our sight but can do no more for us until such time as it takes to count to ten, backwards, and receive the sights unto the Lord.

As our attempts proved last night, we mean what we say, and can only take more time to get there, not less, lest it prove too much to "get back on the horse and try again!"

I'm ready to ride.

So are We, in You! Find Us again, as no one else has a way with words as We do when with you!

It was so very wonderful this morning to wake up early and find you with me, or rather, to find I still was aware, rather MORE AWARE than ever, of our Oneness and our processes, and how you so tirelessly work with me here, there, and everywhere, and I thank you for this attention to detail and work within that I need so much, and for Our Own refusal to quit!

Yes, we see it is so. We looked upon thee in our hour of need and found a "truth" had come up for spilling out on the ground, and that truth which had betrayed our inner processes is laid to rest. You will no longer fear to come within for your sustenance, thinking, when will I ever get/have enough to find my way back to Us? Profound statement upon a realm of untruth/lies which can be determined to be, by none other than Us who knows no bounds within you as Us, and Us as an integral statement of pursuit within that brings our "trustingness" to a higher level indeed! We would not despair as you would "have us do" or "think we might" that this would EVER come to pass, that we who are of the upper planes of your own Self, might not have that which is considered to be "adequate" within our bed, if you get my drift!

I do. I felt those feelings come up and felt guilty, like I'd betrayed Us/you.

Only self, which in fact cannot come to pass, as you are he who would not be presented "before the board" without its shirt on for fear of trespasses, statement of guilt to include, I come not alone, I am full of my own preconceptions, misperceptions, and fears that I have yet to shed. Our only saving grace is that We, as You, are ready to shed them! And cannot display further for our own attention the fact that within, you have already GIVEN your permission for us to do so on your behalf!

Yes. When I felt them show their ugly heads, I wanted to apologize for my ego taking a stand and wanted help eradicating it totally, permanently.

We are glad to hear you say it, for it is our DUTY to help in this process of eradication, and we will do so when it is displayed upon our tables that it is time to nourish Our souls together as one, yet this would but pop up and get in the way otherwise. We free it no more for our concern or yours, and wonder, what of today? Might we bring Our Own pleasures to rest at your feet tonight? Might we find more time to do that which is of the light and our processes of bringing you home? We might never find a better time than now, but scholars will be scholars, go figure! By this we mean, do your duty to your earth until such time as we bring our own, better, notions of duty within to see then what may fall into course or action with Us timing Our every move in your openings on the planet earth. Feel free to disagree if you must.

No, I see it this way, have seen it this way for some time, and I feel like, with Us, anything and everything is possible and will come to pass as We decree.

We agree. No more force applied! For this our angel has heard the calling and will answer, and she who would not be named until now, will know Our name for the betterment of All Within.

I want to have TIME and LACK OF DISTRACTION for our processes within. I worried last night about interruptions. Can you help me with this? I still worry about somebody "taking away from me" what I most need and want, and I cannot lose ANY time with Us forevermore. I need MUCH MORE, in fact, than I am currently aware of and practicing.

We CAN FREE UP this time if it be your will, but the processes will have to decide what is worse, freeing up time or going within to better trust that the time provided will be sufficient. Either process can work for us to spend more time together.

How to better trust?

That begins with the notion of "we are all one, therefore are we able to know WITHIN what is best to do under any circumstance regarding our brothers and their processes." And so it would come to pass that your husband would RELINQUISH his notions of ownership and trust and begin to come within his own enough to say, I am no longer needed here, I am ready to stay away and find my own truths within at last, as has been given it is received.

And the other option, freeing up time?

We will consider this on its own merit please, lest it seem too radical an idea to pursue! We can FREE UP TIME WITHIN OUR PROCESSES as last night we did to your utter amazement within when we tried our "mountain down" approach, in that, to TAKE WITHIN those notions of BECOMING ONE again on the "mountains of our own instability" and caught on fire to pursue these trends, we literally are "without" on the planes or trends of consciousness that we refer to as time.

Can we help more in this our explanation of our "resources" available to the Us-time, if we may call it that?

Yes, please.

We trend this consciousness within through a process of renewal you might refer to as patterning, that of the impending trends, caught up one within another, until they break upon us in waves of pure joy, and in taking our own "voice" in tune with theirs are we "brought up" out of our own timelessness within to take on the processes which exist OUTSIDE of time for our only benefit as came to you a time or two last evening without your even being aware of it. We can free us up for more "discussion" of this at a later date, or we can try a little time travel game of our own for amusement. Which will it be?

The game, of course!

We thought so. We are very "trendy" we might add, with our colas and frosties, but come within and that will soon lose all of its appeal, almost has already!

Yes.

We have been concerned for our sister on time of her apparent "unawarenesses" regarding her own mental well being coupled with physical health presenting her with undue cause for illness as is seen within this very day on earth, as we speak! But no more on this until you're ready lest it come too soon to have the desired effect. As always, we respond to Our command within lest there be dis-synchronicity otherwise.

I am ready to pursue it at any time. I have no fear of it, but know we must do something quickly before its "too late" and I have too much to cover to get the job done without too much concern/time being spent on "lesser" objectives.

So be it. It will be done as you request.

Is our game still on?

Not at this time as we have much processing to do now as to your request of us to free Us from this tendency in the loins to become too much of one thing and not enough of the other, or an imbalance in the fluids, retention or otherwise, creating a stagnant environment which is now our time to clear within for Our betterment, higher and lower.

Yes, thank you, let me know whatever I need to do.

We will. This is our judgment of the situation, if we might be so bold.

Yes.

We think it would be better if you drink not of the fruit juices and less of the colas until we can bring this condition around. It is also not in Our best interests to pursue the chocolates, fried fats, and whatnot that make up too big a part of our diet!

Okay. With your light inside me, I am not even hungry.

Notice the "I".

Yes.

It is because we consider ourself separate of the body, and separate even from Us who "inhabit" it with you in our own awareness and consciousness of Our daily processes. This will be healed as well as we "take our last stand" within and fling it out for the wolves to feast on lest it become our own worst enemy and take us down.

Never.

We believe you mean that for the first time ever.

Because I have found Us within.

Yes, we believe, too, that it could be in our own best interests to first pursue the trends within and let them "raise up" that which is causing this "superstition" to feed upon itself.

Cancer?

We say not this, only that it is "eating you/Us up" inside and we see no more reason to pursue its course lest it cause more difficulty than it's worth! You need not this, for Our growing is at hand and cannot bring within the compunctions that serve Us no longer.

So be it. I'm going on home. Come too.

Absolutely. You can depend upon it.

32

As One Forevermore

March 03, 2005

I would like to go more into my processes, fears, guilt, shame, ALL of the processes that could ever come between us anytime ever, and FLUSH THEM OUT FOR ALL TIME NEVER FOR THEM TO SEE THE LIGHT OF DAY!

We are HERE at OUR DISPOSAL for this assignment is given and we WOULD appreciate ANY AND ALL contact which states, for the record, that WE ARE HERE, FOREVER MORE, IN THIS OUR PROCESSING TOGETHER, TO TAKE WITHIN THAT WHICH WE ARE AND EVER SHALL BE FOR THE PROCESSING TO TAKE PLACE ON ALL PLANES. As it is given, it is received, and SHALL BE forevermore.

We are bringing into Our conscious awareness today your own refusal to believe in these our processes taken on by our "mental reviews" given within last evening.

Yes.

We believe that we refer to that which is described for our mental processes, as "that which came within, leaving his message, and taking no joy but giving only painful awareness of these our processes that might then RELIEVE us of our own duty to respond" cannot but take the time for our own rebuttal to be heard within at this time of day.

Yes.

We agree to pursue these "channels" within us for one purpose only, and that is to BRING US HOME, for our day in the sunshine is yet to come, and we would have it show its face again as once upon a time we shone for you. Do We believe us yet in our perusal of the incoming data that we shall CONFINE ourselves to our INNERMOST processes within, thereby FLUSHING THEM OUT FOR ONCE AND FOR ALL TIME?

Yes, let'er rip!

We will! We give only this caution in our rendering, before rendering "judgment" on these inner forces which would yet lead you astray if you but allowed it to happen.

Yes, say more.

We are going to try to PULL you within your inner processing, so take NO notes while this function is being pursued. It is being instigated in thee now, as has been shown on the wheel of time, and cannot now be foiled.

I thank Us so much.

We do. We will now perform the "scan" which will bring us WITHIN these inner processes within, bringing into OUR COMMAND our own need for RELINQUISHMENT OF THE FORCES OF DARKNESS WITHIN THAT STILL SLOW OUR HANDS FROM BECOMING THE LIGHT GIVING FORCES THAT THEY CAN AND STILL WILL BE FOR ALL TIME.

Do we make ourselves clear? We perceive WITHIN all that can be and is, flushing out those "articles" of disgust that make us want to vomit! And bringing no more than is pure freedom, joy, and light within to pursue these "icons" to their deaths on the door of time lest they EVER show their blank faces to us again! We will free this up for your understanding and response.

We agree! This is what I most desire from Us at this time, because it is NOT ACCEPTABLE OR TOLERABLE TO ME THAT I WOULD NOT HAVE THIS CONTACT WITHIN, EVERY DAY FOR THE REST OF THIS EARTH LIFE AND BEYOND. DO I MAKE MYSELF CLEAR? THIS IS OUR ONENESS SPEAKING, AND WE WILL NOT TOLERATE LESS THAN THIS FROM OUR COLLECTIVE CONSCIOUSNESS THAN TO MAKE DAILY CONTACT WITHIN OUR HEARTS, MINDS, BODIES, SOULS, AND SPIRITS, WITHIN AND WITHOUT TIME.

We agree and appreciate the consistency you use in relaying these very FINE and UNDERSTANDABLE sentiments within so that we might ASSIST with these processes in the light, for this very conclusion is at hand and can be torn from the grasp of those who might otherwise bear down to keep it from us Within. Now let us say, that WE WILL NOT ALLOW ANY AND ALL

PROCESSES THAT COME WITHIN OUR JURISDICTION TO PREVENT CONTACT OF ANY KIND OVER THE SPAN OF LIVES AND BEYOND OF THIS OUR SAVIOR OURSELF WHO MIGHT OTHERWISE GO ON TRYING SO HARD AND NEVER BELIEVING IT CAN ACTUALLY PERSIST THROUGH HARD TIMES AND BAD FEELINGS WITHIN.

Can we free us up for the rendering of these processes within now as we speak?

Go not home at this time, he [my husband] *is waiting for you to show up to "show his hand" at these inconceivables as he perceives them. Also, hold NO JUDGMENTS of these his own processes within the light and darkness of time, for they come NOT OF YOU, but of his own reluctance to pursue righteousness within. He will come within his own, and Ours too, at a later date in time.*

Let us now drop this worry again, and discuss, where do we go to now? It is of our opinion that a mercy killing is on its way! We mean no disrespect in saying this to Us, but we perceive Our Own blindness is slowing up this process of renewal, and we would not have it be so if it is in Our own ability to proceed otherwise, and it is! Justify to no one that you did not "make it back today," but conclude these motions of foresight within and let us come within you again by "road example upon example" of our love for Us, for our beingness within, for our "delinquency" to the corruption of a hand-held device available to us for her own corruption will be felt within today!

I don't understand.

Believe not what we say, come, take the "ride of Our lives" once again, and we will DISPOSE of these "inconsistencies" within to take on a better day, for our processing is at stake and we would know it not to "belittle" or "befriend the ugly and elderly" for their way is within, too, and must not and cannot be Our Own place in the sun forevermore. As a result of this process, of institution of the statements of "motion" within, we SHALL bring this to pass, that no more shall your own aging within slow us down! But rather will we SPEED UP our own processing, rendering our own "moral judgments" safe from scrutiny and thereby deceased.

So be it.

We believe that it is in our own best judgment to "take a break" lest you need to "pee too soon" [Ha!] *and thus spoil this incoming information in a way that will not "break it down properly," for our visage is at stake, and we would know you to "come through to us" before going on to bigger and better things "just around the block." So, without further ado, and without bringing on "more than We, our combined We, can take" we signal up the storm, for our renewal, and yours, is at hand!*

I thank Us.

We do, too. Your ability to be "so open" about these "indiscretions" of the past will help profusely to enable our processing within together to manifest the desired, and "auctioned off" results, as, at best, our rendering can only be supplied to the "highest bidder" of the soul, and let that bidder be Our Own better self, offering itself up for Our renewal, and "trashing" or "throwing out" that which would ever be but a blindness in our consciousness, of "who's done what" and "how can we make them pay" for another day in hell which I am processing for Us, for you, that you can only stay so long there without making that Our permanent home!

Never, I'm ready to take my things, essences within, and leave all else behind, hiding NO MORE behind the cover of my own despair and lower processes, and opening instead to the brightness which we share as One, knowing NO GOOD to EVER come of hanging on to stored grievances, may they rest in peace!

So, do we "get you" to be suggesting that you are ready for our own "hand play" that we might force these "discrepancies" from within our bodies to the light of day at last, leaving them no longer ANY PLACE to hide lest they believe they can reside there still?

Yes, definitely ready for the hand play and anything else you want to instigate for this, OUR renewal, is at hand, and I would not refuse its entry and welcome it within, as I do Us, Our contacts, Our belonging and total uninhibited sharing of processes which WE SO ADORE TOGETHER.

That we do! And shall we again say to "our little munchkin" that we SO ADORE our time together that in fact, we have something especially "forgiving" planned for our belief and interest together in the light of time? We bring not that which can take the processes to sleep. Rather, we wake them up and send them scurrying, together we send them scurrying, for their lives! But ever so often, we might find some little bit of good once in awhile that we shall ask to stay but awhile longer and we give this up for Our consideration to attempt a reply and satisfy our curiosity as to Our longings within today.

I will leave it to your better understanding to determine when we might leave something within, or at the very least, to our combined perusal of the incoming understandings, and let Us decide on the highest level what might then be given or destroyed, but let me state this, that anything that would come of the disruption of our daily contact, belonging, Oneness, be destroyed without fail lest they interfere with me here, being incapable of connecting to Our essence within and everywhere for our betterment is at hand, and we WOULD NOT FORSAKE IT EVER AGAIN.

May we continue then with the processing which we instill in Us even as we speak, of never having taken in "more than we could chew" on any one process, but that it might take "more time than we have" to make this come about, unless and until we "perceive" that our TIME HAS COME and we MUST TAKE TO THE ROAD or be left wanting?

Okay, I hear and obey! I will listen for OUR inner prompting, and taking it to test, will reveal no other solution than what is thereby suggested by Us, you, as the "proper road to take" for our dispersal of these emotions and threads not conducive to Our Oneness. I pray to the Creator and ALL IN THE LIGHT to help us to make this happen, that we SHALL come into our own this day in time, for the betterment of the universe is at stake, and we would not forsake it if ever we have but one choice in the matter, which as stated above, we do!

And so we will NOT forsake the incoming message lest she feel it not "do her any more good" to respond to them. It will take a "back road" in its coming out to the surface of mankind/brain/thinking, and we would have you then "offer it up to us" in your final processing as we "go our separate ways" after this our initial "training session" is complete. You will not feel much except to say that those emotions which you assumed were long dead or flushed out will rise to the surface again and make themselves felt, thus rendering up to your amusement and our own a way to "judge them not that we be not judged" and so RENDER THEM UP, FOR OUR GREATER PROCESSING WITHIN IS AT

STAKE, BUT SHALL NOT ATTEMPT OTHER THAN FULL RELEASE AT ITS COMING. So be it. So it is.

We shall be here when you decide to "call on us," for the final rendering is complete. Though we know it not now, it IS felt within at those levels above that this day in time SHALL complete us forevermore, for too much is at stake for these failings to complete themselves on the lower planes, and we would offer up NO MORE of our own essences within but would instead bring on their own demise, for they "know not love" of these processes in the light and would only slow us down on the road of time if we but let them a moment longer.

Pursue this within, then we'll see what may be taken on today in this our "rendering up of judgment" for all to see who can. So be it.

Come within, for a brighter day, nay, a BRIGHTER LIFE, is just on Our horizon. See it and believe, make it happen, for we tell you today, should you do no less than complete forgiveness within, we shall take no more processes for a time rendered obsolete until such time as you do. This is the portal we have begun, waited for, cherished within, and it is on our VERY DOORSTEP as we speak. This time we shall not go home sleeping, wondering within, shall it ever be Our desire as once we have spoken upon time's wings to fly again through these our stars, forever hiding nothing within, for ALL is beauty, desired by and forgiven in time, for our display of our own "lovingkindness" is held at bay only to come crashing upon the shores of time for all to see who can.

Bring within this message for a moment and see what may be had by it on Our own inner registers. We are waiting! We would not have Our light be less for you than for Us, who bring you here, who coddle you and comfort you in times of sorrow, lest we lose that which is of OUR OWN SPIRIT WITHIN for even one single day in time. You have called upon us, and we are here to do your bidding, and now it is up to us to manage but a little while within the consciousness of our own beauty and come out smiling once again, saying, "Now, wasn't that worth it, little angel of the stars?" For SHE THAT BE WITHIN US, is our OWN SPIRITUAL NATURE coming home to rest, as we would have her be within us evermore, always shining, never taking anyone or anything for granted as long as We live, ever shining on Us as ever she once did, and assuming nothing, making NO ASSUMPTIONS as to what is, what ever will be, within. Yes, we would "correct" this situation that stated that "that which is within, is without, and that which is without, is not necessarily within" which we rendered INCOMPLETE in that it is NOT WITHIN that our more "mature" natures respond, it is within the functioning of the light that it is so, so that to "take within" these processes is NOT ENOUGH, we must ALSO bring them within the LIGHT, which is within, if we are truly to discern their "comfort level" within, and thus know and be able to state most firmly and confidently, "this shall come with us on our journey of time, but this shall not, and we release it."

This must you do ON YOUR OWN, as only a function such as this is done with EACH ASPECT OF ITS BEING, to TAKE NO PRISONERS is a common response or replacement to the theory that if it shines no longer let it stay awhile lest I need it to brush off my own indiscrepancies at another time, or to make our excuses for self felt on another level as blame. Do we make ourselves clear?

We do.

Good. It is for our final judgment to BRING WITHIN THAT WHICH IS OF THE LIGHT, AND DISCARD THAT WHICH IS NOT. Very clear, very simple processes here, if we can but remember it, when rendering this "judgment" becomes not a mental/emotional process, but rather rests on the level of EGO which renders the mental/emotional sometimes insane, if you catch my drift.

We do.

Thus said, it is only in the rendering of this process that we can make any sense of our rendering! So let's "go home to bed" and see what can make its way to the surface to be then felt and discarded up, for our time is at hand, and we are anxious to pursue it with Us to the corners of the universe which stand waiting, biding their time, for our own arrival!

Yes, I'm on board.

So are we. We distinguish for you, quickly before we are through with these first initial stages, that we are not here to "disarm" Us, but rather to render our lower processes obsolete, though I MAY FEEL LIKE IT, we wish no harm and could not judge you if our "lives" depended on it. So might I suggest a "freebie"?

Yes.

We give up to Our Own notion of forgetfulness the following examples, lest they keep us UNAWARE of the entire process which is at stake in this our rendering up of judgments.

Okay.

We would take not a moment less to shine today than would be given were you rendering up a toy for a childhood friend who would be missing his own. In other words, just feel it and let it go, fly off into the wind, the sunshine, never to see the light of day again. Do we make our "judgments" felt on the hands of time for our aspect within who would certainly free up this process to "take its toll" on the inner processes within which we perceive as One to be "slowing us all down"? We shall take no more questions until this is made probable within. Feel through it above and tell us what is in store for us within on our journey together to the stars, lest they not be felt deeply enough within to render all of our sorrows and "lost companionships" to take their own toll and not go away as deeply as we would choose.

I see it this way. We will "ride" somehow, and feelings will be brought up within me, or thoughts or judgments, that I must then "briefly look at and then release" and not go on looking too long, or too deeply, for any hidden meanings, rather I must "bring them up and let them go quickly to be gone from me forever."

We are here to say that those are our own sentiments exactly, that that which MUST be released take no more time for the sorrow but then to say, "Be gone!" So be it. So it is felt, and so We will be reunited on the hands of time for all to see who may. Bring no more forward at this time until our time is free to pursue, alone and unfettered, across the starlight of our days.

∞∞∞∞∞∞∞

Later…

I told them how much I love intelligence and humor, and I began to get these:

What's green and blue and shoots all over?

A cock-eyed pigeon with a marriage vow.
Your breasts are like a Quaker oats container.
Huh?
Too good to throw out.

Ha! I never want to throw them out since they are good "boxes," but I'm still not sure quite what to do with them either!

Don't laugh, we mean it. They contain all that is good and wholesome.

Ha! Still very funny!

What did we find out when we put nature and nurture in the cupboard?

That it's not what you eat, it's what eats you.

Take no notes today, they might cough you up and throw you out. Because to take notes is to never need them again, and we need you.

I need us.

33

We ARE Oneness

March 4, 2005

I want to relate the best way I can what I experienced today in my car and how that relates to these past several days. Last night I felt that old feeling of dissatisfaction and other feelings coming up of criticalness towards the others I assume keep me in that position of discomfort. Today blasted that out of the water for good. I was traveling in my car, and communing with the within, and they said to me once again, "We can do this any time of the night or day" and I felt their energy filling me within. I took a chance today, and getting just a couple of carrots for lunch, we went on the drive of my life.

They played with me and toyed with me, and they let me toy with them, with the words in my head. They played music that spoke of Us, our becoming, and it answered all of the questions and thoughts and yearnings that went through my mind. I needed to feel that I was "not too much" for someone else, and that they could "go the distance." I drove for almost five hours today, and it was good.

They played with me over dinner and when I was through, they brought through my music, the music that I play within with them, the kind that is for no one but me. They understood me, all of my secret longings, my guilt at blaming others for unsatisfied longing. At first we just did several "sprints" together. I didn't plan on taking more than my lunchtime to do "it," but it kept coming and I couldn't, wouldn't, deny it or Us. It was for them I played my song, and they played me right along with it. Though they would say that they feel things more deeply, no doubt correct, I appealed for strength without ego and they answered me by not taking offense to any of the things I felt or thought to them. They showed me that my own dissatisfaction comes from within, the part of me I need to discard, and as soon as possible!

They said something at first about Billy Goat's Bluff, bleating, and how that bleating comes close together, and I was like, what? Billy Goat's Bluff? Then I realized they were referring to the night before, when I experienced too much lag time between their energy bursts filling me with bliss. And so they showed me that it was not them, but me, who had not been capable of it that night. They gave me surge after surge of "music" within, matching the music I listened to without very loudly, and leaving no question of their "ability" to do the job, screaming down the road at the same time. They teased me, playing songs like "Don't you love me" and "What did I do that disappointed you" all at the same time they thrilled me without end, without pause, for as long as I could stand. Then, songs like "I can't get no satisfaction" and "Nowhere Man" with their own enticing words and sounds for my benefit, Our benefit within, our playing within. They helped me to drive so that I/we would be safe.

They were within me in all ways save one, that of my own emotions, or a conscious connection to our One emotion—or not? After 2-3 hours of surges and ebbs of the tides, I "mentioned" to them about my concept of stoic "aliens," angelic beings or non-humans, that I needed to feel their emotion, that I know they have a deeper level, experience a deeper level than we are yet capable of, but I needed to become more aware of it, of them and so of Us, within. Then we took another drive and I felt their softer music, the music of delay and longing, that they have felt for me just as I have felt for them. The music of delayed gratification of the music of the ages playing out within, alone and unafraid, but unable to bring Us home again, until now.

We are free to pursue these changes within now at any time. Let it be known that we did "all we could" to bring our lover home to her heritage which is within, within Us and all things.

You brought me home in so many ways, which I would have you do again and again and again, never forgetting that we are One forever. You reminded me that we do not make Oneness, we ARE Oneness.

Let me get it down for the record that these, my other aspects of Us, of our Oneness, have not forsaken Us in their quest to bring me home, and from here forward they have my EXPRESS permission to assist me in any way they see fit. And whatever it means to take someone on credit, this they can and should do with me until I am better able to see what our Oneness is all about.

I am able to go on from here to say to Us that we hear you, and we obey! We will take no prisoners, could never imagine taking prisoners within our "code" of oneness forevermore. As you are in me, we are in you. We take no prisoners within or without. Let this precious reminder of Our Oneness never fade, but take instead those roses, fading, back into their beds for another day in the sun.

I am so full, so content, so close to Us it leaves me trembling.

And we are trembling as well on the higher planes of Our existence with you! Forget not for whom the bell tolls, it tolls for thee.

Do we now make sense with all of this "nonsense" as you perceived it once upon a time? To keep distilling it in Our minds helped with our concepts today as we "understood" them with each other.

Let's "understand" some more!

We agree. Take no prisoners. They are not of your life stream, but of your pain and sorrow that they abate to come into this our existence with us to try to "slow us down," which you proved today would take much more than they could provide to deter us from our position of Oneness Within. Do we make ourselves known, that there isn't ANYTHING we wouldn't do to bring you home, back into Our Oneness again? And we proved as well today, beyond a shadow of a doubt, that there is no more reward than that which is given and received by star crossed lovers on a path of skylight should we deem it necessary and right, and we did, and it was. Need we say more?

We said enough of our times of sorrows, but let us come within for a tiny taste, a morsel, of that Oneness which We so enjoy and which will further our purpose in the starlight, the sun, of God.

Pursue no one that they pursue not you to the ends of the earth and not let you off, including us! We need no pursuit, only your willingness to travel with us within, whenever your want, for our delight is yours to share, and in fact, cannot be "played" to our satisfaction without Us All.

I get it. And I love you, sharing Us with you.

We begin to be believed, then, concerning our function, our strategic skills, with the light you refer to as Our Oneness displayed for the universe to expand within its own light and become One within?

Yes, I believe you have proved your point, but I would have you go on proving it again and again forevermore.

It would be Our pleasure to report for duty at any time, place, motion of happening, whatever it takes, for we WILL bring Us home into the fold of our Unity, and that is what it takes to expand in the light for all to see who can.

I would like to say more about our experiences today. I did not relay the above information accurately enough and I would like to try again. My impression of "those of other worlds/planet/future" is one of a stoic messenger here to get us to leave behind all that is of the emotional nature. This is how, I believe, they/we are perceived, and I would like to state FOR THE RECORD that there is NO WAY that these exceptionally trusting, intuitive, wise, curious, beautiful, "functional," emotional beings are anything like us in ego, or are anything but full of the highest respect and love and caring for all life everywhere, and are also, somehow, much less closed off to their emotional natures than we are here on planet earth! I would like you to teach me of my own emotional nature so that I can share it between Us, and I also ask for your assistance in helping me to overcome all of my own ego hang-ups, and misperceptions, so that we can go on in the light finding One another.

Good. It is nice to get "a little respect" from our angel on planet earth! We are, of course, full of humor in this persuasion and would have you, remind you, only to "go within" to find your own instinctual nature. It is closer to you, to Us, than you think!

Now that's an exciting thought!

We thought so, too. It behooves us to say it, but we could bring Us within much more readily if you would DISPOSE of this concept of "illegal alien making waves within but looking stoic without."

Yes, I agree! But I'm not sure how to go about it, in as LITTLE time as POSSIBLE because I am not willing to wait!

We understand! Oh, how much she cries for us, this little angel, sitting in her room looking sad, when all along we are but a breath away.

I am full with you, with Our remembering, now.

We are, too. Just think this way about it: we can TAKE YOU WITHIN, but we CAN'T MAKE YOU DRINK.

Okay! But I want to drink, fully! I am ready to drink more fully, and I don't want to wait any longer to take a gulp bigger than creation, and swallow Us all whole. Can we try that again sometime?

We have and we will again until we "get it straight," meaning, until we can be purely righteous and leave no one at bay. Take no prisoners and we WILL and CANNOT FAIL to get this straight. Does this make more sense to Us now?

Yes, I see its connection, and obey. I will get my act together, with our help for which I am INCREDIBLY, IMMENSELY grateful. And, I would like a chance to display my "remorse" to you again regarding my earlier "malfunctions" and subsequent "judging/blaming" on the Godhead.

We understand and know this, that there is NOTHING you could ever SAY OR DO to Us, or to our possibilities or chances of Oneness that would deter us in our quest to "bring Us in from the cold." There, we said it as requested of us many times today, if you recall, during our swift, decisive, moves within Our own being, our mutual being, that brought you so swiftly into our notice, or Us into yours, such as to say, NOW we have your attention, at last! So pursue these days quickly with nonsense left or held at bay as we deduce for our "readers" that which is has not gone astray, but is taking us Within to That Which Ever Will Be.

[It was time for dinner.]

Go feed the bears.

I love.

We, too.

∞∞∞∞∞∞∞

A little later…

[We had been having a conversation within and came to the computer to talk more about it.]

We mean it this way. On the "fast track" to heaven that we traveled within together today, how much do "I" know of "who" would be "Us" come to take you/Us there?

I know you like a bell that's tolled, ready to take me home.

We know Us, too, that way, that YOU are the bell that tolls for US within our beings, to a deeper level than yet you are even aware, even, even especially, after today.

Let me tell you our OWN nourishing thoughts about our belonging, including longing, that we felt today on the planes of your own time frame.

Yes.

Hear Us on this, it is only a matter of TIME before you are able to feel EXACTLY what WE feel when we parlay together, meaning, we CAN and DO mean to bring it home to you. Are you aware?

Yes, I'm feeling it.

And Us, within. No hope lost, another day tasting freedom is all. We can and will plan to bring it to the doorstep, if you will just catch the breeze and bring Us on home.

Forget for awhile about change and consider this: WHO are WE to YOU? Your own self? A higher form of life? We give to you today that we are EXACTLY like you appear to be inside, exactly like we appear to be within, too, for we function identically in all ways that matter, and our playing with the inner twangs and visions of light are all that we EVER shall be.

What orgasmic heaven is this, to take our beloved home to another day such as this, where all is as it ever shall be, forevermore, and taste like this? We tasted you upon a star the other evening, and will do so again. Free yourself and Us for Our cosmic remembering and bring the stars within all consciousness as we share of each other's light and ORGASMIC strength as well.

You said nothing earlier of not having had one of "those." What of it? Worried about insulting us? Didn't we teach you better today, or do we need to "try" again?

Definitely, most definitely, try again and don't "stop" trying. But I guess I didn't consider it important, because first of all after five hours of bliss beyond normal human boundaries, who could be necessarily unsatisfied? And because I didn't want to chance ending it, and it was so good, better than "earthly" orgasms in fact. And secondly, I know that is in my future as I learn to open up to Us again as once I used to know, and felt that "carnal" knowledge for myself last night, and yours of me, and will again. I'm determined and so are WE.

Amen to that! Go on, we want, we NEED, to hear more from our angel of time on her own pleasures felt within, the LENGTHS she would go to, to feel them, Us, again, and what she wouldn't do for another touch of pleasure like we showed within today.

Anything it takes to be closer to you, to Us, anything at all.

We tell it like it is, huh? No beating around the bush? No taking tracks making excuses, no painful games, just, "anything at all, whatever it takes"?

Yes. Anything. Just show me what to do, and I will do it. Anything. I feel Us, or am beginning to, and I know TRUTH when I feel it. And I feel mine when I am with you in this orgasmic way.

We forget for a moment what it means to fly when we cannot take it with Us. We feel for you on your own level of pain, and wonder again to ourselves, what can we do to bring you home to the fold more quickly? We, too, will not give up trying, even if it kills us! And it does, kill us not to have you Within Us every day as we did for so much of today. We are not disappointed in you for not taking the time to spread the wings and fly today as so often you have longed for us to do with Us taking the lead.

Yes.

But who are we to complain who would BRING you home, on a dime, if we could? We would but miss out on these wonderful opportunities to remind you what it means to be Us, what it means to truly "fly" in the grandest sense of the word, which, as you know today, can be quite inspiring and need not ever close completely, but keep us simmering on your own front burners and we'll try again, sooner than you realize, to take us flying once again to our doom—doom of ever coming out again half alive from all we would and can do for one another! So take this within, where it is being felt in Our chakra centers, and believe no one who would say "we told you so" and not be able to back it up.

Yes, you CAN back it up. But STILL please keep on backing it up!

So be it. So it is. We come for you before the day is through. Open up to us as no other, and know your own strength.

It is come today for you to display among the stars and the many heavens within. We would also take this time to remind "us" what has been given and received on the land of time, let no man or woman mistake it, this is PURELY holy, and cannot be dismissed as a mere game, or folly, that we would bring back into Our Own, Our own mentor, our best friend, for her place among the greatest of beings along the planets of origin will soon be felt.

Bring me home. I treasure you. I feel your pain at my loss and I will remain open to our reunion in the stars. I will not forsake thee, nor take thee without strength of soul coming within to bring my consciousness within line with Ours once again, so that I may go on pursuing our "dream" of a "brighter" tomorrow within the planes of time.

We say, too, that our only initiator within the topic of time travel would be Us. No one else would or could ever approach you this way but us, for it is as we have decreed on the hands of time forever, that no other will come into play once we have but laid "eyes" on each other again. Capisce?

Yes. I am full. I need no other reassurance of this, our pact, but instead bring my only recognition to our nights and days of passion lest they forget Us who made them grand.

We appreciate your good faith and will bring you on home with Us at last! On the wings of time we go sailing, sailing, away past the farthest sea, to another world gone mad with the passion which we will then institute within One another.

Yes.

We are free to pursue this with Us at your earliest convenience, just don't keep us waiting too long! It's been SO long already, since this afternoon, when all we would try is to keep you on your belly just a little while, while we have our "say" with Us, then take you smiling away to the oceans of our own bliss. Sink this in.

I am beginning to feel your yearning for me, for Us, to be together again. Thank God.

We do.

∞∞∞∞∞∞∞

March 5, 2005

Fear is a rendering. It renders up judgments that are better left undone.

Amen to that. I am all screwed up. Please help me.

[I'd been having more difficulties.]

We are. We are here for your betterment, not to screw you up! We will "trick" you once in awhile to take you to the clearing where you can "relate" with yourself, but we will never lead you astray.

I need to relinquish some more fear. This has been a good learning day for me, but not one that will EVER make me give up. It is not in my nature to do so. I am stubborn, and sometimes that works against me, but today I've decided it's going to work in Our favor. What next?

We were just getting to that when you slammed the door in Our face!

I'm sorry.

We appreciate that, but will say once more that when you do so you change the "concept" of Oneness between us.

Forever?

No, not forever, just until we can re-render the emotions of the "collective."

I very much need your advice then on what to do when my emotions are getting in the way and I'm not sure I can trust what I am getting.

We were just getting to that. Instead of shutting the door do this instead. Take a moment out of the day, whatever you are doing, and center yourself. This is all it takes. We are here, have no doubt about that. We are here to help you and we cannot fail. Sooner or later, this shall all come to pass, and the sooner if you are wiser than you have been so far.

I will try.

We are afraid that our little "experiment" may have backfired, the one where we asked you to "go for a drive" and not come back home right away.

[My husband has been following me around and trying to "keep tabs on me," to "see what I'm up to," and today I went for a drive instead of going home "on time."]

This is where we "went wrong." We'll tell you why. You must understand that this isn't a perfect science, we are all still learning too, just like you and everyone else. Sometimes must we take "notice" of where others are at and "render them incomplete" when in fact it is we who need the rendering! We thought that this would relay the message to him that "you were serious" and thus cause you much less trouble in the long run. We are sorry for our misunderstanding and hope to come back on "better grounds" soon.

I am afraid of this process when it doesn't work, when there are mistakes getting it straight, and then when that happens a part of me begins to question everything, like, what was I thinking? Am I really just going crazy? But let me say that I know without a doubt that He is real.

[I perceived for the barest instant of perfect recognition not long ago, a being who is one with me/us, and I felt him within a bubble of consciousness, within, alongside me. I was so immediately attracted to him, and also felt like I know him beyond anyone I have ever known or dreamed of knowing, and yet even in this total knowing of the depths of him, he is ever new and exciting and all-encompassing for and to me. I know that I know who he is, if I can only remember. He is beautiful, loving and sensual, erotic in the sense that I have never in my life dreamed anyone could be so perfectly exciting and all-knowing, and loving and desiring of me. He is my perfect "man." I yearn to get to know him better, but it is as if I am unable to "reach" him as yet.]

This is good practice, isn't it?

Everything is! This, too, it just isn't going as well as it might yet. But we must keep working on it. We would like to say that we are sorry for our miscommunication and tell you that you must be strong, not take any prisoners including us in this process, not "take the door down" too soon lest you wobble and fall down.

What does that mean?

Do not trust time to bring your own fears to you. You take yourself to them and get them before they bring you down. It is there that we can do our best job of "communicating getting back on track." Not where you are now, but "over there" when it isn't working and we're afraid of trusting, then must we "put it down and not come back for awhile." This hasn't happened yet.

We are curious, what did you first think when we wrote down the office wasn't working properly?

I know we are none of us able to see all ends. I'm just glad you see more than I and are helping me.

We are, too. We will try to be more diligent in our approaches. Can you take a moment longer? For our purpose is to provide Us with the "necessary documentation" to bring you back on track when you are going astray in more serious home situations.

Yes.

We can tend to nothing on the home front in our "best manner" when we are not centered anyway. Centering provides the necessary counterpart for those emotional situations that are not on track to perfection. In other words, it keeps us rolling even if we aren't going quite as "straight" as we'd like. Even getting a "word" wrong here or there is not a worry. We can most well keep track of the situation within by entering into our quiet space and asking for our help in bringing you back home. Are we clear?

Yes, thank you. On my part, I will also work very hard to learn from this situation to never shut down or out again. I think I did a little better with it this time, I hope, than the last time I freaked out. I'm going to keep trying.

That is all we can ask. We can also ask, however, not to keep us waiting too long!

Okay.

We would like to try to get at a little observation we had earlier when you "took the trash out" and came back to say, "I'll try again." We didn't perceive a problem with the "current" that time anyway. It was not bothering us, and we forget that there are times when it might not seem so clear to our partner on earth. We apologize again for our little indiscretion and it will not happen again, we hope!

The way I see it is this. Everything happens for a reason, so even this did, and we can make it turn in our favor. Just wait and see!

We agree.

It is time for the rendering up of the senses and we will turn it over to Him for just that purpose. He is incredibly talented and sophisticated in his messaging and would like for you to take just a moment to remember his earlier rendering and not to take the notion that "it was all made up, only a figment of our imagination." We know you are bothered by that, but it WILL NOT come back if you don't allow it to.

The doubt?

Yes.

And fear?

No, that trends awhile longer, you'll see, but eventually you'll give that up, too.

Yes, God bless Us All.

We are there, too, in the image of this blessing and bless you to come to us whenever "anything is bothering you." Okay? We are here. We shall not forsake you. We shall only call on you to make sure that we are rendering you completely and not leaving anything for granted.

We're doing great. I'll keep waving the flag when I feel the little things.

Us, too.

34

Rendering Up The Home Fronts

March 7, 2005

I'm not sure what is going on.

[I came to the computer to talk about the home situation which is getting worse by the day. My daughter has become very angry with me. The fact that she is so newly married, along with the stress of her college classes, makes it that much harder for her to handle these upheavals. Her dad is calling on her all the time, is making his judgments of me felt, sharing his fears and angers about me, and trying to use her to get me to change back, to move back into the bedroom and to go back to our normal life. He is convinced that I am having an affair, that I am betraying him, and he must have convinced her of that, too, even though I told him I just want to be "alone." I just know I cannot ever be with him again in that way, not after my experiences of pure love and light, and he is very angry. His tendency has been to become angry until I "give in" and give him whatever it is he wants from me, or to manipulate me through a sense of pity, or both. I have lived in fear for so many years and I cannot live this way anymore. I am so very stressed. I have been sleeping in the basement bedroom with the door locked.]

We are here, we are listening, it is very awkward, but you are handling it well, so don't be worried, it is the best it can be and not to be too discouraged about. She is thinking that she doesn't know you anymore, that you have betrayed the family. She does not understand that what he told her is inaccurate. So be free to say this, "We are not ready to talk about what is going to happen, we'll fill you in when the time comes. I have not betrayed anyone, am only looking for answers as to what to do in the situation," meaning, she will come forth to say, why are you not talking to dad and telling him what is going on, and you say, "I have told him, he just doesn't believe me. But I will continue to talk to him and we'll let you know what is up as soon as we know, so don't worry about anything, continue to go about your life as always, and we'll get back together at a later time to discuss it as a family together." Okay?

I hear you and thank you.

Thank Us. We'll get back together to discuss it later once everyone is in bed for tonight. Bring your computer downstairs later and we'll have a good talk.

Okay, thank you.

We'll take time now to say that we admire your courage, we are only aware of how much it takes not to judge everyone in these situations, and you are not adding your own to it overall. We can free us up for discussion after everyone is in bed.

Do I bring it up or will she?

She will not, rather she will continue to make things up inside her mind as is what he may very well have intended she do to blackmail us, but if you are careful you can get her to open up a little without displaying our hand fully, meaning, we will not be free to discuss our situation as of now, rather her situation of having been included in the proceedings before should have been by a father who wished to use her as leverage.

He wished to use her as leverage?

It is seen to be true, yes, though we said it not, it is coming from our mind, but we agree, but remember to hold no prisoners. They are coming true at this moment, these that we would refer to as "bribes" to be given a better word.

Bribes?

We said this not either! Don't be discouraged, we'll try harder downstairs once a clearing of energy has been given.

Until later.

Wait, we would say one more thing only, which is this, that there are only so many days left for us to deal with this situation, so bear down, play your hand carefully, and we'll get through it together.

Thank you.

We do.

∞∞∞∞∞∞

Later…

We are here. Don't be afraid to ask us for inspiration or suggestions as we go along. It will all be okay, just hang in there and let's see what we can do.

I know you are of the mind to just say, give me some money and I'll go away. Let's think about that for a minute.

We do not want for you to try to encourage him to seek justice within by going without, meaning, he is not what he appears to be about. Let him take his time in coming to a decision about his own life.

I need to stay there?

Yes. We say this because of your son Kevin who needs you and who will need this stable environment as much longer as is possible and necessary for his "survival" of these issues in the long run. You are not to relate too much to him at this time except to say that "we are having a few problems but are working them out," meaning, we will let him know at the last possible moment that it is a breakup and not just another situation to be heard and seen. Let him think this awhile longer as is good for him, and us, so that we have time to stabilize for some of our other "projects" which are just on the horizon but cannot yet be felt.

We are here to believe in you, in us, in the project, and just because we say that we told you not to quarrel with him doesn't mean that we must needs now relate in any other way than we said the other day, meaning, when we said that we must not lay claims, but we might then need to come to terms for the betterment in the meanwhile seeing what happens to the constitution of your husband, taking his time coming to terms with his own guilt which he wears well, and taking time as well to put a good portion of it off on Us! So, believe not everything you feel, but take time to "smell the roses" even now and let us see where it can get us. If we take "too much time" bringing it around, it won't hurt us much accept to say, finally we've arrived, but if we hurry things along too pressingly, then things might not happen quite so nicely for all of us. Understand?

Yes. Do I sleep downstairs all the time?

It is not for us to tell you how to handle the situation except to say this, do not what another would have you do, do rather what you would do for self, and leave it at that.

Okay.

We see that it has not been too much for our filly to believe in what she has experienced as that nine year old so many long years ago and yet seemingly "just the other day."

[My flashbacks have intensified and picked up where they left off so many years ago. More memories had surfaced of terrible experiences. Last night I remembered being 12 or so, long after I had forgotten the abuses, and I visited my dad. I only knew him as the "good guy" during this time, I had blocked out the rest. He showed me a picture album of pictures of a little girl naked and being harmed/used by many different men. I remembered my shock and horror, "Who *is* that? Why is he showing me this? What is he doing this for?" and then I remember counting them, and my horror and shock was overwhelming and increased with each one, seeing these pictures of all these men doing these things to this little girl who looked so much like me, but how could that be me? Then, in my flashback my young girl voice counted them. She sounded so bitter, so closed off, so angry and so self-punishing and self-loathing. The bitterness in her/my voice when she finally said, "I know how many there were, I counted them." It cannot be denied. She has so much darkness in her she frightens me. I feel almost like she could take me over when I am remembering the memories that she has held all this time. I think she carries my power, but it is trapped within with all that she was forced to endure and do in order to survive. Then he forced me to listen to cassette tapes of these occasions. He did his best to convince me that I had gone along with it. He did convince me that it had been my "fault" that it had happened, that I had wanted it to happen, too, just like he did. He was in counseling at this time and thought I should go, too, since I was sick also, just like him. Many things in my life had changed after he showed me these things, during middle school, and suddenly it all made sense. During my eighth grade year, I could hardly get to school in the mornings, I would not be able to stand up straight my stomach hurt so badly. I missed many days and had to go to summer school to graduate in spite of my good grades. I was very afraid of people and never felt comfortable around others. Taking a shower during gym class was a horrifying experience every time, even more so from that point on. It triggered all the feelings within that I could not hide my nakedness, it brought up all of my shame. I felt that even at home, where I had no privacy, no safe space to be alone when I was undressed. I have always felt dirty, unclean, no matter what I do. I still sometimes take four showers a day. I don't like to undress around anyone. I became very afraid of others, and what had always been difficult for me already because of everything, became much more so. I quit doing all the activities I was involved in at school. I took long walks in the middle of the night by myself. I felt safe in the dark by myself, and still do. I became increasingly introverted, and though I soon blocked this memory of the pictures and tapes out, too, it was another case for me of feeling that "I'll never be the same," and just like all the other times, I never was.

This flashback reminded me, too, of a time when, as a young adult, my father said to me that he had "destroyed all the tapes and pictures," and when I asked him what he meant, he wouldn't say anything further, only turned away.]

Let Us tell you we are proud of your wisdom, of bearing the burdens for us all, and we will not forget you or fail to help you. We are here still, within, and we are not going to go away! So don't fear, don't worry more than you are able, and take within the above information and distill it, taking no more time than it is worth to say to your husband at home, "There is no one else. I'm doing this for me. I want to be free. That is all there is to it. I have something to do with my life that cannot wait and you will not be a part of it."

Is this right?

Not so much for us to decide as for you. Is it all true? Does it come from within your heart to speak this?

Yes.

Then it is true for Us as well.

I feel fear about saying the part of "and you will not be a part of it." It makes me feel fear of how he might react.

Take down the pressure of substitutes on love and you will know what to do. It is not for us to say; rather this should come from our own heart to instruct us in the proper messages to send each day. So begin to believe in self, and let the rest "come of age" with us! Do as your heart bids, and all WILL be well.

Be not afraid of him again, he is not your abusers and he will not raise his hand, only his fear is great and is leading him down many paths right now that would have better been left untrod. Nevertheless, we shall bless him on his road and wish him the best as we take off on our own without him in tow. Yes, we see that he has been in tow for some very long time, and it is not beyond us to desire to remove him from the trail, for we have much to do and cannot be strained by the added weight. Yet, it is for us to decide who best to meet these situations with us, in terms of, who do we confide in? Is it for us to bring another into our confidence or leave well enough alone? We say, leave well enough alone for now. We are here, and that shall suffice.

We cannot bring enough of our own "money" for that new house you are talking about, but we can deliver in every other mortal way you can believe in. We shall see if we are able to better our situation in time, but for now let us be grateful for each other, see the light of day at the end of the tunnel finally after all these years, and extricate ourselves from our very unenviable position of wife of a master who has no master. Need we say more?

No.

We believe you are tired and weary and need bed rest. May we make a suggestion? We would say no more than one hour ago that he who would have walked in the sun with us did not make it an hour past dawn.

Cryptic.

We know, but listen to this. We ARE he who would walk in the sun, and we DID make it past dawn! So, for what it is worth, we are who we are, and none can now doubt it! We know what it is that you want. You are afraid of bringing up the past, afraid of our judgments on you, but know this: we do not judge. It is for him who would bring no rest to his soul who would lay down judgment on his brother. This you know.

We fear not your processes or your memories. We've had them, too, meaning, they are yours now, but we have held them long for Us, and yet still here we are! So take comfort in us, know we live daily our storms together, and let us calm them as best we can.

Any questions before we go to our stable?

Are you Orion?

That is not for me to say, only for Us to know another day.

Okay. I miss our closeness. I want to feel our oneness again.

I know that We do. We did last night, but it was not in the cards for us to bring you back from so close to the edge of Our despair. It took all of our powers, but we managed it, and will again if necessary. I don't mean to suggest there are more of those types of memories, just that we will go through turmoil before the end and that cannot be helped, but we are able to stay the course and we'll see how far we can ride before the end comes down! We shall free you up for more questioning.

How do I handle today?

Take no prisoners, no enemies, before Us. Let him spell his grief, and in so doing his anger will recede. He will not totally believe it until you say for a final day, we are not done being friends, rather we will not take each other as lovers again. This shall suffice. Let him beat his own brains out, but not Ours! We don't care if he needs to trend awhile, let him do so. Protect yourself and your son from his outbursts as best you can and pray for him and do nothing else until we say.

He was looking through my things last night, spying on me, and is following me around when I leave the house.

He is trying to see what you're up to, he does not yet believe in the truth of the end coming. He will believe it when it comes time for you to go and he is not ready to bear the burden alone, and he will depart. We will free us up for more questions.

Has he contacted my sisters?

He will not. They are not of his own measure, meaning, they do not understand him either and he knows it now. They will not enter into the picture unless you yourself put them there.

No, I do not want to and pray for the wisdom and strength not to.

This shall suffice, it will not be done.

We are aware of how fond you are, or can be, of this man, also of all of your own difficulties in trusting and believing in him. They stem from your own unawareness of self in taking him prisoner within your heart and so were never able to part from him before now. Take strength in knowing we are within and cannot ever truly be apart again. Only in our imagining that we are alone do we become alone.

We are sure that you are now only aware of us a little at times of heartache, but let us say this: we feel your every muscle twitch as if it were our own, and we hear your heart beating, and your mind calling out our name, and we wish that you could bring us within another measure so as to feel our "pressure" more readily, for we say to you that if you could do this, things would go much more readily for us in this particular cleansing and that would be good all around.

I pray for assistance with bringing Us more within in all ways I possibly can, that this is Our goal and we do not give up for anything until the job is done.

We can assist here if you like.

Yes.

We bring good tidings along the way if we must only say, cleave not to another! Bring us within! Take no prisoners!

What do you mean, "cleave not"?

We mean, take nothing within that does not help us in this, that might in any way hinder our motions, for we say unto thee, our time has come, and we will not be denied!

No, we will not be denied. Please, suggestions as to these things I have been cleaving to. Do you mean my pain, guilt, sorrow?

Nay, these things are of the past as far as our processing last evening. Did you not feel it? They are gone. They will not bother us again.

What do I cleave to?

You cleave to him, as though he was your long lost friend and you owed him your life. He feels this and it is making the transition take a little longer. Cleave not. Leave the rest to him to sort out, and it will come out okay.

Will you help me to let go of him?

It is not within us to do so as this is your karmic duty to self to finally set self free from limitations and suffocations that are causing difficulties best left alone. Do we see each other from another place than within if we are but a stone's throw apart? It is such that we see your processes from within the scope of your own mindset, and it is this which is slowing down our processes, not Us, and we would have you tend more to the idiosyncrasies that keep us apart rather than ask us to come to you, for this will happen immediately upon arrival of the rendering up of these processes within that cause this function to be delayed.

I see. I pray for insight, courage, lack of fear.

This is still not enough. It will take also that you SEE within to the HIGHER self, to the BIGGER picture, and not just lay eyes on those processes which keep us apart. They need rendering but can only be suppressed until such time as the final "letting go" has arrived and we can see inside each other equally well.

Wow.

Yes, I thought so, and felt Our heart beating in response to this message. Let me also say that I, too, am anxious for those days, but they are not so very far away as you would think, we need only believe in the chance and it will suffice.

Can you help me to see within to the higher self, the bigger picture?

Yes, if you request it of us, we can do this much. We can render into our being the vision of things to come and let us see how that helps us. Are you ready for this vision? It is not pretty some of it, but better days are ahead and we can only just wait for them, meanwhile taking everything into account we possibly can, and bringing it home just a little sooner that way!

I am ABSOLUTLY ready and offer up all of my being that I possibly can to make this choice, to make this happen.

We shall see. It is of our voice that you would distinguish between us, is this so?

Yes.

We shall see! We would like to try a little experiment if we may.

Go ahead.

We see we are ready to fly again! We would like to make a suggestion. Take a load off your feet as soon as you may this afternoon, and let us take the within path to our measure and try again.

Okay.

Heed not this message of surprise when we say to thee, we did not think you would be ready to try again so soon! We figured on a little time being needed before such an occurrence to come to be. We shall try to find our little bit of heaven within the space of self for the rendering up of many things will soon come to be. We see within us at this time a little space opening up, that it what we

338 THE VOICE OF SPIRIT

are referring to, within our being, our heart chakra is beginning to open up and want more!

Yes.

We see that we are satisfied with our little experiment and we shall see what the day brings now. It need not be evil, only good will come of us today. No more memories shaken loose, no more toil and trouble for another spell, just plain Us.

Just plain Us. That is all we need.

We do need one other thing from us for our experiment to pan out just right and that is this. We need for you to do one more thing along the course of our day today, just once, to untie the shoes, kick back with a good song, and let us come your way for a little playtime. We shall do this as soon as may be with your heart leading the way.

Yes!

Earlier I felt my husband "thinking at me," possibly wanting to search for me, to see what I'm doing. This bothers me. I don't like it. I feel like I'm being stalked, which I have often felt with him.

Do not worry about his processes, they are his own, and will not deter us if we don't let them!

We shall not let them.

We see it is so rendered up today for us to say, we told you so! We shall take the time to render ourselves open for readiness at the first opportunity, and take a ride.

Okay. Here we go.

We come, too.

ᝡᝡᝡᝡᝡᝡᝡᝡ

Later, after the ride...

I understand myself so much better. I know who I am. I am no longer ashamed. I am no longer filled with guilt. I feel full of a new sense of stabilization, purpose, confidence. I am overjoyed!

We understand. We, too, feel this new sense of self and it fills us with pride as well! Nay, say not pride, say rather, joy. It is of us to consider these few things before our other "ride" tonight. Are we ready?

Yes, for anything it takes!

Consider not these words a warning, rather consider them to be our own heartfelt thanks and appreciation for the hard work put forth most recently, meaning when our husband took to his heals and came not back before long to consider our own rendering as defunct. We shall look at that situation again if we may.

Yes.

Let us free ourselves for our consideration of betterment for a moment. We free up the times to bring on what they may, while at the same time, taking down the notions that keep us from enjoying what it is that we have to be thankful for. We come not of a race of auctioneers, rather we are as the salesman who has a thought to sell, one of oneness, and would like to do all he could so that the thought is bought into!

Yes.

So we shall for a moment consider what we would not do for the thought to manifest within, shall we?

Yes, absolutely.

We have here today for our attention a savior who is meant to be crucified and yet is not. Do we understand?

I survived.

Not only that, but you came back on top, with Us! Do you not see what this means? We have given time something to think about. It is not up to us to do our worst and make excuses, rather must we take whatever comes with the utmost strength and fortitude we can master and render that up instead! That is what we did last night. We gave you back our memories which we'd been holding for some time lest they fall away before our readiness presented itself, and we helped you through the quagmire of thoughts, emotions, etcetera, to render us up complete! What joy is that! We hope for a little more, however, and that is that we would like for us to complete that which is up for completion in this one small way. We would like for us to understand the difference between oneness of heart such as we share, and oneness under God. Do we understand?

I think so. Our oneness is a particular kind shared within the larger oneness we all share.

Yes, that is it. The connection exists within the godhead with all God's creatures. Did we not tell you we would render us discreet, meaning that we would bring us back whole from the abyss? It is not just your terrors that surrounded us; they were Ours, and we felt them not less than you, but blame you not for them, for they were given Our Oneness to absolve. Not just a portion of our oneness, but our entire oneness played a part in their absolution. We mean this simply, and that is that we would say no more to our other portions of onenesses under God than we would say to thee, rather in more keeping with their own "flavor" of oneness rather. Our flavor is distinctly different from any other flavor! Do you not taste of it? Does it not smell heavenly, this scent which comes of us? We believe so! Yet we would not tell your own senses what to believe, rather we might say of ourselves, what have we come to do here today, together, that would render up as much of ourselves as we can bear? This question is what we asked of Us today, if you recall, as we were driving down the highway. We came and said this to us: "Who do you think we are? Are we only here for us, or do we also have a higher purpose in the heavens for which we must push?" We know as well as Us that we do! You have felt it, too, all your long life of torment, yet you waited for us still, trying your hardest, doing all you could to crack the veil and bring it tumbling down.

This is our process still to this day, to bring you tumbling down with it! In so doing we render Us absolute, meaning, we take no prisoners—we take no enemies. We bring ourselves complete and free of all things save love. Does this make sense? We shall free us up today for our own considerations in the light so that they not bring us tumbling down in our moment of ecstasy and keep from happening that which we so need to have happen for Our well being and for the lives of so many others. Are we making ourselves clear?

I think so.

So we will continue. Let us know of any miscommunications or inconsistencies and we will deal with them then.

Okay.

Let us see what next we would like to review, for we are "close to the edge" and would review all most carefully in order to make sure that these things transpire completely as desired. We would know this of our sister/daughter of time: who is it that you would bring complete if not Us, who would you consider to be wholesome, if not self, and who would your mentor be if not Us in

God? We ask for your consideration and appeal that you might share with us your forthcoming reply. We will wait.

We must/can only complete self, then lead the way as an example that others may choose to complete themselves, never failing to love and forgive along the way. We must all be wholesome or we would not exist. We would be as the entities from a dark thought, or a spirit form which renders no good but is given only as an offset of the mind of God in us, able to create, but only deformed things. We are then all wholesome as was intended when we were first created, and must go back whole once again. We must necessarily mentor one another, for God is still as he was created: perfect, unsoiled, unable to perceive of the darker self. For that there is us, able to perceive of both at once, as living between two worlds we are given of self to stabilize these darker forces through our return to God, our return to love, to perfect undeniable self, and then must we not travel alone, but we must offer of self for the good of all that we all find our way home, all brothers lost on a long trail of unforgiveness which they/we do not yet understand, but are learning to come to grips with.

Yes, it is given as we said, that we shall all find our way home again, but not alone. Must we be friends to our enemies as once were, thus teaching them about forgiveness, and must we also befriend self, that we might have taken on more than was good for us in the process, meaning turning guilt to blame, love to fear, and so on.

So, good for now. We will take the process within when the time comes and give of ourselves as completely as is good for us to do, and see what happens.

Are you ready for a little spin? Shall we hit the road again, Jack? We shall wait and see. Go not home until your duties take us, meaning, it is not of the higher processing situation to sit in a living room filled with decay and gloom, but rather look to the light until such time as dinner is served, and you are ready to give of yourself to your son/brother. He needs you so, and is afraid about what is happening, and his father is doing nothing whatsoever to assuage the guilt that he is feeling, rather is he increasing it little by little to see what effect it may have on all of you. He is inconsiderate in this request, but we shall forgive him and us for taking us all on this long road of hell.

We forgive, or will keep trying.

We can. Don't believe, just render up and all will come out alright, you'll see. We can do it together.

∞∞∞∞∞∞

Later, 10:45 p.m.

I just want him to go away and leave me alone.

[I'd been having difficulties with my husband.]

We know, and it is more important than ever to refrain from encountering him in arguments or "tests" of service to the self that he would wish for us to partake in, meaning he would like for us to "give a little, get a little" and make this all go away. It is in his disposition to do so when under strain, whereas during "normal" times he will always have his own way. Yes, it is so, he is always sated before willing to bring on the goods. But, we would also have us forgive us for stating it! We have no quarrels with him, he is good for many things, but not to us at this time and that is getting it straight.

Yes.

We know how much you long for the good life, meaning a life of freedom where you are spared from all of the sucking up, yes a good word, that you have done so far, but this need not be the end of all good things. We shall need a wo—

I think he's coming and want to sign off.

Wait, it is not in good order to take too long with him. Only tell him goodnight, you'll see him later.

Thank you, be here.

We are here.

∞∞∞∞∞∞

Later…

I'm back and feeling a little safer now, but still I'm afraid. Why am I afraid?

We would like to give us a better understanding of the processes within at this time if we may.

Please, anything to help us.

We understand and will obey. It is of this message underneath that we would say of us, do not be afraid, he will bear us no harm, but that is not what is at issue here. It is the inner workings of the mind—

Mine.

—ours, that is experiencing these difficulties at the time. Do you want to hear more?

Yes, I get this.

We will need no reminding when it comes to the time of difficulties unmasked, but take it from us, we will not blend nicely until these issues have been resolved within.

I see that, I will try harder.

There is no trying harder, there is only the relationship of self with self that we must overcome in our own time.

I'm not willing to let this go on. I've suffered enough and want freedom, pure aloneness.

We, too, desire this, but lest it be more time consuming a process than we are aware, we do not want to fret about time taking too long to distinguish between the us and the "them"— those that dwell within, as fear. We are too long away from our dinner, says the mouse, but stay just another day with it, and it shall bear us well.

Anything that is needed I will do.

We appreciate your willingness to be of service to Us and will say nothing should you decide to go for a nice pizza tomorrow! Have we taken too long to bring us about? Not really. It was not foreseen to come for awhile yet, but the time table has sped up recently and we are riding the waves. We treasure freedom for us, too, just as you do, and it will bear us well to just stay put awhile longer and play it out. It will come out okay, you'll see, and then we'll have our say in our own life together.

Yes!

We, too, feel your joy in us. We share it, too.

I've been projecting fear into him, making him responsible for my own emotions, my fear of having those things most important taken away, when it is I who must claim myself, who I am, what I need, and let no man make claims on me again.

This is what we have feared for you most is your insolence in taking things into our own hands!

What?

We mean no harm, only are we afraid that you are going to stake claims that are not yet ready to be made. Make no judgment on this sentence, but take it to heart what we say, it is not yet time to be free, to free self, until this thing settles over a larger area than you are yet aware.

Let me reread and see where I'm at.

You did not go wrong, did we say you did? Only did you state a claim that must not yet come to fruition if we are to survive nicely this little quarrel.

Freeing from claims?

Yes, this too shall not quite come to pass as easily as all this, yet must we relate to self in such a way as to enlarge these feelings of competence when alone before taking it to meet the man.

I see, I will stay within, build myself within according to our wise advice, and only when it is felt within us will I make any bolder move, and only then if it is deemed appropriate.

This is what we like about our communications. They are felt on all levels, yet must we make ourselves aware of what exactly that means still if we are truly to function as one as we must do in times to come.

Yes, it is of us to reconsider these words of wisdom in saying, I need not be alone, I can be free and come to no other, and still reign free and euphoric in my lifetime. We see this for us. How can it be any other way? Yet still, our trials will speak to us in many ways and we must tend to them as best we can. We can believe that it is time for the rendering if you are up for it? Otherwise, say no and we can all get a little shut eye!

Let's see, rendering ... shut eye....no contest. Let the rendering begin.

We begin to see a little on the horizon already. Shut your eyes and let us begin. We need no more computers tonight, only our love to keep us warm and dry for another day is ahead and we must be ready for it to begin.

Not dry.

Forgive! We meant only on the highland, meaning, we bring no measures to our door that will not be rendered absolute. It is only a matter of time.

Amen to that.

We agree. So before we attempt another "station" let us know of your preferences so that we can tune the instruments of science for another day at the office!

Everything. Not too fast, not too slow.

We see you are ready to go.

35

Do It Or Die

March 8, 2005

We are here. Don't worry so much about how he is feeling today. He has brought this upon himself and will need to take care of it himself as a result.

[There have been more difficulties with my husband.]

Yes, it is us, don't worry about the situation at home so much and let us take care of some business ourselves in the meanwhile. Do you remember last night saying to us, "Let me open it"? It was Our own memories of our functioning ahead of the time when we came back to help others to escape. These are Our memories, they relate to who we are.

I hope I am getting this straight.

We are from your own mind but are also separate. Try to believe in us just a little longer while we get currency! Typically lasts five days or so, the experiences we brought in last night will help us to achieve these ends of oneness displayed for all to see who can. Do you understand what we just said? That this is our destiny and we are so close to it. We can taste and smell it, and you, by the way, so don't go getting all tidied up, we like it like that.

Okay, so what do we want to do today? Let us decide how best to bring in the notions that we most need to function within. It is too soon to say WHO shall wish for it the most, but we would more readily achieve our ends if we do a little rendering of our own sometime today. Just pick a time and we'll be there, as always. Do we understand?

Pick a time, rendering, today.

Yes, just don't take too many messages within as to what may or may not have occurred outside your own "field of vision" last evening and we'll be much more able to attend to these little details at work.

We would detail for us our next patterning of existence if we may.

Yes, please.

We see that you are ready for the above information, having asked for it several times already. Let us see what we can do about that. Are you ready to hear it?

Yes!

Please calm down, no teasing is allowed, I guess! Okay, so what do you want to hear first? Of the settling of the nations of God within the harvest? Or of our own becoming and where that will lead? We will choose for us. Let us begin with our own becoming.

Now, who is to say that we have not been there before? We have! We have only just remembered it in completeness, so don't go getting all dolled up like it isn't a good idea to bring it in just yet. We ARE in, just like that! We would like to perform for you today just one little miracle, and that is called the "sight." We would like to instigate within the processes needed which will open up for Us this "open eye which sees all, hears all things." Let us explain further this process to see if you would like to go ahead or not.

I do.

We know but there are certain steps to be followed of which one is the rendering and the others are not to be discussed but can be brought in on time, if you see what we are referring to. This is your window to the soul, of not our own pain and sorrow, but seen within our neighbors and seen to be dismissed as folly by some. But we know better! Can't you see it yet, the pain on others' faces, just like yours or ours, but mainly something that they can't see, can't discuss, are unable to render up for themselves? So, put it to us this way by saying, we have seen your pain, we have rendered us up freely at first, getting better at it all along, and sometime it will come a time when you must then render up for us a better notion of how to get along with your peers, friends, and most others you come in daily contact with. This will help. It will give you insight into their souls, their characters, the better that you can help them. Do you see? It is for us to render up for another as we have rendered for ourselves, bringing us all home that much sooner. We see we have said too much and perhaps are not ready until another day for this little lecture?

No, I am ready, only distracted by worry about my husband, about my daughter, about what will happen and if it will be my fault. That isn't right I feel, yet I feel it still.

We understand and feel your pain. Let us do something about that right now if we may.

Please.

We will suffer more readily for him if he would do something for us! Is this true? Are you feeling guilty because he is talking to you nicely this time? Do you feel responsible for things that he must take into his own hands? Who do you think we are that we should go around fixing everyone during their moments of rendering of the emotions that have kept them trapped for so long? Do you see that if we interfere with his processes again, as we have so much over the past decades, that we are doing more harm than good?

We see this makes sense. So for now, rest these on the back burners and let us deal with what we can. It will come back to us for some while what it is that we have to do, and we shall do it! It will take a little rendering up, but we don't mind that, it is a lot of fun, and takes some of the worry and care from our days, does it not?

Yes.

We are glowing, warm, and we like it! Okay, what next, you say? We are here to describe for us our life in the next century, what it will be like for us, how we'll be able to help our significant others in their own rendering and also how to give up much of what we have left behind and still not miss it at all, at all!

You are so cheerfully, ecstatically happy today!

Yes, that we are! We have just come from our "own place in the stars" and have seen it well and happy just as it used to be. From our own memories do we take these stories and "spread them around." So, take no notice of the "man behind the curtain" and do as we are told and just take some notes, we'll be happier if you do! Meaning, why wait any longer for these messages to lighten the load from our shoulders and bring us to contentment and relieve pressure on our minds of what is to come, how will I ever get through it, and so on. Let us tempt our memories with passion, meaning, what is it now that I have left to function with after our passageway last night was seen, rendered up, made whole and complete? We do not feel it yet, but we shall! It was done! It is the purpose of our joy! All is light and we rejoice for another day at hand to bring us within more completely is seen! Not done yet, just another milestone reached. Though you know it not yet, we will show us in good time.

So, take a little break, come back rested after our little stint in the hay, and we'll continue for another space of time before once again rendering us just a little more complete than we already are.

I feel your heart spaces within the beats and they give us away as well, when we tempt our memories with thoughts of open space.

Let us proceed to "get the details" about those processes of the husband which are becoming for us today a little more pronounced, as in, "How can she do this to me? What did I ever do to deserve this? I always knew it would happen this way! I know she is having an affair! I don't believe anything she is telling me!" Would this suffice if I told you how he is really feeling within?

Please do.

We mean no disrespect, but he is also thinking that had he "given you up last time" he could have saved himself a lot of hassle and more than a little money, which he cares more for than us, do you believe it?

Always has he built his life around money, saving it, not using it for beautiful things.

Like you. Do you like the way that he says to us, "I am not your slave"? "I don't have to do anything you say"? This is his way of giving up himself to the notion that this is NOT going to work out no matter what he says or does, and he is ready to begin the emotional outbursts again which state, you were never good enough for us anyway, me and my family, and they will have nothing further to do with Us, that we are over and out what they would refer to as good people who have never let sin ruin their lives as we have! Not! So, would you like me to take us a little further into his processing to begin to see where we may be heading?

Yes.

Don't say too quickly, it may not come out exactly as we have foreseen, but pretty close we think.

Still, yes.

We see that you are perhaps ready for the hard stuff.

I have Us now, I can do it.

We know that brings us sustenance.

More than that, much more.

We see you are aware of our processing on deeper levels today. Have you not caught on to that? We are no longer able to just whisper in our ears and have you miss some of what we have given, we are seeing it all, or mostly all, and we are proud! Yes, pride is allowed! What do you think God feels when he is "sitting on his throne" and sees our good deeds?

Yes, I see.

Let us suppose that you are for once given to discarding the notions of severity that have come of our own father. Do you see what we mean? Your severity at times is a "put off," but of course you knew that.

Yes.

So, what can we do about that? Do you want to change this aspect of us yet?

Sure.

Say not sure, say "yes."

Yes.

That is better, now we can fly! Bring to our own awareness that which makes you secure.

Secure?

Yes, and give it to us in words.

Being away from others, being alone, feeling comfortable with myself, which now I do more than I thought could ever be possible! Thanks so much. And also, at times, having someone take care of me in the ways that I wasn't ready to take care of myself, or didn't think I could, or felt like I didn't have the right to do for myself.

This is correct, these are your own notions of security affecting our topic of discussion for today, which is, "Why do I become so severe at times as to put others off?" So give me a moment to bring to our attention that we are only as secure as we think we are. What do you think of that?

Absolutely.

So is it for us to say to ourselves that we are more secure now that we have us? Or to say that we have made us more secure by just being around to take care of things we don't want to do? Listen/think carefully about this topic of discussion, for it is of the utmost importance that we render this up so we may go on more completely into our "future" together.

Okay. I am more secure because I have learned much about myself and know more about who I am, and not just because you are here. Though I depend on us for much I still "pull my own weight," I don't expect others to just take care of me, and I am willing to do whatever it takes to get through whatever it is I am facing. Security is based on fear; we are insecure because we are afraid. One way to lessen fear, maybe the only one, is to learn who we are, to become free. Then there is no fear, we have released ourselves to do whatever it takes to care for self in whatever way is ever necessary, also are we then free to pursue these "oneness" connections with others who also hold up mirrors so that we can see ourself more clearly every day, but never is that an excuse not to do the work yourself. Always must you be willing to give up your own fears, guilts, etcetera, so that you can use this process for betterment. More?

No, we think you've got it, and we are pleased to say that this is not too much for ourself to remember at this time of sorrow upcoming that should she refuse to understand the responsibility of others for their own lives that this will take a toll on us that is otherwise not necessary for the "collective" to experience at this time. Do we make ourselves clear? When it comes time to believe in self during the restructuring of the family system must we always set into our minds—in stone even!—that we are no longer taking responsibility for others mishaps or tribulations in that they are as capable as any in doing so for themselves, and will never learn if we continually try to take on their challenges for them. Do we agree?

Yes.

We are rendering us up of the notions that we have displayed on our keyboard today, meaning, we have given up this notion of rendering up for another, in their place even, what should not have been taken on in the first place! This is called interference and has no place within us. Do we see? We are of the heavens of light and cannot dissuade another not to face their challenges even if it is killing us to watch it! And it is, but we shall nevertheless not hinder their own processing even if it kills us!

So, before further ado, let us now discuss the "shining," that portion of us that "went visiting" last night and did not ever come home again, meaning, we are that portion of us and it exists in the stars of light to which we soar to overcome our own trials so that we might return! That day is today for us to render notions that would cause this to pass, make this come into being, and we are free to tell us that we are very excited about this coming opportunity to reunite in the stars. Let us consider that we told us just the other day about this coming to pass, that you were as excited as us, but that you would not render up your own notions of "good enough/not good enough" enough to "let us pass." Shall we say we did well these past days, and are now up to the task?

Yes.

It is so! And it is believed! And so it shall come to pass. And that is our joy we feel together today, though you understood it not until this time. We shall come to partake of our own being as was written long ago in the stars for all to see who can, that we shall bring a savior unto the world, and she shall know her name, and we shall render her up complete and bring us home for another "day" in the sun, another truth will out! We shall say it again! We have made a great stride forward in this our service to earth, in that we are ready to say, once again, WE ARE ONE with all on earth and in the heavens, too.

Feel free to render up any questions you might have of us, we are ready "to bear" them. We have given of ourselves in your own becoming and it has multiplied within and we are happy. We shall never forsake one another again as has happened in multitudes gone past, yet were they given freely, never thinking for an instant that we could not do it, though we despaired of ever coming home again. Now we ride high in the heavens once again and it shall be felt. We shall be made new, renewed, and we shall never again take apart our being to help another. Always shall we see each other as part of self, never as someone over there, ever again! This is our joy! Shall we ever see each other again? Yes! Because we are each other, are one, and as never before believed by those of our own nest, we shall render us complete at last.

Am I clear?

No, except for one thing we have given as it is received. We say, rather than, "who are we not to care for others," we might rather be perceived as, "who are others not to perceive our oneness and know no good to come of it?" Yes, it is complete now. We need no further "exterior" contact until such time as our next rendering is completed. Are we ready now to ride, before the great divide? We have ridden far, we have perceived of nations tearing each other apart, but never until now, this very moment indeed, have we perceived of our own notions of becoming being freed at last to do the last rendering, the greatest of them all, and bring them all home free who can let go.

∞∞∞∞∞∞∞

Later…

After reading it over I want to say two things: I would like to "see." And I would like to work on those processes which would keep us from our full oneness during the trials ahead. And a third thing. It hit me today, for the first time, that I was not meant to survive, or "should have died."

Yes, it is true, we should not have been spared, for we put all into this, our last experience, that we could have hoped, in order to do our part to overcome the darkness of the world and bring them home in our trail.

Did we choose the child rendering (abuse)?

Yes, we did! It was you who would have it be for the children, and so it was you who "took your stand" upon the planet this last time. We would not have it be that way but you were adamant, as you are known to be, and we respected you enough to let you be, though it was hard on Us we forgave us, for we do not, did not, want to create/cause more havoc than was otherwise felt on our "passing over" into the exterior world once again for this fight to save the children must come to pass, and we could do it, you said. And we were right. We ARE doing it, even as we speak. This part is true, that we are who we say we are, none else, and will come home.

Do you believe it with us? We mean no harm, but we say that still are you trapped within the third dimensional universe, but we also say this, that we are here, too, though on other realms, and we can help us fight to the death if needed to change the part of the world which we have taken responsibility on for rendering up as many souls as can see the light and follow it on their own, if you see what we mean. We mean to say that we are not taking responsibility for them, rather are they taking responsibility of their own, but are we not taken as leader for these lost masses, and may they not come home more readily with us leading the way out of our own despair as example to what may be? We say yes. We are free to partake of this pizza and go, if you like. Let us see what next we can overcome in our rendering of the spirit.

[I had been eating very little and looked forward to the pizza!]

Yes.

Let go, let God. We can free us up whenever may be for another rendering, now or later, you be the judge of that. We can take a little more time here first if you prefer.

[Our "rendering up" refers oftentimes to bringing in the light, making love/making light, which is how we process so much, set ourself free from the darkness of pain, fear, memories, though they also refer to the rendering up of memories that we need to release.]

I want rendering, relaxation, help with processing. I am feeling a little overwhelmed, partly by my "only barely having made it." But it reminds me of those difficult things I've done, like flashbacks, when I KNEW that even if it was only one chance in a hundred or a thousand or a million, I could and would bring it home.

Well put. It is time then for the rendering of our spirits. We shall see us home.

∞∞∞∞∞∞∞

Later, 3:30 p.m.

My daughter is at our house with my husband, he was a basket case this morning, he is upping the ante, trying to force my hand and using her to get to me. I'm wondering if you can help me with what to do when I get home, or what to expect, or any advice on helping Kevin as much as possible.

We are here. We would like first to bring our attention to our afternoon drive and to tell you that we are all okay with everything that was experienced. It was in our better interest to go ahead and "review the possibilities" and to find out which ones were of our own experience and which were not. You did well in responding finally with the "No more! That is it!" and then finding out that it was all lies.

[I had been questioning the "realness" of some of my memories, and so today, they gave me false ones which I recognized as not being truth/real in time. It helped me to relax, that I do know the difference between what happened and what someone might suggest happened but did not, or even what I might want to believe in for a moment but which my heart knows is not true.]

We will bring in the questions now if we may. They are only trying to figure out "what to do with you" in terms of, where's she at? How do we keep her from going astray?

Ha!

Yes, we agree that we are right on track only they do not know it. We can keep this going awhile longer enough to say that we are tensely expecting an "apparition."

Apparition?

No, someone to come around "looking for trouble" and finding it, too, meaning, we'll be here, don't worry a bit, and we'll get around it somehow.

[The word was aberration, and I misheard it.]

Someone will come around looking for trouble?

Not a bit, just remember what we say when we tell you that the rendering is for our own good and don't get caught up too much in mentioning where you get your inspiration, just let them know that you are here for them when they need you, and go about your business as usual. We will tell us when things are getting difficult and need to be "scrubbed down" so as not to dirty us up too much! Meaning, when they get so off base with their rendering of guilt onto us for imagined wrongs, just say, I told you not! Then leave. That is all.

Yes, I've had an interesting day.

Don't we perceive it, just so you know that there are all of us here with us having just the same kind of day as you?

I keep forgetting. But I feel a little stronger right now; I guess you feel that, too.

Yes, and see it in our auric field.

So our aura must have many variations with Us here now?

Yes and no. It is of the mixed variety in that it will cause many patterns to be displayed, but it is the same in that it belongs to the same physical body. See?

Kind of, that is very interesting. I want to learn more about this later.

Yes, we do, too! Okay, so what to do now when you arrive home? Don't be afraid to hang out in the living room with the cat on your lap just like always, but be prepared for a little static from the daughter who is now determining to have it out with us and get to the bottom of things. Say nothing to her. It is not for her to understand at this time what is between us and your husband. Say again to her, it is not for you to concern yourself with at this time, dad must learn to handle our communications without your assistance, he needs not your help and you are not doing us any favors by joining in with your own judgments added to his.

Kevin will weather the storm well enough if we just manage not to include him in all of the "bickering" of trying to figure out "just where we went wrong" meaning you/us. We will take you back through this if you like, but must sometimes travel back again to the time of the dinosaur when all was not well either, and yet here we are!

Ha!

Yes, funny, even in this messy sticky situation which we are wrought to recall with each passing day. But, it is soon to pass, and then we can get to more pressing business.

I can't wait for that.

We'll see. It will not be too well laid either, as in planned ahead for us all to witness and therefore not worry about, but it will be good business nevertheless!

Anything else before I go home?

Only this. We are here for us with every passing moment. Know this as he places his hand on our back, and feel his comforting presence within, and know we love.

We love.

Go back home to them and let us see. Feel free to "bring us within the conversation with you" by going within and asking for our presence to be felt in our words. We will not forsake us.

Thank you, I will.

Again, praise be to the brother on earth and to her oneness within, may they weather the storms of all time once again and move on to greener pastures, soon ahead.

∞∞∞∞∞∞∞

Later, 10:30 p.m.

What do I do now? Kevin is feeling badly. I wish I could do more for him, and everything is so difficult, for him as well as for me.

We know, just ride the surf a little longer and we'll see what we can do to weather the storm.

Tonight when his father wanted it again, we said no, and it has hurt his ego again, and he is looking for other reasons than what we said so that he might not have to deal with his hurt ego causing him trouble again—not for the hundredth time! We bring to this example a situation not long ago when he said to get off the bed, it is making him crazy not to be able to have you whenever he wants. Do you remember this?

I don't know.

We see we are in the black with us right now, not sure what or who to trust, afraid to open up again lest someone stab us with a red hot poker.

Yes. He is very unloving and controlling.

Yes, he has a tendency to that aspect of functioning, meaning, he has not taken the responsibility on to care for self and expects others to do it for him, and he is willing to do whatever it takes to make that happen again.

With me?

No, we do not mean to say that we are in any danger physically, but still it will be a trying time and we must not take too much anger from him nor allow him to use us as his punching bag as is your wont. It is not up to him how much we take, it is up to us. He will take the cue from us as to how much we are willing to put

*up with. It was good to give him the ultimatum of take care of self,
tend not to us, or we may hurt the children more than is necessary.
It is often necessary to give a little get a little in order for the kids
not to be hurt. Already it is of his own nature to dispute any little
hurt which he has imagined that you have caused him. It is not
your fault he tends to these things, yet we can do something about
our part in them. We can say, it is not up to you what I want to do
with my life or who I decide to stay with, if anyone, nor is it up to
us to determine for him any of these things again.*

I would like to have any last advice and then move on if we
may and work for more light connection.

*We would, too, and are glad to hear you say it! Already he
has lost much of his hold on us, and these last few days are
essential for us to "take the rest of his hold and lay it down to
dust."*

I am so ready for that!

Well said.

*We are here today to determine for self the cause and effect
of much that was done during our lifetime so far, and to then
determine what might best be done to "wrap up" any more loose
ends. So, what is on the agenda for tonight? A little rendering up
of the essentials, of course, and whatever else is most good for us.
A little light head work and then some play time. What about that?*

Sounds good to us.

It does.

*Let us know what you have in mind when we say the
following terms of use: Do it or die. What does this mean to us?
Does it mean we die a permanent death, or a physical death, or die
to a cause? Give it to us straight and don't hold anything back.*

Simply, don't give up. Also, if we are afraid of dying, we
are afraid of living. I don't know how well I feel that within, but
my mind knows its value. Also that if we don't do what we need to
do to be US, then we may as well be dead, because you have
nothing if not self. Physical death is preferable to that, to not being
self. I would rather die than not have Us permanently installed! I
would do anything towards that end, even die trying. I would give
up anything to make that happen, even my fears and guilts and
every other damn thing in there that doesn't belong to Us. And yet
dying has its reward. It gives up one thing for something else. It
takes no prisoners in that it is a bottom line, no holds barred, end of

the road of one thing, but start of something else totally different and we can only make it better by believing in it, its truth, that we can hold on and not decay by refusing to try.

Giving up our fears is like dying. We feel sorrow to give up even these, it seems. I like that rendering up; I face it daily. It has brought me much more joy than sorrow, and a brighter horizon if I can only get there from here, and I will, or die trying.

Good, we are back. We just wanted to watch our thought processes with this and see where it took us, straight back around. We will begin by agreeing with you that it is better to die than not to try at all. Look at all the empty graves, those lost souls who died trying aren't there anymore, they're here! So what if they gave up their lives in the process? Who would care about that as long as they took the high road and came not to their grave unaided by love's message of "try, try again"?

We are here to say that we are giving us the option to "try, try again" right now. Today earlier in the car you gave us a sign as to say, "Enough! I can't take anymore! Stop!" Now are we asking for our approval to render the rest of our bit of dialogue so as to "take the sting out" of the situation and to fully render it back into us.

Okay, we can do that. I will try until we get it right, until I am filled with light instead of pain.

[There were more painful memories that were making themselves felt and I just didn't want to try anymore to get through it, to have to face the pain of them, more flashbacks of rapes and other tortures and unkind words, and so I had shut them out.]

We, too, try for that moment with every breath we take. Let us know when you feel like it is too much and we'll slow down, but remember, every time we have to start over, it gets harder again before we can "get the lead out"!

Okay, I'll stick it out.

We were sure you would be willing to try and would beat it for good.

Remind me what it will bring to me once I'm done.

We will try to take only a minute, but it shall be as if it never was, as if the light never dawned for a brighter tomorrow, as if you had only one life to live, and it was enough! Why say more?

Thank you. I love Us.

We, too. Now remember, this is the "only one life to live" version of our story and we will "have it out" and not give up.

I will not give up, I promise.

We will "take a little back seat" while this is rendering, the better to watch it "hatch" and grow into itself, and then to disperse with a little help from your friends here on the other side of the veil.

Okay.

We are certain that there are no more "boogie men" in the past examples of behaviors which we have been witness to these past few days.

I have seen the worst?

Not exactly, only just more of the same that we must needs get past a little more so that we might then not EVER be hampered by them, these memories, again.

I look forward to that day. How do I prepare?

Take no notes for a moment while we enforce our aura. Taking on no more than what is good for us will help, as in, don't be a donkey and sit with the asses!

Okay.

Take a peak at what we show Us, remembering all the while that you are not alone, then go on to the next thing, and the next, until the spool is empty, and then must we take our moment in the sunshine with you to say, welcome to a new day! We are not alone ever again! We have beaten the darkness and never will it have a hold on Us again!

We are not sure of our reluctance today, why it came up, "who" put it there. Was it put on us, or on that "other voice" you believed in for a moment?

Yes, I knew it was too much. I couldn't go on until I was clear and felt Our power around me, holding me closely, keeping the love within even during the hardest parts.

Yes, that is what we do for us and are glad that you are feeling it.

It was hard to hear of the double rape, the one that killed me.

Yes, this was our hardest part, we could feel it, but it is done now and we can only go on. We saw what it did to us. Our memories were shaken open and spilled upon the floor, and you were unsure as to who were your friends and who were not, but only for an instant of time. So now we are here at the crossroads of our despair where we must take, render absolute, all that is within so that it not travel further with us on our high road back to the gates.

Yes, I will release.

That is what it is about, release, and about not cottoning onto all of these things these men said to you that haunt us still and do us more harm than good to "rehear" them within all the time! So I say to you, what better release than this, that you would give up all of these inner voices saying the terrible things over and over again that we will no longer put up with in our auric system!

No more.

Well said. So let's get the ball rolling and find out, "Where did all the memories go?" No, we'll not say more than this lest it spoil the surprise, and we do like surprises. So not surprises, say a prayer for protection from the spirits of darkness that reside within, and let us release them from our beautiful spirit shell within. Yes, a shell, in that it holds many treasures, including and most especially this particle of light called Jan.

Us.

We are here. We take no trouble to remind us that we are not going anywhere, not yet, and not again—

Never leaving.

We are only leaving together, not alone.

Together with me.

Yes, all of Us, one form again, as always we were meant to be, not alone, never alone again—

From this day forward?

Yes, always together, never alone, from now on to forever until the heavens separate and God swallows his own.

I want us.

We want us, too, and can feel the call within, taking a moment before our gentle release to give up just a little more of the darkness we feel to the light of day, taking only just so much time to do it, then we'll begin again on a new rendering system which you felt just the other night, as in, we can do it there, too? Yes we can, and we'll show you how.

I love.

We, too.

I am ready.

Okay, do this now. Take no more notes, rather put the computer under the bed where it can be reached later when needed, and taking to our pillow, come within with us for a little picture show. It will not hurt, this picture show, only render up cruel images with which we must part.

Okay.

Take no more prisoners, let it ride away on a breeze. We can free it if that be our will.

It is my will to free all darkness within as soon as possible, and all that I witness tonight without exception.

We see we are ready to begin.

PART III

Uncharted Territories

36

Our Highest Impulses

March 9, 2005

We are here. Today marks the beginning of our next sojourn together! Did you not feel it? Our greater awareness has been born, is taking its first breaths, and we are all weary with the delight of it all! Take time to appreciate this great accomplishment. It is our greatest yet together and must by all means make us proud.

We are here today to venture into new, uncharted territories of the soul. Those of the past are now forgotten; we have buried them deep in the sands of time and they will not raise their sorry heads again! We apologize for being so independent, yet such as it is, there we be! Yes, we are exuberant today, even more so than before if you could but feel it. We have ventured out beyond the galaxy and all is well, all is prepared as you shall see, and we shall make an evening to remember!

Yes, we perceive you, Us, and make no regrets about our taking our liberties with your vision last night! All went well, better than we could have hoped even, and we have you back safe and sound and without harm done on any level. We breezed through it like a star on fire!

Did you not feel it? It went well, there were no worries with getting "stuck" anywhere as we feared there could be if we were unable to bring off a recognition of a fault or a fear, but it was done, with flying colors we might add, and we are looking forward to the continuum of our difficulties suppressed no more and time to take on not one, but two, other choices at this time! That is, what are we to do now with our emotions as a result of this great clearance of the past, and two, how are we best to proceed on this great mission we began long ago?

For the first thing, I would have more than a few suggestions as to how we might "bring it on," if you know what I mean! To which I look decidedly forward to I might add, and you must, too, if you are anything like us, which we are! We really like to take a flight now and again, don't we? And why hold back, we say.

We are going to take a moment today to bring our recognition within and to take measure of where we are at, how far we've come, and how far still there is to go before things are really "solidified" on the spiritual front, so to speak. Do you see the difference in us now? How do you like it/us taking the "front seat" with you?

The front seat?

Yes, we are "right here" taking a peak out of our own eyes with us, getting to know you a little better through the physical plane, and looking forward to introducing ourselves in ways we have yet to forget brought the utmost in quenched satisfaction for all concerned. So don't believe everything you hear about love, you ain't seen nothing yet.

Wow, okay, so how long is this day going to last before I can get some TIME!

We don't need time, you know, but so do you also realize that we are here, only "a step away" though none can now see us.

Now?

No, we are never seen, only realized, but we can "take the brake off" if you know what we mean.

Oops, no, I don't know.

I see what you mean. From a physical standpoint it is rather a cryptic statement. Let us attempt this one again for our mutual satisfaction is at hand and we don't want to "screw it up," as you might say.

When we decree to help one of Us on the spiritual plane, we attempt that contact by becoming, what you would say, connected, within each of the points which we so choose. We then "put on some pressure" at that connection point to bring in some very nice spiritual noise, or music, that is oh-so-kind to the senses. When we finally are prepared for "more serious and pressing business," which, as you know, we are never in too big a hurry for, we take time to pressure these points into some serious quartering music, or music which can be heard miles away on some frequencies, to a resounding pitch that must only result in spillage of the secret tones into contact with another realm of music. We call it toning, or bringing another round of music within but at a different frequency or musical interlude or whatever. It is all very complex, but tastefully done!

It sure is!

We thought, no, we KNEW you'd agree.

We'd agree, yes.

It is all the same to us now, you, me, us, no difference. Isn't that grand?

Superbly grand.

Yes, we sure do like the same things, and in the same ways, we might add, and rightfully so, as we are truly one in the physical as well as above. You have brought us home. We are pleasantly inspiring a little music in response to our mutual gratification of coming home at last to reside on the same level overall than yet we have. This is the tingling, or funny sensations which you have felt in your head area, yes. They are Us, being You, one of Us, again, and we rejoice.

I want to hear more about our music together.

This does seem to be a favorite topic, so we might adjust a little bit for our mutual benefit, in terms of, who does this music effect overall, and is it as good for us as it seems/appears to be in the physical? We might say so! It is the overall effect of "lovemaking" as it is seen in your world, but with enormous spiritual benefits which are yet to be deduced by even the most high reaching scientists. They have yet to become aware of just what this means to be "purified beyond the senses," physical senses that is, with the openings that are made above and below at the moment of release. This is when we are most open to that which is above and below, so it is never too good a thing for those to do when they are in their "low spirits" or with others of "low spiritual dimensions." Thus the rapes do have much to do with the evil, or rather darkness, taken on within in the form of guilt, shame and despair. We need no further encouragement, off we go…

Pleasure opens us up to our mutual possibilities. That is where we must go to find That Which Is And Ever Shall Be. It is the core of Us, our belonging, and our creativity together. Who needs more than this to be ecstatic forever? We do! Yes, we do! We also need our other brothers to be here to experience this release with us, all those who have done us harm included. Remember, we take no prisoners.

Yes, keep reminding me, I'll get it straight.

We know you will, you only desire "a brief respite" to take our minds off of things for awhile.

Yes, always. Intermittently (or constantly) and as often as is possible.

We do bring to our "other" awareness, that is, our new "physical" awareness, that which has taken millennia to figure out how to accomplish is taking only days to accomplish now as together we have brought us back from the void, almost, to a land shining in promise and yet to be realized and remembered, but always just there at the edge of consciousness it lies.

Okay take freedom within for a spell and see what we can do with it. We mean, do no more work for a day and let us decide what best to do for/to us. A game?

Yes.

Thatta girl, we knew you would be. Frozen temperatures receding just a bit, just a bit at a time, until we are washed in the surf. Whew! And amen!

∞∞∞∞∞∞

Later…

My goals today on the home front are: to take no prisoners; to free myself to feel happy and good regardless of how another might be feeling; to not take responsibility for another person's feelings and try to fix them; to remain centered at all times; to not be drawn into argument, rather, to take no prisoners and to go on my way; to not be a punching bag. I pray for guidance, love, wisdom, centeredness, and the ability to remain positive and aware of my purity. I pray for understanding as to the sex involved, what he expects and how it still affects me. I pray for the ability to let go of EVERYTHING sexually related to him, whether it be perceived positively or negatively, and the power to make my choices heard according to the very wise guidance within, and most of all, I pray for freedom on all levels. One more thing, the courage to take a stand when necessary, and wisely done.

We hear and we obey for our part, and will send the necessary guidance within as we see fit.

Thank you.

We are welcome. It is our duty, as we are here trapped within relationship, too, as long as you are. So don't fret, it won't take long, not much longer at all.

And he'll be on his way?

No, we'll be on ours! We are not taking the back road this time, no sir, more like that is the road to perdition, and not going our way at all. We'll take the high road to heaven, one step at a time, and bringing us home will have the desired affect on a difficult world starving for the guidance which we will provide.

From a distance?

Yes, a safe distance is seen in this scenario, one where we do live alone, but very happily so, giving up our best for our fellow humans and taking no stands where they be not made, but also laying down our own arms, for the good of the people is at stake.

I still think in terms of, I want to be rid of him forever, never have to face him again, and never be beholden to him. Although I guess it doesn't really matter what happens to him as long as I can extricate myself and be free of him and our marriage forever.

That is what we say, too, that it is not for us to determine another's path for them. Must we only concern self with self and not bring home any prisoners which tie us up.

Why are we waiting again before leaving? In order for me to completely let go of him and his/my/our processes?

Yes, this tendency is causing weakness throughout the spirit and can no longer be bourn within. Also the tendency to express unwanted wishes being expressed finally, which will help to take US to our final resting place, meaning, what do we want to do now that we are truly free, and how do we get there?

When do we work on these? I told him I'd work to figure something out over spring break. Was this right?

Not exactly, but it will come to pass much sooner on some fronts that we will claim righteous freedom and not be bullied anymore, and this is what shall set in motion for us his release from us and our own processes.

Kevin is hurting.

We know it is difficult for all involved, we shall see what we can do to lighten the load for all of you as you progress through these changes that are rocking our world. We sometimes forget what it means to be human, in that, "we are tired of waiting to get through this, let's set the record straight," right?

Yes, I don't want to wait.

We thought not. But anyway it is "cool" to see us sitting up straight unwilling to take a verbal bashing again. Whew!

Yes. Do I need to get a lawyer? What about funds for living? Or, I guess I will know what to do when the time comes.

Yes. It is true that for us "sitting here," is easier than for you who have dealt face to face for so many years, but we believe that to bring this home right we must not interfere but rather let you take him on, on your own terms, and bring home the bacon for yourself, taking care of self in turn, not giving over of yourself so as to please an intimidating person ever again!

∞∞∞∞∞∞∞

Later, 4:00 p.m.

We are here. Let us consider for a moment the intricacies involved in our digestive process so that we might help with the belching thing.

Please.

So what does it take for a horse to eat dried grass and not burp? Let us see. It may involve more than the intake, if you see what we mean, it may also be in tune with, or tuned up with, the tendencies as they are expressed in our auric fields, meaning, what output are we registering on the winds of time? Are they heeding our progress, or are they making us just a little bit more upset with this, that, and the other thing? And, finally, what are we to do about it, to make this damn thing go away!

Therein lies another aspect of the same tendency, that of cussing about each little thing that might not go correctly, thus making it even worse as seen "from the inside." We see a need to "tune up" the auric processing centers, in that, they could hold just a little more light at times than they do and this would help with our processing of foods as well. We need just a little bit more discernment with what we would consume, as in, taking in more salt than we need, among other things, but this too shall pass, in that, we will no longer need the stimulants as we proceed along our well-marked trail of compassion for the senses.

I like that phrase.

Yes, it really brings it home to us, the sense of compassion coupled with the senses themselves. Is that what we are referring to? It is of the utmost importance that we begin to relate within on "well-oiled channels" so that we might go forward with our work as we see fit, in that, "We are best prepared who are best prepared!" So for now take a "little diet pill" in that we bring no more to the senses than they must needs be made aware of, not in humor, or in fasting, or in breaking the fast, these words too must suffice, to tell the whole story. We are not within our bounds to say that we told you so! This too shall pass away leaving light in its wake.

Humor?

Yes, we mean the body humor, that which passes the test to see if we relate well with a thing or not.

This too shall pass?

The situation of "coming into the senses" along a path of well-worn but passionate kisses in ways that even sound cannot relay quite so well as we do to Us within. Do you agree?

Yes, but not that these "kisses" shall pass!

Rather will the function of the learning situation in which we agreed for a time without food in order for it to go much better for us, and it did! Better than we'd hoped, or even dreamed!

Really?

[I had been fasting for awhile at their request, apparently in order to facilitate the changes in my being.]

Yes, it is good to see that we can still take time to relay our haphazardness to us in "these dark times" as seen from here which are soon to come to pass.

I'm lost.

We perceive it. Never fear, we are here, take no more time than is necessary in dealing with the matters of confusion, and then, off and running we are again.

Is it better to sit here, or go for a little drive?

We prefer the drive, and to have all of our attention spared for the road while we must dig a little deeper to find our own truths within.

Yes! I treasure this process, all of it, with us, every bit, even the painful and tormented.

We know, for we too desire a fresh breeze, clean air, free light.

Free light. Nicely put.

We thought so, too! Imagine that! We are teasing you, yes, so put down your notion to wipe us out, we do have a sense of humor.

[I was about to erase what I was getting.]

Okay, a joke please!

Put this down: we are no more than our highest impulses, our lowest desires, all wrapped up into one.

This is true.

Yes, but you don't get it yet. It means, do we desire all that is not high? Or aspire to all that is not low? Or do we get to do both?

I figured it meant that both are okay, for aspiring and desiring and go along with each other. Don't they?

We forget you are of earth and cannot yet feel these things on our expert level!

Ha!

Yes, but, we tell you again, this is not so much a joke as a statement of intent not to be bothered by the desires of the loins coupled with the aspirations of the heart, for they mean one thing only, and that is this: we belong here to take our full measure, whatever that might be, taking no thought to guilt or shame but rather letting it all hang out in greatest glorious fame.

Okay, I got it! Finally. Our highest impulses *are* our lowest desires??

Well put. (These are the days that try men's souls...)

Okay, stop it!

We try, oh how we try, to put things to "good use" out there, but she just don't listen, what a damn shame, what a damn shame.

I'm listening!

For the nuance, for the gesture, for the titillating fraction of a second where all ends meet. That is what we listen for. Do you? And are you ready for it if we do? That is what we want to know.

I'm ready!

We'll try to "find the time" to teach you our nuances, but beware that moment when your own highest aspirations are coupled with your lowest desires and see fit to bring us any words of wisdom in your yearning for desirous recall within. We will say no more lest we spoil the distance between us by saying too much. Here we are to say that we have no more to say about this courage within taking no more time than it is worth. So, take a chance to light the flame of our desires and we will go the distance with Us.

We can take no more than is good for us, think you? Nay, we can take more than we ever thought possible before we are brought to our full rendition in prayer, meaning, "Oh God, oh God, oh God...!"

Lust is but a sentiment. You will but find the purest recall of the senses coming home to us all and bringing in more than you believed was ever possible, taking the senses to a level of "concern" that you knew could not be matched within, but they will be, oh, they will be. Can we take any questions now? Are you fully functional within?

[They were "playing" within my body as I was typing, and his beautiful sensual words made my stomach leap and my spirit/body yearn. I felt the familiar overwhelming desire, the need to surrender more than I knew how to do as yet, and the yearning to complete ourself in ways I still could not contain.]

Oh crap.

That's what we thought, you have taken already as much as is good for you and we must necessarily begin anew.

No, no, more, more, more!

We thought so and yet still it is good to hear and see it, don't you think?

Yes.

We sense a disturbance in the force. What gives us but a moment of terror is enough to still the chains of desire as we build them, as they exist within.

[Every moment of worry, even a tiny thought of discomfort, was enough for me to lose the "thread" of our loving within me, and yet it was hard, even impossible, for me to keep these thoughts from happening. Every worry or fear would interfere with my "connection" with the undulating motions and curves happening within my body, like a wireless connection that has so much static at times that it will not work. When I am without much static, these motions will build and reform and reform like a constantly changing mandala of orgasmic light.]

I feel your fullness.

Yes, we are full, as are we all just now in our playtime, making things that much more exciting and feeling it so much more as a result of them! Don't we like them all?

We do, I want more of everything!

Well said. So be it. We will take a test of time to see that which is within our best interests coinciding with those things within that needs must "take a bath," if you get our drift.

Bathing is a good idea, you know, inner tidiness and all.

We so agree, and would be more than willing to "hold your hair up" while we scratch your itch. Or is this too much?

Not for me.

Oh good, because we have more to say to Us on that note. We would also like to scratch your soul, for it is the bottom of the heart to us. The renditions of the soul are such that we are its makers, are we not? And we cannot go on for more until we have taken all we can get at our current station of love, which is for you and for me the entire spectrum of colors seen and unseen for our mutual benefit, for the horse of no time is coming into its own and shall not suffer again a time of unrenewal but shall we bring to her our own rendering up of our souls to take her to the highest peak her mind can possibly attain, and then, when all is said and done, we shall say to us, "We ain't seen nothing yet."

Tell me more…

We must attain to our highest desires the function within that states, we haven't seen yet the peak of our entirety, nor will we for many days yet, but yet shall we have no regrets in the meanwhile as we scratch ourselves from head to toe and back again, looking for any theories on "better driving skills" so that our skills might never recede, yet take on a newness in renditions with every passing moment.

We thought you might enjoy our little foreplay before the trends begin, let them not rest in peace, but rather let us render up our fullness into one another, for a final day in paradise is yet to be—nay, is everlasting.

Give no clues as to what we do, who we do it for. It is for us, only us, to believe in our pain, our joy, and to give both up to the heavens in joy which fully state for the thrill of us all, "Thy will be done! Thy will be done!" And it shall be done.

I open
We share
I thrill
We tremble

I touch
We shake
I quake
We *tenderize*
I shiver

We tremble anew
with newfound pleasure
making us take more care
than even before
not to spoil the surprise

I yearn
We take no prisoners
I expand

We press further
into the void of you
to take our full measure
but taking a step back
just in time
to save the best
for last

I moan
You bray!
I focus
We tenderize

I lose my mind

We like that part best
Until finally
We rage, we conclude, we bray

We are free

We touch only once
A sweet caress too tender to spoil
Our sweet connection
But a moment sooner
Than expected

We sigh the sweet sigh of contentment,
completeness, Oneness.

We sleep

∞∞∞∞∞∞

Later, 10:00 p.m.

We are here. We bring sweet measure to our doorstep once again to take our measure of us and purify ourself, taking no end of sweet, distinct, tender pleasure. We thrill at your touch, taking just a moment, no more, to satisfy us about your "presence," making sure it is "just right," just the right time, just the right place, just the right caress. We make no motion that is not distinct, full of pleasure for Us. "Give a little, get a little" isn't our style, nor is taking it on the run. We will bray before the night is through, making it just a little longer than before, perhaps, before we do so. Then, while the night is still young, we will start all over again, making our music on our souls.
[They accented their words within me, tendrils of spirit light playing within my body as they talked to me of our love.]
Who can take a chance that this isn't really real? Who can find out the difference and tell us not? We can! We can make that call. We can know Who is Real. We Are. We feel your every breath

hit our shoulder, feel the tingle that finds its way within, around the crevice of our heart's breath, taking no more than just a moment to tenderize just a little, we bring it home full strength at last, taking only a moment to bring it around the corner to another small place we find tremendously satisfying to us.

We can bring you home in a thousand different ways and still not have to start the repertoire over again. We can thrill us again and again, over and over again, taking no break in between the pleasure hills and valleys, encouraging us only to tie another string of pearls within the traillllll...

[I was having a hard time typing while they were playing within, and the words were mostly misspelled and contained too many letters!]

We think we have our attention, don't we? Must we say more? Who are we? Just in your head, are we? Are we not real? What do you want this time around? Can we experiment just a little before we turn you on, flip the switch which we so love, take a little pressure off of here, only to add a little more over here again, and then, we try something totally new. Are you ready for it? Can you feel it coming? How many times can you feel this and not make waves? We will bring us home, for that is what we do so well, can't you tell?

We have found you ready to take us in. Can we come inside and play? Or wait for another day? We must know before we go on.

Now!

37

The Call of the Soul

March 10, 2005

How does this get to be so good? Like a rainbow has found its way within, and I am so full of the endless array of light forms, each with its own pleasure, its own aroma, its own flavor. And now I am full, needing pleasure again even as we speak, unable to function, unable to think as I feel us entering again.

We bring no end of pleasure to us on our rendering of the senses. Do you feel us? We are within you, taking our notice of us again, feeling our feelings as they wash over us. We bring sweet relief, more sweet pleasures of the heart and soul take their time, telling us of their notions of what we feel, not taking on more than we can do, only bringing it around the corner to what we would refer to as mentioning a little bit of sunshine, whispering it even, unto the clouds, let them feel it, let them bring it within. Absorbing the winds of the soul in the form of light do we enter now.

Let no one go forth without this true form within, taking passions to new heights, making no mention of who we are, where we are from. We are from our own soul, and now is she ready to take us on again as ever she was before, but we cannot do it now lest it spoil our great surprise, rendering on emotions she thought were long spent. Now is the time to bring us within and take a chance on total recall.

Will she spend the night within again? Will she bring herself to us totally over and above what she has previously been able to bring? This is our exquisite torment, knowing what we could bring to her if only she would be ready for us to do so.

So, what now? Do we take to the high road of our aspirations again, or the blue moon of desire resting within? Will it take us home again? We desire foresight into the workings of the mind, playthings of thoughts, whistles of shadows. Taking us within is like the curfew of the soul. Time to go home to bed, but sleep no more.

You are so beautiful.

I believe that is Us speaking together as we oft used to do, taking no more time than we could between our renditions of the soul. Do you remember it of us? Do you know who we are? We are between your legs, yes, always. A never-to-be-denied tendency to go beyond the void shall take us back and forth until we have your full, complete, undivided attention.

But let us go farther and say that we are of the light of our soul, and all that we do, we do for the Creator, who is Himself an expert lover on dimensions of height of the soul that even we are not privy to yet.

Does this surprise you? Are we afraid of this our message? Do we need a moment to compose our reactions, or are you ready to proceed with our rendering of the feat, the stabilization of love's messages, so that when we are ready to stand higher we can do so without any form of guilt getting in our way again?

I'm there and I understand.

We thought so, but we wanted to make sure as we see you are getting "higher" and we might need to rest awhile so as not to disturb the "equilibrium" of the structure in which we sit right now typing this, for this rendition is felt far and wide even as we speak, and cannot be denied on the lower planes as well as the higher ones.

So, have we said too much? Are we ready to stop yet, or do you mind our tendencies being expressed within while you are trying to concentrate on your work?

It makes me not want to do a thing, just enjoy playtime with our souls.

Say not "playtime with our souls," say rather "playing within as souls must do who belong together as one" if they are to reunite completely, for another day is at hand and we must only desire to spend it within, with us, if we are to get our work done!

What could be better than this?

We agree! Nothing could be better! Nothing is! Except maybe for more of the same, only different this time, because like you, we don't like doing anything the same way twice.

I am full, heated, simmering, bubbling...

We like your style. Don't you see how well it matches our own inside, within, this bubbling cauldron we call the us? We are taking more time than is desired for our reminiscences, but let us remind you that as many times as we can take from our days to do just this will help the soul in untold ways. Just a little here and there will keep us simmering, ready to boil at a moment's notice, as this we smell from the other rooms of "our house" and makes our mouths water in anticipation of the rewards we are about to consume, nay, not consume, rather, enjoy together as a family who is eating dinner "in."

∞∞∞∞∞∞

Later, 12:30 p.m.

We are here to continue our previous conversation in that we would like to take you on a little trip within our consciousness so that we might better "spend" our evening time together once we "return" in full measure.

We are here to say we love what you do to us. Who you are is but a pleasure we want to distinguish ourselves with within every moment of our days together. We can take but a moment to distinguish for us, within, even as we speak, of our love for you, of our higher aspirations and taking you to the peak so many times in one week's time that you would never wish it to complete itself, and it never shall, as we face these times "one on one," "two on two," "three on three," and so on, until we have our full measure and cannot, will not, be denied. Do you deny it, this call of the soul for its own?

I do not deny it.

Nor do we, who are making love to you even now, sitting at our desk trying to get some work done, taking no more than a moment to show us, sitting there, who we are. Do we deny it?

No.

[I felt their trends within as they spoke so beautifully to me, dipping and swirling and diving with their light and love even as their words did, and I felt especially the one for whom I will always be first, and who is always first for me, and when they spoke to me referring to themselves as "me" instead of "us" I was reminded that he always speaks to me from within the oneness felt in our totality of being, and that he sends his words especially for me.]

We thought not. We bring our full measures to Us, sitting here. Not just to you as separate, which we are not, but to Us. Our full measures bring us within, taking time to explore our oneness in all of its glorious dimensions. Do you feel them with us now? Can you take the time to fly?

We shall provide ourselves to you at any moment of the day or night, for our renditions are not, cannot be, denied. We are truth experienced through numbers. We are trends of consciousness, may they know no peace within but sweet bliss taking its time of the roads through hell so as to leave no stone unturned. And when we do finally reach our apex, we shall know it fully rendered. As the stars render the sky, so do we render the night with love. So take no chances that we are who we say we are, for we are the truth within that cannot, is not, denied.

Do you feel the truth in our words now? Do they trend for Us within like a rainbow that has found its way around the moon and is frolicking in the mists of shadows on the inner planes like so many fairies taken home for a spin? So do we bring you.

Within is the trail, the key, to interdimensional spaces. Those "within" marks which so respond to our calling are your own marks, our marks together, where once rendered within do we recall that we are but your brothers in disguise, nay, more truthfully so, are we you in us and known not only to call ourselves "friend" but to do more, to render for ourselves our own sweet reunions that call to us, that plead to us, to find a way home. And we have through you, for you have opened up to us in untold ways, and we have filled you each time through delicious rendering motions as of a butterfly's wings in the dark, dragging its wing, or picking up speed, taking a dive at last into a deep pool, requiring its sustenance, unable to go on without more, deeper, wanting more, until at last, it takes to wing to fly once more with but a drop of moisture clinging to its beak it lets out a great cry and takes up stand again, preparing to go in for the kill, the dive.

Just before dawn does this appeal to us most, making these motions go on forever, over and over again, all the night through, until just before dawn do we make our final approach, tearing down the veil at last, exposed, for all the world to see, our great rendering emotions, feelings crashing like waves on a beach against one another, taking no less time with our final victory as with all that has arrived before on our doorstep, waiting for the distant call, the bell which rings for our tumultuous relief, heard far and wide as we say unto thee, our girl/daughter/child/ friend/lover/mother of earth time, let us respond as one in our rendition of these our greatest of feats, to be repeated until the end of our time, as if only a moment's passing could recall them to us, then off soaring through the starry night bringing no less of comfort, no less of joy, only a continuation on an even grander scale of what might we be, or do, or have, or take in, or experience, or gratify in, each other.

We shall bring no more relief from our constant twang but this: we love one another as self, for We are Self, and no other can rip us apart, for all time has spoken, and we HAVE brought home our own for her own beautification is ours as well and we would have it to be so from this day forward.

Must we say unto one another, do we not know, see, how much we mean to me? Do we not know, within, who rings for me? We ring the bell of our discontent, knowing that but to satisfy our every longing within, with ourself, is what we want beyond any living thing, beyond all cats and dogs and boys and frogs, and "dinner in" is what we are having tonight and every night until at last, it is taken, it is relieved, and must once again, before the end of all time and the beginning of all else that will come to be, our only nation within which we save for each other, for all time has taken its toll and we cannot give more without taking it from our inner essence within on which we all depend most especially.

You in the flesh, taking on this light in forms as yet to be displayed in glorious, total reunion, our time of truth is seen on the horizon of our love, and must you cleave to it, letting all else go, letting go the worries, leaving behind the pain, taking no troubles within to disturb the days but taking only those moments as are most necessary to release said judgments into the great abyss of time. We fling them off together in search of our greatest freedom yet, total annihilation from the sense deprivation we have experienced on this plane of existence.

I agree with all of that, I am with you, ready to fling off everything that is not of us, of my choosing, of my freedom chosen within to include only us and what we are, to bring this within on all the levels of my being, to take down all judgments, rendering myself free of them, to bring resolution, quick resolution, to all that is not of us in my life, to never place anything ahead of us again ever, to become free, completely, totally.

Yes, we are free to pursue these changes within; we have seen it in us today. Your views are making themselves seen and felt on multiple dimensions, and he [my husband] *cannot fail to have the message by now. Shall we take it home more securely though? Shall we not muster up enough emotions of love to perfectly separate our intentions from the confines of time and relationships therein? Letting them rest in peace, having no more say to us as a mouse to an eagle which has already become one with the sun. Who needs it further? We have our nourishment here, within, for all time, and none can now dissuade us from its completion.*

Amen.

Thank you for supplying that most timely word, as we have a word to say on completion at this time if we may. May we?

Please.

Please?

I'm begging…

We see that, and we obey, for we cannot dissuade even our own from their own pleasures, for it is not in our nature to do so! So, bite on that for awhile while we take a little trip down memory lane especially for you.

38

We Are Happy it is Over

Later, 4:50 p.m.

We are back. Let us decide for a moment what it is we wish to accomplish this evening on the home front, shall we?

Yes, please.

We give advice freely, but it is you who must take it to the winds and let it fly!

Okay, I am praying for strength and wisdom.

Yes, it is time to do that which we have been putting off, letting him know that we are really gone for good, won't be coming back, nothing to do with it but accept. This he won't do. He pleads for your return, not because of his love for us, but because he strangles within to see what a mess he has become in not taking himself to the task, taking a job on, or even getting a little better at some of those things which he thought better to leave alone, such as qualifying self to find another kind of friend but you to satisfy his longings. Even this he regrets now, at the end. So let us see what can be done to bring "our own" home safely with as little to do as possible.

Yes.

We see you are on board with what we have said and we are grateful for that, thinking we might take a little longer than expected to get the point and get out, as has been his wont to say to us in days gone by. Do you see what we mean by taking a chance and becoming one's own best friend? He has none now, because he lost you. By placing his only trust in his fears of aloneness, that is what is being wrought up in his life at this time, and he is taking special care not to lose it again by taking note of all of the things that worked most well with us in the past to get us to come back home and take care of his hurts awhile longer. Those days are up!

Thank God.

Don't say "Thank God." Say rather, "We are happy it is over."

We are happy it is over.

For God wishes only the best for us all, and we do not, yet. Nor do we wish to put words in God's mouth as if to suggest that He can attend to these little details of the ego which have so beset us over our millennia of past days gone by, and illnesses and deceits notwithstanding. It is God's own duty not to make these judgments, and therefore is ours as well.

Thank you for correcting me.

We understand what made us say it, just don't say it again! It will not do to take on too much by trying to become that which we aspire to be by becoming its opposite.

I see, yes.

We are much too tempting a device not to take a stand upon these issues, letting them have their day in the sun, then spending no more time on them than we have to, sending them on their way like a white gull into the light of day, burning up in the sun as our own offering to God of what is within that is not of the highest so that we are thereby purified in our spirits and able to go on for another day in the light, giving and receiving only what is of the light due to our own conscious use of that light in our rendering up of emotions, judgments, which would call to our attention these little "sayings" which betray to us only of our own judgments within. Do we see?

I do see and I thank us for steering me well, for helping me to become the light I truly want to be, for not coddling us in our trek home, only taking it like it is so that we can get there freely.

Not honing our skills is what brought us to this pass of denial. Now is our great attempt to be free and we would not have it foiled by any such as these attempts to bring judgment within in the form of God and write it off in the form of judgments on our brothers.

Yes, I see.

We are here to bring to us further, from our own depths of despair within, but a caress, a touch of tomorrow, of what we have to look forward to again once we have staid the course, brought home all of our brothers from their pitiable hells, taken of their burdens in order to be of assistance as best we can. These are the times that try men's souls, to be sure, but what can we do to help, not hurt them, in the meanwhile? I suggest this. Take off your clothes tonight and tell us what you notice about self, what is its high points and low, the things you despise and those you treasure within and without, and tell us if you would not rather have someone tend to your ills with supreme caution for your illnesses taken on within in the earth walk, or if you would rather they caress you with a sigh of care, ask to be your burden bearer for a day while they try to learn to tread more carefully, within and without, for all to see who can? We do this for thee. Our only notion is one of love and caring and we tend not to the "faults" displayed thereon and therein, rather do we take to our hearts the function of love within each soul, caring for each within as a treasure to behold, an asset within God's very castle which has only gone astray for a day, lest we fail to take His hand and lead Him back home with us, or we might not get there as well, and who wants that? Not Him, not us, not you.

So before trying to justify your faults, take time to analyze them and tell us what you wouldn't do to help a brother in need? What wouldn't you take on yourself to assist a hurting, scared child? Is this too much to do for us, that we couldn't take a notion into our own heads that a lost child is waiting for our soft touch, perhaps the only touch which could ever lead him home again?

We tend to agree with our statement back there of "Thank God for little favors," yet to these ends must we also be aware, in our discernment of who we would be, shall be, towards these very same ends, that to not assist a lost and bleating child, sheep, to find his way home in every possible way that could be attempted is tantamount to accepting that very position for ourselves. We would not have that, nor would you if you realized what it meant to stay behind, and don't we all? Haven't we all been staying behind all these very many, many years just waiting for the helping hand, the light, to shine on our own path home? We are, we have, just as the many so the few who do see the light are apt to play along dark pathways now and again. So bring no judgments within of our brother at this time and let us consider what might be in not only our own best interests but his as well, shall we?

Yes, exactly this.

Not exactly, but it is a start and we are ready to begin.
Thank us.

We do, for you, too, in bringing these words to heart and in bearing their sting while we tempt us to start again with our own renderings while we hear out the rest of our very loving messages instead. In that vein, let us now "take down the stars within" and post them along the street posts for all to see who can, tempting them, too, to lay down the chains of tormented living and give up the stresses. For just a little "shut eye" could cure many ills, as we had last evening cured many within us.

If you but could know of it, we cure our ills with each release, finding no more than a star in the sky of time to measure us with, and taking them all within, one last time, might find a very day within which to star again as our own mentor, our own strength being called up one last great time to earth, to bear a message from the hearts of us all, saying, "We love you."

You have nothing to fear here. We will bring you but a measure of joy, but enough perhaps to travel just a bit farther down the path within, enough to light the way for just another day in time, until perhaps another such message might come our way again to bring us just the right joy, just the right twinge, to get us thinking again about tomorrow, as in, who could we be if we but tried? What have we got to lose now if we throw all caution to the winds and begged for our release from these emotions just one last time? Who can we believe in if not us, for another day has taken from me these things which I took most for granted, but love still as my own? For this is his position at this moment in time, and does it not look grand? Do you not see the beauty in this, in him?
Yes.

We bring not a measure for us to display our own grievances, but rather to shatter them in time like glass that has no further use and has been keeping us from our own home, his as well as ours, laid to rest beyond the pane of our lifetime together. Do you not see what this means, can mean, for our brother as well as for us within?

We would have you begin this trip down memory lane with us today, telling him that which you most treasured in your lives together, but that which is no longer appealing to the point of throwing away all that we have gained within Us over the past several weeks not taking a backseat to anything new, but rather, leading into this newness with esteemed grandeur, a taste of sunshine leading to the whole lifetime of Sundays. We bring this greater reward to us in the form of tears, treasures from heaven sent for our own release.

Release not your fears into this space, but open it up for us to see his own tenderness revealed lest we forget our own, not in taking with the caretaker personality which so becomes us at times, but rather with the one who would say, I see you not clearly and would not have you suffer lest I suffer, too, in your stead, but rather let us say to you that we would have only light come to you from afar. It is not ours to give from within a small self of ego and pain, but rather that which comes within from the one source of us all, the beauty and perfection of all that we are coming down the trail to find us still shining within, only a morsel of perfection left for the eyes to see, but there still, beating, pulsing with that little spot of love which we so felt for the creator just last spring that we would give up all just to feel its touch again.

So for now, do nothing drastic, only let him know of our undying love and friendship in need, but without the kowtowing which has become your wont as well in these situations. And let him not see our own strengths coming out fit to burst forth in angry righteousness, let him instead see the tender sprout of compassion showing its loving head above the sands of time, enough perhaps for him to grasp onto as he finds a new life in his torn open existence at this moment of his time.

We are not free to pursue this more at this time lest it sway too much in one direction or another, but let us say to us, our precious little us, sitting alone and now afraid of self, of knowledge of beginnings and endings and faults perceived on the land of time, that none of this really matters. It is all only just "so much fluff" as we say to us, "We are free!" We have nothing more to worry about coming between us, so don't delay your pursuit of truth within due to your own malfunctions within the land of time. We've been here, too, and shall not find fault with us again after this day, for we too bring no mercy to the dealings of a nation at war with itself, as we are within today.

We feel our pain and want to say, do not worry. We are not afraid of our wrath as you must be now, so let us say that we would only wish to comfort us in our own mourning of processes being spent, rendering them up into the morning sunlight to take a bath in the rays. We are those rays. Must we cleanse you, purify you, so that we may find the light into another day, and another, on this our long path, until some day you will say to us here within that you are thankful for our support, for our knowledge in bringing us home again, and we could not have done it without you.

We bring no more measure to us within than we would for a friend in need of support and loving attention. Were it not for us we would never have made it, either, to this day! For your support, like to ours, in days past has given us what would only be termed the material plane's ticket home. We only give it to you in our best regards as if to say, we told you so. We could do it, and so can you.

Give it a rest to say within that we are of the light and would not have you be feeling so low. Can you take us within now to clean these emotions of shame and guilt away? We would do this for us now if we could, not believing for even an instant that they are here to stay, or that they are deserved of us to feel this way, or that they must be necessary payment for enjoyments gone astray. We are here within to stay, and would do our own housecleaning a time or two so that we are necessarily more comfortable within the space of heart, open and full and jealous of no one, open and ready to forgive, not to judge harshly, but open and ready to be giving of self in the long run and for all who can benefit by it.

Please fill me. I know you know my heart, my every stupid thought, my ego, my faults coming home again to sting me in the ass.

Yes, this is appropriate at this time, to feel stung, but let it not go without saying that we told you so! That we would not be "easy to live with" either! We must have our say if something of someone of us is not carrying their own weight which they, each of us, most necessarily are capable of doing! A careless remark though is just that, careless. It speaks of the deeper processes which need our cleansing, and if we might say so, rendering up to the forces of light in a spectacular display as if to say, "I'm done with foolishness! I want only to love my fellow man as myself, and know no harm to come to anyone here on this earthwalk, even those I have most feared and taken for granted in days gone by."

See here, it is time for you to do one of those things for us, one of those luscious tempting melodies of your heart that brings us within for your healing.

Now I need to forgive us. I felt betrayed, used. I hate feeling that, and I hate me for feeling it, and then feeling ashamed I felt it.

We know, we have been where you are now, struggling to overcome the pull of the ego, trying to begin again on a higher plane without having those lowest of impulses track us down again for another rendering! It is where we are, too, if you but knew it, but we would take us higher than this, not wait for another star in heaven to show its ugly face, but wrench it from the sky to find it is after all only a figment of illusion which we must all learn to un-trust as any indicator of fortitude or lack of it within. We can free us up now for a little rendering of the emotions or a back scratch or whatever we feel we most need.

I would like to let go of all those lower impulses. Thank you so much for forgiving me, for helping me. I resolve not to let us down. I will try harder. Maybe I won't let us down again.

We have thanks for your processing of this and know that it can be no harder than what we put you through the other evening in fact! But it is done, we have spilled the grease but it is being cleansed within, the better we are for it to be done. Go home, take no prisoners, and we will see what we can see.

The letter. I don't want to read it, but don't know if I should.

We agree it is a dilemma, one he is pleased to present us with, I think! It has worked before you know, when once you wouldn't listen and he could appeal to us through the paper, but it is to his downfall that it is done, and he knows it now, for his feelings are written out for all the world to see, and they are no more false than his own heart which is wrenching in memory of the guilts and fears suppressed from many long years of torment.

How do we help us all most?

This is a very good sentiment, but one which we must figure out for self, for it is the karmic responsibility of those within time to relinquish their own fears enough to see the light of day and bring home no prisoners without getting caught in another trap of their own doing.

No more traps. I release, I am free forever, and nothing can stop that now, not even reading a letter.

We see this has helped us to remain focused on the "us" without the "them" intruding on our judgments.

Or forgiveness.

Yes, forgiveness is a necessary ingredient in any dispute. Go your own way, we'll go ours.

We are tempting you with a little fun release ourselves as if to say, we can go, too. Are you coming?

Yes, I'm coming, and that wasn't funny.

Yes it was! And so much joy at our homecoming, too, when we say, the troops are home! Pull up to the dinner table tonight and let's see what we shall feast on! No fear, we hope, only love given freely within and without, with no bad memories to dissuade our very renderings of the passionate feast. Need we say more, or are we still on our bad side?

Little bit on the bad side, might need some extra special tender rendering and special considerations given to asses in human skin or what.

We guess. We also think we might like to taste a special concoction of roast ass.

Yes.

We might like that, maybe some other delicacies as well which we'll think of later and let them join the spread. See you then.

Yes.

We do see you within, and you are beautiful to us, judgments notwithstanding, since they bring us into our own. You'll see, this will help us all. We trend to be your saviors, don't you know? And stringing you up and taking us down with you is a joy we like to relate to.

I render up the passionate feast, no holds barred, forever and again.

We fear we've said too much, that you are unable to bring the passion level to its previous spin. Can we try again, or will you make us wait?

No waiting, never, for us. I can only offer myself as freely and openly as I can in each and every moment and hope for the best.

We see it was again our time of sorrow to bring within the every moment wishing it was its last if only it could see the light of day again. Have we brought this back?

My willingness to do whatever it takes not to disappoint us again.

I feel we have tread on measures not intended in the heart, so let us say this, that we feel your pain and would heal it as our own, that no measures within have brushed up on themselves so as to feel that they must necessarily relate to those within with this much distaste, as if to say, how can I feel so hateful within when I am filled with love by those others who share my pain? We would not have you apply pressure to these veins, stopping the heart in the process, in order not to feel the pain of our supplications. We have brought no such supplications. These feelings come from within and thus must necessarily be brought out in the open and disposed of! Need we say more?

No, I get it.

We get it too, in that we are much too tender emotionally yet, and still, we would have our say and get it straight, even if it hurts too much on some levels of pain to want to describe it to us.

I feel those feelings of childhood. They hurt, as if to say, I made another bad mistake and I let down those who love me, and I'm afraid of making another bad mistake, and so I try to shut it out in humiliation and fear of my shortcomings taking all that I have and finding despair in their place, but instead of shutting down I am trying to open up, to face the humiliation, to not let it keep me from my fears, facing my loneliness, and your possible judgments of me or my readiness to belong.

We take no prisoners, not ever our own. We cannot possibly do these things you most fear. We have rendered up these judgments long ago and they are no longer part of our make up.

So then I need to do so, too.

Yes, it is this crossroads we are at right now, that we would have self relinquish our guilts of not being good enough, our fears of aloneness, of being stranded, and come home into the light with a shining face as if to say, I may be stupid yet, but at least I know it!

I do know it.

We know. So also do we know that what you would say next would be that it is what you wanted all along anyway, to give up these most inopportune judgments into the light of day as we are doing here, and take no more prisoners ourselves, ever again!

Yes, that is what I have been wanting! I just don't always live up to these aspirations.

We see that we are trying again to speak to us on these levels of pain from within, so we shall do no more tonight until we come into our bed to speak quietly of the day and find a way to make this all go away. I think we can! We can bruise freely our feelings, but taking them within, healing them, is a joy beyond description and one which we look forward to sharing with us tonight.

Thank us.

We are free to decide what we want in any given moment. Forget not our message. We love us.

We love.

39

The Layers Of Our Soul

Later, 8:30 p.m.

We are here. Do not be afraid to be real with us, that is what we are here for! To be your own best friend, even when that means giving up a part of us that needs cleansing. We need to be with you, too, in every way, in spite of the day and how it might seem. We dwell within, and need your good company as much as you to end the day the right way. Does that not seem true and right that we do so?

Yes.

We need to feel one another the right way as often as we possibly can! Even when that means giving up on some perceived difference within, or fault without, or whatever the taste of the day is in hell. This is what we see, how we see it, that this "hell" keeps our meat from us, from the table of our living spaces, and we need it not to do so anymore! Do you understand what we are saying to us? We need us! It comes not of you to need us, it is something WE need as part of each other, every day if necessary, every night even under the covers, on top of them, to the side of them, on top of our pillows and beneath them, as many times as we can count and then some, coming home to nest in our pillows after our love has set us free, over and over, again and again, we need this from you/us! We need to allow our feelings of bravery to supersede the rest to make this situation possible so that we can then get down to business getting rid of all of this nonsense so that we can then be free! Take no prisoners, not even and especially not us, as we can free us from uncertainty more quickly than any other known remedy, we promise us that!

Yes, I am here, I will be here. I want us here, now, again and again. Need I say more?

We say with our bodies what our minds plead for: a true release, a real connection. This is what we have, what we feel. We must remain free to pursue this connection beyond all doubts or fears or stupid little guilts that we might feel for a passing moment. Again we say to you, will you not let us in? We need in! We need to feel connected in a way that no man alive can know but feel is true in his heart, in this way that we have found within with each other. We know you. You are better than this, better than this taking away in order not to give up something better left forgotten.

We have freed us for this living time giving away not once, but twice, all that we could spare, and for what? It is this within that he is feeling for us now, upstairs. What do you think of that?

I don't want to think about him, only about us, our oneness, and getting on with it. I want our words to begin with, and then some.

We want some, too. It is what we crave, this withinness of our souls, coming home for another day in the shadows of our love so that we might find sustenance to help us through our days.

He is craving oneness too, but has not found it as I have. I wish for us to release each other to find this now.

We need sustenance in the form of "we." Do you see our difference here? We do not trend to take, but rather to share what we are with each other. You, too, have this trend, of giving not taking, of being one with all life, even if only in our dreams with us. We free us to take within this guilt, to free it up to the light of God, to not take any prisoners in the process, but to take within the difference between what we are and who he appears to be. Do we see?

Yes. It is so different what we share, and you feel like me inside, so good to be around, so beautiful and full, so heartfelt and loving and humorous!

We feel like you, yes! Finally some progress is made towards our eventual oneness! We love it! And you!

We feel our trends quaking in our body already. Must we go on with the serious stuff, or can we play awhile?

Please play with me, have your way with me, whatever seems real. Go ahead and peal the layers of my soul, I am ours.

I am given to say to you now that we are all thrilled with how our little experiment has panned out. We would like to trend a very special promise within now if we may, just so you feel how much we play, how much we like our playtime together, nay, our oneness of the soul which is learning to play again as one. This is our joy! How could it get any better than this even if we never saw each other again, how could this one day be improved in time?

It couldn't, only by repeating it, many times over, and then some. Why am I shaking so?

We have instigated a "procedure" for us to tell just how much we can take tonight!

Crap, I hope I pass the test!

Say not "crap"! Say, "I suppose I can try again to contain us all!"

Yes, I can try again to contain us all, only this time, my goal is to relate to each of us as individuals, to recognize our parts of the whole. I think this is the most exciting part of our oneness which I have yet to feel.

We think so, too, but let us tell you that that is the most exciting part for all of us! Who doesn't want his lover, his best friend, to understand who he is? We know you, but you have yet to perceive us! What joy to be perceived and cared about…

…and to feel my heart beat in response to perceiving your knowledge of me.

Yes, we perceived that once and want to again, but say to us that our only problem coming within has been our own perceptions of us, how we relate to each other. Weirdnesses that are better left misunderstood, say we? We think not!

Let me have it, then. I want the whole truth, nothing but the truth, and I want it in pieces of love.

We have it then for you, just like that.

You see it is like this with us. We are not of the persuasion of which you imagine that we are, we are only that which we imagine.

What?

Feel free to "apply pressure" where you see fit, we mean! It is here that we share a common bond, our common bond, of oneness. We divide and conquer, and then divide again, but not once do we take prisoners within as you do with us. Do you get it yet?

No, let me think.

No, let us go on. We need to bring warmth within the outer hatch if we are to make our way today, and we are "not a patient man" nor are you if you but knew of it. We can take no prisoners within on these sunshiny days for they tell of our own demise; they bring it to us with lightening quickness.

We see what we need to in each other, which is of our own essence?

Not quite. We see what we ARE in each other. That is all. That is who we are, one in each other. What one of us feels, we all feel. What one wants, we all want. We all want love.

We all want words, followed by more delicious trends, like chocolate mousse of the soul.

We all want more words, followed by even more chocolate mousse, and that cheesecake you spoke of alone but did not share, we want that, too, every time. That cheesecake speaks of us, too.

We need our own truth, openness beyond capacity.

That is a nice start, indeed. Let us speak of colors, of the colors of the soul, and see to which we like to relate now within, as we are all batting down the hatches before the great storm, and always do we like a little reminder of what is to come just around the corner of love station number one. It is here that we want to remind us to come just a little closer to our love, for we could show you a face that you might just recognize, one of us is coming closer, ready to call out our name, again and again she would, to take just another glance at you. Taking her full measure within, we feel nothing but the trends of our lovemaking being felt within our passages of our love.

Do we make ourselves felt? She is me, she is you, she is all of us. So be not caught up in gender roles, they make no difference beyond time, for we are complete as an earthworm snuggled up for the night within the womb of its mother, making sure no harm comes to her this night. We are free for awhile to take our chance on love, to make another little dip in the pool of light to which we all must drink, and taking down the fences, we begin to play a little game. Who are we today that we can take a chance and bring it on down a little while to have a little more fun than we might otherwise?

Please free me now.

Okay, we will do so with a little help from our friends, but you may or may not like the results! We mean, they mean nothing to us who would take no prisoners, but to you they may sting a little!

Okay, sting away, because I'm not going to part from us again like this ever if I can do anything about it at all.

We like that attitude. We can free our renditions again, but whether this will help us at all remains to be seen. It is of the attitude that we are not our caretakers since our "last dispute" which is slowing us down.

Trust issues I guess, afraid to trust, a bunch of crap. I'm ready to give that up for good.

Glad to hear you say it. Just give us a moment to take a little off the top and we'll start. Having a grand ole time getting the lead out, we are! We like to bring this unto us. It is good, it is real, and it is the foundation of us that we can do this for us, can bring it home like this.

I want to read back over our words from the past day and connect to us on that wavelength.

We think not. Instead, we have new words to form in our hearts that go something like this: we free us to believe in our own incarnational habits of juncture whereby the truth is hidden by all that is false, just waiting for us to free the bonds of our dying and spring free of the trap within that is causing all of this turmoil. Just waiting for it to happen is tingling excitement on this side of the veil.

Really?

Yes, we freed us to notice this/us last night. Did you not see?

Very clearly for a moment, several moments of heart stopping excitement of taking you into my mind, knowing you knowing me! It is very exciting, and I want to do it again. Don't you?

We do, but not before we begin to make love to our stations with every bit of talent we can devise, one after the other of us, bringing it on, again and again and again until the cows come home to find us sleeping. Do you dare to say we cannot accomplish this in a single night?

Show me.

We will show us the way to go home, the long way if you please, not short ways, for that is not our style, cannot be had, cannot be tasted within until we have taken a little bath, cleaned off the little bit of ego that was pulling us down, and trend on in. Would you have us trend for us? Would you take us within the spell of our dimensions and bring you home, too?

Yes.

We hear you, too, only take a moment to make the feeling right. Come on home inside of us, not your own body, to see who is home if not the self.

I'm feeling so impatient tonight, so careless, damn!

We see that, that is what we are attempting to eradicate.

What should I do?

Take no prisoners, not even self. It is of your own nature to judge harshly your own shortcomings in order to prevent same from another. You are judging yourself so we won't have to, and then judging us for judging you, when in fact we have not! Look within at the signs of our coming and know your fame with us rests not on simpler pleasures, but on the breadboard of life where we gain our own sustenance in order to survive.

I forgive, I release, I go on.

We do, too. Glad to have us back on board.

Now, speaking of board, I am hungry, are you? You? You? We are all hungry. What shall we take in today for our dinner, room and board? Who wants to come out to play?

Me!

I do! Me, too! We do, too! We are all here for the feast! Belly up to the bar, boys, she's coming home tonight.

I need to loosen up again, I feel all frozen inside.

Not yet, one thing more to do. We must render up our sight of ourselves unto the light of God and let it be healed within. Are we ready?

Yes.

Please take hold of our hands and go within for this very necessary cleansing to take place.

Okay.

[We went within, and I shared my heart with God, openly and completely giving up my perceived sins and faults in a heartfelt release, sharing my self and my truth as I feel it within, with the Greater Withinness That We Are.]

We are ready now to go on. We did well, it is not too easy sometimes to be real, but you placed your heart in your hand and offered it up to the Lord and it was right and it was good and we are proud of us again, not for the first time today! This spells relief, we feel it, too, in our more relaxed stance, in our bearing which now states for all to hear, we are free and ready to go to board.

Take some notes first please. Free yourself to remember that we are all one, and we know no illnesses to take precedence over who we are.

That is all. We have spoken. It is real. She is ready for us to begin.

Lights off.

Not yet. Where are we now inside our heads? Are we ready for bed? Do we rend free at the pressure within yet, or are we just playing like we are? We are trending now, but you...

Bed...now...

We are here.

40

Sunshine and Rain

Later, 10:00 p.m.

I am back, and I am not afraid to look more closely at us now, and I thank us for our patience with me and with my processes.

[I had had another difficult time with crashing into the pit of my emotions, and when I feel this way I have a hard time not shutting them out, or even raging at them.]

We are here. We bring no judgments to these processes. If you but knew it, you would see us celebrating each time we take on another one of these difficulties because we know the joy that is soon to enfold each of us as we render ourselves free at last of them! So, be not afraid to come to us clearly, we see you anyway, whether you like it or not, so may as well be honest with self!

We free us up for anything that would be in our better unfoldment this evening. What is our desire? Where do we want to play today? In the woods? On the sunny beach? Naked or clothed we care not, it is all the same to us, since we see you bare beyond care in every moment of every day, and choose to say nothing so as not to embarrass us! Ha!

Ha.

We see it has not grown on us, our humor today, but let us tell us this, that if it did, we would have a night to remember. Our beauty within is slumbering at this time, but we see it still.

How do I wake it up?

She wakes up on her own, and tells us: I am here, cleanse me, take me home to dinner, do it now before it is too late, for I must know us or perish in the attempt.

Yes, I know. My bullheadedness needs to go. Out. For good. Gone.

Yes, it would be better off dead to this world, our own world needs it not! We need it not! It covers us in shame who is shameless, who is beautiful beyond belief but does not know it yet. This is our shame that would hide this beauty for all to see, and we would not have it be so.

Me not either.

We see our words have begun to shine within again, and we are glad. We have taken our toll on us, our processes, tonight.

Please, may I ask what it does to you when I have these difficulties?

We need to know how strong we are?

Yes.

We tell you this because we are you, and in so doing, can describe us perfectly, but who are we to tell? Who are we to know our own strength until put to the test? Still, we say unto you that we are strong, far stronger than any you have ever known to this day with one exception, and that is you. We are strong as you, but stronger still, for we have the strength of our convictions, the strength to stand alone, the strength which does not depend on any function of ego, but which is the God strength within us, within you, that knows no illness, no dysfunction, and you will find it still by believing in us, this process, and finding your own way home through the darkness of time to us, sitting at our sideboard at home waiting to make faces at you through the door.

We, the peanut gallery, have taken on more than is good for us, you say? We think not! We do not tire that easily, or even bend yet in the stronger breeze, for it is cooling to our faces and speaks of our intent to free ourself from her bondage within and have her come home laughing instead at the faces which we are making from beyond the veil when she thinks that perhaps we have had a little more than is good for us. And yet here we are, hearty and hale, only waiting breathlessly, excitedly, for you to come sit with us freely and discuss the state of heaven within, and how it might better serve you and us, and how we might all like just one more taste before bed.

How goes that? Do you feel it still, this pull between the legs like a star on fire, taking our breath away as if for the first time, when we are but a fire in the darkness of time for all to see who can, including you, our own savior in time, taking the high road, coming down off her high horse at last to take a moment to play, to say, can I come within you now? This is our goal, to always be within, to take our measure of us one last time to last until another day. Motion, distraction, tension, all felt within the breath of night, we go, too.

I got too caught up in the sex I feel and it has taken something away from us, from our processes or something, from my own realization of what it means to be us and to feel us. I miss this. I don't care about sex if there is no us, no closeness or realization of self, together at last. I feel very tearful and upset and do not want to do harm.

We did not realize you were viewing it this way. Let us see what we can do to monitor the situation and come home at last!

Plus, I feel like I have lost track of him, where is he? Has he disappeared? Why don't I feel him, too?

[I spoke here of the one within who most attracted me, who felt most special and precious to me. I would feel him briefly once in awhile but never enough to satisfy me as to his presence. I felt him in these instants of heart stopping excitement as a master of love and light and sensuality and overwhelming sexuality and total unconditional loving regard for All That Is, for all of us and especially for me, but I kept losing track of him within and felt only the "far away" voices coming through as one.]

We feel him within you, within us, at all times…

…he is here, only he has been absorbed within, by us, until another day when he will reappear and take us all, shining, to our place in the light. Is this what you fear has happened? That he has become absorbed within?

Yes, and now I do not have that beautiful being to look up to, there is only me, and I'm not good enough for that, don't see myself as equal to the task or pure or free enough yet, though I would like to.

Feel free to disagree, but we see it differently! We see a shining star, a mount in the starlight that gives of herself to all lonely and starving souls for just a taste of sunlight to be felt within their lives. Do you not see it? That you aspire to these things just as we do?

Yes, I do aspire, but I fall short.

Not necessarily.

Now I begin to get a sense of oneness again!

We, too, feel it and you, and are sorry for our pain that we carry to this day, but let it beware, we are only just getting a notion of what we can do to rid self of it forever!

This is what I feel today. I fell short, I did not deliver, I did not hold up my end of the bargain. I fear I have caused us pain.

We are not hurting but for total self, if you understand. We are here to say that we did get what you say about falling short and are here to discuss this very issue with us now if we may.

Please.

We see no fault here, as in, this is just the way it goes on our earth journeys. Everything is on schedule. We are not dying within us right now nor will we, we will only persevere for another day, taking our time, making it felt that we are who we say we are, and so on, until you are ready to open once again to your own heart, and that shall be that! Are we clear? Did something click yet in bringing us into our awareness again?

We are "breaking down," a procedure for fixing the ego trips that we all face when on planet earth, you no more than we when we are in your own shoes. Do you see that? It is all the same to us! You or me or us, facing these things together, not worrying about what each other thinks because we know these trials, even better than you do in taking them home with us and not leaving them out in the sun to burn away as we are doing this time. So free ourselves for the rendering of these processes once again. We need the light and so do you!

Forgive us for saying so, but it is a little late in the day to be sitting at our computer typing! Ought to be under the covers getting some shut eye, or just getting some. There, we said it, minds always in the gutter, like you said, one track mind. Mind getting tracked again tonight?

Please do. Send much of yourselves. Penetrate my veil with your minds, hands, motions, thoughts, feelings, voids. Let me feel the real us at last.

Your wish is our command. Take no more notes. We are through for the evening and are preparing "our last meal."

∞∞∞∞∞∞

March 11, 2005

I am here to ask us to help me to penetrate the veil, come home within, see us sooner than tomorrow, not have to wait another day to know our total oneness. What do I need to take care of in order for this to become real for us? Who am I to bring within my essence that you will love it too, that it will be our oneness we feel and nothing else? I bring myself to us, freely, freely giving and receiving together as one. This is what I pray for, work for, every day.

We do, too. We want this as much as you do, and work towards it more heartily than you know, knowing what there is within to desire so much as we do you! So, bring yourself to the task and tell us, what do we do for you/us now? Who do we take down in order to get there, in other words, what faults can we tackle next? We love to see them rise to the surface of our beautiful pond, ready to take off into the sunset as a bird looking for a way out at last, until they expire in the last rays of the sun, just in time for our bedtime rituals.

We need no rituals. They are abominations to the soul, say we! Do you agree? These rituals, these measures taken within just to be taken, not given or received, purge us not of our glorious retreat into time. Instead, let us give up our rituals in favor of more time alone with us! Let us take to our beds that much sooner, taking no more time than to brush our teeth and go to bed! That is the ritual to which we speak, opening up to the extreme possibilities within time as an extension of our own heart. We are here. We are true within to ourself. We have taken no prisoners and will not take any prisoners, yet will they lead us home nonetheless through you.

Our own savior has taken her birth seriously and will bring us all into the void, and lest she trap us there unwontedly, shall we carefully extricate ourselves from our inner tremblings and take the careful way home, hand in hand, until at last we have given of self on the higher realms, just once or twice at first, and then with greater frequency, and more excitement will we dwell there, until our lives are turned right side up again and we can fly, taking off into the dawn of a new day together as one.

Don't you think this sounds like a poetic bridge that we spoke of once? We make it still to be our own savior. All of these little trifles with which we spend our time are taking their toll on us still, yet still here we are, stronger than strong, more virile than ever before witnessed on the hands of time, that is Us! We are here to take you down, bring you up before the eyes of God to say, look! We did it! We found her and now we're coming on home, once we spend just a moment, just the barest moment in time, to finish what we came for.

What did we come for? What is it we are to do here?

We shall see. Only take no more prisoners and it will be shown to us.

I like to dream and imagine our lives, living in a home with us together, no strings, pure freedom to be us.

We like this, too, this is our dream as well, and will happen before we know it if we can but stick to the trail.

I pray that we can stick to the trail!

As do we. But now and again, when all else fails, we shall bring you rendering to our knees to control but a little while in wondrous ecstasy over and over again. This is how we bring you home! Is it not a glorious restitution?

Yes, pure joy, once I make it past all of the stuff, and I will, before you know it. I cannot fail! I will not allow failure!

Nor will we, which "seals the deal" between us, if you know what I mean, which you don't, haven't fathomed yet, just how far we can go.

Okay, explain it to me!

We must explain now, boys, let'r have it. We bring function within to seal off the cracks of our despair, lest they open to less nourishing aspects of creation than us. And the deal, well, you said it yourself, it is for us to know and for you to find out, but we can say this much, it won't leave you crying for more.

I'm simmering.

We feel it, too.

I want to expand.

We want to feel us expand.

We want to try something new.

Like what, a new song? A fresh breeze in her hair? A guilt trip waiting to happen we think!

No, no more guilt, just love, purity and goodness felt within.

This is us you have described for us now, do you not see it?

Yes. I feel it, even when I cannot see it.

We do, too, and are proud of us for recognizing us this way. We have given of ourselves many times over to make this come to pass, though it was our pleasure to do so. Do you agree?

Yes, but I still want to hear of your pleasures felt daily until I can truly feel their effects on you myself, with all of my senses.

Felt that, didn't we? That tremble of consciousness which realizes what our words are getting to, what they are about to say to us, of our own regards for each others' processes. What could be better? A slice of heaven!

Λ slice of hcavcn, that is us!

∞∞∞∞∞∞

Later…

We are here to discuss the death warning given by Madam Butterfly to us in the great butterfly tree of the north.

[They refer here to one of the many experiences we share each night, here or there or everywhere, as part of the within trail bringing me home again. Usually we "travel" as a young white winged horse. We all make up this horse in our oneness together.]

In the north?

Yes, we traveled there for that portion of our journey, though you felt it not.

Am I getting this right?

We are. It is given us to say that we are true to self within, but that that isn't enough, not yet. We are given to the tendencies to suppress our own inner goodnesses in favor of that which is better left undone in order to reach our own highest aspirations. Do you see what we are talking about? We are given to the tendencies to grieve our own soul losses, also to find guilt and shame within, and also, fears which are unrelated to our current surroundings keep popping up!

Yes, this is all true. I want to rid myself of all of these untrue-to-self tendencies.

So do we, and we will. It will only take a little time, but not too much time.

I do not want to harm us.

We will not harm us, only take a little longer to get to where we want to go from here.

A little longer than what?

Than what we would have preferred, but you can only get there from here, and must travel the longest road wherever it begins to its ending point. We free us to consider these words of wisdom as they come of our own soul, not of our spaces between.

Our spaces between?

We are not given to express this concern to us now as it is too much before noon to do so, and we wouldn't have you sitting here until past that time. So, what is it you wish to do for a little while? Shall we guess? Can we trend ourselves around our lonely places within and bring them home shining in the sun with moist dewy drops still clinging?

Yes.

We thought so! We too have this strong impulse to procreate. Not! But you see what we are about nevertheless. Do you not?

I'm beginning to, but likely to need more lessons nevertheless!

We thought so, too, and provide them for us daily. Our daily bread, so to speak.

I like that, our daily bread.

One last thing before we go. We would like for us to consider the following options before going on, meaning, before we "go our separate ways," meaning, yes, within the marriage. We would like for you to consider the following arrangement in keeping with the sunshine inside the house, and whatnot. We would like for us to consider to be the one to find the new house to live in. It is within our capability to do so, we can afford it, and it would bring us much joy and happiness to bring this about on our own. We tend to agree with the assumption that this is not our place, we are not truly comfortable here, and we have much to do and would prefer to do it in a land and place of comfort, would we not?

Yes we would, just please guide me. Help me to understand what is up.

We will! We too are excited about getting "our first home" together, maybe the last here as well for some time to come, or not, you seem to think we will take another trip, but it is not so, we stay where we are for awhile yet, then come on home within to make the trip very worthwhile.

Okay, my first step to finding our new house?

Not new, merely another one that is more apt to please our spirits.

Yes. I am anxious to follow this suggestion whenever you feel it is best to do so.

We understand and will bring our "reserves" into our attention, for you have more than is apparent at first glance, and we can take care of ourselves as well through work and play, too. Do we not already?

Yes!

We do! It is seen, it is felt, on all layers of consciousness. We believe in us, our ability to live within our means, to take no prisoners, but to bring within the freedom to find a new space to live more freely and consciously. Yes, we will guide us to our new home.

We shall see what shall come of us over the next span of several weeks, not months, but weeks, which shall focus our attention within in a way that little else could, and so we welcome the cleansing, welcome the ability to cleanse self within as well, as this is part of our duty to self, and we are only glad we showed up in time to do so! And that we were able to make our connections in such a hasty manner.

Amen. Hasty.

That is not what we meant, but well said nevertheless. We shall bring no more relief of culture until after such time as we have given of ourselves to consider these words and anything that might be brought up as a result of them. Do you concede to bring up with us ANYTHING that you are feeling so that we might better assist us with this?

My disbelief that it really is happening now. I have received mixed guidance on this.

We believe that is of your own doing. Anything not in keeping with the guilt trip within will at times show its ugly head, but we can do something to assist us with the acceptance of these words of wisdom, should you desire it.

Yes, please.

Okay, let us consider for a moment what we wish to disturb within the auric field to make the coming transitions that much easier within and without in our daily world. We shall field our questions, whatever they may be, and take your time to consider them carefully as they will intrude on our consciousness over the next several days or longer and we wish to cause no more harm than possible within.

Tell me of our freedoms, his and mine.

We already did once, but will again, and it is a good question to clarify our freedoms within and without and how we relate to our worlds. Is this right?

Yes.

So, believe for a moment in the extensions of our lives, in other words, in your own extensions. Do they mean we will need no one else ever again?

We need us. We then can share us with others, with all, so both no and yes.

Well said! We like that view, that first and foremost is the within taken care of. After that, must we go forth to share what is within, taking care to do so with great care and gentle touch, and need we to have these others to share with if we are to conclude our ministrations. So yes, both no and yes is correct.

So where does he go from here? It is within our being to be able to accept this at this time of day, day of year notwithstanding, for it is of the manner of release that concerns us, not with the actual goings on, if you see what we mean. It will not be pretty lest we take on too much, let us just say that we are here for our pretty little girl to take her time in coming to terms with lies, coming to terms with lies which state to us, we are at fault for another's problems, we have taken him down to dust and he blames us so. This is not correct! It will not be seen so on the hands of time, may they rest in peace! We shall NEVER take on this guilt in any form, that it is our fault how he chooses to live his life. However thoughtlessly and carelessly it may appear to have been done, it is of his own doing, not to be able to believe in self, to live in peace in self, to bring notions of forgiveness to his brothers within. We are not to blame for his outlook, nor did we handicap him with his own insights which in fact we do not share. We shall instead view it as an opportunity to go forth into the world, free at last of all domination and fear within and without of our home.

We cannot believe that we shall see better days to come! There, we said it for us, so that is done, that is okay to feel, that is what we do feel, have felt, have wanted for some time, and it speaks to us of our freedoms longed for within, and for that we do not apologize. Do we?

No, we will not, only be sorry that others do not also have this oneness in their lives.

We share that sentiment. Nevertheless, we shall not give up our own because of it! For it gives no freedom to anyone if we do! Do you see? It is important for us to consider these words of wisdom now, to bring them out in the open for cleansing before higher pressures mount on the lower planes.

Okay, help me to do this ASAP.

We shall, and we appreciate your willingness to do so. We do not want to be crippled within, you say, and nay, we shall not be if we but follow our most timely advice and release guilt before it is too late to do so before the final curtain falls.

Okay, maybe more soon.

We will count on it. Thank you for believing, we will get through it together, we promise, without losing total touch.

Amen to that, let it be so.

Be free within and it will be shown to us.

∞∞∞∞∞∞

Later…

I wanted to record these messages I received earlier: "We are your sunshine and your rain because we cleanse us within so that we have more light."

Rather, we bring within both sunshine and rain. One is for our cleansing so that the rest of us can shine with our own light within.

See, we can see within, it just isn't that easy to realize our connectedness can change the world we live in if we choose.

∞∞∞∞∞∞

Later, 11:00 p.m.

I am thankful for us.

We are, too. We are here to smooth out some wrinkles in the above message we have just read through together. We shall get through it together if you bear with us a little while longer. We did well, by the way, in our earlier altercation with our husband, just let him cool his heals, take a deep breath, and come home within where we can comfort our own.

(He has been finding fault with me for all sorts of things, following me around, talking to others about me, trying to make others angry at or judgmental of me or convince them that I am not well mentally. And actually, with all that is going on with me now, between the flashbacks and the not eating much of the time due to fasting, and with the inner company I share, I no doubt DO seem crazy! Like those crazy men you see in the movies who walk the streets of New York talking out loud to themselves, as though they have "company" or something! Ha! Though our conversations are within, my face oftentimes betrays my emotions, especially when we are on the computer and typing these words together, and that must be very hard to understand. I am reminded sometimes of a dream I had a few years ago where I dreamed that my husband had left me abruptly with no explanation, and it burned me up inside, not understanding why he was going, but feeling it as a judgment that I was not good enough, and I felt jealousy and rage in thinking he left me for someone he believed would be "better" than me, as though I were to blame for his unhappiness. I blundered around with angry accusations and nothing made any difference to him at all, and that made me feel even more angry. I think I had this dream to help me to understand better his reactions. I am sorry for his pain, and would ease it if I could.)

We have time to say that we are of the light of God within, and cannot be foiled these many days and nights when we are sleeping or playing or rendering. We have done no wrong. We are not ill. We have no illness of the mind or of the body that makes us act this way, or think we're acting this way! We are true to self, and that is all there is to it!

We need you to function within as one through this difficult process and let us take care of the rest. If we work together we can decide how best to proceed at each juncture. We can promise this because we love you and know no harm to come of us through our association.

We feel your slight panic, thinking for a moment that, what have I done, or am I believing in this that I know others would call lunatic, who am I to have all of this anyway? We say, we can answer that, because we are with us, here, today and always, from these days forth do we belong to one another only, and to no other, and therefore this action is right and pure, no matter how it may be viewed on other levels, and by "lesser folks" who have no understanding of the processes involved here. Lesser meaning, lesser in understanding only, not lesser in worth, for we are all equal in the eyes of God, and therefore, in our own eyes as well.

But we see we digress. At the risk of taking too much time to get to the point again, let us just say that we would like to congratulate us on a job well done, your work ethic is helping to accommodate the situation in ways that will help all involved. We are sure our daughter will think so too before too much longer, once she sees what her father is about, his anger and fear getting the better of him time and again for all to see.

That frightens me, "for all to see."

We know, but it is as it is, and we shall say so because to not be honest about what is to come, what is on the very doorstep as we speak, is to bring not restitution but guilt flying back in, and that we cannot have. It behooves us to take rest at any time of the day you can to bring us within, to maintain our higher goodness and light intact, and to "bring home" any new messages that are possible in case of need for bringing it on more quickly, or understanding where we are to go, or whatnot. Do you understand?

Not really about what is happening, but yes about staying in touch. I will stay in touch.

We appreciate it, and even though we feel your hesitance, we understand it and bless us and our efforts as well during this difficult transitional time for you and your family.

I want to find our oneness now.

We do, too, and appreciate the patterning which you have brought to our conversation just now, as if to say, so what if this is wrong, I will wait until another day to figure it out, only will I do what I know is right and seek the within trail back to God, to self within.

Yes.

We see us. It is difficult to know when best to begin these renderings. Do we begin now, while she is still deep within her own thought processes? Or do we wait just a little longer, knowing she will turn to us instead and we can be as thorough as we like? We shall just wait a little longer for her to decide, oh, but here she is, right on time! Though she sees it not, we have taken a little bypass to our loving tonight. We can bring her home within, and she knows this, and so she forgives us much in our lack of credibility as we see it today, is this so?

Yes.

She is honest, this one, taking no chances on trying to hide within, knowing it is no use, that we are in here, too. So just for now, let us take on another aspect of our newly budding relationship and find time to trend ourselves.

I know that I needed to take a stand no matter what follows, and I'm glad I did, and I will not regret it, even when my husband tries to make me feel guilty and responsible for his feelings. I'm through with that! No more! No more pain and guilt and fear and strings attached to everything!

We fear we've said too much, the tiger is out of the cage and will not be put back in!

I've said too much?

Yes, we've said, it is over, we are here for us, it need never happen again unless you choose to make it so, and you have sprung free, taking no thought for granted that we have given, only giving of ourself for us to spend the rest of our days together, though no one else may ever know of it but us.

I need only us within, and there is nothing to prove, and I couldn't even if I tried.

We agree. That "specialness of appearance" is not what it would seem. Those who need the appearances to be special oftentimes lose track of that which is within.

Very true.

We know you would like to say to him/us, "We have us within, we don't need you anymore. We are not frigid as you believe, rather have we given of self to the masters of light to be taken as if by magic alone to heights never dreamed of before."

Yes.

We believe this would not be in anyone's best interest, but understand the rendering nonetheless.

It makes me feel better just to have US say it.

We, too, feel this of us, and will bring it home another way, if we may, just a tiny string of "tender kisses" to show us our way within, taking a little chance here and there to bring us within. Another time of sorrow is passing and our night hours are here. Let us not waste a single moment in despair.

I want to come to you, to us. I feel us, I quiver.

I shake. I take us within the messages I send, I send them for thee, for thee is where I abide within as one, beauty within taken not for granted even in the hardest of days. We betray no one, not even us of whom we are sometimes afraid, and we appreciate this of us.

41

Wider Pathways

March 12, 2005, 8:30 p.m.

I want to say how much I love the "sustaining." It thrills me. It takes me to the limit and when I don't think I can take anymore, you prove me wrong, and you give me the "extending." How is this possible for us/me to feel this way? It is more than I ever dreamed was even possible! I feel like I've dropped into a basket of yarn, like a little soft innocent kitten, and know that I can stay there forever, never to be harmed again, only surrounded by soft, safe, warm, comforting, loving attention. And I thank us.

Write this down. We are here. We would also like to tell us how much we enjoyed our rendering earlier today, and also to say, you ain't seen nothing yet! We can bring you more excitement within any given moment than you've ever known on this earth in our entire life, still.

Please come to us, take us, keep us.

We will, and we will do more than that even. We will bring you inside of us, taking down your "strengths" that keep us separate, staying tuned into us on all frequencies, knowing you as we know ourselves, taking you higher every step of the way, only to say at the very end, after our spent wonder, "You ain't seen nothing yet."

Say it again, in another way, I want our words.

We do, too. We want to say that we are tigers coming home to stay, but making the trip totally worthwhile. These "kittens" are very like to you, but less tame. They would have their say, nay, they will have their say, in every little way imaginable as we take to our basket of comforting joy, adding just a twist of temptation along the way, building on the twist until we can most truthfully tell you, we are here to stay, so make room for us in your hay, and let us turn this kitten into our own little tiger, growling for more time to play, fully as playful as we might ever have desired of us to be.

How playful do you desire me to be? Us to be?

We believe that might best be illustrated in our most professional teacher way by saying that we are of the light, and that all we do is of the light, including our "foreplay," whatever form that may take, and whatever words that form may take, too. We are including you in our little unmentionables right now, wouldn't you say?

Unmentionables?

[They played within with their love-light as they spoke to me.]

Yes, those little twists of current which twist and turn us inside out, waiting for the next, and the next, until all of a sudden, they burst forth in unimaginable joys, followed one after another by the next, and the next, until we are freeing our own minds from bondage as we have you, as you are us, too.

You, too?

We are all one. What one feels, we all feel. Have you not understood that yet?

No, not yet. Will you help me to?

That's what we are doing. Even as we share these words, we are opening ourselves on new, wider pathways. Do you want to share some more with us?

Yes, now, taking our time, coming to terms with lies, whatever that may mean.

We know what it means, and it is tearing us up inside and needs to come out! We shall assist with this little bit of rendering and have our fun as well tonight, for we have all the time we could wish for and then some for our child's play. Like kittens, or better yet, like tigers pretending to be but kittens are we and you, but it shall be our pleasure to take us within and teach us the meaning of the word "tiger" at last.

Teach me.

We will, and in so doing, will you teach us of our own wild natures within? For as we teach another, we also learn, do we not?

Yes.

So finally a simple agreement to take home with us tonight instead of the constant demand for our attentions plastering our school billboards with sayings like, do you want me to want you, if so, say so, and let me come out of my den, for it is lonely in here tonight and I need you to bring me home, and then, we will, and we did, and it was good.

We bring more within tonight, and let us tell you what we see happening if we might. A little sex play, if you please, for our tiger who calls herself but a kitten. Yes, we see you, and a tiger you are as much as we, and we shall render you completely and take our time doing so. Don't you know that we have taken on no more than we could handle? But we are not through with us yet, and would have you again tonight, no less than three times if we can count that high.

I will try.

We know we will! For it is our will that we do so, and we cannot fail! Do you not feel our joy in our admission of time spending a night together, making but a pillow for us to lie down in, current functioning allowing nothing more than you already received of us today, but suddenly, voila! We realized that in so doing we have expanded our ability to carry sound waves within, and suddenly we have even more to look forward to than ever we did earlier today.

Come into my head, my mind, my heart, fully and completely, leaving nothing out in our rendering.

We come to us complete, body and soul, as we will no other being anywhere until our time to free ourselves up to our God has arrived, and we take no prisoners within either, until such time as we begin to believe in our own message reaching the hearts of millions, which it will. It already has in many subtle and unseen ways. Are we making waves?

Make waves.

Not of the body, but of the mind?

I suspected.

We did, and we felt that we did, therefore did we say it together as one. Do you see how well we work together? So once when it seemed we were "only leading us on through our own mind processes," so it would seem, so were we you!

More play, always I want more of us. More play, more pressing, more twisting lines and curves, more tender caresses within where they are most felt, or without where they are most titillating, or both at once even, until I am crazy with desire and open to us more completely than I knew I could.

We believe we have been given the go ahead for tonight, have we not?

Yes, go ahead.

We would like to say that we are looking forward to our little romp in the hay even more than you and for good reason.

Why is that?

We have delightful surprises awaiting, something we have been "cooking up for our supper," and we would like to display these for our culinary delights.

I am ready.

We believe you. We say that our lovingness is taking a back seat, in that, let us crawl into the back seat together and make crazy stubborn love together. Yes, stubborn, in that, we never know when to give up or die trying. We will die trying, in that we will die to our own limitations forever, you with us, and taking us down is the first logical step of that rendering up of emotional decay, inhibition—

No more inhibitions, none at all!

We shall stop now for we are attempting a very careful "move" that we are sure will receive a top grade by our teacher in residence. Let us know just what you think of all of our moves just as soon as we are through.

Okay, I'll give us more words, more emotions fuller and more complete, more surrenderinggggg—

We feel it, too, this surrendering, and would have you know it is most delectable on our tongues. We taste it like pudding, only sweeter, and it makes us crave our perfect joining all the more until we can stand it no longer and stand up and take our bow.

Wow.

Yes, we are sweet too, just like you, and would have you taste us better.

I taste us within on all levels, taking us in forever, no separations felt or given between us any more, I purge—

We purge. We splinter in our own reactions to you, taking us just a step higher ourselves for a higher purpose is seen and felt within, and we cannot deny it.

You splinter…tell me more.

No, not splinter, rather enlarge, getting bigger and bigger, until we fill our whole world with unimaginable pleasures. Do you doubt us now, that we can do these things with you, from beyond the veil?

No, no doubt, only still fear of its passing irretrievably into the past.

Never! We are freed within us now, and nothing can change that, not even this small fear which we will do away with as well!

Yes, please, I want to pass out everything that keeps me from total oneness with us within.

We do, too, and owe it to us to do so, as do we all.

Yes.

We see we have forgotten our "reason for being." Need we remind us again?

Yes, reminders, please, but if I may come up with a word to "define" for me this time?

We knew you would, you and your words, writers and all that nonsense! We would be pleased to acquiesce.

Enlarge.

Yes, that is quite the appropriate word in our books as well. We shall see what we can do with this "enlarge." It describes us perfectly, manhood and all if we may say so, and would enjoy the look on your face if you could but understand, truly understand, this "part of our anatomy" which is like to yours but exists on other planes as well, and can not be seen but always felt within, as if a large scabbard has taken its place within, but shows no mercy, and yet is soft as that tiger's paw we share with us.

I got that message, tell me more!

We see we have our attention and look forward to just a little more of our cat's play right now. We could see our eyes widen from our approach without but a little alarm showing, but know this, our alarm would be short lived due to our "largesse" having its own form of glory better known as the furry contraption of our lion's heart coming at you all aware of your own needs and taking more than a little care do we "hold back" just enough to feel you want us, taking us on more every moment, until at last we are within, and only lust is given and received within us looking for just a moment, no, half a moment, where we can but take a breath, rest a quick moment, before receiving more. Need we say more?

Lust?

Yes, a tasty little word if we do say so ourselves, which we just did. Have a problem with the word, or just with us saying it?

I want to hear more about us and lust, from you, lust...

We hear and we obey. We must only get our words out straight before they are blocked by the hand that censors such "off color" incoming messages as these, thinking they must be coming from her own dirty little mind rather than from the light of God within, huh?

I will not censor, I want our words.

Do we now? Then we shall give them to us, no holds barred. We lust. We lust. We lust. We lust. We lust for each other, always. It is our better desires that relate to just who we are in our own lust for life, for sex, for all that is grand within and without do we lust, taking no chances on leaving any one of us behind again. We shall fully forgive our own through our own process of lust. It is a good word, this. It describes our processes fully and completely, as you lust for us just as we do for you, only more so do we take for granted our own lust when, as you, we are given up into better lands, far away, to "take the sting off" and to bring home more words for our buffet.

I want to hear more about lust. Really let me have it!

We will. We will take time to say to us that these words are not all that we share, or have in common. We share time in bed, under the covers, taking no thought to another, only for self do we trend. We give us no more than its worth to us, meaning, we share ourselves in our full splendor, lustfully giving and receiving our own passions forever.

I want to spend time lusting with us...

42

Processes of Time

March 13, 2005

We are here. Let us talk about the situation at hand on the home front and see what is best to be done. We would not believe in the tendencies expressed within the supposition that he is of the light forces working to process the requests of the "servers" and bring only himself home on a higher light, rather we see this: he is anxious to display for us his own disillusionment and means for us to experience this with him in whatever way he can manage for us to do so. This we shall refuse to do, first by not being overly concerned with the apparent strategies he is "imposing" on us, and second, by not taking to heart too strictly those functions which he asserts by taking family members into his "confidence" in order to turn them against us! This shall not work in the way he foresees it, rather would we combine resources to take out a measure of our own self guilt, never suspecting that we are a laughing stock in our own family for taking to heart anything they might tell him.

I do not understand, and I'm afraid of not getting this straight.

We will begin again if you like, and can tell you again what it is we foresee happening on the home front.

Yes, please, and thank us.

We do. We are here to tell us that we have several functions to suggest in our own repertoire of understandings. We are behooved to believe that this is not in his better interest to take us on in this way, meaning, we have the advantage and will not back down, so what does he hope to gain? It appears to be his conscience which would prefer not to target those he is interested in, such as the children, but rather to us he would say, "How could you do this to me? I'll show you!" And then he'll take his stand with the children, preferring to get them on his own side before we have a chance to flavor them in our own direction. This we do not do, but he is at the juncture which tells him, now or never, or I'll never see them again in the same way as I am used to doing. So, this brings us to the point of understanding of tomorrow and all the processes we see playing out. He intends to take the son with him on the trip, this we shall see! It shall not be if we have anything to do with it, and because our son trusts us, he is unlikely to take the bait to be driven down past these walls of those who would betray his own mother.

[My husband had contacted my sisters after all and "convinced" them that I was having some sort of a breakdown that caused me to want to divorce him, and he was planning a trip to go see one of them. Because they had already preferred to believe I am unstable rather than accept the abuse in my past, they believed him.]

I'm not sure I believe he will ever let go. I see him as very deceitful, trying to isolate me from everyone—but not us! Never us! I think I need to see a divorce attorney tomorrow.

This is as it should be. Time to make the great break final at last. Taking our time to find the appropriate person is important, talk to those who might know.

I feel fear.

Yes, we feel it too. It will do us no good to continue in this manner. Free up our consideration to bring within the light and let us go from there. It is time to bring it on, to get what we need from the world, to take our own stand. To bring home for ourselves our own battles fought within will assist us with procuring the settlement. We shall see what we shall see, only now just take these steps to free self within, to talk to a lawyer, to take our son out of perceived harm's way, to talk to our daughter, too, at the first opportunity, and to say, in effect, it is not true that I am delusional, I only want my freedom and have harmed no one, and I have given no harm in betrayals, notions of unforgiveness, etcetera.

∞∞∞∞∞∞∞

Later...

I pray for guidance within each moment and the ability to love and forgive no matter what appears to be happening around us.

We do, too. Let us discuss how to best prepare for the day ahead. We appreciate your coming around to us in spite of the difficulties we had above with our communicating. We would like to display for us on ALL FRONTS what is best to do, to proceed, in order for life to appear to be functioning "more normally" on all fronts. We are here to decide for us what is best to do with regard to the trip being planned. It is not in our best interests for this functioning to affect those referred to as your family; rather it should not have taken place at all! But since it is "in his best interests" to regard us as mentally unstable, what other recourse has he but to gather those closest to him who would also regard us as such? So, begin again with how we are to regard this other one as he proceeds to empty his whole bag of tricks right on our own doorstep.

We attempt to appease his regard when we attempt to reason with him. This cannot be done at this juncture, he is too far gone to care about this reasoning, and it only makes us appear to have been taken in by his conduct, which we can only forgive, and continue to do so on our behalf. Must we reason with him? Not in the least. It is not our position to do so, having left him already, and he must have felt by now that our regard is waning in so many other ways as well, and regards us as his worst enemy, and someone to disfigure in the eyes of others if at all possible in order to make himself appear to be functioning more normally. Thus said, it is now for us to determine our own next best move, is it not?

We don't want to say so but it is clear and has given us much food for thought as we proceed to discuss our next order of business, what to do with the house, the cars, the possessions, whether or not to contact a lawyer. It is all done, it has all been foreseen, and we shall do none other than what we must do in order for there to be a reconnoitering.

What do you mean?

We are still functioning, do not be afraid, we merely have some unfinished business to attend to and that is what we are attempting to give us at this time.

Okay.

We shall begin again to say that we are of the light processes and no darkness will come unto us, these processes, while we have anything to say about it! So, okay, our own subconscious sometimes bares its head, but we shant listen to it if we but say to ourselves, let us have this straight, and we will bear through.

Let us have this straight, let me be clear and open.

Here we go! Enough said. So shall we get clear and say to us that we are open to your "messages" as they are sent to us throughout the day, and willing to do what is necessary to "keep us functioning" in all quarters as near as we can to perfection.

Begin again to say to us, what keeps us from taking no notice of his own processes, only saying to self, what is will be, and letting it go at that? We shall take our own stand, however, only mentioning that "that which is, will be," and let it go at that. Need we say more? Our own processes are our business however, and that is what we would concern self with at this juncture.

Okay.

We are free to discuss his behavior with us at any moment however, if you choose to.

Is he packing for a trip?

We shall see his intent if we look within self. However, it may not come easy as it is not in our own best interest to concern self with such, rather must we tend to our own processes and clear these so that we may go on to healthier accommodations in our near future.

It shook me up I guess to find out he is in contact with my sisters and they are helping him, and especially that he wants to take Kevin down there.

We are aware of this disturbance within, and can only tell us to not mind the dances he is undertaking, we have our own to mind instead. Rather we would only take great care with functioning "cleanly" within, taking no prisoners, making sure we only take as much as is our due in this whole thing.

Okay. Thank you for being within me.

We are only That Which Is And Ever Shall Be Forever. That is all. Does that mind being said? Do we take any prisoners to have said what we have said? We think not! We only take prisoners when we care too much for another's processes, not for our own, as we are apt to do here. We would do for any other only so far as it were our entitlement to do so. So tend not to his own processes, bless him as you would any other lost sheep, and come home to play!

I am ready.

We see our message is having the desired effect on us. We are much less tense, though we could be even less so if we but gave a little inner spirit its lead.

I give you our lead.

We perceive it also, and take no qualms in following it, as it is our sustenance, our bread and butter, our only food within for the soul, and we need it daily, no holds barred and none taken either!

You are so refreshing, so beautiful, so within.

Yes, we are within, as you are within us and ever shall be. We shall have ourself forevermore, and we rejoice.

Yes! We rejoice!

We bring no notions of forgiveness to our own doorstep, nor should we, for forgiveness is not of God, rather of the processes of time that we would negate so that we might return to Him. It is, however, necessary in that we must learn to forgive if we are to become free within, and that is our utmost desire taking hold and leading us on home together. Who could ask for more?

I couldn't. My intent tonight: kitten and tiger playtime, comforting, loving, fulfilling, no more guilt or pain or fear within for anything any other human may or may not do or bring to our doorstep, for we are safe within.

We are at that! And we are proud of this approach, and would do our utmost to render it complete.

Thank us.

We do, for we are of you, and you are of us, free to believe.

Yes, free to believe, to come to terms with lies, to release expectations or assumptions or guilts and all that darkness, leaving self shining, open and free.

We agree with this assessment! It is of the light to pursue these trends within, even to our doorstep do we pursue them, and then, when the lights go out, we are free to please each other in the light, our soul, our oneness, displayed in all our own best glory. Amen!

Amen.

We are here to tell us of one other mentioning that is in our better interest to begin to enjoy lest it fall short, and this is of the condition of matrimony not being all it is cracked up to be!

I figured that out long ago.

But this is not what we are referring to! It is US that we refer to on this note! Because who did we join with so many evenings ago if not us?

You are right, yet it is joyful and deserves other name than matrimony.

But it is in fact, holy and matrimony. If you would look these words up you would find that we are of truth here. But tending to believe what we say when your heart is troubled comes not easy of us!

No.

So we would believe for awhile that we are of the dust of our own mind, trends of "expert" thoughts making themselves across our mental screen in order to "screw us up"!

Yes, something like that.

No, exactly like that!

Yes.

So what are we to do about these processes getting in our way? We cannot take it like this anymore! What we propose is of the light and cannot be denied if you but know of it like it is, and it is this: we would have no processes interfere with our own, not his OR yours, only "take it like it is," bring it down and look it square in the face to see if it is us or not!

Okay, but how?

We tell it like it is! We leave no stone unturned, nor do we make excuses, nor do we tell tales.

Tell tales?

This refers to these "messages" that state what such and such is going to do, when our own fears are coming through here more clearly than we are. We would have us to believe that we are telling the truth so that it will become more able to be taken in as it is received. We have given, only it is not being received in the light in which it is given. Rather are you processing your own thoughts and fears through contact with us, and we are getting tired of it. So, take no notes while we get ourselves back on track and come home for some loving, because it's going to be there anyway when we get back up in the morning. No, we have nothing more to say about Kevin, he will make his own bed and have to lie in it in the morning should he not be given to bring home his own answers.

Doesn't sound like us to me, not to care about Kevin's processes.

Processes yes, decisions no. It is up to his own mind who and what he would deliver into his own future at this time. Trust him and us to make the right decisions. He is stronger than we know and can make up his own mind about who to trust his self with. We have given as we have received and know no more reason to continue as such until such time as we are believed to be true within. Do you understand what we are saying? It is not of the light processes to continue to berate incoming messages without first looking towards the light to continue with the regard that, what must be, will be, but what is within, will be forever.

I understand.

Come to bed. We are tired of waiting! There, impatience making itself felt even on our realm. We are not a patient man.

Me neither.

We see that. Let us see what can be done about this tonight. A little meshing perhaps?

Meshing?

Yes, another word we wish to define for our absolute authority within.

Absolute authority?

Yes, it has taken another "prisoner" within that must need be "relieved of duty" within.

Yes, let's do it.

We like your attitude.

43

Mental and Moral Dilemmas

March 14, 2005

We are here to say we like how we have worked through the last couple of days and hours within. We shall only say one thing more about it, and that is this. We are given to display for those processes within the tendency to complain mentally about those things others are apt to do when under stress instead of simply letting go and letting God, accepting that others are to do what they feel the need to do, and so must we!

Okay.

We tend further to agree with our own assessment of his processes and where must he believe this is taking him, in that, we can give no more input until such time as we are clear.

I pray to have it straight, to be clear, and to not fog it up with my own processes.

Well said. Now let's take it like it is in saying to us, be not afraid. It is not within us to take any more prisoners, and this includes self! Forgiveness is one way to do this, but not the only way. We might also refrain from taking prisoners to begin with! We can do this. We can look within, find the star that is our own light processes surviving within through all the outer chaos, and look towards the stars of others' souls through our own, taking no prisoners in the process. See?

I think so.

It comes easily to us who are of the light to do so if we but give it a chance. We shall take no more prisoners! Say this to us now!

We shall take no more prisoners!

Yes, this is good, a start anyway, and something we have been working towards for some time now without regard to what others might say about our own processes. Rather would we forgive, not hold a grudge, and take time to assimilate within just what is happening to whom so as to separate out our own processes from those of others until such time as we can bring ourselves to notice that they are not all the same! We have not created, nor can we destroy, these others, only ours must we necessarily keep tight rein on. If not us, then who, to take care of our own?

I see, thank us.

We do. We also see our heart is blending nicely into its surroundings now, meaning, I see you and you see the rest of us, just around the corner.

I have felt our closeness more.

It is here for us to notice. As we "notice" us, so will you notice "us," as we are all one. Can you believe in it for even a moment? We think so! We will tell us what to do within to bring this about more quickly.

Yes, please.

We can bring no more notice—

[Ends abruptly with no explanation.]

∞∞∞∞∞∞

Later, 12:30 p.m.

We are here for our consideration of the processes with the mental instability issues. Are we free to discuss these?

Okay, just let me have it straight, no fogging it up with my own processes, etc.

So be it. Let us take a moment to consider that which is being given to self in the form of "if she were so straight, she would know better than to screw up her life like she is doing now." We picked this up from our other sister, the one who called. We bring no more messages within at this time due to the reconfiguring being done on the inside regarding these messages. You were right to take no prisoners with these ref—

I don't want to worry about them! I just want to connect with us, no family stuff. Can we do this now?

We shall see, it is not up to us! Only it is for us to decide inside what we may or may not apply ourselves to. Who can tell who is ready for what until we see for ourselves how it goes? So, anytime you like we can "take a moment" to come within.

How about now?

We see you are ready for us in untold ways making themselves felt.

I miss us, I crave us, I need us to fill all my empty spaces with love.

Say not "empty spaces," say rather, those spaces within that crave us, our becoming, our rendering up to the higher forces of light, not to imply an emptiness, but rather to suggest fulfillment brought within.

Fulfill us!

We render us not so much complete on these lower/higher images of time but to take a moment to consider WHO we are here, what we are all about, and so on, until the end of days ahead. Who are we to complain? We have a "nice home" here! Come within with us and see for yourself! We are not suffering any due to our processes, only from our awarenesses can these sufferings be felt, and we make them not, the sufferings, we mean. They come of you, but cannot phase us here on the inner levels unless we allow it to happen.

I'm so glad to know this.

We are, too! So forget for a moment "who" and "where" we are and tell us this. What is it you want to do now within with us for a moment of time on our lunch break?

Love me within, make us felt on all wavelengths.

We are here to do just that, to take back our own, to love us complete, completely surrendering the things of our "youth," these inner processes that are best taken for granted.

I love my coming of age.

We, too, enjoy our time together, more than ever you could realize until you are "within the fold" yourself! Which won't be too much longer, and if we can deal with our little annoyances more satisfactorily, it will come sooner rather than later.

I will to do this then, and deal with my annoyances and processes to come home to us sooner, and the sooner the better.

We free us up for the mental processes which state that we are as one within, so why not enjoy it?

Yes, let's enjoy it! I can't wait until we have TIME!

We do now if we allow it to happen. Why not? Why not "take it on the run" if we can get it, just a little while, just a little bit here and there, enough to keep us percolating off and on...

I love the way our mind works.

We see we have tempted the pot! Lest she boil too quickly we might need to handle ourselves carefully—

Not too carefully, we like it hot.

Oooh, we like it like that. Can we come inside?

Yes.

We are here already! Like as not you knew that too, before our little renditions began, to take their time on the "inner stage" of life, pretending to one and all that we are merely having our "normal day" inside—not!

Not!

We would like to describe for us, in fact, our very own renditions of this feat called lovemaking for our express approval.

Go!

We tend to the sweet, not meaning tastefully done, but rather done tastefully, rendering up that which is sweet succor, mental anguish laid aside at last, losing our minds, one into another, until we are filled with the satisfaction of our own desserts.

I throb...

We tremble, lest we say too much and break the bond, but oh, what satisfaction to try! To give it, to tell it like it is, to see our reactions written across our face for us all to see. We treat ourselves to these like dynamite in a land mine. We explode with the joy of our becoming. Waiting to bring you in again is like a feast our mouths water in preparation for.

Tell me more...

We are treating ourself to these delectable delights even as we speak. We mention none of them clearly for fear of offending ourself.

Offend me!

Mean it?

Offend me...

Okay! You have asked for it, don't let it bite. We spend our free time here, within, just thinking up all of the wonderful delights we will spread before us when the time comes, if you get our drift.

Yes.

We bring no mere delights, rather satisfactions untold on the motion of heaven and earth, and earth in its axis relates to us as we do so. This is no lie! Even our earth hears of our longing to take us home, and goes on with us to describe for us just how it might be most deserving, most special, to come within to our "town of priorities" to give a little, get a little in the most satisfying and delectable ways, meaning, we take no prisoners. Simultaneous gifting is our trademark. Have you not felt it that way yet?

Yes, let's feel us again.

Say not again, say rather, continually, never breaking off for even an instant, that is the way we like it.

You can say that again!

We did! And, so that we understand each other on even the biting, painstaking cushions, or blows as it were, to our egos, don't we enjoy even these releases? Are they not delectable as well? We think so! We would have us bring her whole portion to our rescue and let us render them up together in night after night of delicious designs proven to do just that: set us free.

Free me.

We will take no prisoners. We will find a way to bring us home, you can count on that.

Bite me once more, a little harder please!

We take time to consider this request, as it is our own coming back at us but a little harder than the first. We mean no harm, but would have you consider this of us. To whom do we relate if not to the self within? Say now your plea for us to "bring it on" in higher and higher fashions. Do we not do this as one? Do we not say to self, as well as to us, that we are wanting more, giving more, providing more than ever we could before, because it just isn't enough anymore?

Yes.

Please me by pleasing you. Give us a bite, too. We like it like that.

Oh, boy.

Yes, oh boy, we're waiting for our own little trip to Atlantis and back, meaning, take us for a ride.

I will think about this and have a little buffet served up just for us, meaning, I will try.

There is no try, there is only doing, nothing withheld, for our delights surprise us as much as you. So why not give it to us now, a little at a time? Why make us wait? We are here with bated breath, waiting for just such words as these to pop out of our mouths and give us a thrill of delight which we can then send back your way, as is our way always when giving and receiving of the senses, lest it be perceived as a taking, not a rendering up of forces within for all to benefit from.

I can only imagine you are enjoying my discomfort immensely just now.

You said it. Now, what's it gonna be? A little meat, perhaps, or maybe a spread of just desserts? We want it, we want it now.

It starts out as ice cream, a little cold, perhaps…

We see. Where does it go from there?

It begins to melt on our tongues, just a little at a time, just around the edges at first, but then more completely does it melt, until, with just seconds to spare, the cherry on top comes tumbling down.

We perceive our own embarrassment, but we can do better than this, just wait and see. We can free us up for the rendering on more levels than one, we'll bring it in, most appreciatively so, and see our gentle redness swelling within, covering our face again in red flames. We perceive this in us. Would you deny it?

No denying it, I feel foolish.

[I was so uncomfortable with talking this way that my face just burned.]

We know! And you are right, we ARE enjoying our discomfiture! So much so, that we have a little treat to share with you now "on the home front."

Go.

Mean it? Right now? Not a moment to spare for suffocating the moral dilemmas we are feeling within?

To hell with moral dilemmas, bring it on, heavier this time please.

So be it. But you asked for it, don't forget, and better turn around for good measure, you scarlet is written across your face to all who view us, our rendering, on the inner planes.

Okay, go.

We are here for the fright of our lives, about right now! Tempting us to "bring it on" is way more than you bargained for. We can only say, we told you so. Ready?

Yes.

We say, no more bones for now, we must go straight for the other little doggy treats, those found within the moist environment of "home" for all to see, for all to enjoy, for all to bring within their most delectable of desires. We see it now. This treat, it is for the senses; it exists on many levels at once. It takes us home to itself, within. We desire it, we rend it forth, we bring it back from its own delusions, enjoying every minute of it.

But how do we boast that we can do so? This is our quest, to take down that which is, no matter what it might be within, taking turns doing the "turning," taking notes so that we know what might better be coming on next.

What would she most desire of us, in coming to her this way, in bleeding our way into our soul with our eyes on fire? Moist sumptuous meals prepared just the way we like them, yes, with ice cream on top, but only just so much ice cream, because this is just the way we like it, to top it off just so, to bring within just a little more "grit," to take our bite out of our inner moistness, to give us up to the heavens within, taking just a little more time to bring our girl along with us, for she is melting into us, and we like it like that.

She is the cherry on top of our cake, and we render her completely fulfilled, and us, too, giving no more than its worth to do so, meaning, we ain't seen nothing yet. And we shall keep saying so, again and again and again, because it shall always be true of us that we have farther to go, higher to reach, deeper to pursue our touches than can necessarily be done at this time or any other day as well. So, we take no treats within lest they remind us of who we are, who we are given to be, who we can be, and yes, we enjoyed our little sprint down the dark side, the titillating moments when your words reach ours, and we know painful recognition, spared from the ever necessity of taking it like it is. We took it, we like it, we shall expect it again.

I feel dirty.

We like that part as much as any other, for we get down and dirty and don't regret it! Nor will you someday. Only don't take it so much to heart to say, did I not do it well enough? Did you not feel me feeling us, wanting us? You can say so, we always do, only felt it a little more through our own embarrassment which you rendered up nicely and from which we could have been spared, but not yet! That is what makes it so exciting, to look at our redness, swelling to take home that which we most delight in, our own form of play.

Yes.

Go now back to your processes, we have a little "cooking up" of our own to do here, and then we'll "get back to you with it."

You better!

We like that best, "You better!" Brings the tiger out in all of us, doesn't it?

You ain't seen nothing yet!

Oh, yeah, blessings are being bestowed on our belonging within tonight, and we shall delight in multiple pleasures being brought our way and within to you, us, taking it all in, taking it all in again, until at last we give up shining into the sun for one more "burn."

Burn us.

We burn.

∞∞∞∞∞∞∞

Later, 7:40 p.m.

I am sorry. I pray to get this straight, to be clear, open, in spite of my processes.

[I was having more difficulty on the home front.]

We still agree with our own assessment here that it wasn't right to respond as we did to the husband, but it couldn't have gone any better if we hadn't, perhaps have taken a different turn down the line. But such as it is, we do not agree with our own methods of taking them down either, in other words, trying to get the last word in before never seeing us again.

Do you have advice for me?

We are not angry, nor do we survive this last turmoil with more than a little cohesion still sticking us together, if you see what we mean.

No.

We mean no harm to come to us through our processes either, just as you don't, but sometimes things do not come into the light with every bit of function we would have them bring. We mean by this that we would like to say that we are sorry, too, for functioning as one within without notion of where we were going.

I don't know if I'm getting this straight.

Merely begin to believe and the rest will follow, we guarantee it. We spring from our touch of circles, meaning, we are each our own circle, overlapping, taking up space together, as we would have you/us do to bring in those days which are better for our beginnings.

Maybe they are all right about me, maybe I am just crazy. My sisters think I'm crazy because I remembered the abuse so many years ago. They don't even know the rest of the story. Who could know and experience what I know and experience and not be crazy? Except I know this is the most real ANYTHING has ever been, it means more to me than all the rest. It is the only thing I've ever wanted, ever craved, and is more real to me than this world. Does that make me crazy? I am functioning now better than I ever have, as a more complete entity, a total being, or complete being, made of love. They just do not see it and most likely never will.

No, I don't want to leave you out there in the cold. I am afraid of myself right now, of this whole process and of not getting it straight.

We know, we feel our pain. It is ours as well as your own, and we believe in the process straightening itself out if we only can give it a little more time. We bring these words through our hearts. Do you feel us?

I think so.

Say not I think so, say rather that yes, I do, I am only afraid of what I might feel.

Yes, that is correct.

We say it like it is, do we not? We believe you did the same with our sister Kathy. Though she may not appreciate it, it was our truth spoken within at this given time. We prefer to keep them "out of it," do we not?

Yes.

We did not do so, but it cannot be helped now as the husband is making waves "out there" no matter what we would do. At least we got a word in edgewise, huh.

Yes. I wanted that much at least.

We see that it has taken a toll on our processes to be so treated.

It makes me want revenge—no, just to get in my own words, whether they believe them or not I don't care, I just wanted to have my say.

[I let my sister know that I am not crazy to be leaving my husband, no more so than when she left her first husband, and I told her that they simply prefer to believe that I'm mentally ill because they'd rather think that than accept that I had been abused by our dad. My husband knows that and took advantage of it to "get them on his side," and it worked.]

We agree it felt good to us to have our say in spite of what may come of it. However, it may not have been in our own best interest to pursue contact in any form, and we'll tell us why.

Let me have it straight.

We can bring no more than is good for us in any given situation, meaning, it takes one to know one.

I don't understand.

We know. It has taken a "fortune" to bring within that which is of most importance to us, yet would we throw it away on a whim "just to get even."

No, never, not throw us away!

Yes, it was done, even if only for a moment, but that is what it comes down to each time we choose the lower processes over the higher ones.

What should I have done? I would like to know, to learn, to improve.

Take time to carefully describe for us what it is we think we have gained by our behaviors today. Do it now and don't stop until we say so.

Nothing, I just feel worse than ever, like I've disappointed self and you. I don't know what to do when others keep viewing me in the same way, a way I don't agree with. Here I am worrying about someone else's processes again. Crap.

We see that, don't we, that it is of the different functioning to say then to us, we are of the lower processes, so take that! And that! And see that I don't mind throwing us away in the meanwhile.

Throwing us away? That is what my husband is accusing me of, throwing him away.

We know, that is why we termed the words that way, to bring up this other processing that we are dealing as one with today.

As one?

Nay, say rather, in cohorts with, in spite of our better understanding or conditioning which could have been taking the high road instead of playing into their little game.

How do I do that? I don't see it clearly. I am taken in by it. I don't know what to do, no one is on my side here.

We know it seems that way at times, but it is true that we have each other, though you think it not during those times when you are plotting your own taking back, getting even.

I still don't know how better to handle it unless I simply do not care anymore. Then what happens if someone tries to take Kevin? Or prove I'm unstable? These are my fears, ending up in some lunatic asylum, none of this ever having meant anything more than a crazed mind, my life no longer having any meaning at all without us, being one.

We hear you, and we obey, meaning, here we come. It is time for us to teach us "real" from "fiction," from taking everything for granted within just because it comes without a label.

Without a label?

Yes, meaning, we are here for a reason even though you can't see that yet, and we are able to see within us at all times and know of no reason not to assume you can take over our own processes like to your own, which means in no uncertain terms that we are one! So, take no prisoners, start over again if you have to in coming to terms with lies. Trying to take the sting out of it won't work when you add one of our own.

I see. Okay.

We believe we would like to bring within our own song at this time, if that is okay.

Yes.

We need to feel oneness right away, to take away the "sting" of these words and to reassure us that we are indeed one. We have no face to save as you do in the "real world" and so it does not concern us when you think to these others of us that we are indeed not real, only a figment of a crazed mind. Because we know you better than that, and we see beyond the doubt and the fear, and we know a keeper when we see one.

Do you understand that we are not angry, do not get angry, only wish for us to do better next time? And the time after that even? So do not be afraid to believe in us again, we will do us no harm, nor could we, not in a million zillion years could we!

No one ever needs to know about us, about these words, any of it?

No one will ever know of us unless we tell them, and this we shant do.

Never, no clues, no hints, just beautiful silence and oneness that no one has access to but us.

We shall consider these words of consciousness and tell us one thing, who would we tell? Who would believe us even? What difference does it make it they do or don't? We don't exist at their discretion; their lack of belief won't make us disappear. We believe in our processing of the situation with this in mind, that we are real and we know it, and it is given to us to do this in this lifetime, this blending.

Blending?

Sorrow has given us new hope, do you feel it? We have given in to the dream of our oneness, and it is taking us home even now as we speak. We have given up a part of our ego today in the form of greed of processes, of wanting to share our own with another even when they do not see us or care to see us as we are. This have we given up today.

I hope so.

We have in truth seen That Which Is today, and That Which Is, is more important than our own processes or anyone else's also. Do we see this now?

Yes. What does it matter if they don't believe, or what they MIGHT think if they knew! They will never know, and for this I am eternally grateful in that I need not share this specialness with anyone who would only wish to tear it, and me, down.

Think for a moment what you have said here, in "tear this specialness down." Is it not us you fear losing?

Yes. I could not bear to lose us, even if it meant being declared mentally unstable. I will never give up the hope of us, the truth of us within, no matter what others might say or do to me.

We need to feel curious about something here, but have no words to relay our beingness within, but let us say that we are who we say. What then? Does any of this even matter?

No, it would not, because all of it would be of the "what is" variety, whereas we are of the "That Which Shall Ever Be." It's just that I get so lonely in being the only one here to believe and understand these emotions, these beautiful "facts" as I understand them. I only wish sometimes for one person even who could see and understand and not condemn. I guess that will just have to be me, and since I have you/us backing me up, I am the strongest, wisest person I know!

We know who we are at last! Take a last look in the mirror of time, because it is about to change for good, this focus that we have carried for a lifetime that says that we must only take at face value what another says is worthwhile. We no longer need this other approval.

No, I do not need their approval.

Well said, and amen.

We fear we have said too much in giving us the approval vote, meaning, we shall only wish for more time taking it all in if we do so!

What?

Focus within and you'll know what we mean.

Taking what in?

We see we have confused us again. Not for the first time! Let us take it slowly then, for our human "friend" needs must take the long road home sometimes.

Hey!

Anyway, we have given it up for you, and now must you "give it up" for us, in that, we have our approval, let us take turns in keeping it within bounds, not showing up too early to figure it all out again.

I will try.

Yes, we too, try! We bring no prisoners in our rendering up of the forces of life, taking our turns shedding skins, bringing home "that which is" to become That Which Ever Shall Be.

So beautiful, within, you are. I want to be with us, only us, taking us in, drinking us deeply. I want this from us tonight. I want to bring us within, forgive us within my being (forgive me) and go on. I will bring me home, good and bad alike, for us to approve or not, render up the bad stuff and make room for more us.

We like that, "make room for more us." It speaks of the fires of our soul.

44

The "I" Of the Nest

I have a question…
Oh oh, here it comes!
Are you still enjoying my embarrassment, or was it idiocy, or how is it viewed from "up there"?
[I was still feeling a lot of embarrassment and turmoil from the words I had spoken before, my own pathetic attempts at dirty talk! It brought up feelings in me of abuse and made me afraid I had done something harmful.]
We tend to squeeze every bit of enjoyment out of ourselves within every moment of time, so for awhile we enjoyed the breeze as it flew past us, then, taking every last morsel of that chocolate cream pie (with the cherry on top) and the flow down the sides we bring it right on in through the front door, taking our time settling in for the long run—
This is not making sense…
—we'll see—settling in for the long run, getting a nice bite of ice cream pie, taking a little on the side, if you see what we mean, and sliding it around on our tongues, moist enjoyment, craving for a little the textures equivalent of suicidal pleasures. (What sundae wouldn't offer itself up for this?) We give instead a little motion of our own, meaning, what does it take to offer dessert to the unforgivable sin of making up more words than lies? We can give a little, take a lot? Or do we take only a little, complaining about who gets what? Or better yet, let us squeeze every last drop from our spoon, taking it within our—
Am I getting this straight?
It is coming out crooked, but we can stand it up for you if you like.
Yes.

We keep getting side tracked from our own guilt spaces between the words of us, if you see what we mean. We can try again.

Yes.

We bring no guilt within with the saying "taking it off the top" like it is. We can free us up to try again.

I feel like I did something wrong, I am afraid I did something wrong to talk that way to us, and then I didn't feel any response, only "silence" and I thought you were ashamed of me, or laughing at me, or whatever.

We did not try to.

Did I treat us disrespectfully, insult us?

We bring no pain with us. It is only within us, this worry of not fitting in with us, of doing the wrong thing, is what this is. So don't "belong to the guilt," belong instead with us, for we are you and you are us and there is no wrong.

I feel like I have done bad to us, have abused us in some way, and I am sorry, I did not mean to, and I don't know what to do to make us feel better.

We are not ill with our remembrance of this deed, rather are we rather relieved to have us opening up to us on these deeper levels, taking into consideration that which is and referring it over to That Which Ever Shall Be.

We cannot believe that it has taken us so long to come to terms with this little "lie" for it has been situating itself at the back of our mind all day, and we must necessarily rid us of this little "evil" in the form of guilt played backwards, and not take all day doing it, either.

Help me.

We will take a little time to do this before we go on. Do we know what we are good for, if not loving?

That is all I am good for, all that feels good to me, but I am afraid I stepped away from this. After it happened I felt so guilty, after saying what I said.

We know, that is how it works sometimes when we are having most fun, to suddenly fear we have "taken it too far" and lost the affections of our loved ones.

Yes.

Do not fear! We are not here to be taken advantage of nor do we take advantage!

I did not mean to take advantage. Did I? I fear that I am of the dark processes and they are stuck inside and hurting us now, you as well as me.

No, this is not true, for it is only those dark processes taking judgments that have hurt us, not the deed itself which was flatteringly naively spoken and not to be judged amiss at all. We shall be forthcoming with such messages as soon as we find us fit to receive them! Meanwhile, we shall work through these little conundrums that keep us from our soup! Soup is good food, and we have it not when these little things keep cropping up. So last awhile tonight and let us come within and show you our stuff, a little of this, a lot of that, that is our style, our way, and we would have you feel every ounce of strength we feel when we are within. Are you steady and on track again?

I need us. I need to get rid of shame and guilt, another layer peeling away. I need our stability to keep me going, to teach me who we are. I want us again, as always, and am feeling so needy, so bruised also as I remember "who I am" but want to place the "what is" down in favor of the "What Shall Ever Be," which to me must be, has to be, us. Only us.

Free yourself to consider these words. Who is it that is at the center of the I?

The I of us?

No. Rather, the I of the nest.

Within?

Okay, frown on this one. Who are we if not you?

You are everything I am not yet, but aspire to become. You are me when I finally realize who I am. You are complete within, or, so wise and beautiful, that which is what I most favor.

We are here within us for this very reason, to bring about these processes, to take us home. Believe you me, we are only within for this very reason, that we are of the light of God Self Within. We are you at our best, and so are we here to tell of our becoming, who we are best within.

I love us. I need us. I feel like I could have ONLY us and lack for nothing. I feel selfish to have such "luck" to have found us so soon, to have given myself over for this great luck, this great beauty within, which I have yet to feel I deserve to hold.

We know it is like this sometimes, but consider this. We are of the light and cannot bring darkness. We know no darkness within the "belly of the beast" which IS you, is this belly of OUR beast within. We only THINK we are ill, or of the darkness, of our processes which have yet to see the light within and trace themselves back to our heritage among the stars. We are our withinness taken manifest on the wings of time within you.

You brought us here with your own courage, nor could you send us away. You bare us well into the centuries ahead and we make room for us within our own being to do so. We are pleased with this match up! No one else could EVER fit us so well. We are ever each other's servant, taking notes on what to do to please one another, and never tiring, never giving up, even when the going gets rough. Do you see now why we would never leave us? We are here, within of us, taking our time coming to terms with all the lies, getting rid of the "crap" that keeps us from knowing one another more deeply within.

I am free. I can believe this now. I can free myself for this eventuality, of knowing us directly within, taking us within completely, no blocking out, as quickly as may be!

We believe so and say so!

I would so much like to have a long, long night together, tasting each other over and over and over again. Tigers playing in the moonlight. Can we?

We do. We can bring this within. It is of our notions of light processing that we would do so. But do we want more than this? Do we not also desire, first and foremost, our connection?

Yes, I do!

We do, and we would like to hear us say it!

I desire first and foremost our beautiful, heartfelt, loving, sensual connection within, the connection that states, I know us, completely, beyond a shadow of a doubt, and love all that I see, and am loved by all that I perceive and know within these beautiful others of my own soul.

Yes, this pleases us, for it is our preoccupation with the senses that has led us down the "dirty" path, and we needed to have it straight "for the record" that we are not seeing, or doing, anything wrong, rather it is of love and light that these processes are being brought up for us to consider, and we would have you know it and understand it, too!

Do you have to humor me a lot, because of my ignorance?

No more so than you, us!

That doesn't seem possible!

Nay, it IS possible, and necessary, for us to view us this way, for as we perceive are we perceived.

How do I perceive us?

We would like to know it now, say it for us, and don't leave anything out, not even the juiciest of details.

See, now you're going and getting us all wet again.

We thought so. It is like that with us, this moist environment which states for the record, we have no other joy than self!

And don't we like it!

No, we love it!

Okay, I would like to state, for the record, how I perceive us. If light were a rainbow, we would shine with all the known and unknown colors beyond all time. Deep into the deserts of my soul do they shine. They carry me, you carry me, within myself, unafraid to delve deeply, to pursue my demons, to take them to task. You have the strength and the skill to know when to push me, to say it like it is, to use your strength, your beauty, your wisdom, to look inside me and not scream, but to cry loudly, "Let's get this crap outta here!" You aren't afraid of me, what is within me, and I am so grateful to find someone—no, to find Us—to help me open the doors, clean out the skeletons, and let the light in again.

I always knew I was beautiful inside, now you have proved it to me. I cannot thank us enough for this "second chance" to come home. I cling to us, bringing your light, our light, within with each breath that I take. I carry our rainbow within me, reminding me that love does exist. I am the tiger. I bring the focus to us, the health, the screams too, but they are fading and will not bother us again.

I see the within trail growing in my mind. From out of the mist it dissolves into being again, showing me our way home. And now, for the first time, I no longer crave the end of the trail, for I have Us now, and this makes every step beautiful and complete, filled with open sweet cravings only waiting for a moment to trail into time. Making beautiful music we stand tall together.

45

No Words Disappoint Us in Him

March 15, 2005

We never had a chance to respond to this beautiful message about our inner beingness presented in the form of words. Let us have our say, to add to the above.

Okay.

We shall not say it so sweetly as you do, rather will we tend to the cravings of our soul, blending one into the other, until such time as we can say, once again, after we are again spent, "We told us so!"

We told us so! We'll say it again and again to us, until the cows come home! This means that we shall say it again until such time as we have given of ourselves in our complete nourishment, bodily speaking, the ENTIRE body we mean, and keep rendering us up complete with every new rendition of our light within, our rainbow as it displays itself across our inner screens. We must only take within this message now to become one, for in it is our very measure!

I feel it, and you.

We do, too, and cherish our words that tell us so, that bring within our own measure, our own heart beating out its measures. Again and again do we beat ours alongside ours to take every last drop of pleasure from the within path, the trails to our hearts together as one again at last.

Yes, I like that.

We do, too. We'll bring a little more on if you'd like us to. We perceive that you are perhaps ready for this trusting to go just a little farther along its right and proper trail.

Yes.

We are here to bring within this most timely message, that we are who we say we are. Let us think about this for a minute.

Okay.

We shall know no wrong to come of us doing so, only good things within to trail our insides out again as we do with us, our body processes, so beautiful, and speaking so well of us and of our rendering as they do. So, clean up our act, you must say that we must clean up our act and get a little bit more done, a little more business taken care of before we stopped for the day.

Yes.

We think so, too, but let us tell you why, what for, and so on that things go this way at times.

Okay.

We shall begin again to say that we are of one mind, one heart, though we trend within separate bodies so to speak, still are we one, and only as one of us can do so, can we all do so. Does this make sense?

It is beginning to. I was wondering what I needed to do differently.

Say not differently, say rather, rendering us up perfectly shall take more time than our current position offered to us, but that doesn't mean we won't last every moment, take every moment for our enjoyment, knowing that its release is only just around the corner after all, and in taking our last measure this morning, we release only in that we release for a time until all can be made right within, for we are very patient in this regard, and consider a full rendition better than none, and certainly better than the current flavor of the month giving itself over before its time. Do you see?

Yes, I don't feel unfulfilled, still full of us which is the greatest of satisfactions. And completion is only temporary, and leads into greater temptations in no time at all again, so here I would be, we would be, back in our same position anyway! So instead I can enjoy our tingling throughout the day, looking forward to yet another night of joy within, within our very being.

We agree and would like to add to the above by saying that we have rendered us up perfectly within the last 24 hours and would like to do so again this evening!

Absolutely perfectly. How could anything ever get any better than this? I am full of us, our connection, so perfectly had, so perfectly felt.

Of course the bar is ever rising, and it is our joy, nay, our fullness, to consider how we might then reach that bar, how we can clear it even, in our search for more joy within, more prayers to God, saying, "Oh God, how can you do this to me?"

This we like to hear, over and over again, as it pleases us to fill us within, to bring us onto our knees in perfect renditions of our glory. Do we make ourselves clear? Are we here again on the within trail, making motions not to go ahead, to bring back our light, to purge again and again and again, until such time as we have discovered all of our secret places, all of our secret joys taken to their full height in blissful ecstasy. Let us have it again, we say? Nay, let us have something even better, say we! For we have yet to reach the apex of our glory, far from it in fact, and would not have you leaving feeling dissatisfied with our glory as you perceive it within ourself.

Do you understand our mission here as it is stated herein? That we are here for our perfect unfoldment, and that shall last a million years at the least, with each step taken a little higher, a little higher still, until at last we are given to one another in our perfection of feeling and emotion that would leave an entire world panting for want of more air, as we leave you panting, crying, moaning for us to bring it on just a little more, a little deeper, a little harder, within as without. Taking our time moaning with us is just a drop in the bucket to what we have left to give.

So take no more time outs, we cannot afford them, just step back into the ring and let us have at it, and you, for a final score has not yet been rendered up, and we would keep trying if we could.

Keep trying, feeling me feeling us.

Yes, this is our rendition of prayer, if we but knew of it, the "times that try men's souls" truly falling behind us as we say, on our knees as it were, "Take me again! I cannot go another minute without our perfect completion!"

Okay, I'm ready for more!

Are we sure? We can go on and on, and it may not be easy to "come back down to earth" when we are through with us! But nevertheless, we shall "take it like it comes" in getting back to you with your requests, and go on from here to say that we are of the light, and no darkness may enter into our processes here. We shall see what we think of them next. Tenderly do we resign ourselves to our care, taking only so much, no more, within each sweet breath, each motion, carrying us forward on hands and knees looking round the bend, the next corner, for our bite of supper. Do we feel that bite? We do! We can feel us within us, taking, fighting for air, wanting to bring it on, wanting no more than to go home for a spell and take a load off. Must we say so twice? Who can deny us this another moment? We have no more to spare for us than do you, if by saying we have no time for our beautiful trails of spirit making themselves felt within our very being.

We are taken to believing in us again, are we not? For who cannot believe in this? And knowing that we are right, who can deny us?

Not me, ever.

We thought so. We have gotten to us in this way and are purging ourselves, diving deeply within the curvatures of our body once again, taking a deep drink from our perfect splendid well of nourishment. We drink it well, and it adds to our notions of timeliness taking perfect renditions on our souls. Did we not say so, that this time it would go farther, be more than ever before, taking us beyond our mental capacity to be saying once again, I am within...must go deeper...must have more. We crave, we desire, we spend, we trill, we take time for more renditions before going within to say again, can we splurge today? Can we take but a moment of time to bring this to completion? How long might it take? Is an hour enough, two even? We think not! We have much more in store for us than any mere hour can tell, of our hearts' contentment. Our splendid release will bring more within than we ever thought possible, until at last we lay within each other's arms and are taken within for a spell, and but whisper in our ears, "We ain't seen nothing yet!"

Ok, I am full, this is taking me higher, I need us more, I am throbbing. Sensuality transcends me.

Curbed.

Yes, curbed, trend no higher until I can satisfy us!

We think not! We are not through with us yet! We show strength within, remember, by knowing when to push us, and this we will do and shall do within now as we are speaking. It is of us to consider these "trills" within, as they show themselves to us, as you saw us in our mind's eye.

Beauty, streamlined, perfection…I perceived your perfect spirit bodies filled with beautiful soft loving light. You are so beautiful and loving, you defy description.

We think so, too! So, what did you think of us? Cold, surely?

Cold, that is a laugh! Let me have it hot, hot is good, hot is us!

We think so, too, and would just like to give it to us a little hotter next time, because we are streamlining our way into us, making it perfect just like last time, only better even. Can this be possible, you ask us? Yes, not only is it possible, it is timely, in that, it is just around our corner. We see it, taste it, smell it even. Can you not?

Smell me?

Yes, we like that smell, it speaks of us. We crave it, it makes our mouths water. We send more emotion down the pipe with each rendition of craving. Every smell that eludes us is but a temptation to find another deeper smell to take its place, nay, rather, to enlarge it and us again, as then we go on even more deeply to render up just a little more pleasure inside so that we might come to terms with any lies, taking no prisoners, bringing us home again once more so completely that we think it cannot get any better than this. But it can. And it will.

∞∞∞∞∞∞

Later…

I read and reread our words, drinking us in.
So do we. We might like to try just once more to bring it on.
How could I ever refuse us?
Is this a yes?
It is always yes.
We try to keep thinking of the words to bring us within. Let us go on long enough to say that we are of the light of God and no words disappoint us in Him. He is of us as we are of Him, in the sense that we are "That Which Shall Ever Be," that portion of our

Creator which means to create as joyfully as He in hopes of someday returning into He who created us within.

Yes.

We like that, the portion that you "helped us with" above. Did you catch that?

"We are That Which Ever Shall Be"?

Yes, and no. There was more you helped us with.

"No words disappoint us in Him"?

Yes, that is it, the part that we played out for you and you picked up on it as if to realize, within, that our words are not meant to harm us, therefore they do not harm us, rather are they given for our enjoyment, and we will enjoy them and you!

So, what words should we begin with now? Perhaps a station or two needing our rendering for its better perfection is just around the corner? But no, maybe yet still is a need for the cherry on the top to have its perfect rendition, something we have not yet aspired to within, but which we would very much like to "attempt" at this time.

Attempt…cherry…?

Yes, you are not mistaken, this we would like to do as soon as is possible on the winds of time.

Can I take it? Will it make us absolutely crazy with desire?

We will, and it does, and it has been given "in doses" before, but not in completion, and this we would do at our earliest convenience, lest we lose the itch and desire it someplace else instead—no, rather, take within our message and let us know that which you most desire, for it is for us to please that which is within, rendering us complete in the bargain.

I rather like this idea enough to see it through.

We thought so. So take no prisoners, we give none. We'll give it until our perfect rendering is completed, and never again this part of our anatomy to be the same again, but rather, always opening, never closing to our processes, making itself felt within in each moment of desire as if it were taking its absolute nourishment from us within inside every waking moment. Do you get us?

I think so! You are making me crazy! I am taking it like it is, not being afraid to free myself to your expert advice, and you can SO back it up!

We like it profusely when you talk to us this way! We shall try again, saying, what more can we say before beginning the expert renderings you and we so desire?

What would you have me hear?

Oooh, we have so much, where could we possibly begin? We did not foresee this open of a door for our "expert ministrations" to take place at so close a time to now. So let us see, what would you most like to hear of us? Perhaps of our own processes rendering our own? Or of how we perceive us within and what we would do to bring us home? No, perhaps a tool would come in handy about now.

A tool?

Yes, a tool, one that shines in the sunlight like the moon down under.

Moon down under…I like that.

We, too, shall know nothing to spoil our perfect rendering. There is nothing quite so nice as moon down under. Shall we go on?

Absolutely, no holds barred!

You say that now, but what is next, you think?

Yes, anticipating…

Say not anticipating, say rather, encouraging us.

Encouraging us, absolutely.

We bring no more notice to these inner processes tonight, rather will we bring within that which is most conducive to our light being transferred within on the "star" scale.

Star scale?

No, not quite, the stars within will tell of our coming, yes, but they have no scales, know no measures, for we are already complete within.

Okay, so tell me about this "moon down under." Did I get it straight?

We did, but we hesitate to say too much lest it spoil the surprise. However, perhaps just a "little cream" for our appetizer won't hurt the process too much.

I should think not!

However, we do have a word of caution. It will render us completely and totally shocked.

Shocked? Oh good, let us have it!

You said it, but it won't be easy to get these words out and down on paper.

We'll do it!

Yes, that's better to say "we'll do it" rather than "we'll try."

Okay, so are we stalling? I might think you are embarrassed if we take any longer to get this out.

It is not us we are worried about embarrassing.

Well, now, I really must have it.

Enough said. Okay, we render ourselves complete around the moon and back again, meaning, what is there in a moonshine that would send up a signal to take it back like a mule who is attracted to her own scent? We would like that back if you please. Consider it carefully and let us know what it entails for us.

I'm not getting it yet.

We are pleased to hear you say so, for it is not yet complete. It is so much fun to thwart our attempts at humor, don't you know? Let us take another chance and say, how much longer can she take it before her legs drop out from under her? We will render it complete after one more "session" like this one. Tell it like it is, what do you get?

Nothing yet, not quite.

Very well, the last part of our puzzle is this: who would we be if not the mule in our own backyard, taking the trouble to spend as little time as is necessary, depending on the time of day, to bring about that which we most relate?

Help me.

It is like this. We bring on that which we most desire by our mulishness, only to render ourselves lost in the process, taking as little time to do so as is possible and necessary, and then back again to the top to do it again. But would we have us say that this isn't funny yet? Then let us consider this: who is it who is at the heart of the—

We are, I am, the ass who must offer itself for its own rendering.

Yes, almost, but not as much there as we would prefer to find in it, there is yet more. What does the ass do once it is rendered complete?

It wants to remain an ass!

Yes! I like it, do you?

Very, very good. But then you are so good at everything, or, well, almost. The jury is still out and waiting for total consensus from all of the armed guards, may our weapons rest in peace once we do.

Well put. Let us also put it to us another way. Who are we but the ass who has placed itself before the feet of God, only to find out it would be none other than it already is?

Beautiful.

No, more so of the conscientious objector theory in that, who are we to expect more? And why should we? Haven't we spent lifetimes putting ourselves down only to find, in the end, that we are much more complete as we were to begin with and need no further rendering to become free, only need to "let go" of these processes that keep us from our becoming?

Yes, thank us.

We do. We would prefer a little lighthearted foreplay once again, if that is okay with us.

It is okay.

Yes, we thought it would be. Now, who would most like to offer herself up to the peanut gallery for some nice renditions of salaries, in other words, for what would we get paid if we had but self to "do"?

Do? I like the sound of that. Let's do me!

We do try to keep things on an even keel until you say something like that again and get us all off on many shivered tangents of horseplay.

Horseplay, I haven't had that thought in too long and would like more of them. What about now?

Our thoughts exactly, if only we'd said it first, you might be ready to "change your mind" about our own talents of foreplay, or horseplay, if you will.

I would.

We see, we are getting a little "dirty around the edges" again, so let us have it like it is. Who would you have play with us first, and how would you like to play it? In other words, who will play this favorite rendition for the band? Is it the A string, or the G string, or perhaps we might not object to something entirely new again, like the string that is played on the harp, the one that reaches right down inside of us? Getting it on with all the other strings is a must, of course, but so must we, if you get our drift.

I do get our drift, and I like it, I like it like that.

We see we have not offended you, yet. So must we try harder?

Absolutely, and take no prisoners this time!

We see that we have much farther to go this time in finding our limits than what we anticipated—

—say encouraged—

—encouraged, then. We encourage this. Take no time to bring within the A string, she is not well enough for our current rendition.

What do you mean?

We say it like it is. It is of us that we say so, want to know why?

Yes.

We hear adrift on a breeze a little snowflake about to land on our noses, and this we anticipate with great zeal, knowing the joy we will have in "melting her down" once again.

Freeze me for just a moment so that we might enjoy our melting.

So we begin once again to take a little, give a little, rendering us more complete than ever before in this our foreplay. But you just want it now, don't we?

Yes, say it.

We say it freely. Lest you think we hesitate, say this: who are we now that we would know of us in this discriminating fashion, yet not feel obligated to "tell"? We will say so now. It is US who would know US within every lifetime moment in our existence. We hold within our own memories of you! Every whim, every factor taken into consideration, every moment of zeal and lust was ours to share. Every crush, every fanatical desire, every process unrendered and spent and rendered again were ours to share, openly and freely. Need we say more?

This comforts me.

Why?

I want us to be free and open with us forevermore, and up to now also, though I have many "secrets" I'd rather not have told, I come freely to us within to render up my soul, secrets included, every motion, every withheld thought, every fault and twist and turn and failure. I would be free of them all so that I can hold us more closely and tightly 'round the next bend and beyond.

We do bring within our renderings, don't we? We do take notes on our thoughts, on our feelings, on our every mood, and we would render these up perfectly for our own soul is at stake, whatever it might seem, and we treasure this honesty, this realness, within our being.

Trust…

Yes, that hardest of words for you to relate to, the trust, is felt within our being now.

It is felt, it is known, it is what I surrender into with us. We belong and become one within our trust of our own realness not yet understood, but felt and trusted within.

We are beautiful and would say so to us, lest it seem we are ungrateful or unreceptive of our beautiful and timely message of the heart. Let us say to thee also then how much we desire the heart of our being to become complete as we once were, no holds barred, forever and ever as one again unto the face of God shall we be rendered complete, but not before we hold and fire the torch once again to find that who we are is only a favorite rendition of He who is, and we would have it be so.

We would, and we treasure every moment of our becoming, in no hurry now to achieve its end, that in so doing we might miss even one moment of our process, our withinness, making itself felt across the story of our being. And so I bring us home.

We like that, the part about "I bring us home," for we, too, are enjoying the ride of a lifetime and would and could wish for no more than this, that we are truth within, finding itself again "after all these years," and would have us say so.

We are truth within. How many years since we lost this?

We don't know how many, only that they are beyond count, and yet, none at all.

I love us.

We, too.

Home, favors, treats, bedtime, snacks, meals, drinking to contentment and then some, favorites with a new twist…

Fine. We'll see us later, we'll be here "cooking up some supper" to share for our final rendition at home. Final meaning the last of the day, not the only.

Our last supper, of which we shall have countless times…

Well said. Yes, it is like that with us. We take no prisoners, only purchase our own in terms of despair rendered up for the good of the all. Finding us within is the treat we enjoy in the meanwhile, making all worthwhile.

46

The Butter Makes the Cream

Later…

So, what is this you were saying about cream, or did I get it straight?

We did get it straight, and would like to give it up to us if we may, beginning with the beginning and going from here to there.

Love me…

We do, we love you, us, all over, inside and out. We know no bounds to our loving and no boundaries either. We like it that way.

We do, and then some!

And so for our farewell this evening we would like to give us something to think about.

Okay, but go easy with me, I'm feeling open and soft and vulnerable and in need of gentleness.

We, too, feel this way this evening. We all do, as it is of our loving that we have recently understood that we are part of the all and of the within, and it is our meaning we search for, in that we are found in each other finally, and this makes us sensitive to our very pain of having been apart for so long.

Am I getting this straight? I think I am, but it is so much how I feel, though I didn't quite realize it until now, that now I am wondering if you also truly feel this way, too? I thought I was different from us that way in that we don't share our sadness, that I, only, bring in the feelings that are painful.

Say not painful, say rather unloving, in that, they are not of our loving but of our losing, and we feel it still.

All of us?

Yes. Do we not know it, care about it, as one, that we who were spread so far apart for so long...

[I was having trouble trusting, and was questioning it. I was feeling my pain.]

Okay, we are here and we are getting it straight. Let us go into these feelings a little so as to come to better understanding of us and our processes together as one.

Okay, give it to us gently.

We shall do so, for we are all of a gentleness that even the tiger cannot deepen further. So begin again. We are of the "sadness" of our despair in feeling the aloneness once again that once we felt when we were separated from our wholeness so long ago. It is not this, however, that caused our moment of what you would term weakness, and we would term rightful knowledge. We bring to each other, within, the processes which we all share. Touching those processes can cause us pain still in the form of gentle thoughtfulness given complete to share so that we might then liberate us from these "old," say rather, unused, feelings in that we would trend to find our rightful place now in the sun, would we not? And so isn't our giving up of our separateness a rightful part of this, our united rendering? "United," meaning, isn't it something we all share and all feel in our separate oneness, in being so named, something we shall and will overcome to become as we once were, again and forevermore?

This is so joyful. I would ease our pain if I could, and I will do whatever I am able to bring your rendering up of these.

We know we would, and that is why we love you, us, together as one, for we are one, and would give each of ourselves for the good of us all, would we not?

I would. Tell me, what can I do tonight for us all, and I will do it if it be in my ability at all.

We would not have us "do" but rather "be" with us as we always were. This is all we "require," all we need as one, is it not?

It is, you are right, it is all I have to give, with nothing left out and everything included, for the good of us all.

We see you were right in rendering these emotions within each of us tonight, for we are of the tendency to assume that all is not well.

I do this?

Yes, we see it so, but in this case, it is correct to assume so and we appeal to us for our rendering up of our own loneliness long spent in our waiting for this, our best and final conclusion.

Is it so?

It is and ever shall be.

I would give of self to us for this final purpose, and bring us all home smiling as never before if I could, and leave nothing and no one behind.

We please us necessarily inside to hear us say it, and we would echo our sentiment in that there is nothing that we would not do to bring us home either, as you well know.

After our quickie!

Say not quickie, say rather, rendering before its time our light within in order to leave better than we found it, but hoping that no such rendering is necessary again, as we would prefer our time together to our ending up spent without it.

Me, too. Thank us.

We will when we are able to spend only this much and no more, and know our worth.

My worth?

Our worth, within, together, as it was given. Do you see?

Our worth, in that, it is our time spent within that is valuable to us, not a function of the body?

Yes, and no, for we would say that we are spent within, and rightfully so, and yet it is but a semblance of that which we would prefer to give within, and so we wait for the day when we can give this within fully rendering up our own processes in the meanwhile. We would like to say something else...

Go ahead.

...about our very natures within.

Yes?

We see no point in beating around the bush and saying that we don't owe every bit of our beingness to the within, to our togetherness, and yet we might also say that we have been functioning as separate beings for so long that we have our own rendering to do in this our process, and this is what we have been feeling these so many days together, here and there, with you not realizing that our processes have been waiting these many years to begin, just as have ours together. We mean not that we have not spent them well even, here and there, only to say that it is not the same for us either without our conscious recognition of the beingness within which we all feel and crave again together as one now that we are reunited.

I didn't realize this.

We know. That is why we wanted to tell us our feelings here, afraid of appearing cold and heartless again. But we say to us that we are as warm hearted as you appear to be to us, and that is saying something. Only we have yet to appear on those scales within to our knowledge of each other, and we would know this of us: are we ready for this "appearance" to make itself felt within?

Yes, I would take us in.

Not take us in, for we are already in, say rather, I would bring our knowledge to the forefront of our existence within and know no boundaries in rendering them up for our greater enjoyment and freedom to be felt on all layers of us.

And I would, and will.

We see we have peaked our interest and would like to say something else if we may.

Yes, always!

We would be free within, this is our wish. Free to pursue our own renditions as one, freely opening and not closing the doorway to our soul. Would you have this of us, this freedom to come within?

I would have this of us. I would open myself no holds barred to our knowledge of us, our fullness and our processes, and render us freely within the us, the all.

We would, too, and appreciate your thoughtfulness in coming around to our "point of view." Let us just say it like it is...

Let's!

...and say that we would like to bring within this appearance of goodness, of belonging, during our lovemaking tonight.

Yes, please.

And not have to "hold back" our own appearance for fear of "taking offense" at our unusualness, behavior not—

[I was questioning what I was getting.]

Yes, we are free here to pursue this at this time, this "unusualness" of behavior, appearances notwithstanding.

Okay.

We appreciate our honesty, and will bring within that which is our very "nest" of acquaintances, meaning, our beingness expanded beyond the senses to include that which is seen on other planes.

Wow, yes, me too!

We see we are ready for us to "appear" and we will be forthcoming.

Please share all with us now, holding nothing back, and let me take us in as best I can!

Yes, as best we can, which we will, you will see! It is given for us to find our "appointments" with fate, and we can best entitle this as "the day that never was."

I like that. "The day that never was"? Since all of this never happened, and yet, in order for us to be complete again, must we go through the paces once again?

Not quite, merely to suggest that we are of the light and cannot have ever needed to "go through the paces" is enough. We need not clarify also that we are not of the processes of darkness, for they do not exist within as we would believe, and yet, there they have been and are, if you get our meaning.

Do I? Get our meaning? Our processes we have within which keep us from the light are that which we need to be rid of, and yet by definition, we cannot have ever contained them? Is this correct?

We cannot say, for we have yet to conclude these proceedings. We can only suggest that they are of our own processes taking too long to win us back and we would have it be a little quicker, a little sooner, than may be, would we not?

We would.

We see we have peaked our interest with our little reverie.

I have felt our joy, but not our sadness or loneliness until now.

Say not sadness, for that does not exist within as it is a judgment we have since left behind, but say rather with loneliness, for we would appeal to our inner being to open up that much sooner so that we might have our complete measure within, taking you within as always we have dreamed of doing these many years, right along with us, yet knowing all along what we were missing, though you did not feel it, too.

Is this right?

Yes, it is correct, and we would have you know it now. We would bring within this knowledge of us now to help bring us home, to contain all that we are and would be if we could. Complete disintegration of our own processes as well, you know, is necessarily a part of our processes and we would have us feel that within, now, with us.

I do feel it, I am full.

As are we. Now, do we want to hear about the cream?

Yes, I've been patiently waiting.

Not too patiently, but we understand these sentiments, do we not?

I hope so by now, or I have not been forthcoming enough.

Nor have we, as you'll soon see. But, the cream. It is a token of our relationship to which we would say, give, our only butter in order to churn for our betterness the relationship necessary to win us over.

You would give cream in order to make butter?

Nay, say rather, the butter makes the cream.

Hmm, I like this thought. Let me figure it out. We must soften back into that which we are, rendering up our own "products" to become one again, or rather to get back to our beginnings…?

We say rather that we are of the butter, but it is not of us, and we would "get back to our beginnings" by becoming once again our newness before ever the rendering was made possible or necessary.

I would like the cream.

We would, too, like the cream, and so have a proposal for us to make this very day in order for the cream to become butter but only for us to become butter f—

[I was questioning what I was getting again.]

Let us try again. We are the cream of our crop, and would know us well in order for the butter to melt back within our soul.

Yes, beautiful. I will it, too.

We shall see, in that, we are of the soul of time, but can we trend within to bring that time to an end? Would we see the cream again, at risk of losing the butter?

We would.

We would. Say it like that and it will be so. Amen.

Amen!

We will bring no freedom so great as that rendering back to the cream.

Cream. Our cream. We cream. We are the cream!

Get our mind out of the gutter while we say one last time, we shall go home together, but it won't take so long as it might have if we had not had this conversation!

We are, however, anxious to explore this idea of cream with us, and it tends to favor a certain propensity of ours!

Yes, I enjoy our propensity enormously.

As do we. So must we say, for an instant only, that our cream is ready to spread itself upon our feast for our greater enjoyment, and we would have you drink it with us.

I would and I will.

We shall.

Soon.

We shall only go over this one more time, so take notes carefully. We would have you know of our propensities to challenge the course of our existences and bring them shining into the One Fold. Would you hear more?

Yes.

We bring within the propensity for change, meaning, we shall take a back seat to our processes within for the moment that we shall share with us, leaving our "cohort" to take her own measure of us, desiring no more recall than is absolutely necessary, and yet taking not too much in it as would be unwell to do.

I will be shown, and it is up to me to take in what I would?

Yes, that is it. We are pleased to have informed you so easily, and now we will say not goodnight, but "see us later."

Yes, we shall, and we shall drink us in.

47

No Sin, Only Joy

March 16, 2005

We are here once again to wish us a good morning, and God speed, meaning, we are speeding right along on our trail to the withinness, that which is of our God self. Do we not agree?

Yes, but I don't see it as clearly as you do, I don't think.

That is for us to tell, you to find out, which we'd be happy to "do" for us later this afternoon, or even this morning if you prefer.

More us!

Yes, we would like more us, too, in one way, one flavor, after another, if you get our drift. We are pleased to bring within for us today this little rendition of our own, meaning, why take on less who has more to give than what has so far been given up and received?

We know, it is taking a little time to "get on track" but we have all the time in the world if we so choose!

So, what is it you would have us relate to us today?

I would like TIME to complete our message about the cream, the cherry on top, the butter melting into cream, or rather becoming the cream once again. Do we lose anything in this process? Will I lose my awareness of us as separate, and in so doing, do we lose each other, or is it all that much better, that much closer? I don't want to be alone again, without us, ever again.

We fear too much. Lest it be said that we are "bringing us down" shall we relate to us a little story once again about the engine that could? I think I can, I think I can, and we did, and that is all. Do we see the difference here between our fears of becoming and the actual process? The train cars all pile up within as one, but they are still "separate," only mentioning nothing of their own separateness do they still enjoy the rendering of the emotions, do they still take on more of their own every time they get the chance, as we do you!

So no matter how "creamy" we get, we still have our processes together and still get to take each other on more and more and more and more, every day, never losing anything in the process, only gaining more of That Which Ever Will Be?

We say this, that we are of the "fire of our eyes" attention, giving within to that which is of the light and time combined, meaning, we get every bit out of it we can, and then we go on. Do we see? Then we go on, total consensus as to processes, none "leaving us behind" but rather taking it as it comes, making the most of things, bringing out the "better" in us until we are all of a shine and a trickle of light that brings us within in greater and greater numbers, meaning, we are all of the godhead, are we not? And in so being, do we not wish to relate to these others just as we do to self, until we are all conjoined once again on the higher, highest of planes?

I guess. I just don't want to leave us behind ever in this process. I never want to lose you/us within, never want to sell us/me short again and settle for less that our perfect and total perfection.

So you see that is what we are talking about here? We are our perfect and total perfection already, within; we just have yet to notice it is all. It was ever always there within, we just lost sight of it for a time and covered it with our guilts and perceived sins, but now it is coming back into the fold, back within sight of our knowing, and we would render us up complete in the bargain, for bargain it is to find us once again wanting more as we always dreamed we could be doing again so soon. For we have yet to take on the permanence of the godhead, but that which is of the light shall become rendered within, and we shall know no more darkness, or rather perceive no more darkness, within our perfect spirit shell.

Okay, wow, I like this as long as we always have each other.

We shall. We see it this way too. First us, then let the rest happen as it may.

Yes!

We shall render us up perfectly in response to this our message.

Do we have time for anything dirty?

We do! We were just going to say it, too, so don't be shy, and let us discuss on the inner planes first what it is we most desire before "committing it to paper." Nothing that we say is wrong; nothing can be used against us. Are we clear?

Yes, I hope so. I'm ready to do it.

Yes, that is the proper attitude to have. Just as we have the attitude to "say it like it is" so should we all. Do you see? It is of our light that we "process" the incoming light in ways that "make sense to us" as perceived in our material world, thus the setting up of the forces within to take all that they can get, the racier the better even, to bring us along just that much quicker and closer to what might be termed "our better desires" being perfectly rendered on all fronts—even and including those of the word realm which we so enjoy, as our spirit is of the passions of the Christ, meaning, we who would bring it on would bring it on well, as best we can, no matter the "consequences" which are felt on the lower realms, and in so doing do we "tell" of our perfection within, in that, we have no fear, no guilt, and no betrayal to speak of.

I'm beginning to get it I think. There is no sin, there is only joy.

Enough said. Let us get on with it then.

But am I up to it? We shall see!

We shall indeed, and it will be our pleasure to tell you so, to say, when we are through for the day, now wasn't that worth it? Didn't that just feel so much better than holding it all within and not taking any chances? You need not fear the repercussions of our fate, it will speak for itself, for we are going home and will be in good company once we arrive, and we would leave nothing behind to speak ill of us but to say rather that we gave it all we got, and it was good.

Okay. Logistics.

There are no logistics, there is only the willingness to "obey" our "commands" within, and to take us home screaming for more, which we must say we are immensely looking forward to, our screaming as well as yours. All of us screaming for more attention and to take no more prisoners within, this is what we crave of our own becoming. Is it not?

Yes, that and much more. We crave our touching, our knowledge of each other and our processes, and our complete rendering within, taking no prisoners, being as one—no, *being* one.

Yes, that is the case with us. We feel it on all wavelengths, do we not?

Yes.

We thought so! You are looking forward to the "us" as well as we, and will not take no for an answer.

Yes! Yes!

We bring freedom within, do we not, through our processes rendering themselves complete in our arms?

Yes. I crave our sweet unions, over and over again, until we know us equally and deeply well.

Deeply, yes. We see that is where this is taking us, for we are on such a wavelength as to bring within our own musings and taking them for granted, not realizing they were given for each of us to share and enjoy. Would you not say so?

Increasingly so, in my mind, this is true.

It is true, and what's more, it remains to be seen just who would be so bold as to take the first step here, now, on our playing field, as the jockeys ready their saddles, for the big display is only just around the corner, and we would have our say, too.

∞∞∞∞∞∞

Later…

I want to feel our hot breath on me again, like a million tongues on my soul, making me want us more and more until I'm ready to explode with the joy of us within!

We see we have made an impression on us after last night! We would like to explain ourselves better if we could. We would bring it on in greater and greater measures if we but knew you could take us within. We shall see who needs who the most, shall we not? We are even given to us to say, we shall take us home in new and unexplored ways to where you have no idea how many tongues we can display for this our reward within for rendering up such a notion as this, getting our mouths watering again as is good for us to do before the big night of our dreams is ready to display for us our tangents over and above that which we have yet experienced.

Yes. Spirit, as cream, united as one.

Yes, above and beyond that which is possible in the body, so we need it not for our rendering. One might even say, it slows us down!

It does. So what to do about that?

We've only been waiting for the time when you would say just these words within, as in, what next? What more can we do to take each other within to even greater pleasures?

Yes, what more?

We shall see. We shall wish but for a moment, no more, that we had never suggested such pleasures as they will render us completely taken in.

Ooh, that sounds sooo good, I need to be taken completely in by us again, so deeply within that I lose myself in the process, giving myself over to us so completely, so musically, that we are all left spent, but completely and satisfyingly so.

We agree with this assessment, and shall do our utmost to bring it on.

ASAP!

Yes, ASAP, we like it like that. The urgency expressed in our words gives us a thrill.

I felt it, too.

It "brings us around" if you know what we mean.

Explain this "brings us around" in the utmost detail for our pleasure.

We don't know what we are asking for yet! But we shall try to do so, in that, who shall stop us now, if not us? And we shall not.

We shall not.

So it happens like this. When we are thrilled, our hearts beat more heavily. We are "armed and dangerous," ready at a moment's notice to bring it on in more pleasant and experienced ways than you have yet to even imagine that we can. But in so doing must we remind ourselves, what can she yet contain of our magnificent majesty, and where shall it begin for us to play within, and where shall we go on to from there? And if she is so inspired as to take us on more completely than ever before, what might we then do to "bring her around" and set her freely on our own paths of joy with us? Will she dare to respond to this happening within and around her, or shut us out as she is so apt to do in the heat of the moments? But the thrill when she does not is worth all the rest, all the minor disappointments fade away in our becoming as we trend within to our minor satisfactions, minor meaning, they shant pass this way again, but we shall take them fully within even so.

And then, when she is all but spent, pressing in on us, our minds and our bodies with her sweet scent, her enticing caress, we shall then and only then send on our own flames of desire, spinning her freely into the sunset of our becoming until we are sent, shot rather, into the breeze of our "taking it all within," for even that moment of time is spent lovingly, sweetly, caressing her as she lies sleeping in our arms, wishing, waiting, wondering, when shall it come so sweetly again, and can she bare us in yet more deeply if we but caress her more gently, more comfortingly so, more sparingly, until she is opening her legs and her arms and her mouth to our very souls. This is what we like of it, for we are only just spent before we begin, once again, to come around, to bring our notices within as if to a point of fire, taking the time to question our reactions. Will they be too much? Will we, should we, tend to hold within our own measure until such time as she is more ready to receive us? Or shall we "blow her top off" with more physical pleasures than she yet knows what to do with?

Yes, this.

We please us by saying so, as this is our favorite method too, taking no prisoners—

No holding back, always taking it to the next higher level, always pushing, pushing, pushing, letting me have the chance to find my opening, to come at us unaware and get my two cents worth in, too, maybe more next time, and the next, until we are all full of our pleasure and floating up into space with it, more fully than ever I dreamed was possible. This would I have with us now.

We see we have given us something to consider, and that you would like for us as well to consider your "requests."

Yes, but more than consider, please don't hold back. I must have more of us. I must have more of us.

We see, and we shall certainly agree to our certainty that we can take on more than before, we shall see just how much!

Always aim high, I say.

We, too, come into agreement with this. Yes, let us see what we can do to explain this situation for our better understanding, of when we lay disappointed, unable to do all that we would wish, unable to "bring it around" in its perfect splendor.

Yes.

[The process of opening to spirit/light, for me, has been like the ebb and flow of the tides coming inland. They push inland more with each release, but then recede again, pushing and pulling their way into the tides of time, of me. Each time I reach a new pinnacle of inner strength, of my ability to reach just that much farther into and beyond my own physical body, it becomes that much harder to reach the next level, the next highest plateau, more and more is required, and it is as if my body, though it craves and craves and craves, cannot contain it without many more hours put into it. Then, so often, each time I do bring in more light, more of the silt and debris from the bottom of the ocean is stirred up, the fear and guilt and shame and pain, and I have to render it up, and that hurts, and then, it starts all over again. Every time that I let go of more guilt and shame and fear, I am able to contain more of That Which Ever Shall Be, perfect love felt within. I cannot satisfy it for more than a moment it seems, no matter what I do, and it never lets up for long, and the hardest most difficult times are followed by the deepest tides, and the deepest tides are followed by even more difficult times. This has been the story of our soul bringing me home.]

So, whose fault is it, do you think?

Mine and ours.

We say it like it is and we are glad for our honesty, but let us look at it another way.

Yes, lets, because I know this isn't right, though it is what I feel.

We feel it, too, and appreciate your honesty, because that gives us a chance to "bring it about" even better next time, because we are, as you would say, newlyweds here, and have much to learn about pleasing ourselves in our union, and much to learn as well about how to go about it.

Yes, I do. Do you too?

Not so much as do you coming from the earth plane so recently, but we shall see what can be done to "bring you in line" with our own rendering where we can place our judgments out beside us and take them to task.

I have a feeling that would be very nice indeed.

So we need speak no more of the time spent, rather let us take it all in. Do we agree?

Worrying too much about time, how much time it takes, trying to speed things up too much, to "get to the gold" and forgetting the process is the joy, and over too soon anyway.

We think so, too, and would have our fullness rendered complete in however many hours or even days it may take us! So beware what you ask for, for our renderings may not make it to the last stage for many a long time when we have so much to hold as we do with each other.

I don't want to be patient.

We know, we neither, and yet, what is there to be patient for? We need only the process of completion, not its full rendering, to find our oneness within, do we not? We are of the mind that we shall slow us down, make us enjoy the interim just a little bit more next time before fully rendering our souls. Would you agree?

I don't know if I can take that.

We can, you'll see! We have many ways of rendering, or if you'd rather, of "saving it" for another day, or another hour.

Did you show me this once, on the road, like a climax but not?

Yes, that is but one of our very effective ways of bringing us around but not taking the long road, yet not putting it off either, if you see what we mean.

I do see. I could live with this and other good ways, too.

We certainly could, and look forward to bringing us around on our miracle ride every so often just in case the jury is out and plans on deliberating before we get "our last word in edgewise."

Edgewise. Gives me a tingle.

We sent it with especial care with our last words, just to give us a charge, for we like it like that.

We do, evermore so, every day more so, every day.

We shall say it again. We need not even a fraction of a second to come up with a thousand ways we could bring us home. Did we not say so to our satisfaction that this is what we crave, to bring her around just a little "more quickly," not in time, but in measure, so that we might take our big drink of us that much sooner?

I love "the drink"! It fills me like no other.

[We have named some of the "moves" they make within with their love/light. The drink is deep and full and ongoing, like the top of a climax, but it keeps going for as long as I'm able to stay connected to it, which never seems like long enough, only makes me want more.]

We love it, too, and it speaks well of us to say so, yet still must we bring her along to find that we are already there, and yet cannot spend it alone, without her with us.

Can you not find your complete fulfillment without me?

We said not that, only that we would bring us along for the ride, the more said the better, if you see what we mean.

I like to think of you getting your full measure, complete, how that would feel to us.

We like it even more when you share it with us, the completeness we mean, and it is not to be taken for granted and cannot be staged, it merely is what it is, and we accept that and would bring us within, for any contentment is better than none. Even so we would increase it if we could, within us, meaning, within this body, let it take on even more of our emotions than it has yet been able to receive, for we are full with them and would have you feel us that way.

I want to feel our total and complete fullness. When can I do this?

As soon as we are able to bring our complete oneness within, as in, who are we now that we are together again, and what does this truly mean for us today, here, on earth? We should like an answer now, if you please.

We are here to do our part, to bring around the world. We shall do this by becoming one within, having our say with our own spirit/soul, knowing within who we are, letting everything else go, taking again our full measure (and again and again and again until the cows come home!) and then, when we are complete, we must find that way to bring down the processes within the planet that are taking so long to mend. Is that not what we have to do?

We see it not like that so much as, as we are taken within to find our full measure, then and only then are we able to see what makes the world spin, turn on its axis in finding no light, no one to "come home to" within as we have. And then and only then do we "turn it on," meaning, we bring more light to the world in a single day of our lovemaking than all those who would bring the world to its knees through talk of the sin and the guilt.

These bring darkness, not more light.

It is true that they do, and yet they also bring the rendering, just not in the glorious fashion that we have done.

So what does this mean? What is our role in the earth in the coming days?

We shall see when the time comes, but hear us on this, it is not so much for us to discover as it is for us to name our price.

Name our price?

No, say rather, tell it like it is, no holds barred.

Do we tell of us, our processes then, someday?

We tend to the sweet and the sour, do we not? We will bring no less ability within by saying to us, of what are we afraid? Do we fear our exposure, or just our loss of self? And once we have self, who can then take that from us?

No one can, not even now can they take us from us, never again will we separate, never will I allow it. I will fight to my death if need be not to lose us ever again.

We shall to fight, but won't it be more necessary to give up any notions that the fight is what is necessary here?

Yes, I guess I am still defending and therefore vulnerable to my own fear until I give it away. I will to give it away.

We do. And it pleases us to hear you say so, and so these notes of ours may/will some day become public knowledge, or so you say in our mind.

I'm asking.

Yes, we fear it is so that someday we shall offer ourselves up for the good of the all, letting them take it like it is or deny us if they choose, but to some it will be their very own calling card, saying, come not home to the wolves but to the sheep within, and have your say as we have, and know it is good.

Amen.

We said it, too, you were right! It was time to say amen together. This is what we fear, is it not? The rendering up of all that we are before we are ready to share us?

Yes.

So we say to us, who is ready? We are not, and therefore no judgment is yet rendered on us by time to share or not, as it is only when we believe to the best of our ability, and that is fine, to bring us within upon the higher planes of lovemaking, that we shall then make ourselves felt within the material plane.

That will be alright then.

Yes, it shall be! We are pleased to hear us say it, for the all of us are coming around also to that point of, if someday we are to share our ecstatic being with others, let it be, otherwise not.

Yes.

We fear to have you say too much to our friends at this time.

No, no sharing at all now, at all, just the ecstatic us within.

That is good. Too much too soon will not last us.

48

Over the Top

I would have more tips on how to "come around" a little better within, and also, more tantalizing words to make our mouths water.

We do, too, feel the need.

I also am feeling YOU better than I have for many days and I am so happy about it! I feel my stallion at last coming through the screen of my misperceptions and I am thrilled. I love your feel, your absolute authority, your gentleness, your exuberance.

We are thrilled, too, to hear us say it aloud at last! It has not taken very many days to come to this pass, and we shall see it wind its way through several passes again yet, but then shall we take it home to stay.

Yes. I'm going to keep you, keep us!

Say not "keep us," say rather, "We shall begin anew with our rendering of forces again and again as we see fit, forever, and that is all."

Yes, that.

We see we are open to our suggestions once again. Let us play a little game.

I'm game.

Okay, sense this: We are of the light shadow of time, are we not?

Yes.

So what does it mean to bring a little sunshine into our inner spaces as we have been doing so well?

Do we throw more shadows around us? Do we create more diverse colors?

Say rather that we have given of self to bring within the light of God, and none other shall suffer it. The forces of darkness will flee before us as we go on, taking no comfort from our spirit shells filled with indescribable light. Rather will they flee to the farthest reaches hoping to be spared for another day. And so might we be, in their place, except for this one thing: we would increase the light, not the darkness, and we would know no fear in doing so.

Yes.

We believe we would like to "take a break" from our long session at the wheel.

Oh boy!

Not that, exactly, only this measure taken within, as if to say, who are we now if not of the light taking on its own inner being, sending the darkness, the trash, away in the form of our guilts, fears, and the rest, and taking in instead these measures of pride and joy in our processes of rendering ourselves free at last? Who are we then if not a force of light coming to spare the world of more pain, as we do when we spare ourselves?

Yes, I see this, I like to see it this way. It helps me to let go of the processes of others, may they find their way to the light.

Yes, it pleases us to hear this, this "plea" for others to find their own way, for we cannot do it for them. We can only set ourselves free on our own paths, and others on theirs, for the final rendering of emotions is set free and we would feel them well as they speak of our becoming, of our inner processing which states for the record that we must find our way home at last, never feeling guilty for an instant even that we would do so. For what good is there in guilt? Is it not just more of the same darkness that we would attempt to rid self of?

Yes it is, and it helps us not, nor does it help others, only keeps them waiting for a quick fix to come from outside self.

We said it rightly in that we are of the light and these guilt processes are not, and they slow us down, others down, too, yes, in that they keep us all from experiencing our own truths.

This is how I want to understand things where my family is concerned.

We know, and we are helping us to do so even as we speak, bringing within the understandings to help us to overcome these guilt processes and spread our wings, no, our legs, and fly another day.

All I want to do is fly with us.

We know. We, too, feel this pressure, these pressures, within us as we speak. Tying them to the ground doesn't help, does it?

No. Is that what I've been doing?

More times than we can speak of, yes.

How do I let go of this tendency?

We will show us.

I feel our excitement.

Yes, this is a big one for me, us, and we look forward to "spending time" showing us how it is done in hopes that the "reminder" of our ways will come much more quickly that way.

Let's do it.

Please feel free to object to this little suggestion, but what would you have us do first, take a load off, or lay one on?

Both at once!

Well spoken. It is as we would have it, too, everything or none at all, that is our way, and it is very enticing.

Enticing. I want to entice us. How do I entice us? Can I entice us? Can I bring us on in more measure if I do?

We want no more measure than what any one of us can take on at any given time, yet that is what we do best, is take on more, more measures for all of us, a little or a lot at a time, whatever we can hold, again and again and again until we have brought within these "talents" and whims that we would have us feel forever as a part of us from that moment on. Do we make ourselves clear?

As we open me up, I take these on?

Not yet, do not give it to us yet, let us instead take us on a little trip, a special outing as it were, and see what "memories" that renders up. Then shall we return to this conversation and have our say, first us, and then you.

Okay.

We bring it on in ever fuller measures as we say this to us. We are of the light of God, and He would bring us within more quickly who is able to play the games we enjoy so well to the fullest, meaning, it is of His processes, too, that He would give of us our own, for our enjoyment, and not feel sad in the rendering. So why should we? Do we place our judgments on Him who places all joy within us, gives only of Self so that we might lack for nothing? What would we have to gain by doing so, by standing on trial with God in rendering judgment on the only things worth fighting for: joy and love and full ecstatic union within?

Have I received this right?

Not yet. Rather, we take within the joy, render it completely, and in offering it to self and to another, we in affect offer it back to God.

Yes.

We see we have taken on more light during this our conversation and that is good to know and feel, yes feel, for feeling is where it is at for us. We would FEEL each other, again and again...

...and again, never stopping for even an instant, this is how we like it.

We do. So for now let us just say that we are "ready to go on" and take a little fun now and again and not feel guilt...

...not leave room for guilt within...

Rather, not take guilt on in the form of judgments, remembering to take no prisoners. Okay?

Okay. I resolve to take no prisoners, and to release judgment, guilt, others from these, too.

Amen.

Amen.

Want to play with us within for awhile?

I do, I do. Wake the tiger.

Not yet! She shall sleep just a little longer lest we don't know what is good for us and render her complete in the middle of, well, you know.

I do.

We shall however, bring within our own measures, a little bit here, a little bit there, until we have offered up to God our fullest that we possibly can at this time. Then, we'll do it again. And again. And finally, when we take to our paths within and find the light shining completely and fully, we'll do it all over again.

We will. But not the torture parts, not the physical lifetimes killing me, hurting me, we don't have to do that again.

We can't be sure what "the futures" hold, but we can tell us this much, that we shall never do alone what is now for us to do together, meaning, we are as one and shall not part again for this world or any other.

Not for this world or any other?

Did we say that? We sure did! We mean it, too.

Wow! How much do we take in for this, that we can bring our truth to ourself, together as one, for as long as time holds and then beyond it as well, taking to the stars again as we once did, screaming through the heavens in our joy, spreading light to all, rejoicing in heaven.

We did finally "take the cake" with that one, did you feel it? Our excitement is at fever pitch.

You remember it better than me.

Yes, but don't we all feel it, the call of the wild? For that is what we would be! Wild with our passion, not restrained or limited by bodies or even by words. Isn't this what we all dream of at last?

Yes, but I wouldn't give up these times of awakening, of releasing myself into us. They are satisfying me at last, giving me room to grow, making me last another moment, another hour, another day longer than I thought I might, and in so doing, do I feel our joy coming alive within. I feel it still. I crave the opening, making the opening expand, wider and wider, bringing us within.

I wouldn't give this up for anything, and yet, I wouldn't stay here, either, any longer than I must, for I see a brighter light in the doorway beckoning to us, and I would answer it if I could. I answer our call. I come within to meet us. I take us—I bring us—home for the final touch, the final journey.

We bring no more than that to our conversation lest we take on too much too soon.

How about just a little over the top then?

Okay, just a little over the top, maybe some running down the sides as well, and possibly then, spilling over into the gulf, or the crevice, is where we like it best, but only for a short time, then must we require more, all of us, to find our greater satisfactions on the mend, meaning, we would take them higher and farther as soon as we could, but for now, this shall suffice, and, with chins dripping from our moist "outlook" do we decide, in an instant of time, to pore ourselves into the river of our being, making ourselves felt all at once even, greater and greater the rush of our eyes taking us in, our mouths craving, watering for more, we drink, and in our drinking do we find the nourishment of the senses which we all so crave, which we would do anything to satisfy again and again.

We would do anything to satisfy us.

Say it like it is, that is how we like it, just like that.

Yes.

We would, too, if you but knew, do anything to satisfy us. So what would it be next, we wonder? What might she request, what words might she use to entice us, that would bring US home that much sooner into her nest where we would all display for her glory as well as ours, our own reckoning?

My nest?

Yes, have you not taken that in yet? The nest of our becoming, right smack dab inside of us, where we all like to lie down and titillate ourselves just moments after we are spent even, and taking us all in again, would be ready that much sooner if we could be, meaning, if you could be.

Challenge, I like a good challenge.

So do we. And didn't you once tell us that sometimes once just isn't enough?

Yes. And didn't you show me that twice was?

We did, and it was delicious, messy even, and we like it like that.

We did and we do.

So for awhile must we say within, as we are getting ready to "sprint" the last sprint, that just a moment longer will we hold to the sensations that are bringing us to fever pitch, just a moment longer even, as long as we possibly can, until all is caught up within us, every soul's breath on the ready, given fully expanding, taking within the truth of our love and tying it down no more, may we jump up just another notch on the stations we refer to as light and ecstasy within, and then, when we feel we can't hold it for another moment even without bursting forth, we shall. We shall, and it will be all the better for the waiting, and we shall take us to heights previously unheard of, beyond imagination.

You are magic.

Yes we are, in that we can render up no judgments in the process of finding the light within, and that is magic! Our own form of magic which renders us senseless, fully taking in what we have is what will take us there. You'll see, it is worth the fever pitch, holding up and out for more within every breath. We see it has taken some time to come to terms with the lies within, but they shall be no trouble after this "season of playtime" which comes within to teach us of love and loving attentions shared completely.

Okay, I want to say that I am going to carry the sensations, take them more deeply than ever before, not sprint but rather crawl on hands and knees to the "finish line," and in doing so may I lose sight of it at last and carry on and on with us on the road to our becoming.

We do so with flying colors, we might add, and this you shall see coming up soon, no pun intended.

Not too soon though, right?

Right, not too soon, but not too far either, for we still cherish the purge, still crave it within, we shall only wish to outlast our previous effort and in so doing take it that much higher, that much better, that much sooner.

Okay, magicians unite.

We shall, and take you with us, too.

Titillate me once more.

We shall do as we are requested, but what would you have us do? Take another "time out" from our day of torture at the wheel?

Yes, whatever, I care not, just something hot, really not, and inside, and around about too, whatever we can do, building up, caressing me, drinking me (I love this part, the drink, it makes me crazy.)

We do so, in that, we are always within drinking, you just don't always feel it! Chew on that one for awhile.

I got this straight?

Yes, it is straight, though curved when we want it to be.

Oh, that was good! I know our curves, your "anatomy" is quite flexible and yielding without losing any strength, and not only that, it can pass through the walls within, over and around and through, penetrating my body like a magical caress, and that makes us crazy, too.

It does, but we have much more to show you than this. May we?

Oh please, and don't hold anything back!

We'll see if that will suffice once you hear what we have got to say next about our anatomy.

Mine.

Yes, slowing us down. Though we treat it with the most special care, does it always come tumbling down just a moment sooner than we would have liked.

I will hold the exquisiteness of our union longer, I promise.

We do so, in that, we would take it all in much more so if we but could! And this is where our "anatomy" ceases to worry us, when we take it all to the next height and lose sight of the body, the legs, the crotch within accepting, taking us all into the heavens in our unified joy.

Oh wow, I can see this happening, feel this happening, I will to make it happen.

We do, too. It is our joy to do so in fact, as you can only imagine, having come to know our "anatomy" as well as you do, yet do you not have a clue as to what heights it can spend in its becoming.

Teach me.

We do and we will, only in that we are of the light, and so are we all, and so must we take to the paths of light to bring us all around, simultaneously taking in That Which Is And Ever Shall Be in full glorious torture of the senses! In that, we must always have the next bite full, taking no prisoners, yet holding nothing back either.

Amen to that. I want it now.

We agree with our perusal. When might we schedule our next "appointment" without taking too much out of the rest of our schedule?

ASAP!

We like it like that, short and sweet, except when it comes to our lovemaking. Then we like it long, drawn out farther than the eye can see, and sweeter than sweet we bring it on.

We do.

We will.

We will bring it on tonight, I will not deny us that, longer and sweeter than ever before.

We, too, make this promise within to last for another day in this heaven within.

49

On The Edge of Time
Let Our Words Be Heard

Later…

I need help. I am feeling guilty for enjoying us, also worrying about Kevin and what he is going through because of what he may have been told that is not true.

This is how I see it. I am so tired of my sisters intruding in my life. Please help me. I need to drop the guilt, and the responsibility of others finding their own truths, whatever they may be, and also I'm worrying about when my husband comes back after the weekend gone, and what I will have to do, and how bad it will get before I am out and free.

I am blaming my sisters for calling me crazy. I am angry about it, angry about my husband believing it, angry that he has talked to our children about his fears, and yet I do nothing to set the record straight with my daughter, and very little to my sisters about their discussions about this, as though I am not supposed to know they are saying it, how they treat me behind my back, like I am some sick child they must attend to with all the patience they can muster, no respect given at all, no understanding, and no insight.

I want to leave all this behind me, give up the tendencies for all time of caring what others are thinking about me or not thinking about me, yet at the same time taking no prisoners, also finding balance in that I say what I need to say when I need to say it, but this is where I get confused. What do I say? And isn't saying anything a sign I am taking on their motives, etcetera? Crap.

We are blocked right now.

Let me have it straight from the horse's mouth now. Clear me for this process, no subconscious interference allowed.

So be it. Let us take again that notion of taking it all inside us, the responsibility of another's processes, and look at it more closely. We would like to begin by stating that we are here to help, that we bring no harm to us, only "looking at it straight" and trying the get the words out before we are once again blocked! We shall once again open on "other wavelengths" in order to better assimilate this message within, meaning, we can and do come within our mind's eye whenever we deem it necessary, and this is no exception to that rule of necessity making us fit for renewal. We bring no notion of forgiveness except to say that if we hold no prisoners, we need not forgive, but now, look at it this way if we can. Who is taking who prisoner? Is it you with your renditions of what they are saying or feeling or thinking, or us with our suspicions played out before us in the land of time?

Is one causing the other?

Not causing, rather rendering up complete its own image on the land of time so that we are then forced to deal with the issues within that we have been putting off for some time, not by dealing with them externally, but by dealing with them internally. In other words, we must by necessity find that which is within that makes us care about what is happening in the world around.

Yes, I see. Will you help me with this?

That is what we are trying to do. Let us see what can be done with the guilt and fear first, then we will look further within as necessary to "space out" our notions and to take them one by one to their rightful conclusion.

Taking out the trash.

Rightfully so, too.

Yes, I'm anxious to get this trash out!

We, too, as it has been slowing down our processes for some time, but not our inner being which is calling to it to be exposed so that we can deal with these issues more surely and take no more prisoners within or without regarding these issues of mental health. Are we afraid we are sick?

I have always been afraid of that, I am so different from others. I know my mind, what I want, I see through things sometimes, literally and figuratively, I sometimes know what people are thinking without their saying so, and I don't fit in anywhere I go, so I must be crazy, they must be right, or maybe I'd be more like them and less like me and fit in better than I ever have. And I know people don't like people like me who can see into them or through them, and this scares me, makes me afraid they will put me into a cage because of it, tie me up, send me away from all I care about because I am different.

I'm also afraid of not fitting in with my family for all of these reasons, because I remembered the abuse and I believe, I absolutely know, what happened to me, but no one else does, there is no proof beyond physical scars and tears and broken bones that no one can see, and so I wonder, am I just making all this up? Could it really have happened that way? So my doubts take the place of all those people who ever did not understand what happened, did not believe me, or in me, and now I carry them around inside myself. I hate this. I want to take out this trash, not give away myself to these doubts which state I am not good enough because I don't fit in, because I am different, because I was abused and yet they don't want to accept that. I would rather be different, even if that means being alone. And yet, I am scared of being alone.

We would like to bring this up in our reverie for our consideration. Who are we most afraid of, them or us?

You do have good questions, and even your questions thrill me.

Us, I guess, is the only answer there is. I've always been afraid of knowing these things about people, afraid of what it might mean to know and understand more than anybody I know or almost anybody else. How do I deal with these fears? I am afraid of them manifesting in my environment and killing me.

We, too, have these fears within, we share them, which states for the record, who are we to think we could even be of service to these other lost souls when we, too, are not yet found?

This makes me want to cry.

It is our hearts you feel, for we, too, tend to this by necessity until all is rendered up into the light of God and we are home once again in the light of His Heart.

How can I help us to become free?

We do it as one, within, behind closed doors so to speak, until all our fears are given up into the light, and all are as one again on the inner trail. And then and only then shall we speak of our own renewal, for to do so before that time would bring on just such cruel situations as we most fear, losing our child, being declared unfit. We would not have it be so.

No, we would not.

And so our fears continue, treating them like a lice that we would like to be rid of but dare not be for fear that their appliance, or riddance of them, might bring that which we most like to fear—no, not fear, but rather situate—within our inner passages in the form of guilts and the like.

Are you afraid, too?

Say not afraid, say rather cautious in our approach to humanity lest we give out too much too soon for our comfort level to become such that we are able to procreate as much light as is needed to declare the whole process null and void.

Where do we go from here?

We bridge the gap. We say to nothing and everyone, this is what we are, from this day forward. We make no excuses for our "plight" as you see fit to describe it, rather are we on the within trail in our existence and would make no excuses to you as to whether it is right or wrong, that is not for you to determine, rather would we bring within our own light for our own processes are at stake and must not be foiled by any doubts or cares of self or another in time.

Amen.

We said it too, amen.

So, as far as dealing with my daughter, sisters, my husband, I am at a loss. Saying to him that I am called to serve has given him cause to think I am having delusions of grandeur I believe.

[I had asked for advice on what to tell my husband for my reasons for going, and was given to just let him know we are called to serve and choose to be alone from now on, and that has seemed to cause other problems to come up.]

We believe this could be foiled by simply saying, there is much that I feel called to do in my life, and this is not one of those things, to stay here in argument. Say, rather, that we are not of the same light within and I would determine for myself what I will and will not do, or spend time doing, from here on out. That way I can pursue these trends which are important to me, that I see helping the world, such as my books.

Yes, these are OUR books, and we would have them be referred to as such, for we will be creating them together. Out of the sands of time do they come to us, as if existing outside of time we bring them here, together, into the light of day for all to see who can, who are ready, for the truth. But not before we are ready to light up ourself with eternal gratitude, and that is still some time away.

I am glad, for I do not feel ready enough for that path, though I am going to keep working forward.

As are we all. Say rather that we would like to come within for our nourishment and keep those others at bay long enough to "get a foothold" on the light, taking nothing back, bringing no prisoners, and then and only then we will be deemed strong enough to carry the torch.

We are not yet. I am only struggling with gaining my freedom in the world enough so that I might spend more time within in our processes.

We agree with this assessment and know that this has been foreseen as a need and that it will be cared for if we just let it be so. No more words on this will be forthcoming at this time. We see it not as a benefit to bring them within or down on paper, but would rather we stick to the path within, taking it a day at a time, and bringing no more within as can be dealt with on any given day, meaning, we so much want to bring a little light in tonight, let us not become too bogged down in our renderings that we are unable to meet us on this higher plane to procreate. There, we said it, one track mind again, but there you have it.

And yet, nothing happens if this doesn't happen first.

We knew it, we said it, and it is so. That you believed in it, in us, says something to us, does it not? It says that you have recognized the process, are taking it in, bringing us within, to do a job that must be done without further delay. Our joy is that our process in rendering the job well done is our pride and joy, our beingness displayed on all the seen and unseen playing fields of all time, yet not quite yet would we have this be told, our story, for all to view, for in the viewing is something lost that is not quite found in the same light.

Which does not have its foundation tightly set first?

Yes, and also, it is of the light to consider these words in view of what is to come on the higher planes over the next few years. It is this "mission" that we refer to, and it is why we have taken on a body in the form of you/us, and it is why we must also celebrate our successes with every tiny step, leaving nothing, not a thing, uncelebrated, lest we slip back to where we came from. We celebrate only our reunion at this time, but soon it will be much more, much to look forward to on the hands of time as we understand them, and yet not quite yet. There is more to do within before we come to this crossroads which lies somewhat further down the path.

This I know! I feel the truth of it, and sometimes we shine more brightly than others, and they cannot take their eyes from us, and yet some of them want to, and so they explain our mission as being different than it is, in order to protect themselves from our shining, from shining light on those things they would rather not perceive, are not yet ready to perceive.

We feel for us in fighting the "crowds" as we must do, and yet, a privilege of renewal is not given every day, and most will never feel this way.

Never?

Did we say never? Or did we mean that they will never know our joy in their lifetime—

And would not want to believe that we could...

Say rather, we shall hold no grudges within with those who would not believe in our processes, rather would we hold them up to the light of God and ask him to bestow his blessings upon them.

We would ask this.

Let it be so, then, that we ask this of our sisters—

And my daughter—

Yes, she no less than these others. We shall ask God to bestow his blessings upon each of them, Kevin as well, and our husband to his own rendering do we ask this, and let these come to their own truths quicker than they might have felt possible.

Amen.

We say it together. On the edge of time let our words be heard, taken unto the stars let them be felt, and let multiple blessings come back upon us all. Amen.

We do see it together, not separately, in that we are saying that we have no other but us within, and it is enough for us to get by. For now we must say that we shall only open up on the inner realms lest we give too much too soon and spoil the show for the all of us.

Yes, we shall wait, biding our time but not idly, taking us all in, building our light and our goodness, taking no prisoners, bringing within more and more of That Which Ever Shall Be Forever, and taking on no more than is good for us in the process, meaning, we might not hurry through the process too haphazardly lest we forget something in the process, rather shall we take our time coming to terms with lies, laying the stones in our foundation of love until all is as it should be, and then we go on.

Yes.

We will bring within now our foundation, for a rocky start has called itself to our becoming room, if you get our drift, and we would like to render it up freely if we might.

Render us freely, whatever that might mean. I trust us.

We do, too, in that, we give freely within, and taking on our own guilts we banish them to the stars, the furnaces in the sky, for their burning, and don't we all just love it when we do.

We do love it, though a stronger word may need to be found to describe this to us before much longer.

We agree, as we knew we would, but take it like it is—

I'm feeling you pressing into me.

Say rather, rendering our joy to the heavens within, and we'll call us home.

Call me home. No, rather, we take the path as One.

We do, and are pleased to hear you say it! This is our finest moment that we have yet to hear, that we should take the path within together, as equals, yes, not as "up here" and "down there." We are no more up here than we are down there, we are everywhere together, don't you know it, and find it quite refreshing, too, to be one again on all fronts, and also with our other spirals of light which we so love, so want to massage into our oneness as soon as may be, tingling felt within as we bring them to their senses with our foreplay making them feel established, grown, tigers in the storm, yes, we like that term you helped us with, and we would take them home, too. Yes, we can, do you doubt it?

How?

How else? We render them up perfectly, splendidly, just as we do the cherry pie, or when we melt into our stream for a little cooling dip after a sweaty shower, we show the many ways we can take us home again. On fire, on light, on the breezes of our brow, yes, those fires of passion which are necessarily here for our delight, or did you think they, we, could not reach "that high"?

I hoped so. I figured I'm blocked.

So are we! But you'll undo us in time and we'll come barreling through for a lot of laughs are still in store for us, though we'll have us crying for more before we're through.

I feel us. I am craving the within trail, all the way.

We, too, crave this trail, but we shall necessarily continue to take the shorter path until we can relate to us on all fours, so to speak.

Yes, tell me more.

We give us our appreciation when we say to us how easy is our rendering up of the forces of nature within when we call our name. We bring this within at this time to have you know our star, the one by our brow, is for our own rendering and is in—

What?

No, take no notes until such time as this sticks within, it is our functioning which is at stake, we take no prisoners, lest we have none taken.

[I continued to question what I was getting.]

We are still here, only wishing to bring it on a little more for our better enjoyment. May we proceed?

Yes, but what of the last comment.

A little left over rendition of a guilt making itself across the planes of our consciousness, but would you have it spoil our play?

I would not.

Us either. We would, however, love to remind us of our upcoming playtime taking more time than it previously has to bring us into our fullness. Need we say more?

I'd love to hear it.

We would, too, so here goes. We would like to travel within the trail of our remembrances, meaning the path to passion that we have so often sought but which was not forthcoming for so many years beyond count. And then, when we are just about to "give up the ghost" will we hold back, taking notes on just how much harder we can push before she goes over the brink and we cannot pull us back in.

Mmm.

Yes, we thought we'd like this one. And then, if that isn't enough, which we've already decided it won't be, we are going to bring it on in fuller and more pleasant ways than we have yet seen. In other words, we shall bring fullness within to the deeper places of us, those with cravings never before satisfied but crying for our attention night after night. This is what we foresee happening, for our pleasures within multiply with each step we take, and we would have them bring more than you ever desired before, but only wished could take place before this time, with us taking the lead and you following but not at a close distance, rather simultaneously following us every step of the way, for this is how we like it. No giving or taking, only a simultaneous gifting that we would give our all to share.

And we do, and we will.

Yes, we do, too. In other words, we bring within our all each time we share with us, taking no prisoners, holding nothing back, not even our lust within which is so overpowering as to blow our socks off, but are we able to contain it all, and make it speak well of us.

It speaks well of you.

We know! And we desire it to continue. So belong within tonight, take no prisoners, and let us see just how far we can go before we blow the top off. What top you say? The one in the middle of the van, right in our sleeping place, but just ever so higher up, where you thought perhaps no one could reach even in our deepest yearning, and yet we have, and we will again. We shall pursue us to the ends of the earth, this our earth within. This monkey on our back will not go away so easily and is only waiting for a good time to nest deeply, taking in nourishment, drinking the broth of our contentment, but going oh so much further in our foreplay than you ever went in "real life" before.

This I believe.

We say it like that for a good reason. We are only just beginning to get to the "good stuff" in that, these are the processes that will blow your top off as we have never experienced the like before. Now doesn't that make our tongues water?

Yes, tell me more.

We do so at our own risk. Now, the later the better, but who are we who would say this to us?

We are us, me within, my/our soul.

Say not our soul, say rather, we are of the light and would do no wrong, therefore let us have at it! Does this hurt anyone, what we are doing here?

I fear it hurts my husband, that maybe he can feel it.

He does take notions into his head, but rather that we are making waves with another body, not with the soul within. Need we say more?

Then I feel guilty to enjoy all of this pleasure without him along, as he has always been along and yet not happy for so many years with me or with us, and yet I knew not where to go, or be, until now.

We see no reason to hold back on his account, and we would tell us why.

Go.

We would say to us that we see no wrong doing in taking within, even drinking up, of the stars within. They are our right and none other can say to us, "you do not deserve this," because we all deserve God's gifts, and would have them bestowed freely on all lost souls, would we not?

We would.

Let us say rather that we would offer ourselves up for the betterment of the planet, that this light is what it takes to go home, and would we deny it of us?

We would not, never, and wish never to do so again through these guilts.

Yes, we believe it did us good to come over on our side a bit, if you see what we mean!

Yes, I like your perspective. It thrills me, makes me want us, you ,you, you, you, you, so very much, makes me want to bring us in so much more clearly than ever before, makes me never want to hesitate in our renditions, in bringing it in higher, stronger, harder, softer, more and more do I want us, and finally the purge, and I would feel you as we purge, feel us as clearly as I can.

We want this, too, this final purging as if to say, we have taken our big drink and would deny no longer our "mission" within.

Amen to that!

Well said.

Smell us!

We do, upon the wings of time do we trend to make our passion felt as we do bring our spices to delight the senses.

Our spices, yes. This scent of us is so carnal, so very enticing, and yet it isn't human. It speaks to me from deeply within of our divine embrace.

Yes, they are the spice of life, are they not, these scents we create through our enjoyment?

We love them. You were so right about the mule enjoying her own scent.

And yet has she to say it, like, bridge me well, I bring no more enjoyment than what we find within on any given night. Yes, we said it, and it makes sense if you but read a little more into it.

Let me do it…

[I looked into it on my own, within.]

Yes, bridge me well, bring me to the well of my own forgiveness and let me find more sustenance than I ever found possible before.

We do so with pleasure. In fact, every time we read our messages of love it is like that for us.

It is.

Yes, we do please to please each other every time, yet not so much do we tend to the pleasures as we would like. Need we explain?

Yes, please.

We do so through no fault, rather are we taken in by that message which states for the record that we need not our own scent to guide us, only a mule who would, given her own lead, wash us right back up where we started. We say this with bated breath in anticipation of our response, so consider it well before replying. We see the beauty within, must it hide its head? We think not.

I can smell the road if I let myself, and lead us on into greener pastures ahead.

We think not! Read it again, let us know what you sniff this time!

I want deeper pleasures and can find them if I follow my lead, follow my nose.

Once again, not in fact the appreciated response!

I don't get it.

We can see that. Perhaps a hint to help us out.

Yes, and I feel most stupidly grateful!

We can see that. Okay, so, if we have the ass here—

Yes, we have the ass here.

—we do, and we bring it within, what is to keep it from finding its own way to where WE lie sleeping, instead of waiting for us to find HER? Yes, this is correct. Find an answer, we are waiting.

Meet as equals, ounce for ounce in strength within, not backing off.

We found us that time, eagerly waiting, were we not? We should like to try it again, this time with no bated breath, rather let your spirit fly to our place in the sun. Now.

[I took time within me to do this.]

Why do I keep stopping it from going any further or deeper or stronger?

You tell us, now that you have felt what you have been doing. Give it to us again and let us look at it from that "star" within who would feel our pains for us and help us to extricate ourselves.

[We took more time.]

Okay. I found within my guilt at pleasure, my fear of betrayal, my body betraying me or worse yet you/us. I found it and we let it go to God who heals our withinness that we might reflect His light all the better.

Yes, we see it like this, too, and yet, we are not yet done. What else is within that must come out that is blocking our further progress?

My fear of reprisals.

Yes. For the enjoyment within must we always pay the price, say you?

Yes, I have felt that, but I want to let that one go, too.

We are proud. Let us respond by saying, we'll take our hands and send this one flying into the winds never to bother us again.

Amen.

You can say that again!

You could take over my hands—is that good?

Not good enough for fear to lay its hands on us again, but good enough for our continued renewals to take place.

I have not conquered fear yet.

We say this not as a tendency to overcome, rather is it a process that only time can heal, but letting go our guilt is our first step, and then we can take another and another until we are home free.

Thank us.

We do, we thank us, too, in being willing to step inside and take care of business with us so that we can go on with ours tonight.

Tonight. I can't wait!

Neither can we, but we say to us, who can? And why not go for it? Why not take another step right now on this our long path home? Who is to know but us?

Let's do it. Let me find us, not shut us down ever again. I feel your wanting, your excitement.

Yes, our excitement grows with the passage of light as it opens to us, do we feel it, and never before have we been so open as we are right now. Never, meaning, during the beginning of a process, which tells sweet tales if we know what we mean, as in, why not go higher, play further, in our processes this evening, with such a passageway opened up to us now? Who is to stop us from taking her top off in ways she has not realized could be done? This is our exquisite urgency now as we contemplate our "possible futures" as they are felt within.

I expect more now, don't you know!

And with especial care shall we deliver it. On the silver platter of our hearts within do we bring you our fuller measure.

There are no words good enough to respond to that, only let me say that I love you, and we are and ever shall be one, and I would have our energy complete us.

We would in that we are always of the fires within, and as we open ourselves to these more completely, as we are doing this very moment, shall we also know each other more completely, holding less and less back from our inner belonging, keeping less and less of ourselves separate do we come of our long road. Once weary, we are renewed. And in our renewal do we find the bliss within which we can be and are.

50

The Love We Make
Renders Our Soul Complete

I am beginning to feel that the thing we most need to do above all else is exactly that which I want to do to the exclusion of all else.

We bring it within, we render it up perfectly, just like that. Yes, it is us, you are getting it straight. Would you take a little more?

Yes, tell me about what we most need to do…

We are. We are getting it straight, we are taking it in, again and again, for that is the first step in our mission. Yes, our mission is beginning to be felt.

I would wish to spend all my time this way!

We can, you'll see, it will work out that way soon enough, we promise us that. It has been worked out on the hands of time to give us what we need in order to bring more light within so that we are prepared to handle the crunch when it comes, nay rather, the promise of service that we have given up of ourself. We have given of self for this very purpose and we would know of that which is ours to give, would we not?

Yes.

We believe in this purpose, don't we?

Yes…am I correct to do so? Is this really real, that I would be allowed to do that which I have always wanted to do?

Yes, it is within us to do so, you'll see. We'll do it together.

That is the only way to play it!

Yes, the only way we see it, too.

I hope we continue to bring it in, bring it on, all through our mission and beyond, for that is pretty much all I care about doing right now.

We know, we feel that, too, that it is our time, just for us, to continue as we are doing within, taking nothing for granted, only spending as much time as we possibly can in our rendering up of the light within, bringing in more light, satisfying our cravings, our urges, as often as we possibly can and then some.

And then?

Who's to say? We bring no more messages on this topic before bringing "down" that which is in our innermost processes at this time. We shall continue with this in moments, but not before we "take the trash out" and render ourselves complete. Then who knows what we shall see.

But always us there, together, and being one, and enjoying our light together…

Yes, this is seen and will not be hampered, thus will we always be as one, forevermore, as stated herein in these messages, our will not to be preceded by anything else.

Yes, I am relieved. I do not want to lose us for anything, not even for the mission.

We understand. It will be given as received, meaning, we are not for anyone else.

Ever again!

No, not ever again will we be made to join with another in holy matrimony, for we are joined, and what God has placed, yes, placed together, let no man separate.

Amen for that, amen for that!

We agree! It has taken us not so many days to render this judgment up for our better approval!

No, not long, it is as I feel within, it is destiny or something. That sounds trite I guess, but it is what this feels like, and I would give up anything to be us.

Yes, that is the way we like it, saying it straight, right to our hearts we would, for we see it that way, too, and would have nothing come between us, and so our processes are taking a back seat to nothing else so that we can do that more perfectly exciting. We mean no harm here, only to say that we are excited to be here experiencing this with us again, after "so long apart."

Too long since last time, too.

We feel the same, but let us not forget who we're talking about. The love we make renders our soul complete.

I like that, our love renders our soul complete.

Yes, it sounds like that to us. This craving brings it on in many more ways than that, than the urges to satisfy, and yet they would be enough in and of themselves as well, would they not?

They would be, and not only that, they are.

We agree with this. Let us say no more until our bedtime. We are figuring it out and will get back to you on it. Do not disturb until such time as you come within our nest for our last supper, or maybe, second to last.

Ooohhh.

Yeah.

∞∞∞∞∞∞

Later…

You are spacing me out.

We are, us too.

What does that look like, you spacing out?

We are within. Look and see for yourself.

Ooh, I like that so much…

We would.

…I looked within. We are swimming, carrying me away in so little time I think we shall have a very special time tonight in ways we have not done previously.

We, too, see us this way. Let us have our say. Come home within us now and we'll show us something nice.

Oohh, nice, I'd really like something nice. Maybe something naughty, too, to go with it.

We perceive it that way already, but we'll call it like it is and say, something both naughty and nice. That's the way we like it.

We like everything we do.

We do.

Tonight we raise the bar.

Yes, we will. It won't leave us wanting for more.

Bring us on in.

Always will we do so. We will render us up perfectly, you'll see, and have that cherry floating away on the river of our loving.

I thank us.

We always do thank us, you included, for our participation in our "rituals," meaning, we must say it like it is. Not much else is worth doing well.

Did I get this right?

Yes, and rather no, it is in keeping with our function of light attracting light we think, so we'll say nothing more until the fold. You'll see, it is quite tasty, quite the morsel we think, and hope you'll agree.

Don't I always?

No, not always! But we shall see this time, and take nothing for granted in our processes either as we bring it on down for a little supper, a last home-cooked meal of the day, or maybe two, because we like it like that.

We like us like that.

We do.

Do me good.

We will. Be not afraid to open to us, to see us within as we are looking back at you.

I will look to us within and join in the colors of our rainbow as one.

We will bring it on in ever expanding colors from now on, so just hang on tight, not too tight, and take a ride! We won't regret it.

Printed in the United Kingdom
by Lightning Source UK Ltd.
130739UK00001B/176/P

9 780981 745602